2

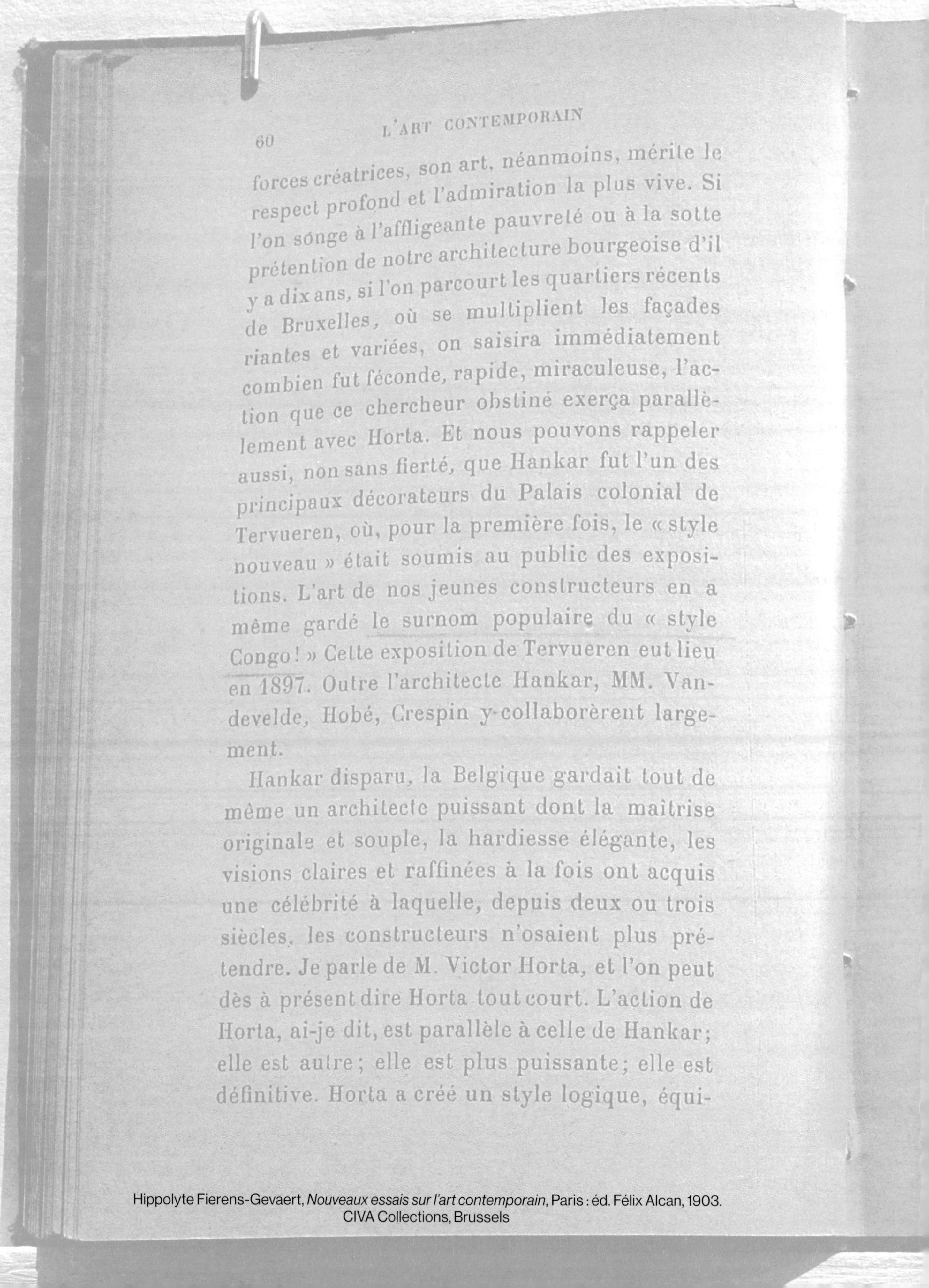

60 L'ART CONTEMPORAIN

forces créatrices, son art, néanmoins, mérite le respect profond et l'admiration la plus vive. Si l'on songe à l'affligeante pauvreté ou à la sotte prétention de notre architecture bourgeoise d'il y a dix ans, si l'on parcourt les quartiers récents de Bruxelles, où se multiplient les façades riantes et variées, on saisira immédiatement combien fut féconde, rapide, miraculeuse, l'action que ce chercheur obstiné exerça parallèlement avec Horta. Et nous pouvons rappeler aussi, non sans fierté, que Hankar fut l'un des principaux décorateurs du Palais colonial de Tervueren, où, pour la première fois, le « style nouveau » était soumis au public des expositions. L'art de nos jeunes constructeurs en a même gardé le surnom populaire du « style Congo! » Cette exposition de Tervueren eut lieu en 1897. Outre l'architecte Hankar, MM. Vandevelde, Hobé, Crespin y collaborèrent largement.

Hankar disparu, la Belgique gardait tout de même un architecte puissant dont la maîtrise originale et souple, la hardiesse élégante, les visions claires et raffinées à la fois ont acquis une célébrité à laquelle, depuis deux ou trois siècles, les constructeurs n'osaient plus prétendre. Je parle de M. Victor Horta, et l'on peut dès à présent dire Horta tout court. L'action de Horta, ai-je dit, est parallèle à celle de Hankar; elle est autre; elle est plus puissante; elle est définitive. Horta a créé un style logique, équi-

Hippolyte Fierens-Gevaert, *Nouveaux essais sur l'art contemporain*, Paris : éd. Félix Alcan, 1903.
CIVA Collections, Brussels

Style Congo: Heritage & Heresy explores the politics of cultural representation and appropriation through both contemporary artistic and architectural interventions and historic materials, primarily from CIVA's collection. Based on the eponymous exhibition, this book chronicles the representation of Congo in international and colonial expositions held between 1885 and 1958, using Art Nouveau as its anchor point.

The Belgian Art Nouveau movement—also called Style Congo at the time—coincided with King Leopold II's exploitation of Congo and reflects a widespread fascination with "exotic" materials and forms. As total artworks, the pavilions of international and colonial expositions illustrate the synthesis of the arts to which modernism aspired, not only through architectural form and applied arts, but also by merging stage and collection, setting a precedent for displays in ethnographic museums. Through their enthralling constructions and beguiling references—each utopian in their own way—the pavilions communicated a twofold idea: Congo as a lucrative African colony and as a creative field for Belgian artists and architects. Through a display of both imagined authenticity and promised progress, they served as a platform for cultural propaganda and economic exchange.

Contemporary artistic and architectural positions question the canonical histories and colonial roots of this heritage, and with them the perception of iconic buildings in Belgian culture, such as Victor Horta's Hotel van Eetvelde (designed for Edmond Van Eetvelde, administrator of the Congo Free State), which is portrayed in the exhibition in photographs by Chrystel Mukeba. By examining marks of colonization in the city of Brussels and in the Congolese urban landscape, artists and architects propose a decolonial resignification of private and public spaces, seeking to rewrite the margins of history into the center.

To whom does this heritage belong? Are artistic movements such as Art Nouveau or Art Deco enclosed forever in a hermetic architectural canon and a homogenic narrative? Or can heritage unlock diverse, even contradicting, narratives, to redefine history as a continuous construction in the present?

In his 1999 lecture "Whose Heritage? Un-settling 'The Heritage,' Re-imagining the Post-nation," Stuart Hall called on diasporic communities to subvert the foundational ground on which the process of heritage construction has proceeded. For Hall, heritage is the material embodiment of a nation and a practice of "governmentality" that must be deconstructed through discursive practices: "Who should control the power to represent? Who has the authority to represent the culture of others?"[1] These questions apply particularly to the communities that "have dwelled for many years in the double or triple time of colonization, and now occupy the multiple frames, the in-between or 'third' spaces—the homes-away-from-home—of the postcolonial metropolis."[2] Since Black Lives Matter gained ground in 2020, Afro-Belgians and affiliated communities have demanded historical introspection and a reassessment of Brussel's architectural and monumental heritage. A call for adopting a decolonial approach in the urban environment and for the re-politicization of historical memory through a reflection on the symbols of colonization in public space has been launched by the authors of "Report for the Decolonization of Public Space," whose work has been an important reference for this project.[3]

Decolonization is a process of excavation, which requires bringing to the surface deeply rooted historical structures and entanglements. In order to push the critique of modernity toward a decolonial opening and to transform the way in which we understand architecture, art, and aesthetic processes, this project centers a rereading of historical artifacts from CIVA's own collections. CIVA's collections contain materials of architects who built in Congo and Belgium on behalf of King Leopold II and the Ministry of Colonies. By examining them, the aim is to shed light on the politics of material and cultural appropriation at stake in the construction of the colonial-modern paradigm and look at the architecture of the late nineteenth century and mid-twentieth century through the lens of the exhibition medium, with a particular focus on international and colonial expositions.

A central element of this book and of the exhibition is a new archival structure developed by the architecture collective Traumnovelle: a transhistorical reading of the collection through select materials. Oscillating between historical research and subversive analysis, Traumnovelle chronicles the representation of Congo in international and colonial expositions held between 1885 and 1958—the first and the last years when Congo was presented as a colony in international expositions. By displaying a historical repertoire of ambitious pavilions that aimed at representing the Africa colony in the European metropolis, Traumnovelle's narration emphasizes the construction of the Other through the exhibitionary machine.

In order to address the colonial entanglements at stake in these histories, we invited scholars Debora Silverman, Johan Lagae, Sandrine Colard, and Rolando Vázquez Melken to provide historical background and fuel possible questions toward the future. Debora Silverman draws from her research on Belgian Art Nouveau to discuss scholarly sources and political events that shaped Belgium's "imperial modernism." Her essay offers a close reading of an example of Style Congo: Henry van de Velde's Export Room at the Palais des Colonies, designed by Paul Hankar for the Brussels World's Fair at Tervuren in 1897. Hankar's Palais des Colonies is evoked in Judith Barry's video installation *The Work of the Forest* (1992), which addresses colonialism in Africa as an engine for wealth accumulation in Belgium. It deals specifically with the constitution of the Royal Museum for Central Africa, which opened in 1910 on the site of the Palais des Colonies, only a few years after the 1897 exhibition brought a trove of Congolese artifacts to Brussels.

In the international and colonial expositions organized around the 1930s, technological progress and modernization in Congo became central as Belgium looked to the colonies for answers during the worldwide economic crisis. In a reprinted essay by Johan Lagae, the author analyzes the colonial sections of the expositions in which emphasis was placed on the ways in which modernization was being imported from Europe into the colonies, arguing for the civilizing mission of colonialism. These efforts contrasted with the representation of Belgian Congo by means of a presumably authentic display of the colony's native culture, made evident in the eclectic design by Henry Lacoste for the Paris Colonial Exposition of 1931. The promise of progress was also manifested in exhibitions organized in Congo, such as the 1931 International Exposition in Elizabethville (now Lubumbashi)—which is central to Jean Katambayi Mukendi's installation—where the participation of companies such as Union Minière du Haut-Katanga (a Belgian mining company with a British stake) was intended to posit the city as a model for economic growth and fertile territory for technological investment. Finally, a vivid contrast between progress and the "primitive" was visible in the enormous section of Belgian Congo and Rwanda at the 1958 Brussels World's Fair. Their participation comprised seven vast colonial pavilions, complete with a large tropical Congolese garden and an Indigenous village, designed by René Pechère, which were juxtaposed with the Atomium, a high-tech world powered by Congolese uranium.[4]

Belgians invested significantly in research and infrastructure for their mining enterprises, and with that the management of natural resources, particularly in tropical climates. The essay-film produced by researchers Paoletta Holst and Johan Lagae recounts the story of Edmond Leplae, the first general director of the Agriculture Department of the Belgian Ministry of Colonies who traveled to Indonesia to study the plantation system. Leplae also studied and advocated for the colonizer's plantation house, which he considered a key instrument for successful agricultural and economic exploitation of the colonies. In 1935, the architect Henry Lacoste proposed a Congolese pavilion for the Brussels World's Fair in the shape of a "panorama atmosphérique" (atmospheric panorama) that would offer the visitor the experience of an expedition crossing the climatic zones of Congo (the savannah, a tropical forest, and the Ruwenzori Mountains) thanks to the latest engineering technologies. Sammy Baloji, in a work commissioned for the 2023 Venice Architectural Biennial and here reproduced, reinterprets this unrealized project and connects it with the history of Yangambi, home to one of the world's largest research centers on tropical agriculture, established by the Belgians in the 1930s. In her text on Baloji's project, Sandrine Colard juxtaposes the desire to recreate the Congolese landscape in Europe, while architects and urban planners in Congo tended to design structures and infrastructures that avoided any contact between colonizers and nature. Nature is also the subject of Daniela Ortiz's *The Rebellion of the Roots* (2021), which narrates stories of the many plant species that were uprooted from Africa and transplanted in Belgium to appear in colonial exhibitions and royal gardens. Most species are still present in Belgium today and act as a reminder of the ongoing coloniality and racism pervading European society. The toxic afterlives of colonialism and how it contaminates the present and future in a transhistorical and fictional perspective also lays the ground for ayoh kré Duchâtelet's installation, *Ornaments and Crimes* (2023), a polymorphic fictional work based on the toxicity of colonial violence represented by a multiplicity of voices. The "hearing room" he designed acts as a healing space—a sound piece bathes visitors in the atmosphere of the old ABC Hotel (Hôtel Alimentation du Bas-Congo) in Mbanza-Ngungu, built in Art Nouveau style and later converted into a courthouse. A novel, which tells the story of bodies contaminated by colonization in the form of a mysterious pathology, calls for repair and justice in the context of extractivist production which deeply unbalanced our modern world.

As Rolando Vázquez Melken affirms, "the question of repair is a question that challenges the function of Western art and Western institutions as a whole."[5] According to Vázquez Melken, the expositions made evident that Western modernity, modernisms, progress, and notions of civilization are implicated in the destruction of many lives and the extraction of Earth's resources. He further expands in this volume that architecture choreographed spaces where people could experience the "imperial imaginary" through pavilions that controlled the representation of the world by mobilizing pleasure and enjoyment as a tool of oppression.

In a conversation that closes this book, Vázquez Melken and Baloji discuss issues of "shared heritage" that have emerged in recent debates on colonial history. Vázquez Melken points to the need for moving toward positionality—that is, acknowledging who is speaking, who is representing, who is represented, who is enjoying, and who is suffering across the colonial divide, while being conscious of a radical plurality of worlds and histories.

By interrogating colonial expositions, this exhibition and book propose a different gaze on these events, which we see as "contact zones"—spaces where cultures meet, clash, and grapple with each other, often in contexts of highly asymmetrical relations of power.[6] By making visible the mutual dependencies and interrelations in the forms and spatial practices that migrated and mutated between Belgium and Congo from the late nineteenth century until the mid-twentieth century, the projects here seek to make sense of the captivating power of design that gave eloquent physical form to fictive projections of the Congo, in situations where subaltern perspectives were, and continue to be, marginalized. The question is whether acknowledging, rereading, and analyzing the role played by these margins in modernity can help construct a new concept of heritage.

1 Stuart Hall, "Whose Heritage? Un-settling 'The Heritage,' Re-imagining the Post-Nation," *Third Text* 13, no. 49 (1999): 4.
2 Hall, 10.
3 Gia Abrassart et al., "Decolonising Public Space in the Brussels-Capital Region: A Framework for Reflection and Recommendations" (Brussels: Urban Brussels, 2021), https://cloud.urban.brussels/s/xbpfRfn82trTGmE/download/2021_URBAN_REPORT_DECOLON_PUBLIC_SPACE_EN_DEF.pdf.
4 See Dennis Pohl, "Uranium Exposed at Expo 58: The Colonial Agenda behind the Peaceful Atom," *History and Technology* 37, no. 2 (2021): 172–202.
5 Rolando Vázquez Melken, "Fragments of Repair/Gathering, On Decolonial Aesthesis" (lecture, BAK, basis voor actuele kunst, Utrecht, June 10, 2021), https://www.bakonline.org/program-item/fragments-of-repair/fragments-of-repair-gatherings/fragments-of-repair-gathering-iv-on-decolonial-aesthesis/.
6 See Mary Louise Pratt, "Arts of the Contact Zone," *Profession* (1991): 33–40.

Henry van de Velde: Art Nouveau as Style Congo, 1895–97

Debora Silverman

"Ouvrir à la civilisation la seule partie de notre globe où elle n'ait point encore pénétré, percer les ténèbres qui enveloppent des populations entiers, c'est… une croisade digne de ce siècle du progrès." —King Leopold II, 1876

"Quelque chose se réalisait, en ce moment, en Belgique…la pensée que les artistes de ce petit pays avaient mission de secouer l'ennui dense dont l'atmosphère pesait sur lui depuis sa foundation….Qui éloignerait le nuage … sinon les artistes? … D'autres facteurs dans les autres domaines de la vie économique et sociale allaient secouer la torpeur: la création royale des colonies, et la fondation d'un troisième parti politique." —Henry van de Velde, 1902

Henry van de Velde is celebrated as a pioneer of twentieth-century international modernism. He is less known for his central role in developing Belgian Art Nouveau through raw materials from Congo and Congolese motifs—what I call "imperial modernism." Van de Velde grew up in Antwerp, where he watched dockers unloading massive baobab tree hardwood at the new "Afrikadok," built in 1887 to accommodate the circuit of streamers coming from the Congo Free State. His brother Willy set off with Henry Morton Stanley to explore the interior along the Congo River and to claim territory for King Leopold II, and Willy hoped Henry would join him there. By 1885 the king had won international authorization to rule the continually expanding entity of what he named the Congo Free State—a vast, resource rich

▼ Gustave Serrurier – Bovy, Import room in the Colonial Palace, *Exposition congolaise de 1897*. International Exhibition Brussels. CIVA Collections, Brussels

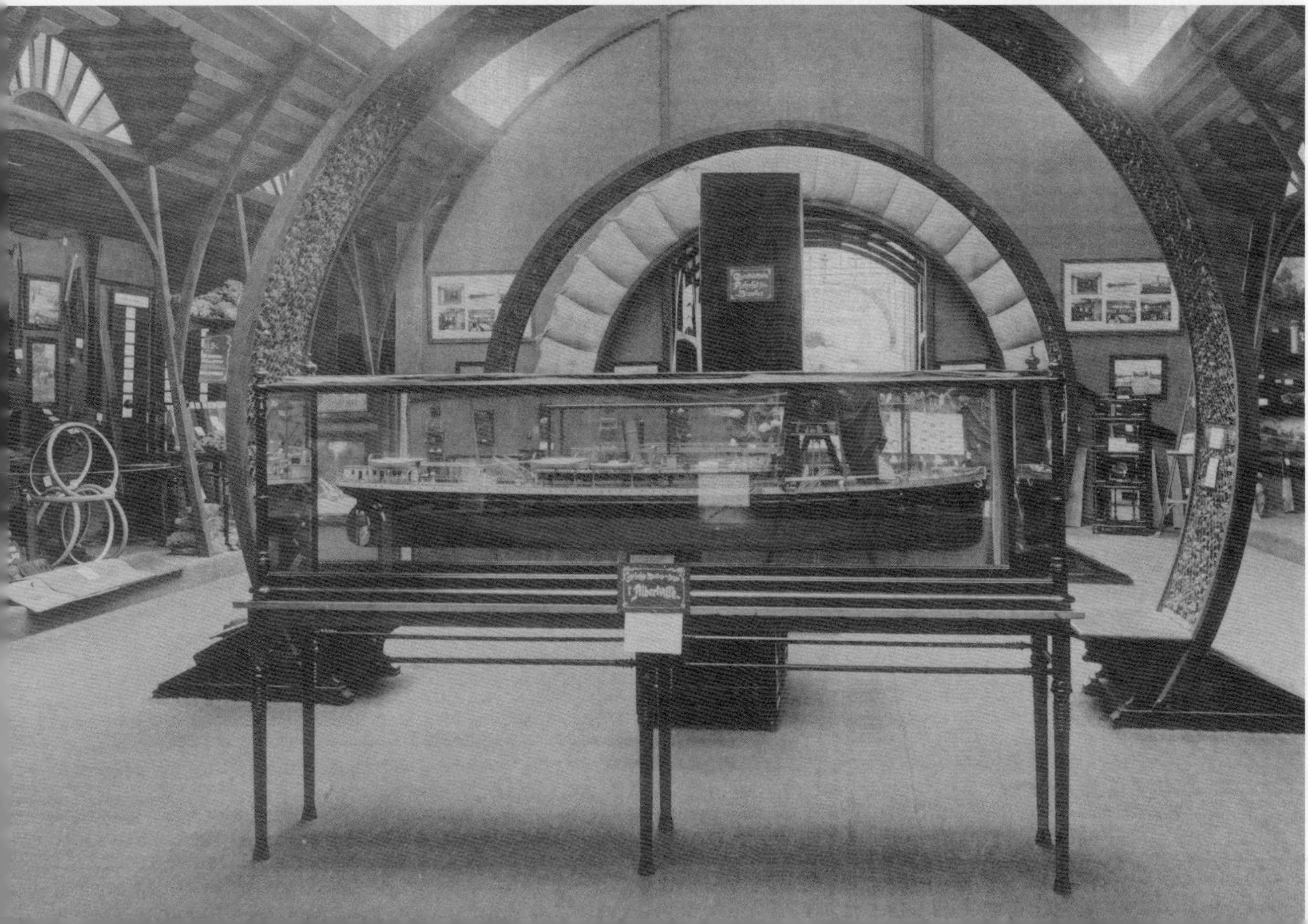

realm for investment and extraction. This was not a settler colony propelled by a national mission, but a private entrepreneurial venture. The abundance of ivory and wild rubber found there brought sudden and spectacular profits to Belgium, the king, and a web of interlocking concession companies. Van de Velde was deeply impressed by not only Congolese people, but by the raw materials he encountered and the fantasies he conjured—all of which would shape his production and career as a designer.

Congo Connections at the Maison de l'Art Nouveau, Paris, 1895

Van de Velde gained international renown when, at the age of thirty-two, he was invited to contribute a suite of rooms to art dealer Siegfried Bing's Maison de l'Art Nouveau, which he opened in Paris in December of 1895. Bing was keen to spur modern design reform, liberated from history and tradition and inspired by nature and the unity of all the arts. Bing had visited and been impressed by Van de Velde's design for his own residence, Bloemenwerf, in Uccle outside of Brussels, completed in the same year as the Maison. Inspired by William Morris's Red House, Van de Velde's large home integrated interior space as a single design ensemble, and he flooded it with light and air. For Bing's initiative in Paris, Van de Velde joined an impressive roster of avant-garde artists and craftsmen: Louis Comfort Tiffany, Henri de Toulouse-Lautrec, and the Nabis painters Édouard Vuillard and Maurice Denis, among others. Van de Velde contributed a dining room and a smoking room. The latter was installed in the gallery, designed in dark wood and nested in the wall, with cushioned banquettes and sculpted wood around windows that looked like sizable portholes.

On visiting the building, Edmond de Goncourt famously attacked the Bing initiative as a "delirium of ugliness" and the "denationalizing" corruption of French taste. He singled out Van de Velde's smoking room for the dark, bending wood alcoves and bow windows that he said looked "like ships' portholes." Goncourt's comparison to the portholes of a ship later expanded into the enduring epithet that came to define Art Nouveau as an international style—it was to be known as the "yachting style."[1] Van de Velde acknowledged and even welcomed Goncourt's characterization of his work. But what the aesthete Frenchman ridiculed and derided, Van de Velde embraced as a point of pride. Responding in his memoirs to Goncourt's comments, Van de Velde asserted that his was indeed a style inspired by sailing ships and their smooth, functional, and sturdy structures, flexible and responsive to the water's course. He suggested an important distinction, though, in identifying nautical sources for his Art Nouveau: his was closer to a "steamer style" than a yachting style.[2] A student of the old and new ships at Antwerp's bustling docks, Van de Velde hailed the architecture and design of the modern transatlantic steamer as his ideal. Yachts, diminutive and elegant, he associated with an indolent world of aristocratic dalliance. Steamers, with their churning engines, fitted furnishings, hefty keels, outsized cargo holds, and blasting smokestacks, he celebrated for dominating the seas with technological prowess. These engineering feats—like the SS *Léopoldville*, built in 1894 to service the new Antwerp-Matadi line for trade with the Congo Free State—were precisely the engines of extraction bound for Central Africa that Van de Velde observed and admired.

Two other factors link Van de Velde's Paris debut to Congo. He composed the 1895 ship-shaped smoking room for Bing entirely in Congolese

1
Edmond and Jules de Goncourt, *Journal: Mémoires de la vie littéraire, 1891–1896*, vol. 4 (Paris, 1956), 893–94; all translations my own, unless otherwise noted.

2
Henry van de Velde, *Récit de ma vie*, vol. 1, *1863–1900* (Brussels: Versa, 1992), 275–77. An important art critic in Belgium, Henri Hymans, made a similar comment on Van de Velde's Art Nouveau, describing the snug, functional forms as less of a "yachting style" than that of a ship's cabin ("le style 'cabine de bateau'"). In Henri Hymans, *Oeuvres de Henri Hymans: L'art du XVIIe au XIXe siècle dans les pays-bas*, vol. 4 (Brussels: Académie Royale De Belgique, 1921), 345.

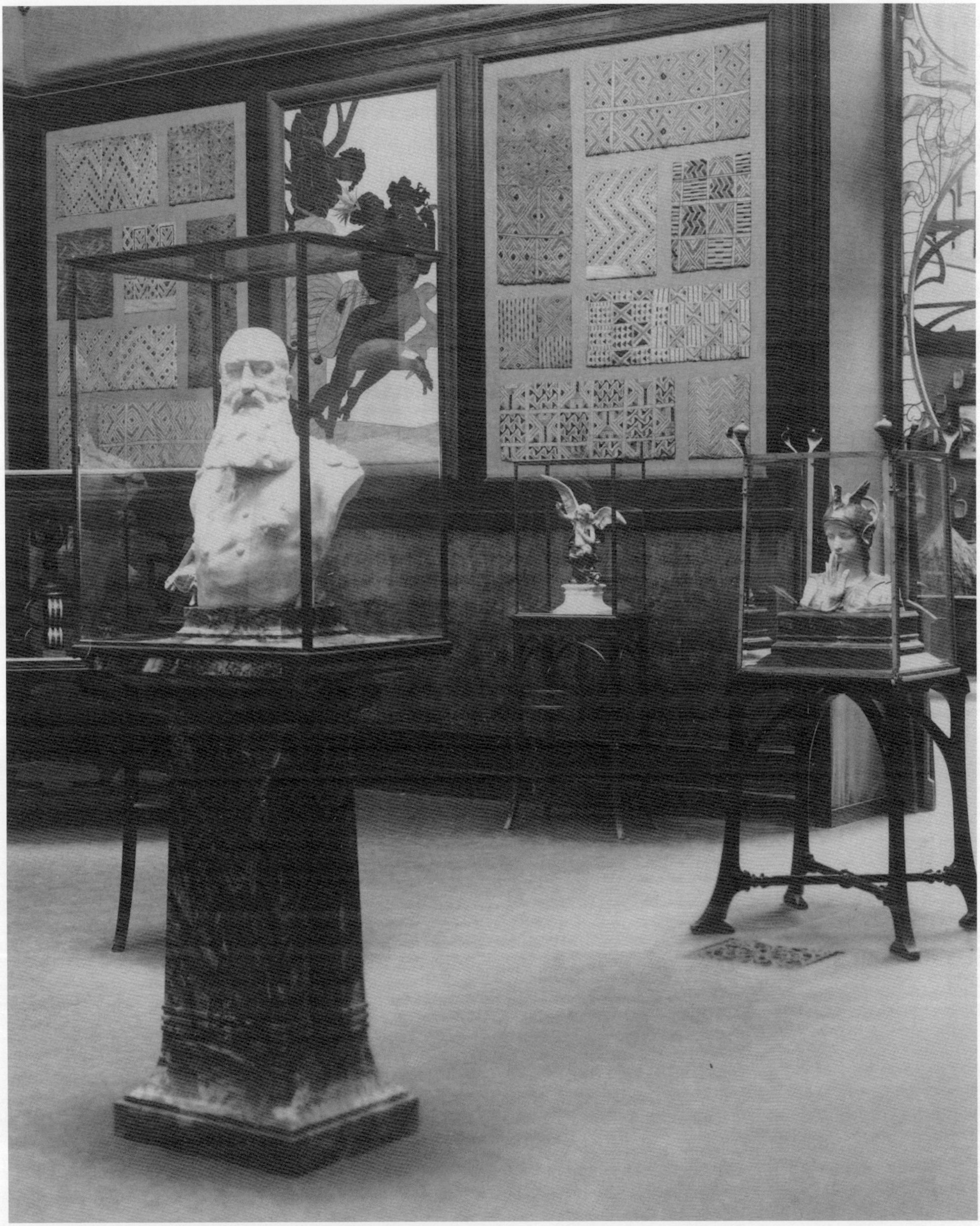

Ivory bust of Leopold II by Thomas Vincotte, with Charles van der Stappen's *Mysterious Sphinx* in the background, photograph of the Gallery of Honor in the Royal Congo Museum, Tervuren, ca. 1898. Collection MRAC Tervuren

hardwood, the same raw material that steamers like the SS *Léopoldville* brought back in huge loads from the Congo Free State forests. More surprising, and overlooked, is another instance of Congolese influence on Van de Velde's designs. According to Julius Meier-Graefe, when he came to Paris in 1895 to work on installing his interiors, Van de Velde stayed with his friend Henri Jaeger. An adventurer and explorer, Jaeger had recently returned from the Congo Free State and fashioned himself a collector of African objects that he procured during his expeditions. Jaeger, Van de Velde, and Bing talked about including some "African" as well as "Flemish" objects in the rooms. What were they? These objects did not appear when the gallery opened, and Jaeger died soon after of a tropical disease.[3] But this example points to the deep and early entanglement of Van de Velde's Art Nouveau and Congolese culture.

Van de Velde's Style Congo at the 1897 Brussels International Exhibition: Export Empire Van de Velde was delighted by his first official commission, when he was hired as one of four Art Nouveau artists to design the Congo section of the 1897 Brussels International Exposition. Housed in an iron-and-glass pavilion built at King Leopold II's estate at Tervuren, the installation gave public recognition to Art Nouveau and led to its inauguration in Belgium as "Style Congo." Railways, riverways, steamers, and locomotives were central components of the 1897 "Export Room" that Van de Velde was chosen to design to promote benefits of and opportunities for investment in the Congo Free State. Early on, Van de Velde had been patronized by Edmond van Eetvelde, Administrator General and Secretary

▼ Paul Hankar, Ethnography room in the Colonial Palace, *Exposition congolaise de 1897*, International Exhibition Brussels. CIVA Collections, Brussels – Phototypie Alexandre Bruxelles

► Paul Hankar, *Exposition congolaise de 1897*, International Exhibition Brussels. Collection MRAC Tervuren - Phototypie Alexandre Bruxelles

3
Philippe Thiébaut, "The Opening of l'Art Nouveau Bing and Belgium," in *The Origins of L'Art Nouveau: The Bing Empire*, ed. Gabriel P. Weisberg, Edwin Becker, and Evelyne Possémé (Amsterdam: Van Gogh Museum, 2004), 107–12, 261. See also, Van de Velde, *Récit*, 317.

4
Such a showcase was urgently needed, as in 1897 the king's private enterprise in Africa teetered between triumph and debacle. Profits soared to astonishing

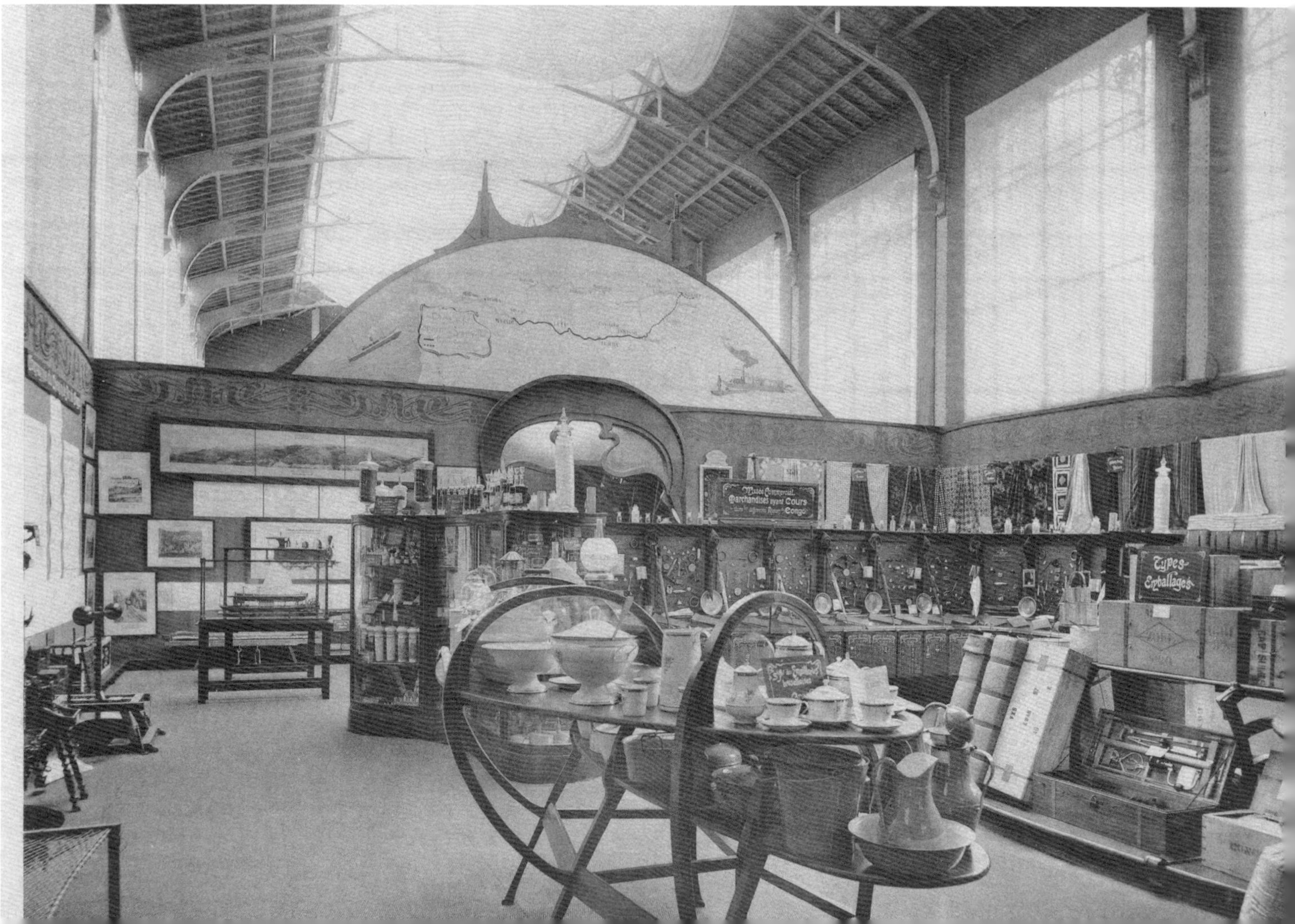

of State of the Congo Free State. Van Eetvelde coaxed the king to commission practitioners of the new design style to showcase the products, promise, and artifacts of the Congo Free State for the 1897 expo.[4] A Hall of Honor featuring chryselephantine sculptures by Belgian artists welcomed visitors upon entering the Tervuren palace. Galleries that followed displayed, in succession, Congolese ethnography, imports, exports, and crop cultivation, all created using raw materials from Congo by Art Nouveau artists and architects: Paul Hankar, Gustave Serrurier-Bovy, Henry van de Velde, and Georges Hobé.[5]

A giant curved mural marked the elevated boundary that set off Van de Velde's Export Room from the Import Room that flowed directly into it. In that room, Serrurier-Bovy exhibited the wondrous imports to Belgium of caoutchouc in manifold shapes, sizes, and object types. Sacks of rubber formed a neat semicircular frame around one doorway, while open counters showed latex disks, cables, balls, and cords, along with photographs and price boards listing the various grades collected in Congolese forests. Dramatic large-scale wooden arcs animated the middle of the Import Room, deftly carved to end in a bench under each side and topped with wire-mesh netting stuffed with lumps of latex, exposed to view. Here visitors could stop for a rest, sitting as if under the arc of a rainbow. In this case, the rainbow bore its pot of gold in the form of caged rubber chunks suspended above, transposing into physical form the widespread adage of the first decade of the king's Congo: that the vast liquid treasures contained in the lianes (the wild forest vines) rained down on lucky Belgium "like manna from heaven."[6]

levels that year, but unprecedented challenges also intensified. In 1896, long-denied evidence of atrocities in the Congo Free State were published in the Belgian press, with Georges Lorand's articles on "mains coupées" (severed hands) appearing on the front pages of *La Réforme*. And as the king planned the Tervuren exhibit, disturbing news of three mutinies by Batetela troops reached the public. Van Eetvelde organized the colonial exhibition as a giant public relations campaign to counteract criticism and overwhelm the public with the astonishing richness of Congolese products, resources, and investment possibilities.

5
See Debora L. Silverman, "Art Nouveau, Art of Darkness: African Lineages of Belgian Modernism, Part I," *West 86th* 18, no. 2 (Fall–Winter 2011). For basic information, see M. Luwel and M. Bruneel-Hye de Crom, *Tervueren 1897* (Tervueren: Musee Royal de l'Afrique Centrale, 1967), 44–67; and Maurits Wynants, *Des ducs de Brabant aux villages congolais: Tervuren et l'Exposition coloniale 1897* (Tervuren: Musee Royal de l'Afrique Centrale, 1997), 96–119.

6
See Silverman, "Art Nouveau, Art of Darkness," 139–43, 162–65.

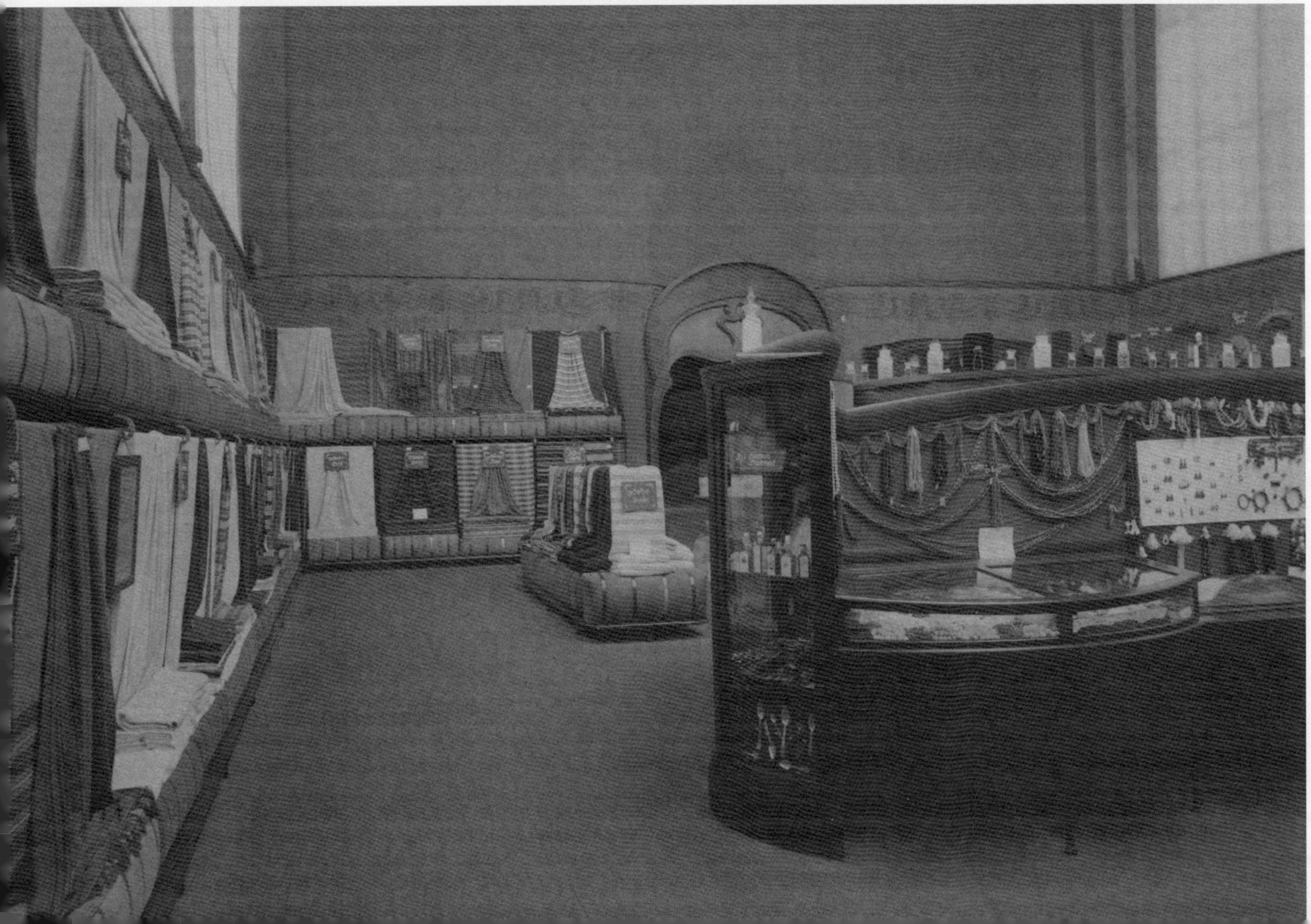

Serrurier-Bovy composed the gateway to the Import Room as a bouncy swerve of Congolese hardwood that both simulated the ramping bulk of the rubber vines and took on some of the qualities of elasticity heralded in the products displayed.

Van de Velde's Export Room announced at its entryway the twin engines of Belgian technological power that sustained the in- and outflow of Congolese products: steamer ships and railroads. The elevated mural depicted the twists and turns of the Congo River from Boma to Stanley Pool. In the upper left corner, a transatlantic ocean liner resembling the SS *Léopoldville* was shown advancing to Africa's shore. On the mural's lower right side a smaller steamer appeared, puffing smoke, while a native stood in a dugout canoe alongside it. The mural's legend and linear marks presented the route of the vaunted Congo Railway—"from Matadi to Stanley Pool"—the efficient modern rail system that was expected to negate the dangers and contortions of the Congo River. By 1897, seven years of work on the rails had yielded only partial completion of the line, under conditions widely known as murderous and Sisyphean.[7] Van de Velde's Export Room's giant signpost neutrally presented the railway progress by marking the map with dark ink, inscribing the portions still to be built with dotted rather than unbroken lines. King Leopold II celebrated what he called the interlinking network of "*chemins de fer*" and "*chemins de la mer*" (railroads and riverways) as the transformative agents of progress that would turn the Congo Free State, like Belgium, into a circuit of international transport and trade.[8] Van de Velde's Export Room mural showed the component parts of this circuit to the Belgian public as it was presumed to be operating in Africa.

Just beneath the elevated mural, Van de Velde created an expansive wood portal shaped into the sinuous forms of two snake heads meeting at the center. The steamer and the railway appeared again inside the Export Room. One wall displayed an oversize drawing of a locomotive; a glass case in front of it contained a model of a paddle steamer, much like the one in the mural. But the main purpose of the room was to present the profusion of products that were now considered necessary for the Congo Free State and the opportunities for companies in Belgium to manufacture and supply them. Primary among these were the commodities for the reputedly more-than-ten-million natives waiting to be civilized.

Filling the airy hall, Van de Velde designed and installed various furnishings and fittings—armoires, display cases, tiered tables, counters, and booths—to showcase the exports. There was a *musée commercial* that included equipment for Belgian pioneers as well as merchandise for the Congolese. Van de Velde's wide, glassed-in wood cabinet contained a number of white pith helmets, while tailor's mannequins were draped with dress uniforms for station commanders and agents. Suspended nearby on the walls were rubberized *impermeables*, or rain ponchos, coverings required for the tropical seasons, made out of the latex materials from the Import Room next door. Van de Velde also crafted lighter-weight and springy Congolese wood display tables with open shelves and elegant curves to house innumerable supplies manufactured for overseas recruits, from pitchers, crockery, and cutlery to toiletries and medicine jars. Along the floor were stacks of trunks, crates, and tool kits, many with the names of their manufacturers visible.

The multitude of products intended for native Congolese fell into two categories: costume jewelry, especially thick strands of pearls and glass beads,

7
The Belgian investment company Société anonyme du chemin de fer du Haut-Congo, headed by Albert Thys, had begun work in 1890 to traverse what would be a total of 233 miles along this route. Technological hubris initiated the well-funded project to be thus completed with alacrity, but the torturous conditions of climate and geography meant that by its completion in 1898, thousands of deaths, among both natives and Europeans, had accompanied the laying of the rails for what became small-scale locomotives that more resembled "the little engine that could" than the industrial behemoth of what Stanley had told King Leopold II would be the called "the penetrative express" of a Congo state connected proficiently and profitably to outlets to the seas.

8
Georges-H. Dumont, *Léopold II: Pensées et réflexions, recueillies par Georges-H. Dumont* (Liège: L'Amitié par le Livre, 1948), 33–41, esp. 40.

9
In 1910 the first director of the Tervuren Museum of the Congo, Alphonse de Haulleville, characterized the work of Belgium in the Congo as one of "invasive civilizationism," through trade and, in particular, the process of clothing the naked natives. Quoted in Silverman, "Art Nouveau, Art of Darkness," 144, 174n18. Alexandre Delcommune's important two-volume book included a series of photographs from 1891/1892 showing the progress of civilization in Congo as a gradual adoption of clothing—fabric swaths with patterns much like those arrayed on Van de Velde's Export Room walls. Women are photographed in Delcommune's book and presented

and clothing fabric. In the middle of the hall, Van de Velde constructed stylish cabinets and interlocking counters where Belgian companies, their names visible, pinned rows of necklaces and bracelets created for Congolese markets. More prominent were the booths and rows of fabric stalls that lined an entire wall and spilled over into the midsection of the large Export Room. Van de Velde found an ingenious and streamlined method to display double-decker bolts of fabric that advertised the wares of the Belgian textile manufacturers buoyed by the prospects of millions of Congolese customers.[9] He also mounted sturdy packing wraps to form the base of these textile booths, reminding viewers inspecting each type of cloth of the mode by which it was to be transported and stacked in the steamer ships so conspicuous in his Export Room.

While jewelry and textiles thrived from the stimulus of the Congo Free State demand, the main impact on the export segment of the Belgian economy for Central Africa grew out of armaments and weapons manufactures, headquartered in Liège. Magnate John Cockerill's empire extended in the 1890s both to the shipyards of Van de Velde's Antwerp, where transatlantic steamers were built, and to the Cockerill Seraing steel- and ironworks in Liège, where cartridges for the rifles sent to the Congo Free State were made.[10] Van de Velde's Export Room contained no displays for these most profitable and continually in-demand items. But one Art Nouveau colleague of his in Liège did devote a modernist facade on a new building to that most important export to Congo—weapons. The entryway with the words "Fabrique d'Armes" showed below it a sgraffito panel with a scene of a pith-helmeted official on shore, his ocean liner visible on the seas behind him in the distance. He is engaged in instructing a local on how to lock and load a rifle, and he is pointing to the trigger mechanism. Beside him is a box with the rest of the rifles marked "Exportation" on the side and bearing on top the name of the manufacturer: "Lambert/Sevart, Fabrique d'Armes."[11]

Although he created no displays for the weapons industry, Van de Velde's Export Room did include one key element that demonstrated the militarization that sustained the king's Congo Free State. In a section of the hall that came after the *musée commercial*, Van de Velde furnished an exhibition area for the manufacturers of army uniforms for Congolese troops, the Force publique.[12] Already 18,000 strong by 1889, the Congolese security forces were provided an indigo blue uniform much like the one for Belgian army infantrymen. Belgium's voluntary army and its status of perpetual neutrality meant that demand for uniforms at home was relatively flat, and the whole enterprise was radically underfunded until 1909. Indeed, recruits and even officers in Belgium's army were ridiculed in the 1880s and 1890s for having to darn their own socks and repair their own fraying uniforms—that is, for sewing and not engaging in fighting.[13]

Initially Zanzibaris, but soon Congolese, formed the shock troops of the Congo Free State. They were pressed into years of service by promises of meager pay or by force. Back in Belgium, pride and incuriosity commingled in public reactions to the news about the recruitment and operations of the Free State's Force publique. But the boom in the uniform business was spectacular. For the Congo troops' uniforms, they blue serge to create tunics and short pants, with variations of the Belgian army kepi cap. The outfits were complemented by leather overstraps and ammunition

first as naked ("barbarie"), then as quasi-civilized, wrapped in textiles: the photo caption read "Vers la civilization: Jeunes femmes indigènes" ("Toward civilization: Young indigenous women") See Alexandre Delcommune, *Vingt années de vie africaine: Récits de voyages, d'aventures et d'exploration au Congo belge, 1874–1893* (Brussels: Larcier, 1922).

10
Reports on the flood of weapons into and militarization of Congo abounded and had been circulating for at least a decade, beginning with Stanley's reports (when he worked for the king in the early 1880s) that he had distributed "1,000 rifles and 2 million rounds of ammunition" to natives as he explored and occupied the region. Quoted in Neal Ascherson, *The King Incorporated: Leopold the Second in the Age of Trusts* (London: George Allen & Unwin, 1963), 122. In a letter from February 1895 from an inspector magistrate to a court president in Ghent, concern is expressed over the fact that more than two-thousand bullets were discharged in a single village raid by the Congo state troops. On the Liège Cockerill Seraing manufactures, see, for example, *Belgium and Holland, Including the Grand-Duchy of Luxembourg: Handbook for Travellers* (Leipzig: Karl Baedeker, 1910).

11
The architecture and facade are discussed in Alice Delvaille and Philippe Chavanne, *L'art nouveau en Province de Liège* (Liège: Editions du Perron, 2002), 32–33.

12
Th. Masui, *Guide de la Section de l'État indépendant du Congo à l'Exposition de Bruxelles-Tervueren en 1897* (Brussels: Veuve Monnom, 1897).

13
The caricature of threadbare uniforms and other derisions are described in Georges-H. Dumont, *La vie quotidienne en Belgique sous le règne de Léopold II, 1865–1909* (Brussels: Le Cri Édition, 1996), chap. 6. See also Lewis H. Gann, *The Rulers of Belgian Africa, 1884–1914* (Princeton, NJ: Princeton University Press, 1979), 18–24; and Émile Wanty, *Le milieu militaire belge de 1831 à 1914* (Brussels: Palais des Académies, 1957), 3–271. Charles Lemaire lamented that officers in the neutral army were being treated like "saber rattlers and old women." For a discussion of the dilemma of the neutral army and Congo as a space for militancy denied at home in the 1880s, see Debora Silverman, "Ensor's Panache: James Ensor, the Army and the Congo in Belgium, 1887," in *James Ensor: The Temptation of Saint Anthony*, ed. Nancy Ireson (Chicago: Chicago Art Institute, 2014), https://publications.artic.edu/ensor/reader/temptationstanthony.

pouches around the waist. These military accoutrements for export to Africa were also manufactured for and used by the Belgian army.

Leopold II Style, Vanderveldische Linie, *1959*

When he died in 1957, Van de Velde was buried next to his wife, Maria, in Tervuren, near his private residence there, the nautical Nouvelle Maison. The furniture he had made for the Export Room remained for some time in the Tervuren Museum of the Belgian Congo, but was eventually dispersed. Some of it was lost or possibly burned as firewood by the invading Germans.[14] The expansive armoire from the 1897 fair, that Van de Velde designed to display exports of pith helmets and officer uniforms, was transferred to the Royal Museums of Art and History in Brussels, where it remains in the storeroom.[15]

14
According to museum curator and anthropologist Maarten Couttenier.

15
The objects were transferred in 1967, as shown in Luwel and Bruneel-Hye de Crom, *Tervueren 1897*.

The Tervuren Congo exhibition, and the museum that issued from it, however, had other significant roles to play in sustaining Van de Velde's reputation for pioneering modernism and for promoting its distinctively Belgian qualities. In 1959, the official journal of the museum, *Congo-Tervuren*, published an article entitled "De 'Belgische stijl' te Tervuren" ("The 'Belgian Style' in Tervuren"). By that time, Art Nouveau had entered the canon of art and architectural history as a pan-European and international style. The article's author, Jean van de Voort, sought to reclaim Art Nouveau for Tervuren, for King Leopold II, and for Belgium. The article discussed the prominence of the "new style" in 1897, republishing archival photos of the chryselephantine Hall of Honor as well as Van de Velde's Export Room; the images captured the dynamic curving furniture wrapping around those booths, the counters for the costume jewelry, and the fabric stalls discussed above.

Van de Voort emphasized two key points. First, he maintained that Belgian Art Nouveau was inextricably linked to what he called the "Leopold II style." This he defined as a wide-ranging architectural initiative by the forward-looking king, who had built modern Belgium in such monuments as the iron-and-glass Laeken greenhouses, the Antwerp Central Railway Station, and the Tervuren palace itself. Second, he celebrated the divergence of Van de Velde as designer and theorist from other variants of Art Nouveau. With its thickly sinuous wood and directional rhythm, the Export Room typified a Belgian modern style. The indulgent excesses of what was known as "macaroni style" and the frivolity of the "yachting style," the author continued, differed greatly from the essence of Van de Velde's innovative work: the "*Vandeveldische Linie*," the structuring "line of force" or "line as a force."[16] Thus, just a few months before Belgium was caught by surprise by an uprising for independence in its African colony, the *Congo-Tervuren* magazine, featuring King Leopold II on horseback on its cover, proudly reasserted the integral connection between Belgian Art Nouveau and "Style Congo," as generated by the vaunted king's imperial and architectural visions.

16
Jean van de Voort, "De 'Belgische stijl' te Tervueren," *Congo-Tervueren* 5, no. 3 (1959): 62–63.

Coda: Style Congo, Belgitude, "Percer les ténèbres"

Van de Velde also designed the wood plinth and the glass-and-iron display case for Charles van der Stappen's *Mysterious Sphinx*, the chryselephantine showpiece for the entry Hall of Honor at of the 1897 Tervuren Congo exhibition. The *Sphinx* now takes its place in the ivories gallery in the Royal Museums of Art and History, without the original stand and case that

Van de Velde built for it. One rare photograph shows the original display in the Gallery of Honor of the first Royal Museum in 1898, where the *Sphinx* is set just behind Thomas Vincotte's bust of King Leopold II, in Van de Velde's case. The *Sphinx* appears to be beckoning to the king. A second photograph shows the *Sphinx* with the Van de Velde case and stand in 1910, now moved to a corner of the new Tervuren Museum of the Belgian Congo. Nearby are other Art Nouveau furniture pieces composed of the Congolese bilinga wood that Van de Velde used; above the glass box are wall-mounted Congolese textiles. Van de Velde sealed the case with four strips of metal, which split at the top with knobby serpent-like heads echoing the open-mouthed silver snake of the ivory *Sphinx* inside.[17] Bracing the forms is a series of visible rivets at each corner, which accent the rampant figures while visually echoing the dotted points on the swatches of cloth above them.

We do not know what happened to the Van de Velde case and plinth, nor when they were removed from the Van der Stappen chryselephantine figure. The *Sphinx* remained in the Tervuren museum until 1967 and was displayed there for decades; photographs after 1930 show the object without Van de Velde's case and stand. Although we have lost track of some artifacts, reconnecting the history of Art Nouveau to imperialism in the Congo Free State, when it flourished in its formative period, can bring many gains: a host of objects to revisit and analyze; the discovery of networks of patronage in Belgium, where modernism, imperialism, and liberalism interacted, linking prominent statesmen like Edmond van Eetvelde to industrialists like the Solvays; and an Art Nouveau known as "Style Congo." Distinctively imperial visual forms, social circles, and cultural mentalities coalesced in architecture and design.

There exists a forgotten article by Henry van de Velde, which sheds light on the collective psychology of expansionism in fin-de-siècle Belgium and the cultural dynamic that sustained it. Writing in the *Wallonia* journal in 1902, Van de Velde lamented the debilitated forms of modern design and celebrated, in contrast, the new work of his Art Nouveau colleague Gustave Serrurier-Bovy. He peppered the piece with general assertions about Belgium that echoed many voices of the period: he pointed to a nation beset by timorousness, incuriosity, and soul-sapping industriousness, a nation shaken to the core by centuries of foreign conquerors and domination, then confined to narrow frontiers and forced to be neutral in the decades after a hard-won independence.[18]

In Van de Velde's view, three sources of vitality coexisted at the century's turn to redeem Belgium with equal portions of militancy and "passion." He exalted these sources at the end of his article: the militant avant-garde breaking through the lethargy of stylistic inertia; the militant socialists breaking into mass demonstrations and organizing public agitation; and the king breaking beyond the boundaries of a Belgium constricted by European fiat by establishing colonies across the globe. The trio of regenerative powers was essential, and it redirected legacies humiliatingly prohibited from expression. As Van de Velde suggested, militancy discovers compensatory arenas "in a country that cannot wage war."[19]

In the 1880s, after fifty years of peace and prosperity, many of Van de Velde's avant-garde comrades embraced the task of cultural renovation; as second-stage liberators for Belgium, they transmuted the political emancipation achieved by their "grandfather" patriots in the 1830 revolution into

17
The double-headed serpent was also featured on the 1897 book cover that Van de Velde designed for Van Eetvelde's Liber memorialis celebrating the Secretary of State's work at the 1897 Tervuren Congo exhibition, as well as on the large doorway mural in Van de Velde's Export Room for the fair. See Silverman, "Art Nouveau, Art of Darkness," 158 and n42.

18
For expressions of the themes of "beset masculinity" and national torpor among the 1890s literary and legal avant-gardes, and expansionism in Africa as a redemptive response to these conditions, see Debora Silverman, "'*Modernité sans frontières*': Culture, Politics, and the Boundaries of the Avant-Garde in King Leopold's Belgium, 1885–1910," *American Imago* 68, no. 4 (Winter 2011): 707–97.

19
Henry van de Velde, "Un ingénieur-décorateur liégeois, M. G. Serrurier-Bovy," *Wallonia: Recueil de littérature orale, croyances et usages populaires* 10, no. 12 (December 1902): 285–86, 295–96. Van de Velde's passage on page 295 about shaking off the torpor in Belgium compares this condition to the cover of heavy dark clouds that dominate the country in the winter months; his rhetoric about dispersing the dark clouds recalls the early public statement of King Leopold II about opening up Africa to civilization. Leopold II said, in often-repeated phrases, that "penetration" of Africa would "open it up for civilization" and bring light by banishing dark shadows: "penetration" would "pierce the darkness that envelops whole peoples" ("percer les ténèbres qui enveloppent les peuples entiers"). This last statement circulated widely and was inscribed permanently on the gallery walls of the new Tervuren Museum of the Belgian Congo that opened in 1910, and hovers in the ceiling cornices there today.

the quest for artistic and literary independence. Van de Velde developed this generational theme, adding to it the twin forces of political and imperial radicalism. His statement of 1902 is a rare contemporary articulation of the interdependence of the three. Art Nouveau as "Style Congo" absorbs, expresses, and transforms this culturally resonant project of activating a new "belgitude" by breaking through limited horizons to expansionism in Africa.

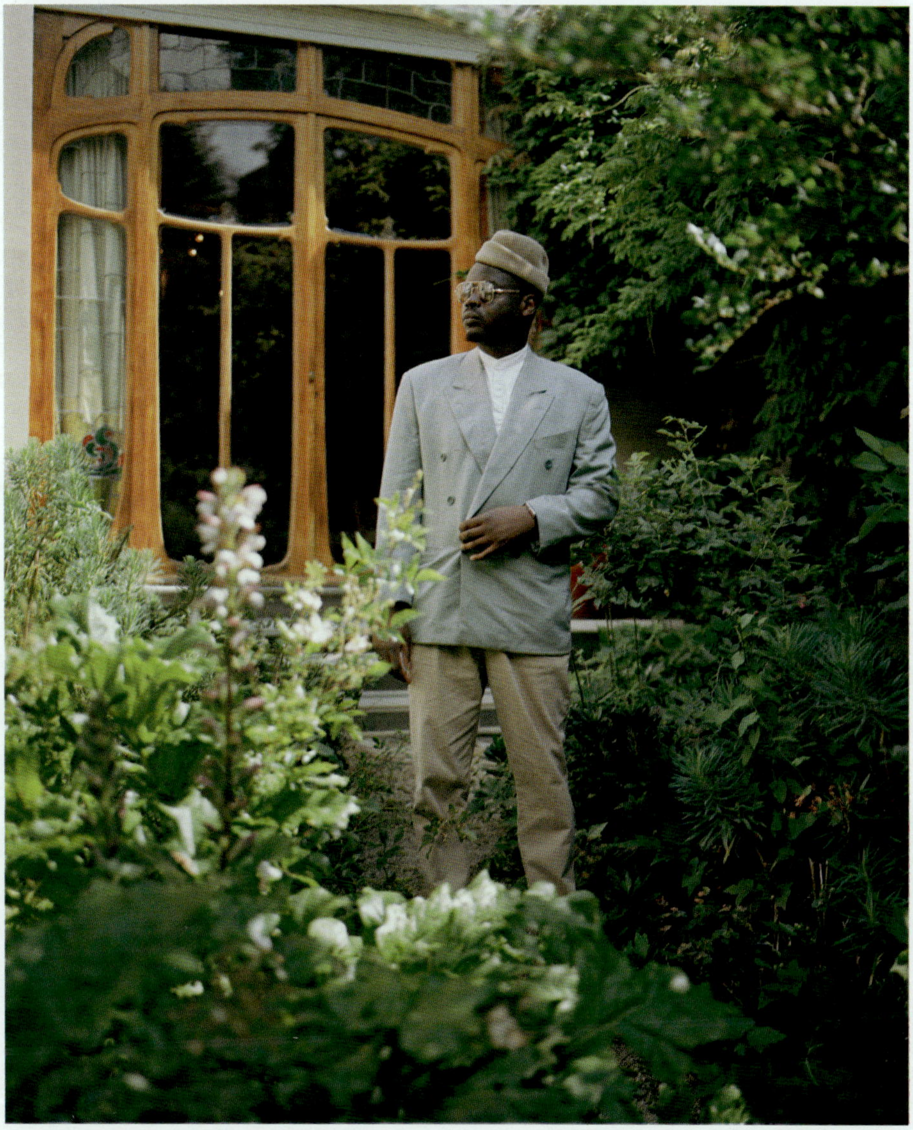

Chrystel Mukeba, *Badibanga Ndeka "Badi," Maison Horta*, 2021. Courtesy of the artist

Chrystel Mukeba works on the links between colonialism and Art Nouveau through portraiture of Afro-descendant Belgians in Art Nouveau buildings. Her photographic subjects include people who carry intimate lived experiences of colonialism as well as younger generations whose relation to the not-so-distant past is but a specter. The photographs were made in iconic Art Nouveau buildings, including the Horta Museum, built in 1898 by and for the architect Victor Horta, and the Hôtel van Eetvelde, designed in 1895 by Horta for Edmond van Eetvelde, general administrator of the Congo Free State. By suggesting a symbolic reappropriation of this architectural heritage, built via the exploitation of Congolese raw materials such as hardwood, the work poses a question: To whom does this heritage belong today? Mukeba's work draws a parallel with Santu Mofokeng's project *The Black Album / Look at Me: 1890 – 1950* (2013), in which the photographer explores the self-representation of Black communities in nineteenth-century colonial South Africa and their desire for social recognition. In her work, Mukeba proposes to make visible Belgium's Afro-descendant communities and to give them the opportunity to be represented within buildings that were built during a period of violent oppression and cultural destruction.

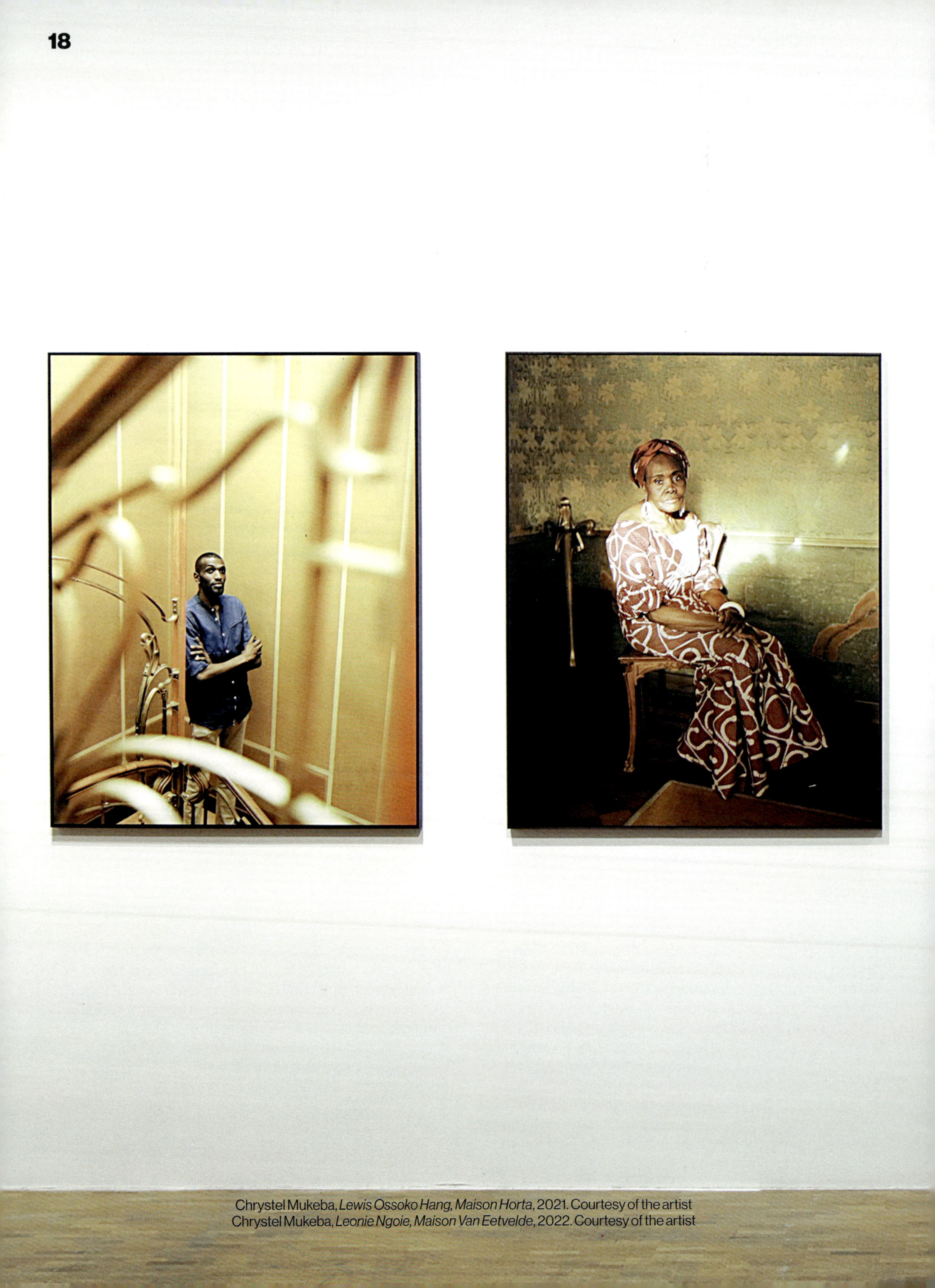

Chrystel Mukeba, *Lewis Ossoko Hang, Maison Horta*, 2021. Courtesy of the artist
Chrystel Mukeba, *Leonie Ngoie, Maison Van Eetvelde*, 2022. Courtesy of the artist

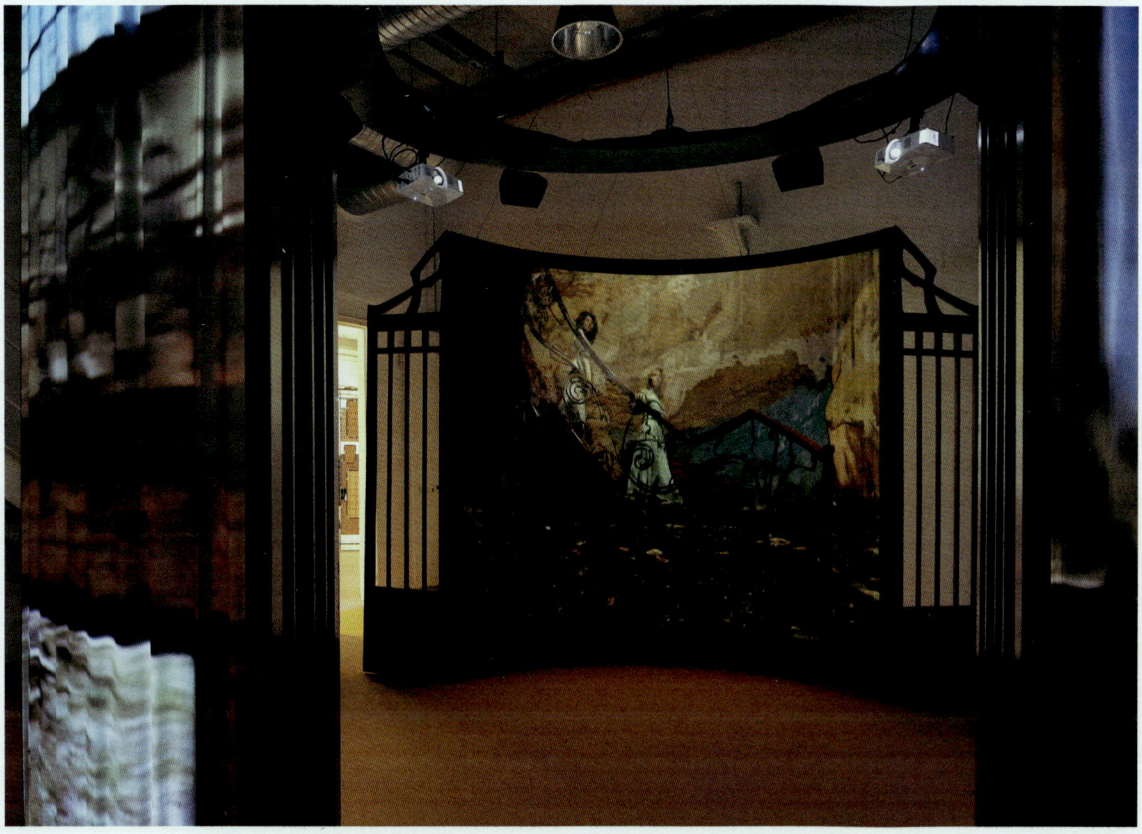

Judith Barry, *The Work of the Forest*, 1992. Three-channel video projection panorama.
Courtesy of the artist, Fonds pour l'Architecture, Brussels

First exhibited at the Fondation pour l'Architecture in Brussels in 1992, *The Work of the Forest* addresses Belgian colonialism in Africa as a major driving force for the development of wealth in Belgium. The piece unpacks the notion of interiority in relation to the architectural style of Art Nouveau. The screen design recalls the folding screens (possibly designed by Paul Hankar) in the Tervuren building of the Brussels International Exposition of 1897, which showcased the Congo Free State. Three synchronized videos playing across the three screens are projected as a continuous panorama. The first section probes the ruins of an Art Nouveau house through a series of phantasmagoric images that relate the colonization of Africa to fin de siècle life in Brussels. The second section investigates the Stanley Archives at the Royal Museum for Central Africa, looking at the relationship between Congolese people, explorers, merchants, and missionaries. The third section discusses the myth of Africa and the commodification of Africans by Europeans. The fourth section explores the gardens and greenhouses built by Leopold II to showcase his conquest of Congo. The fifth section metamorphizes into an endlessly transforming liminal space, setting simultaneous histories in motion as nature takes over, returning the museum to life.

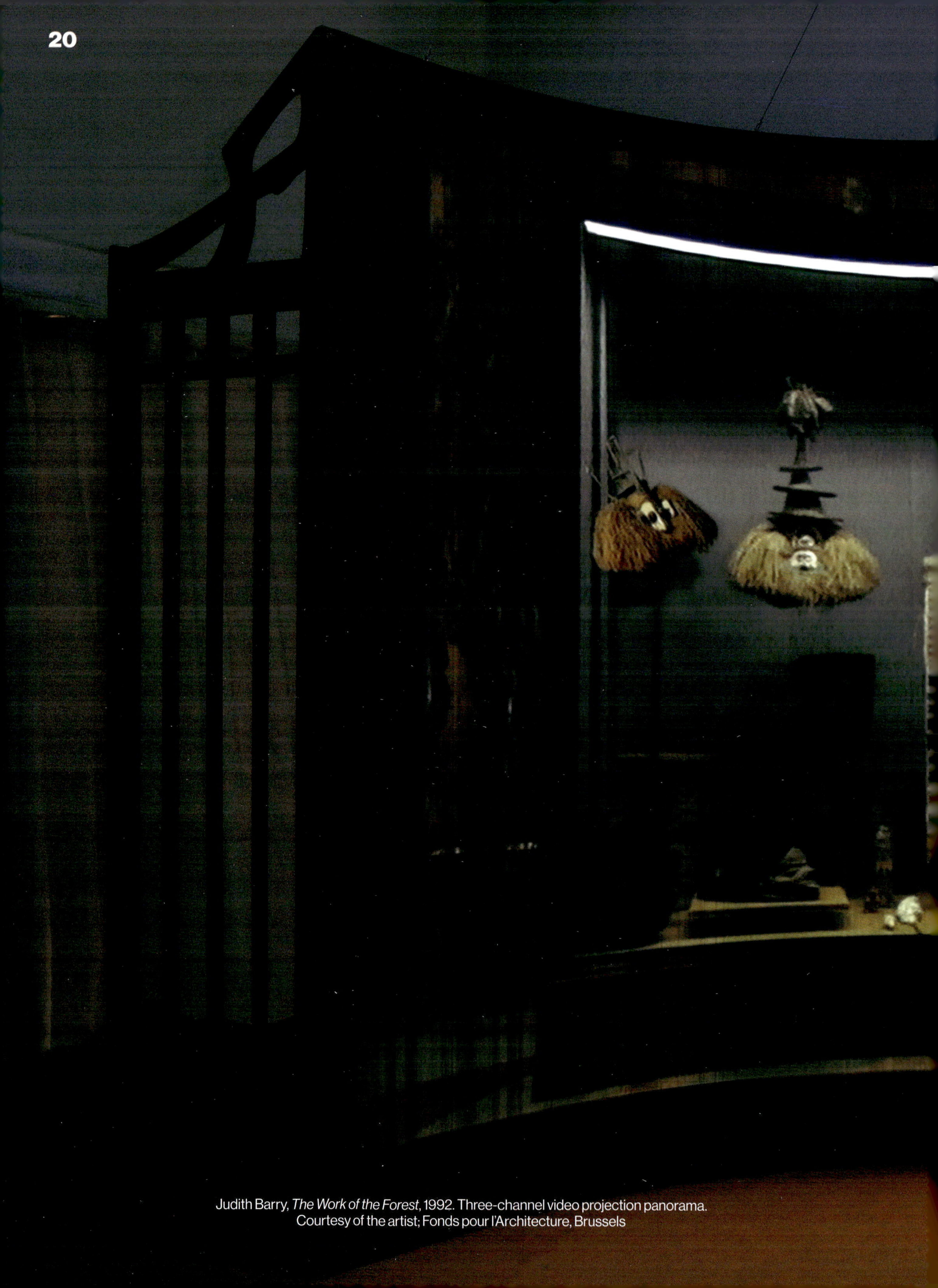

Judith Barry, *The Work of the Forest*, 1992. Three-channel video projection panorama.
Courtesy of the artist; Fonds pour l'Architecture, Brussels

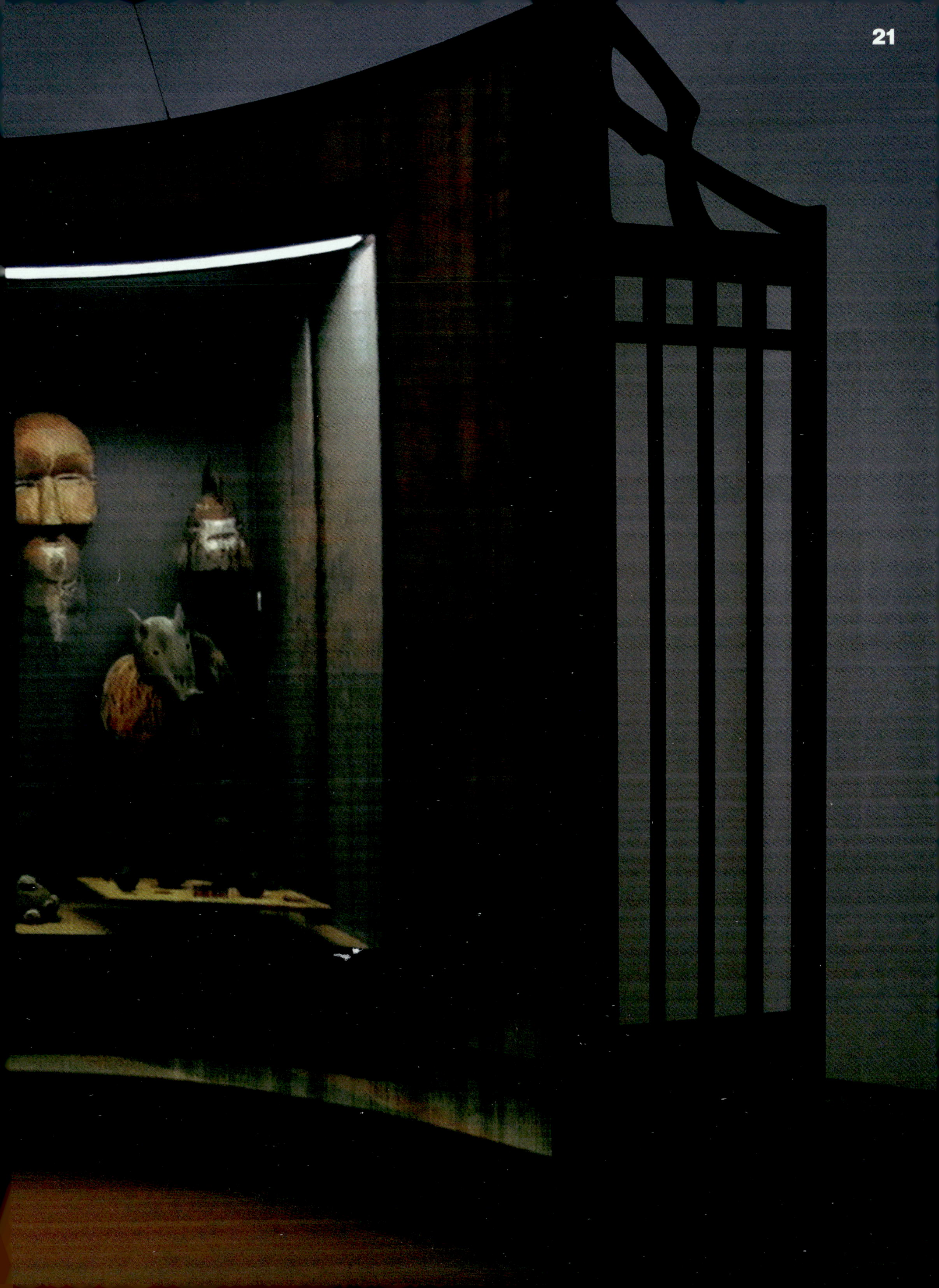

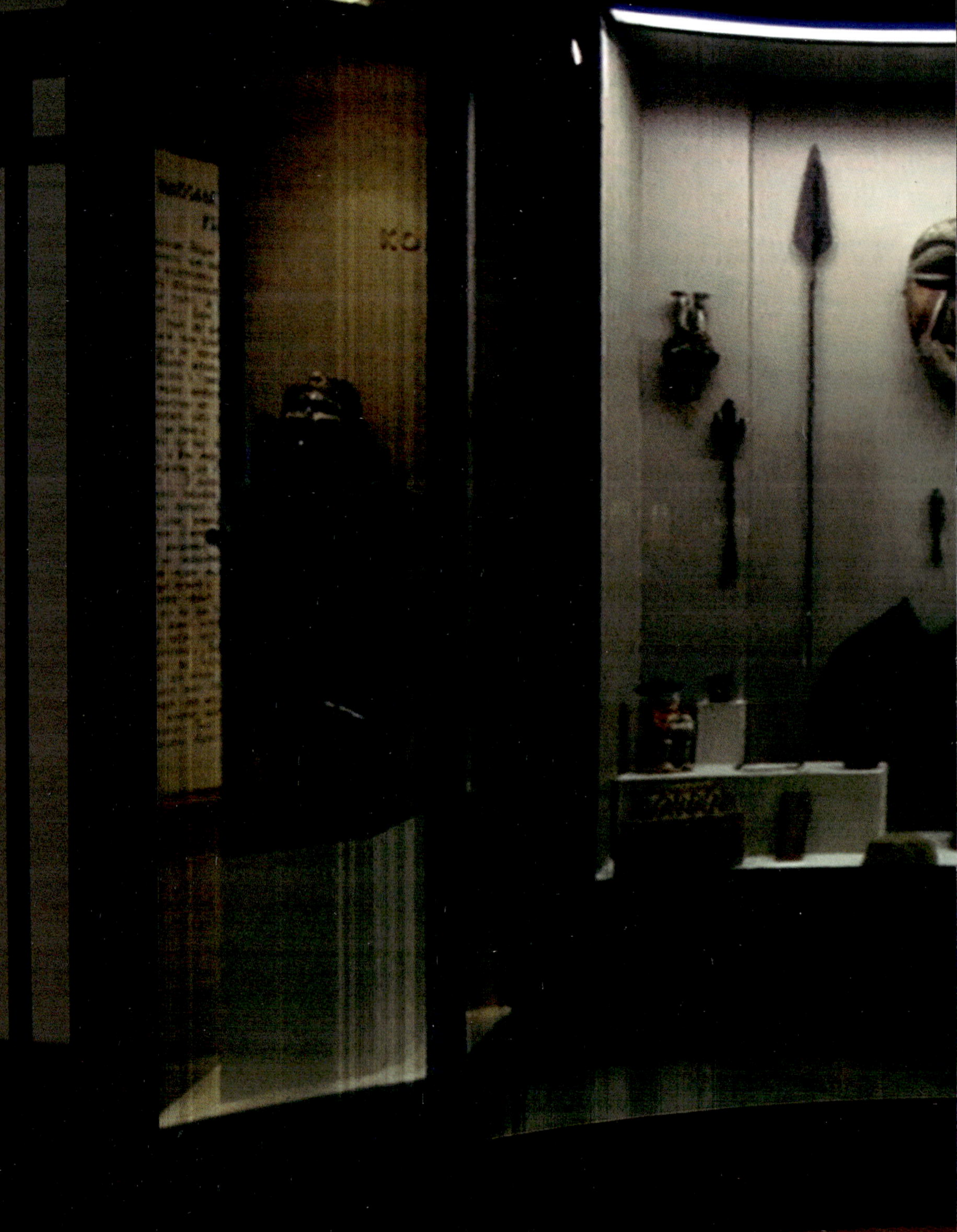

udith Barry, *The Work of the Forest*, 1992. Three-channel video projection panorama. Courtesy of the artist. Fonds pour l'Architecture, Brussels

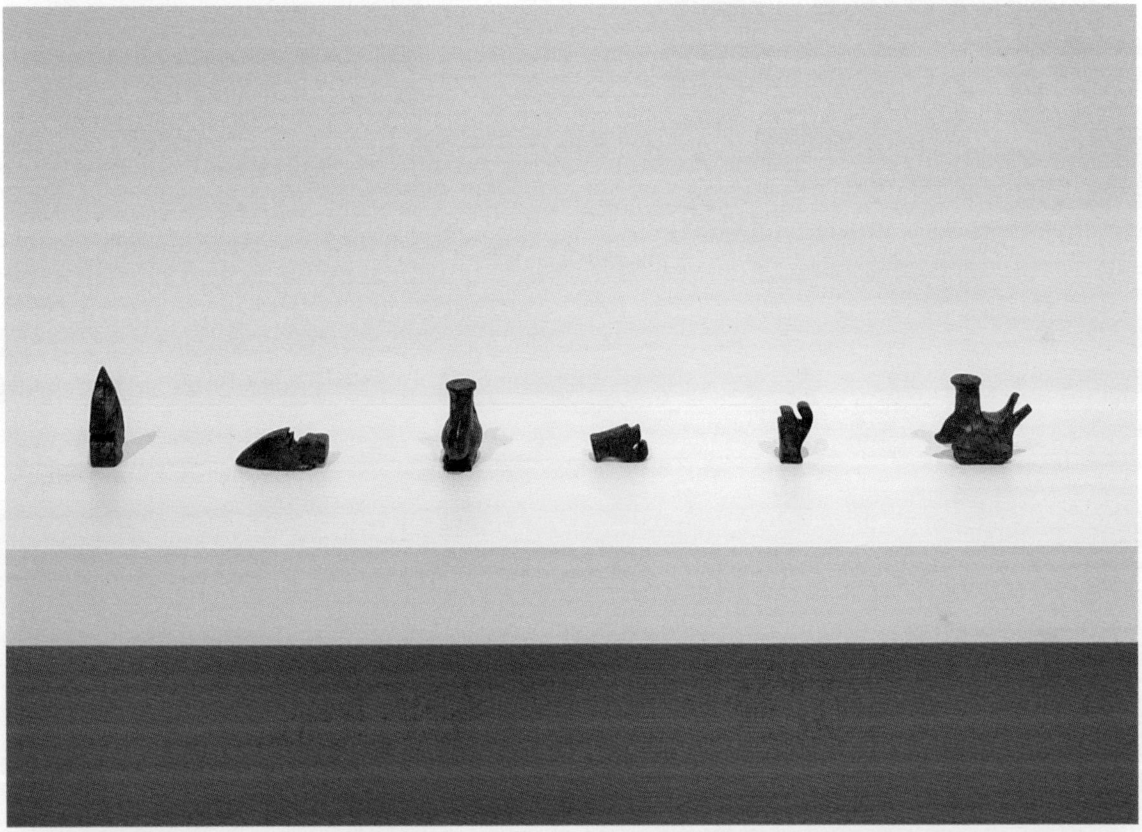

Ruth Sacks, *The Unmade Pavilion*, 2022. Cast iron sculptures. Courtesy of the artist; CIVA Collections, Brussels

Artist and researcher Ruth Sacks bases her iron casts on Victor Horta's plans for a colonial pavilion that never materialized. Horta designed a glass and iron Art Nouveau structure for the 1900 Paris Exposition, after which, the modular pavilion was to be dismantled and sent to the Congo Free State to be used as Belgian administration offices. However, the pavilion was never realized. The impracticality of sending an intricate construction to tropical Africa was not what halted its fabrication; rather, Horta's pavilion was deemed inappropriately luxurious in a political context in which King Leopold II's colonial regime faced widespread accusations of atrocities. *The Unmade Pavilion* isolates geometries from Horta's architectural plans to form object fragments that do not slot together. These iron pieces are the building blocks of nonfunctional formations that can easily fall apart. The unidentifiable iron fragments are rusted and treated so that they stain surrounding surfaces.

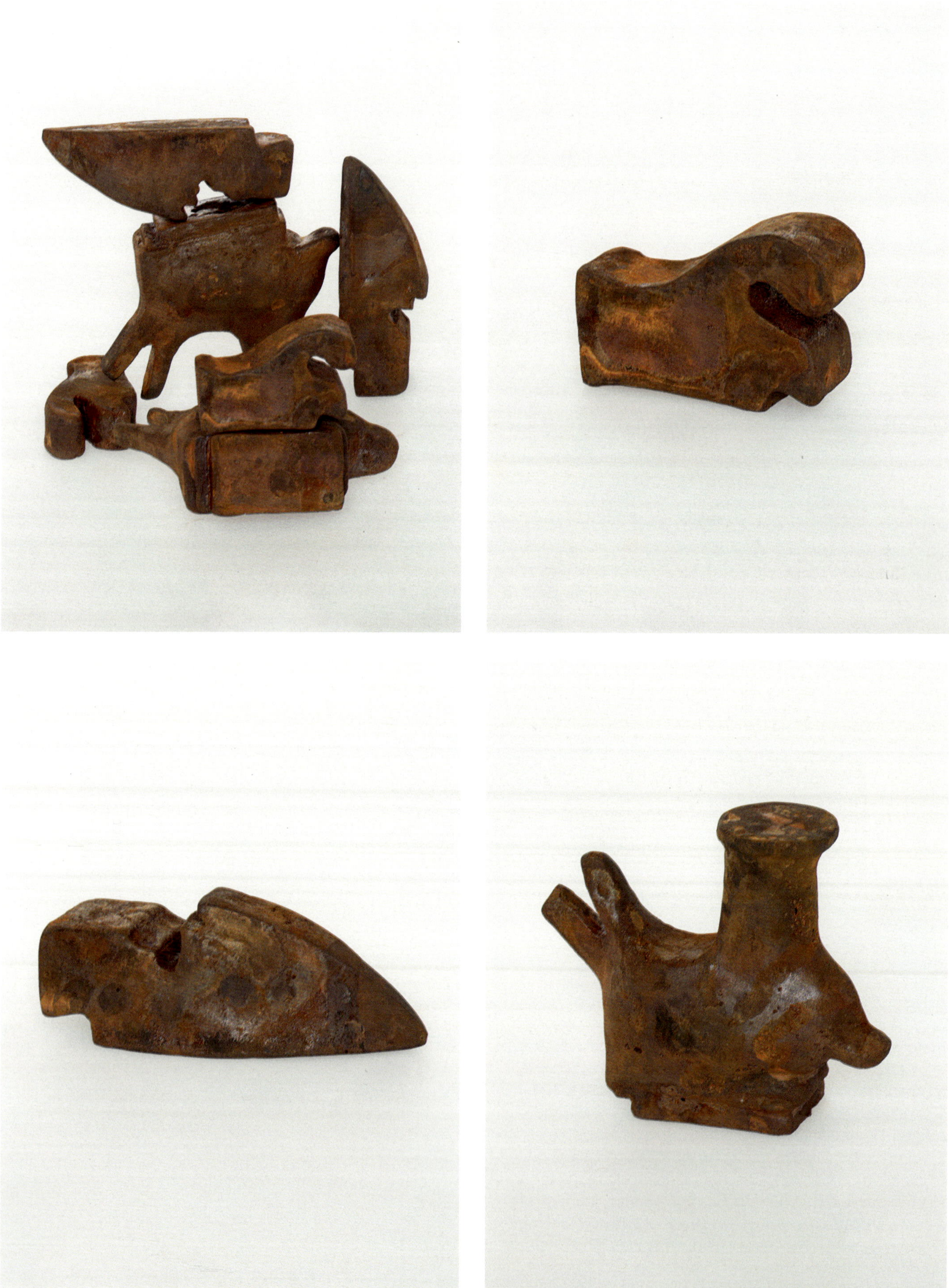

Ruth Sacks, *The Unmade Pavilion*, 2022. Cast iron sculptures. Courtesy of the artist; CIVA Collections, Brussels

What is the Congolese presence in Belgium today? It is from this question that the installation *Congolisation* (2023) was born. When protests erupted across North America and Europe after the murder of George Floyd, people started to demand the decolonization of public spaces. Statues were identified as the main symbols of this order. They were commented on, criticized, and sometimes spectacularly taken down. Yet architecture has remained, at least in Belgium, a space shielded from criticism. A wall is just a wall, right? A wall is never just a wall. A wall embodies a cultural project that always has a political agenda.

Exploring the archives of CIVA, we encountered the pavilions that were built by Belgian architects aiming to show Congo at different international, universal, and colonial fairs and exhibitions. This is where the journey of *Congolisation* began. From this journey through the archives, the answer to the role of Congolese culture and style in Belgium's architectural history appears obvious. We were, however, uncertain about what to do with this knowledge. *Congolisation* aims to share these materials with the hopes of redirecting the question of representation to meaningful investigations about the built environment. Heritage is a precious tool that can be used to better society.

The Pavilion as Speculative Space

Everything is fiction: the world is a collective cultural construction. It is important for us that we be aware of this construction as a way to continue to build on it or to destroy it, or be part of it, to be able to write new fictions. Form follows fictions and pavilions are the outposts of such fictions. They are built as thresholds between what is already there and what could happen. Pavilions are laboratories that propagate ideas into mainstream culture, and the Congolese pavilions that were built by Belgian architects should be seen as such.

Architecture as Means for Economy

From 1885 until 1958, the time frame of our research, the economic and imperial agenda behind the organization of all the fairs is clear. Architecture is used as propaganda to sell goods. At the time of the 1929 world economic crisis, imperialism was a governmental project and colonies represented a new hope for investment—new wealth, new opportunities, new dreams. The archival materials related to international pavilions report the products that were for sale, from rubber to uranium. The architects' task was to shape the appropriate box for encouraging the sale of colonial goods.

Construction of a Nation

In 1885, the first international exposition in which Congo was featured as a colony took place in Antwerp, and Congolese people were presented to the public in what was later known as the "human zoo." A decade later, in 1897, Leopold II asked architects and artists to not only showcase wood and ivory, but to transform the material into new objects. The international exposition of that year, which took place in Tervuren, just outside of Brussels, marked the official announcement of Art Nouveau, which at the time was also called Style Congo. As Leopold II said, in order to be recognized, the young nation-state of Belgium needed its colony. He was also known to have said that history would do him justice.

The Archive as Weapon: How to Look Back in Order to Move Forward

Looking back through the archive is also a means to look forward. History is a construction that reshapes itself based on new elements and new actors, dead or alive. It seems more crucial than ever that we look at our past through new eyes and with new agendas. Congo is not a faraway land; it's a central part of Belgian architectural history. Its materials, its clients, its agenda, and its archival presence have built Belgium.

Spatial Construction and Re-reading History

Architecture always has an agenda. It is from that premise that we researched and developed the spatial installation *Congolisation*. We were hoping to share more questions than answers. The installation is an attempt to recreate the experience of CIVA's archive: a grid system with voids allows the eyes to cross through time, revealing new links. We sought to keep the mediation elements as light as possible so that viewers can also make new links, can create their own stories based on a selected archival material. The installation features a timeline in which visitors can wander in the direction of their choice, slowly discovering that the end is uncannily similar to the beginning.

Conclusion: There Is No Good Answer to a Bad Question

Through the identification of the different proposals made by Belgian architects throughout history, we can see clearly that there isn't a correct answer to a bad question. A box to sell colonial goods might be made of gold or wood, yet it remains in the imperial logic of exploitation. Some voices of the past have tried to address the issues behind these pavilions—for instance, the counter-pamphlet (and later exhibition) published in 1931 by Surrealist artists against the 1931 Paris Colonial Exposition in Paris demanded, in bold font, "Don't visit the colonial exhibition."

We hope that our archival contribution might open a new field of study into the built environment and allow walls to talk. The Congolese influence on Belgian architecture is a sort of contamination. It offers new references to Art Nouveau reveries and the modern movement, and its specter appears in certain pavilions that are still hidden in plain sight in the Belgian environment. Georges Hobé's pavilion built for the 1897 exhibition, for example, long served as an outdoor barbecue space at the Royal Museum for Central Africa; or the Carillon, a brewery designed in Tournai by Henry Lacoste at the same time that he was building Belgium's pavilion for the Paris Colonial Exposition (1931), on whose floors and walls he used Congolese motifs of his own creation. We could also think about the *Panorama du Congo* painted by Alfred Bastien and Paul Mathieu for the Gent International Exposition (1913), now held captive in a military barrack of Ypres. A former pavilion of the 1958 Brussels World's Fair is today used as a garage for used car retailers along the Brussels Canal, or the pavilion built by Lacoste in Paris in 1931 is available for rent with this promising catchphrase: "If you are looking for an unusual location for your events and business meetings, the Belgian Congo Pavilion immediately plunges its guests into an exotic universe by taking them to the site in a 4 × 4. African musicians and dancers can, if you wish, punctuate your feasts with local colors: bison, crocodile, or ostrich meat on the barbecue. A real change of scenery in the Parc de la Rocq."

The exhibition is not over.

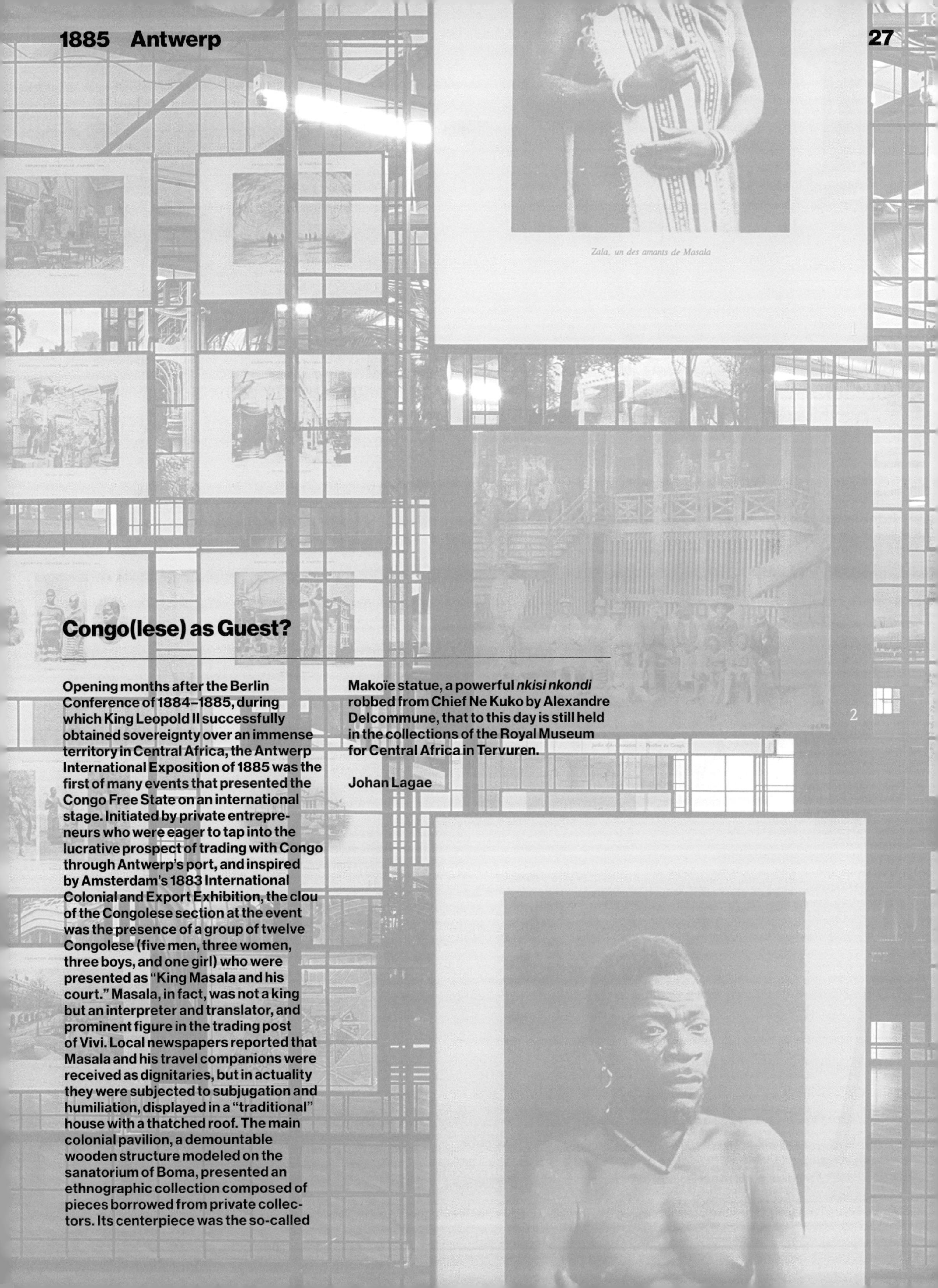

Congo(lese) as Guest?

Opening months after the Berlin Conference of 1884–1885, during which King Leopold II successfully obtained sovereignty over an immense territory in Central Africa, the Antwerp International Exposition of 1885 was the first of many events that presented the Congo Free State on an international stage. Initiated by private entrepreneurs who were eager to tap into the lucrative prospect of trading with Congo through Antwerp's port, and inspired by Amsterdam's 1883 International Colonial and Export Exhibition, the clou of the Congolese section at the event was the presence of a group of twelve Congolese (five men, three women, three boys, and one girl) who were presented as "King Masala and his court." Masala, in fact, was not a king but an interpreter and translator, and prominent figure in the trading post of Vivi. Local newspapers reported that Masala and his travel companions were received as dignitaries, but in actuality they were subjected to subjugation and humiliation, displayed in a "traditional" house with a thatched roof. The main colonial pavilion, a demountable wooden structure modeled on the sanatorium of Boma, presented an ethnographic collection composed of pieces borrowed from private collectors. Its centerpiece was the so-called Makoïe statue, a powerful *nkisi nkondi* robbed from Chief Ne Kuko by Alexandre Delcommune, that to this day is still held in the collections of the Royal Museum for Central Africa in Tervuren.

Johan Lagae

1885 fig.1

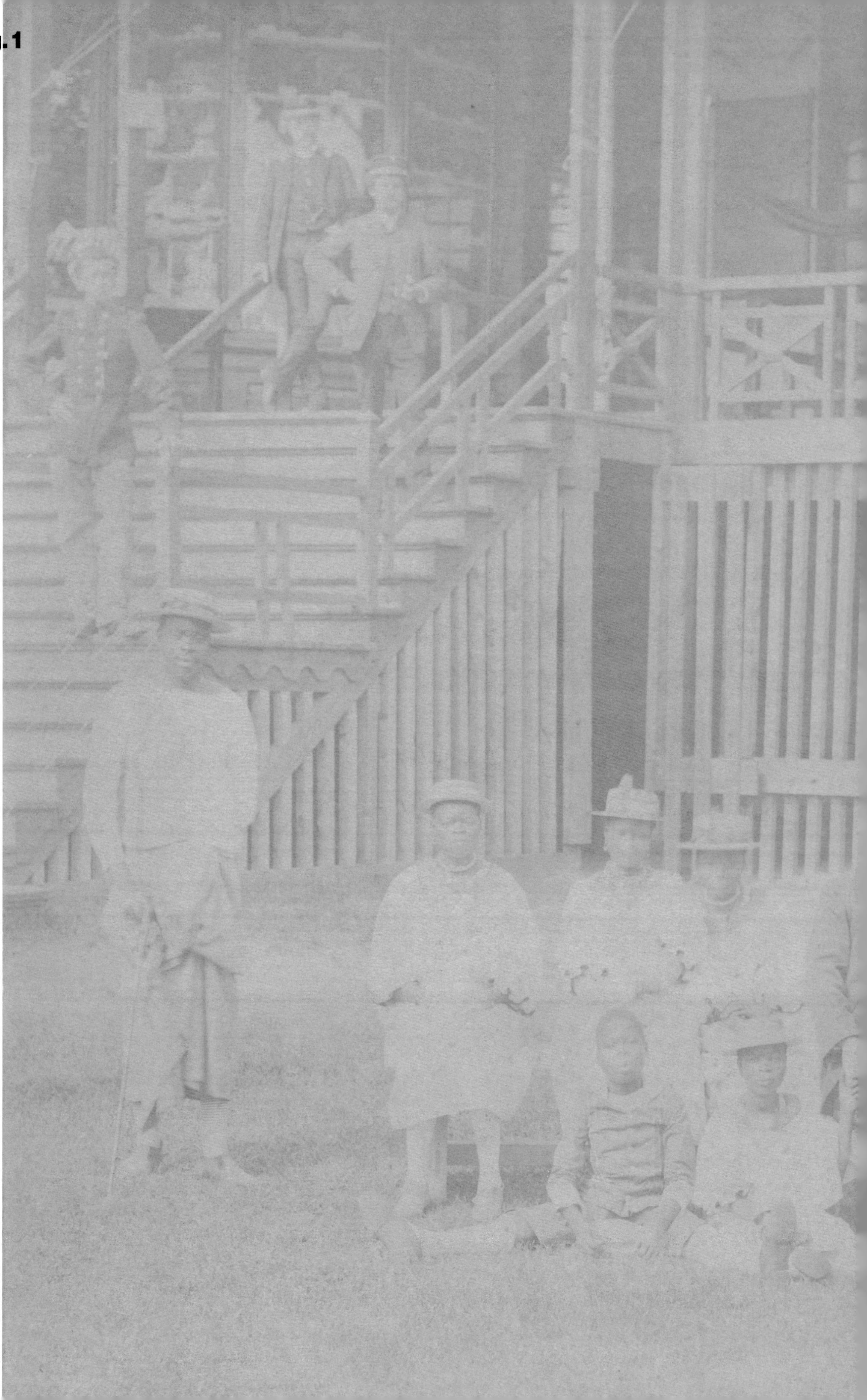

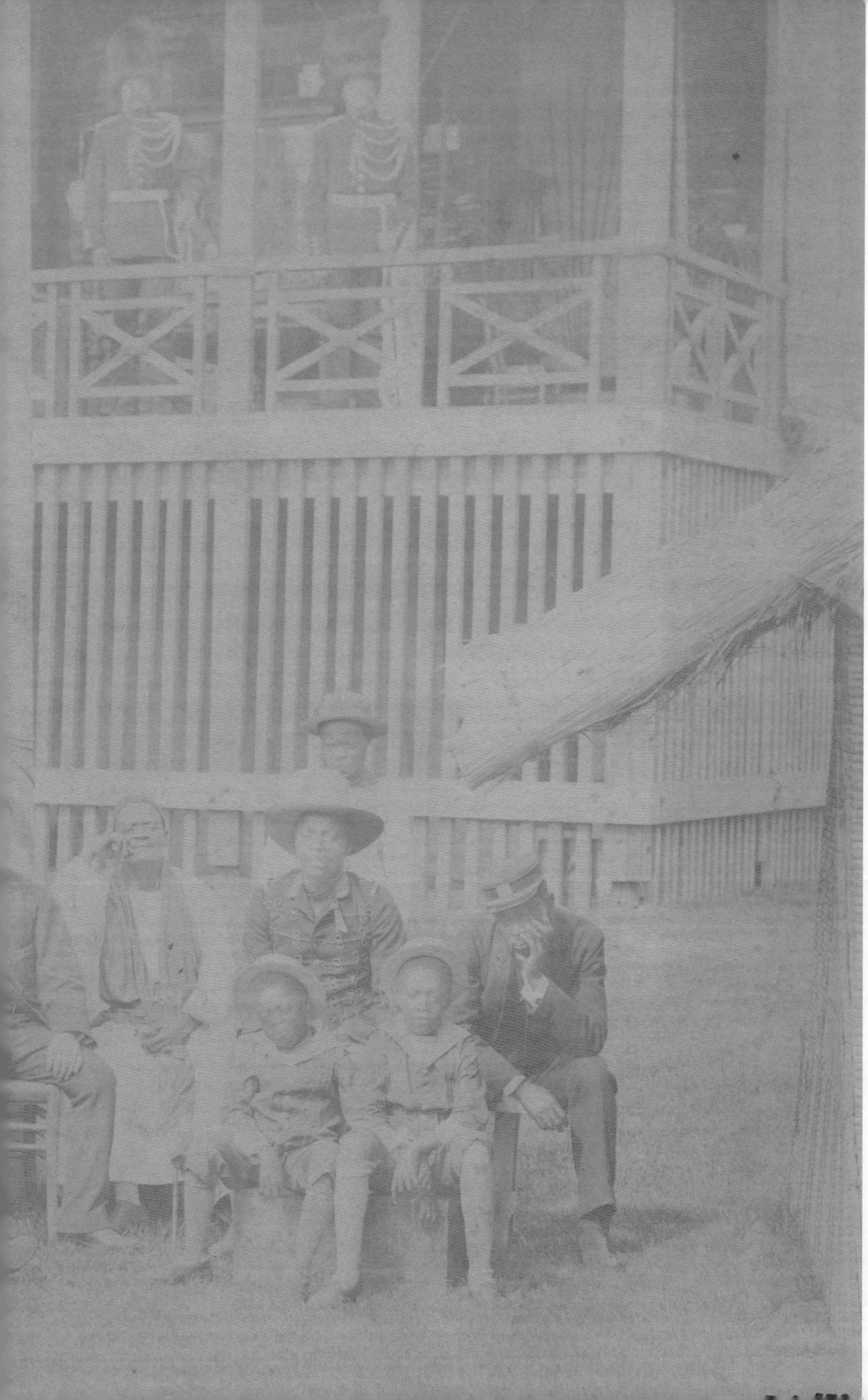

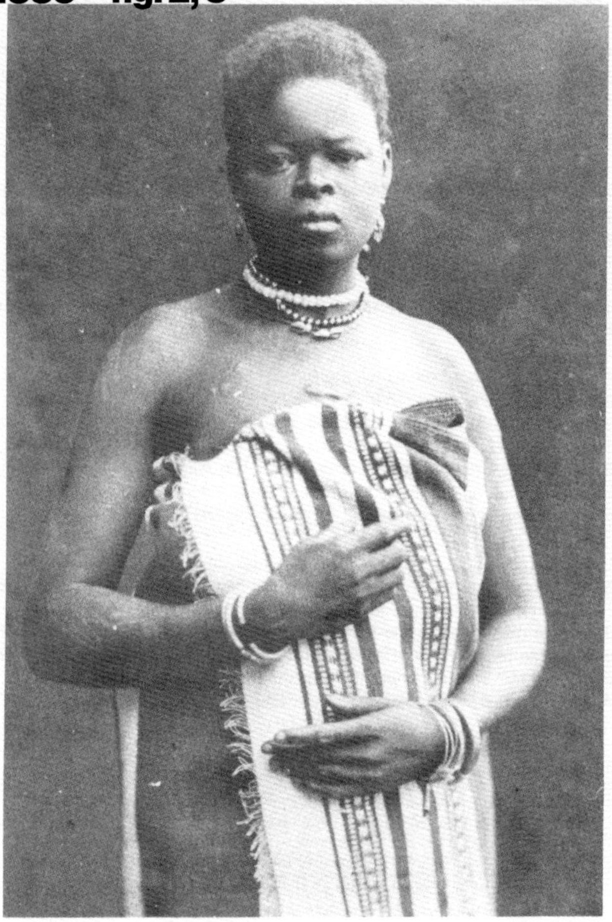

Zala, un des amants de Masala

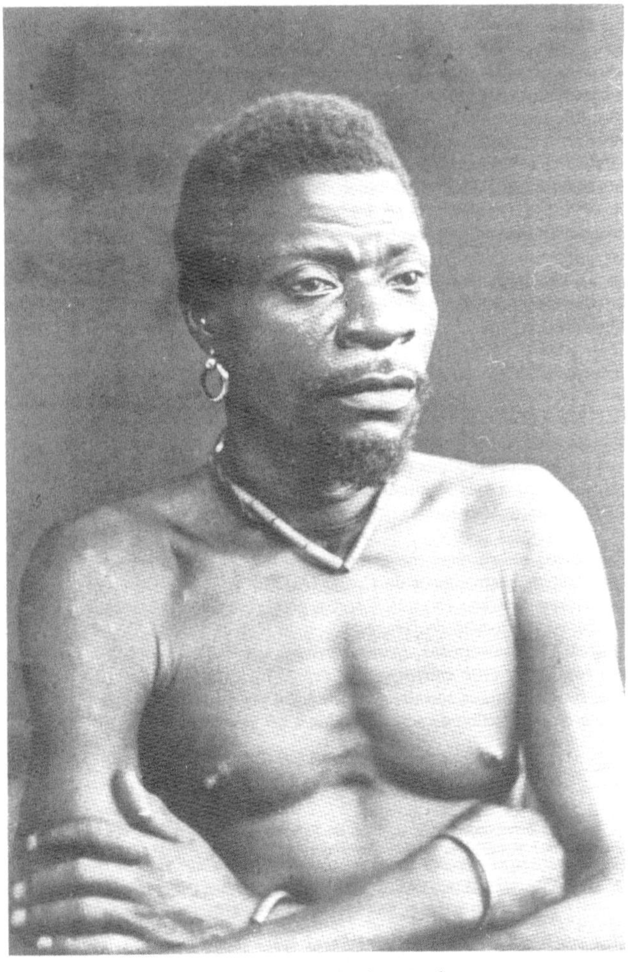

Le Roi Masala chez le photographe

la Compagnie du Chemin de Fer Matadi-Léopoldville, qui a décrit sa rencontre avec Masala, le 25 juin 1885, comme suit: "*25 juin 1887: Ce matin à 8 heures, M. Janssen et moi, nous sommes partis pour Vivi où les chefs avaient été convoqués par ordre du gouverneur général en de grandes palabres. Nous faisons la traversée à bord de la Belgique, le premier bateau que nous avons envoyé au Congo. Nous arrivons à 8h30 et vers 11h, après une minutieuse visite faite au plateau de Vivi, nous nous trouvons réunis dans la grande salle de la station de Vivi Beach.*

Tous les chefs de Vivi sont là. Voilà Vivi Mavungu le principal des chefs, avec sa figure intelligente et rasée et sa jambe boiteuse. Il est vêtu d'une redingote noire ... Celui-là avec sa grosse figure, coiffé d'une casquette de l'armée prussienne, c'est Mambouk le second en importance. Immédiatement après vient Massala l'ancien visiteur de l'exposition d'Anvers. Quand Massala est parti de Vivi pour Anvers, c'était un chef sans la moindre importance, mais les richesses qu'il a rapportées d'Europe et la considération que ce voyage a attachée à sa personne l'ont considérablement élevé et il n'est pas douteux que, s'il survit à Vivi Mavungu, il deviendra le principal des chefs de Vivi.

Tous les rois nègres sont assis sur des chaises ... M. Janssen présente ensuite à Vivi Mavungu et à Mambouk deux jeunes nègres, leurs fils, qu'il fait élever à la mission de Boma. Il dit aux pères que les enfants apprennent à lire et à écrire, qu'ils savent déjà un peu parler le français et il leur demande s'il entre dans leurs intentions de les reprendre ou de les laisser continuer leurs études à la mission. Vivi Mavungu et Mambouk s'empressent de répondre que leurs enfants doivent rester à la mission, mais qu'il est bien entendu que M. Janssen continuera à les nourrir, à les habiller et qu'il payera en plus à leurs pères la redevance habituelle, c'est-à-dire deux pièces de mouchoirs par mois. M. Janssen le leur ayant promis, les palabres sont finies. Le gouverneur général fait distribuer ses présents, c'est-à-dire trois douzaines de mouchoirs par chef et six bouteilles de gin. Quand il arrive à Massala, il lui remet en outre un immense bonnet à poil de grenadier, son cadeau particulier, puis une ombrelle en soie rouge, cadeau de Mme Oesterith d'Anvers et une boucle d'oreille en or, cadeau de Mme Wauwerman également d'Anvers. Les chefs voisins de Massala regardent avec une envie non déguisée les superbes choses que leur camarade reçoit. M. Janssen leur fait ainsi expliquer que ces objets qu'il donne à Massala sont des souvenirs que lui envoient ses amis d'Europe; que si Massala reçoit plus que les autres, c'est la juste récompense de la confiance qu'il a montrée en se rendant chez les blancs en Europe, tandis qu'aucun des autres chefs n'avait voulu y

Ce comité remue ciel et terre pour avoir à sa disposition les belles collections de l'A.I.C. et de la N.A.H.V.. Ensuite, il s'adresse à la Province d'Anvers, à la Ville d'Anvers et au Comité Exécutif de l'Exposition afin d'obtenir le concours pécuniaire qui lui est indispensable. Il est évident que cet argent doit servir à faire venir à l'Exposition quelques sujets noirs de Léopold II et à les entretenir durant tout leur séjour. Ainsi Amsterdam, qui, grâce à la collaboration de la N.A.H.V. a su exhiber 'quelques spécimens de la race congolaise' aux visiteurs de son Exposition en 1883, trouvera en Anvers son égal!

Le 13 mai 1885, le conseiller municipal libéral Victor Lynen et son collègue catholique P. Koch, respectivement président et secrétaire général du comité exécutif de l'Exposition, informent Wauwermans qu'ils interviennent pour une somme de 10.000 francs dans les frais auxquels donnera lieu la participation des 'naturels du Congo'. Ils se proposent aussi de partager entièrement l'opinion de la S.R.G.A. selon laquelle il n'y a pas lieu de réclamer du public une rétribution spéciale à l'entrée de l'emplacement réservé aux Congolais dans les jardins. C'est à fonds perdus, ajoutent-ils encore, que le comité exécutif met à la disposition de la S.R.G.A. la susdite somme de 10.000 francs.[14] La cité scaldéenne offre à son tour une somme de 10.000 francs, tandis que le subside de la Province d'Anvers promet une subvention de 2.000 francs. L'Etat Indépendant ne contribue donc pas financièrement à l'organisation de la section coloniale.

L'arrivée des hôtes noirs à Anvers, 12 mai

"... Ces Congolais forment certes une des plus belles tribus africaines. Les hommes sont beaux, bien musclés, marchant droit et ferme; la vivacité de l'oeil trahit une activité mentale très grande; les femmes, beaucoup plus petites, ont le regard d'une grande douceur, et nous donneraient une assez haute idée des beautés nègres, n'était la suprême élégance de leur marche de canard ..."[15]

---

14. Copie de lettre de V. Lynen et P. Koch à H. Wauwermans, Anvers, 13 mai 1885, in: Archives de la Ville d'Anvers, Wereldtentoonstelling 1885, Copyboeken (E), Exécutif n° 11 (E11: Copie de lettre), 1041/84d.

15. CORNELI R. & MUSSELY P., Anvers et l'Exposition Universelle 1885, Bruxelles, 1886, p. 225.

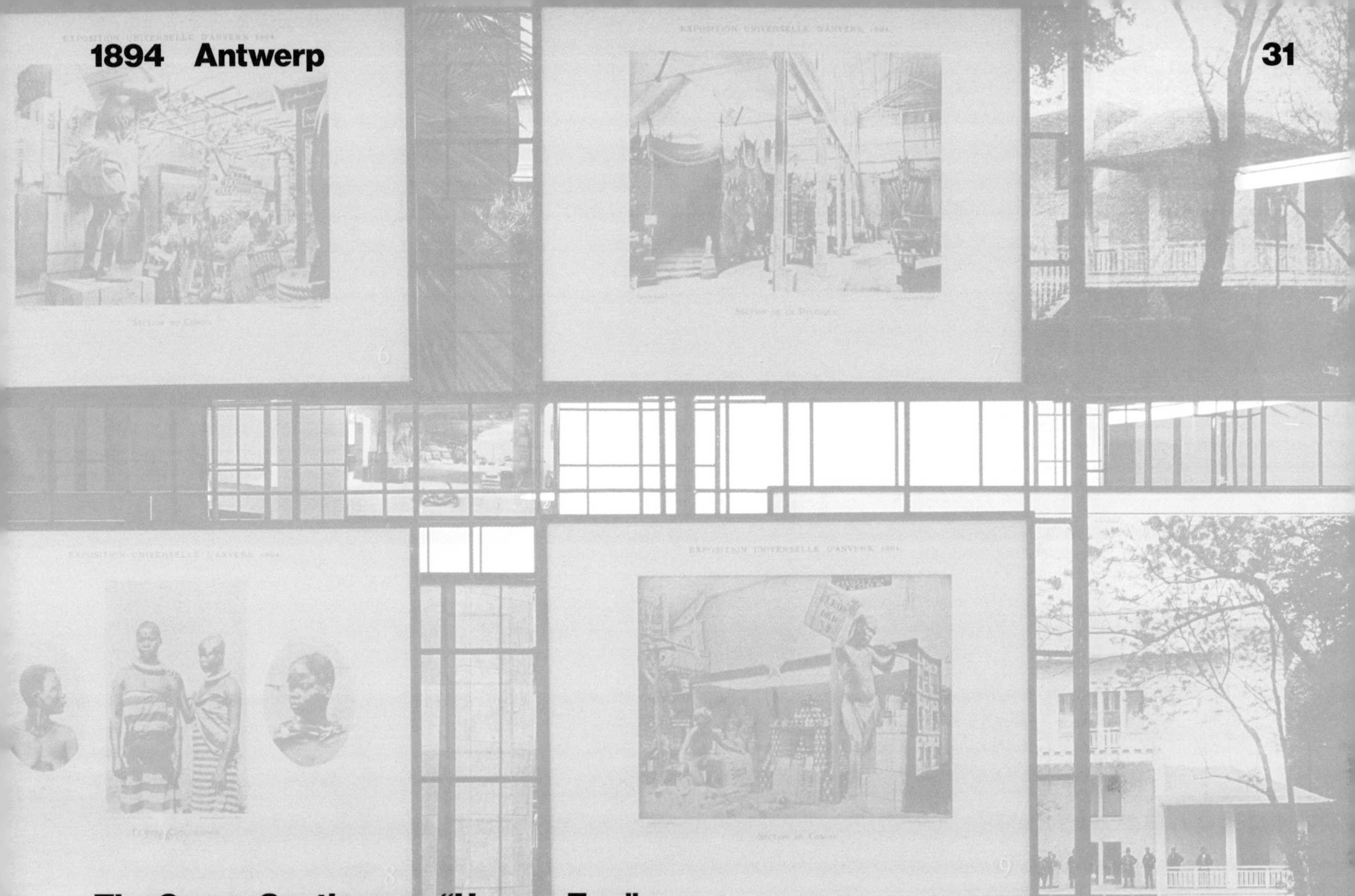

The Congo Section as a "Human Zoo"

Organized by the Congo Free State authorities, under the leadership of Edmond van Eetvelde, the Congo section of the 1894 Antwerp International Exposition focused on the economic dimension of the colonial enterprise. In order to stimulate investments for the exploitation of the territory, the temporary Congo palace housed elaborate displays that presented various imported resources, from different kinds of tropical wood to rubber samples, and illustrated their potential applications. No less than 144 Congolese from different regions were shipped to Antwerp, as well as several animals, expanding dramatically the so-called human zoo display that had been part of the 1885 exhibition. The Congolese were accommodated in a "Congolese village," framed on three sides by the Royal Museum of Museum of Fine Arts, the immense *Halle des machines et d'électricité*, and the Congo Palace, a temporary edifice with strong orientalist features. Consisting of a series of "traditional" houses organized around an artificial pond, which the Congolese navigated on a pirogue, the "village" served as the stage for musical performances and traditional craft making, and it also formed the backdrop to document different ethnic groups through photographic surveys. With their pronounced bodily scarification, the Bangala people attracted particular attention. As recent research revealed, the 1894 exhibition ended tragically: a significant number of Congolese fell ill during the exhibition, and eight of them died. Today, they rest in an anonymous ossuary in the Schoonselhof burial grounds in the outskirts of the city.

Johan Lagae

1894 fig. 4

EXPOSITION UNIVERSE

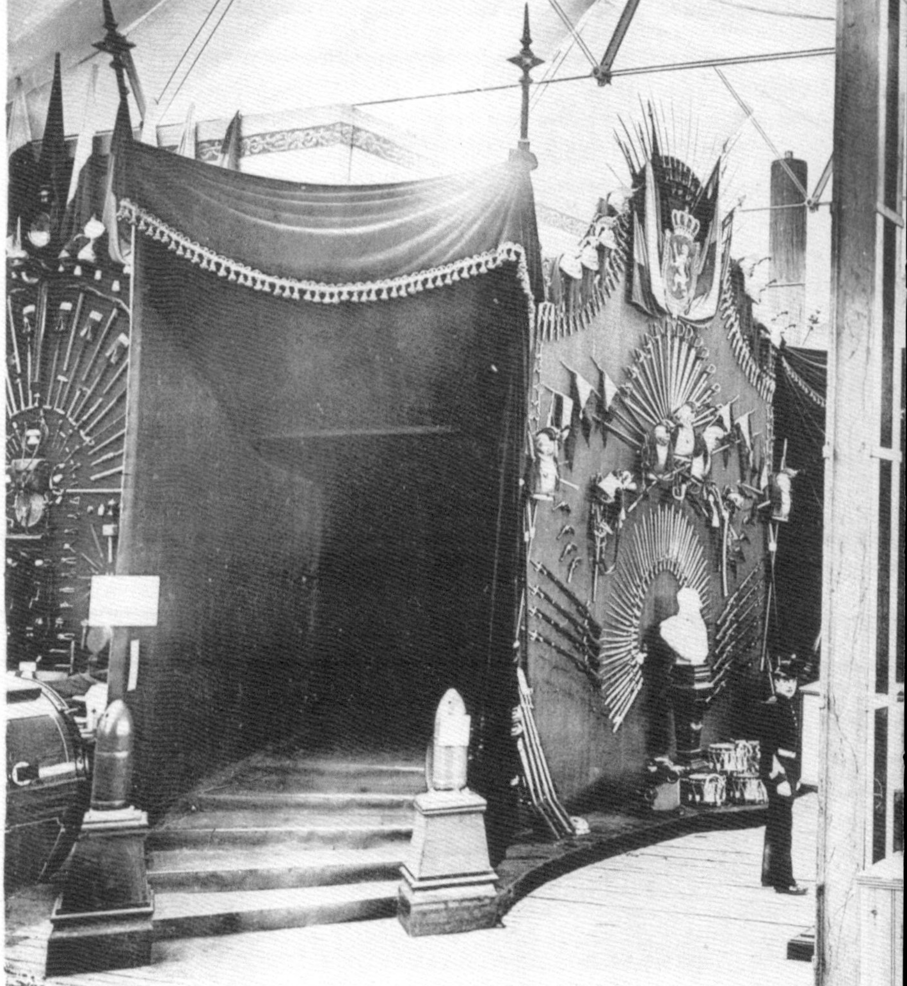

Cliché Th. Lantin.

SECTION DE L

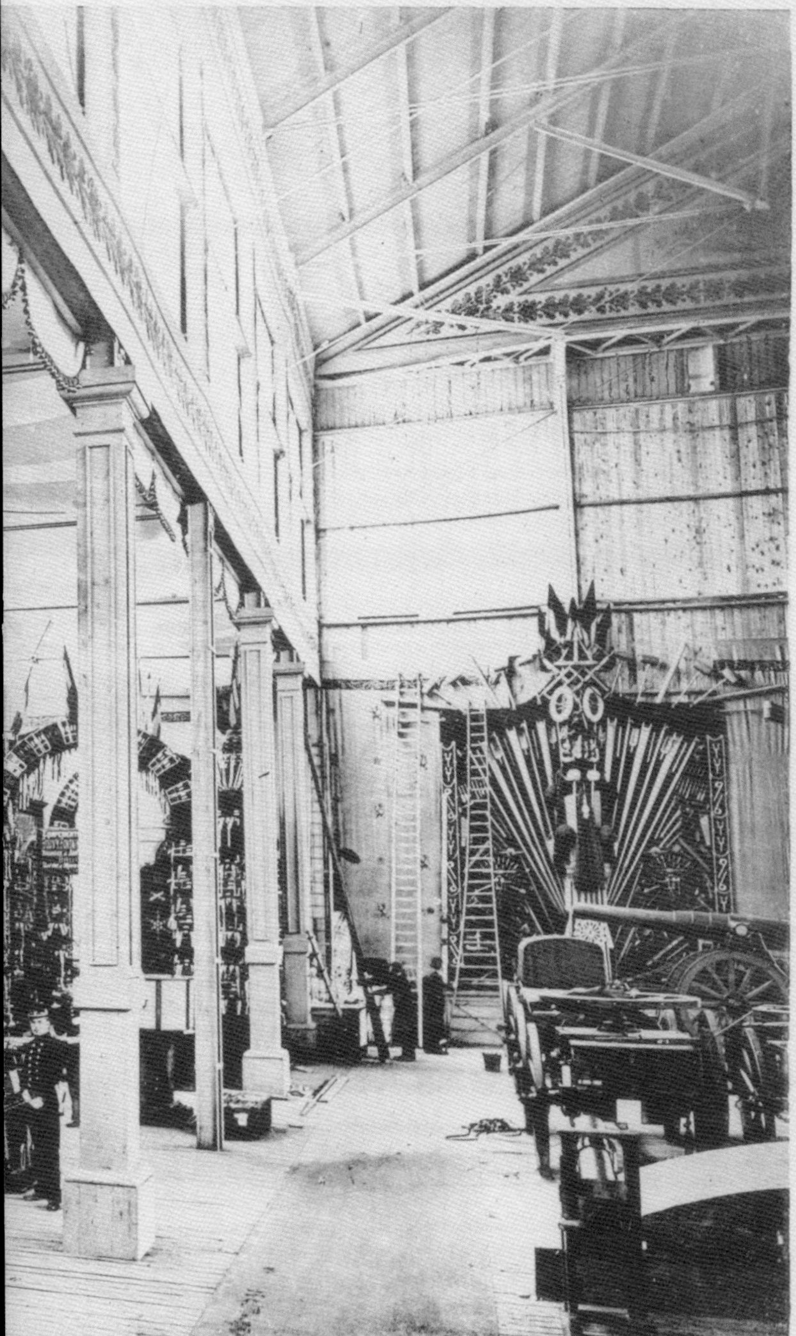

Photocollographie Jos. Maes.

BELGIQUE.

1894 fig. 5, 6, 7

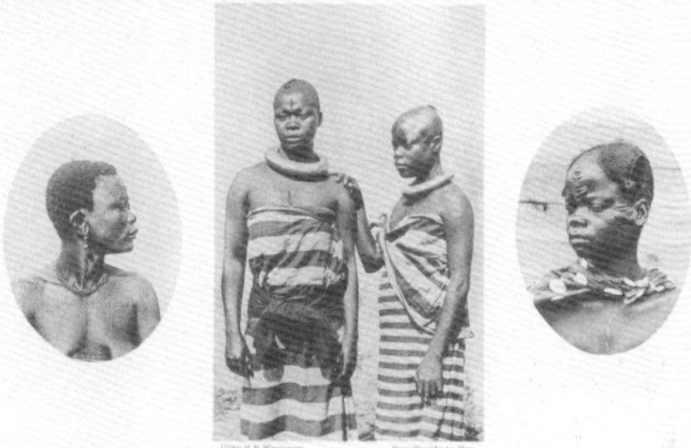

FEMMES CONGOLAISES.

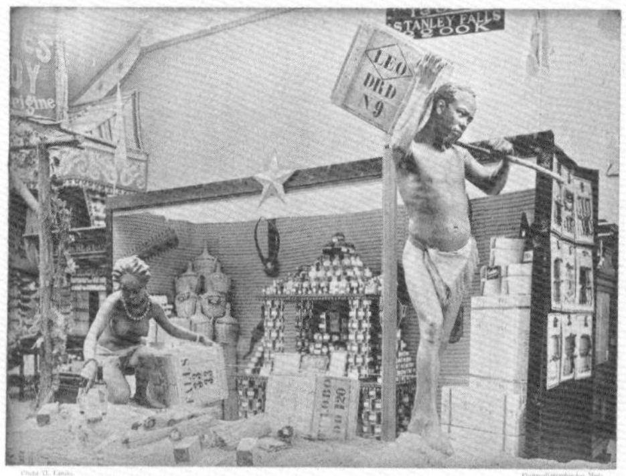

SECTION DU CONGO.

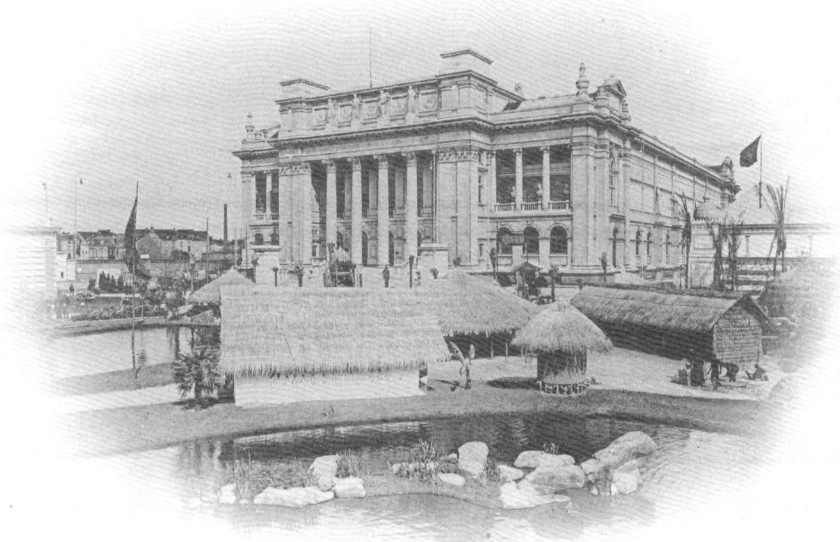

Cliché Th. Lantin. Photocollographie Jos. Maes.

MUSÉE ET VILLAGE CONGOLAIS.

Style Congo and (the Display of) Imperial Ambitions

Organized at the same moment when the gruesome colonial regime of Leopold II started to be questioned internationally, the Congo section at the Brussels International Exposition of 1897 formed a blatant celebration of the king's overseas enterprise. Taking place in the neoclassic Palais des Colonies (today known as Africa Palace), built on the same site in Tervuren where a decade later the vast Cité Coloniale was imagined by architect Charles Girault, the event was considered a huge propagandistic success, attracting over one million visitors. Ethnographic displays were complemented by seductive presentations of the exploitation of the territory, which would expand substantially the following year due to the finalization of the Matadi–Léopoldville Railway, a major infrastructural project that was highlighted at the event. The Art Nouveau interiors of the exhibition rooms, designed by leading artists and architects like Henry van de Velde, Paul Hankar, and Georges Hobé, as well as the presentation of eighty chryselephantine sculptures made by, among others, Philippe Wolfers, contributed to the exhibition's appeal and resulted in the coining of the label "Style Congo," which spoke of a widespread fascination among the visitors with "exotic" materials and forms. In an attempt to evoke the natural scenery of Congo, three "villages indigènes" (native villages) were constructed in the park, with the houses conceived and constructed according to information collected from doctors and military officers with substantial field experience in Central Africa. Peopled with 267 Congolese, including mainly soldiers of the Force Publique and members of the Bangala and Mayombe peoples, the village formed, as in the previous exhibitions, the most popular part of the Congo section. However, the death of seven Congolese, to which the still existing graves near the church of Tervuren testify, would put an end to the practice of bringing over Congolese people and displaying them in a human zoo.

Johan Lagae

1897 fig. 8

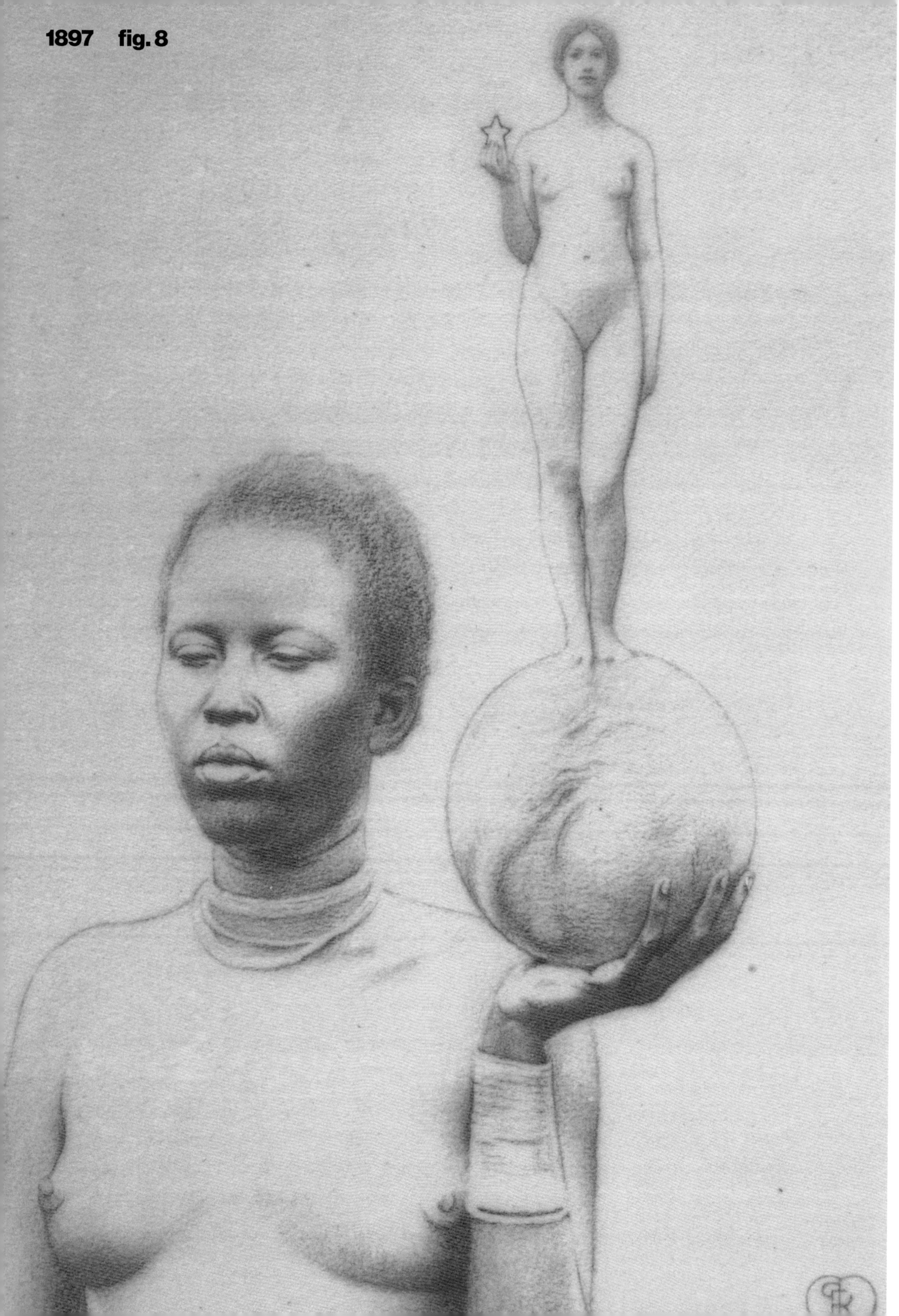

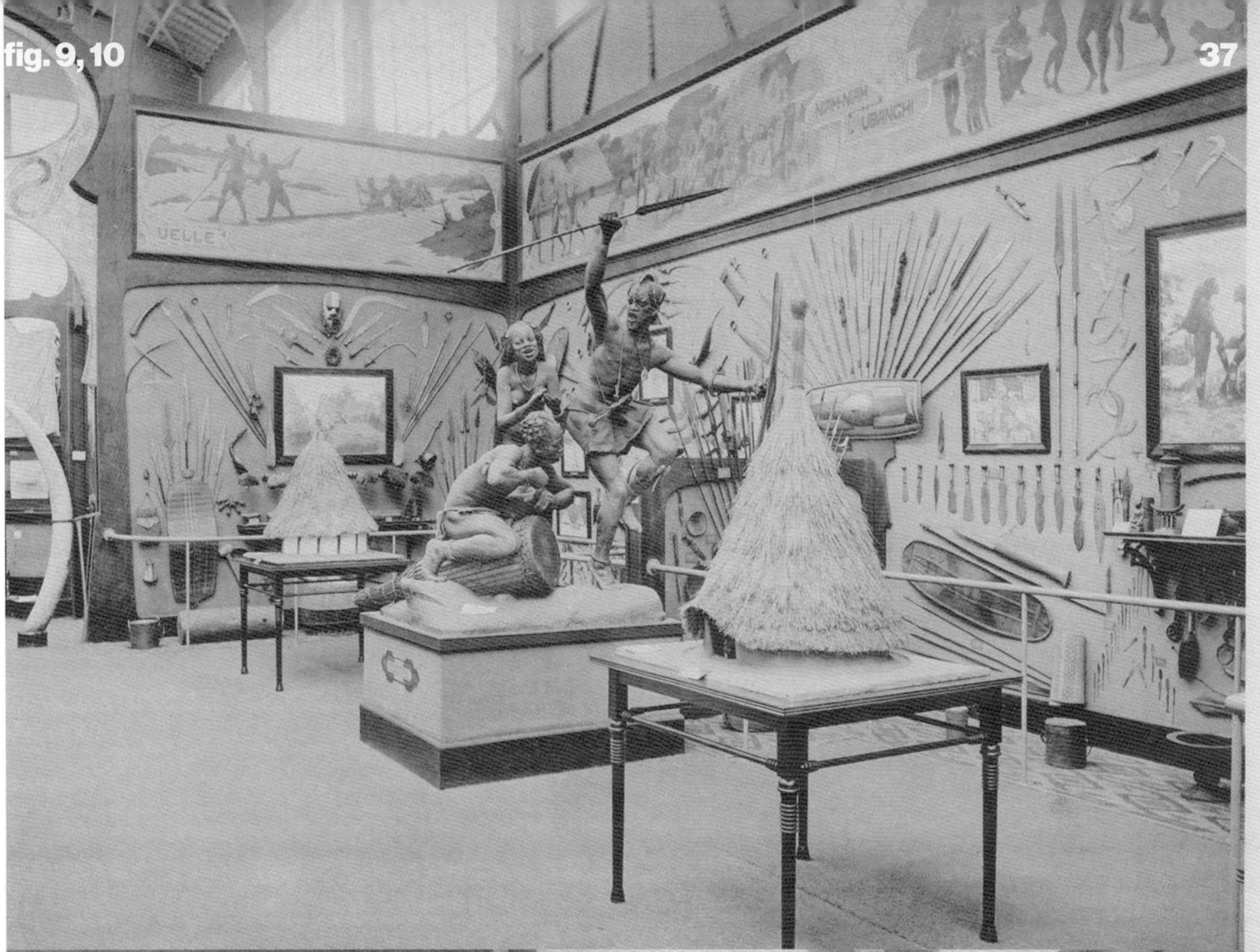
UELLE

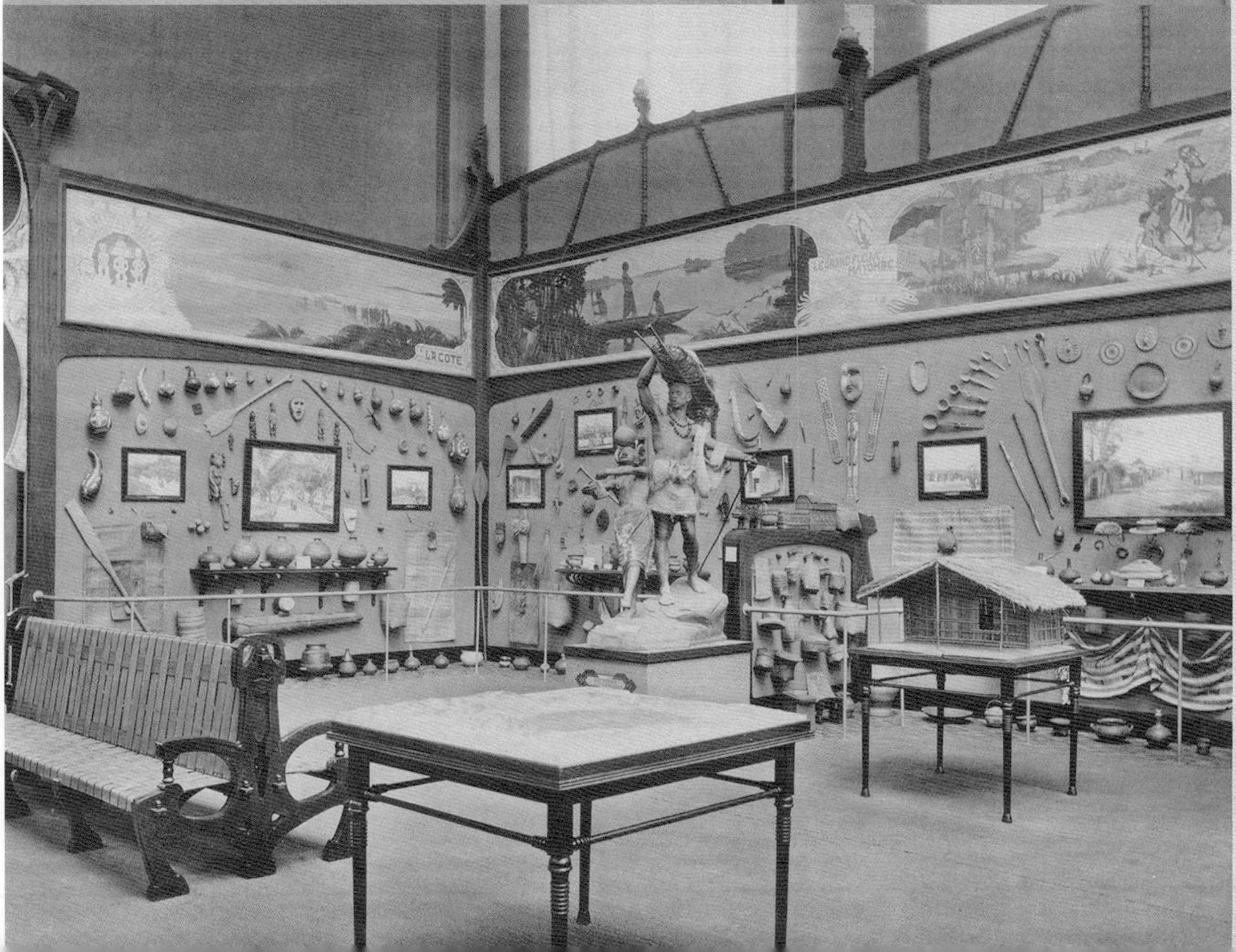
LA COTE

1897 fig. 11

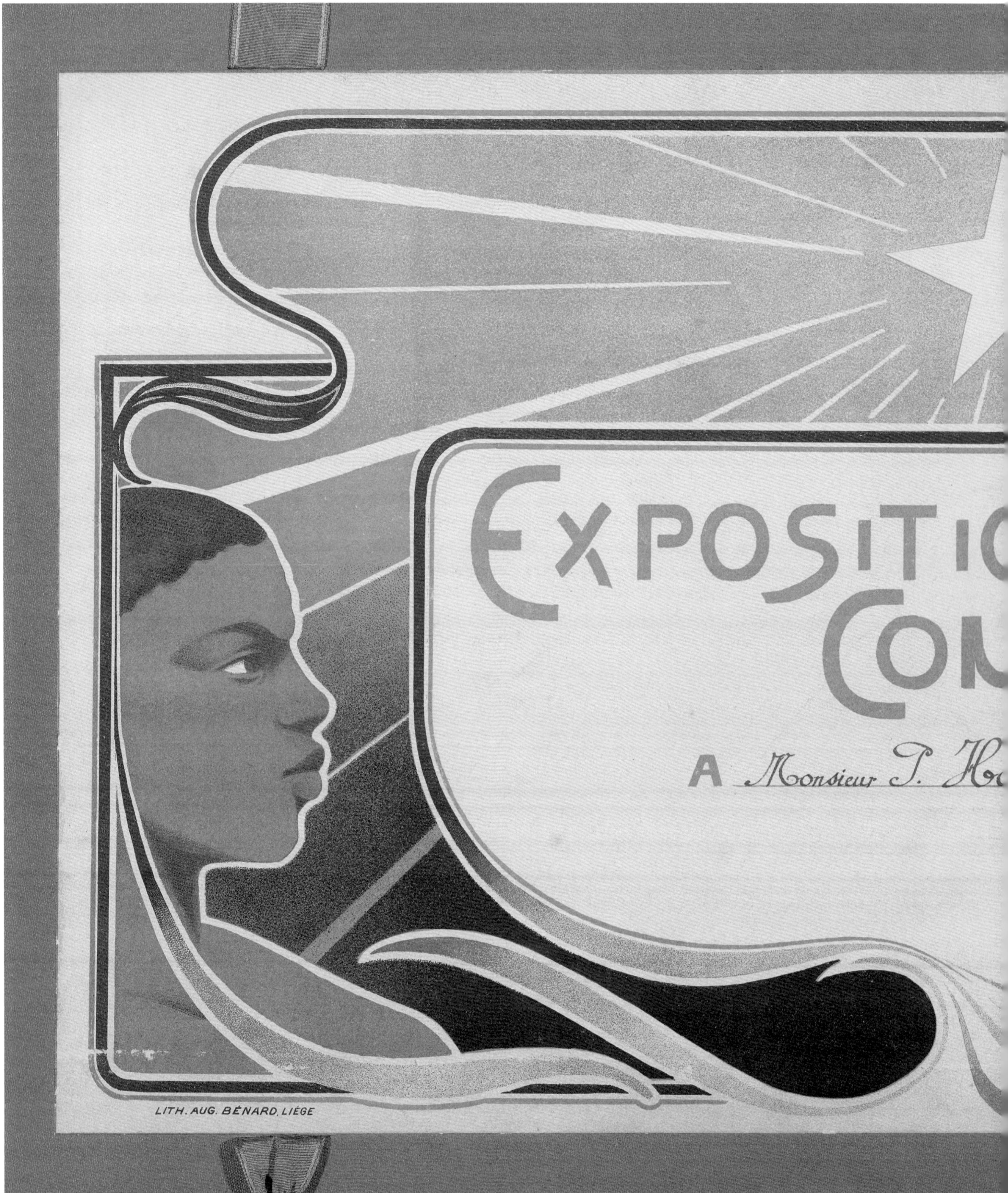

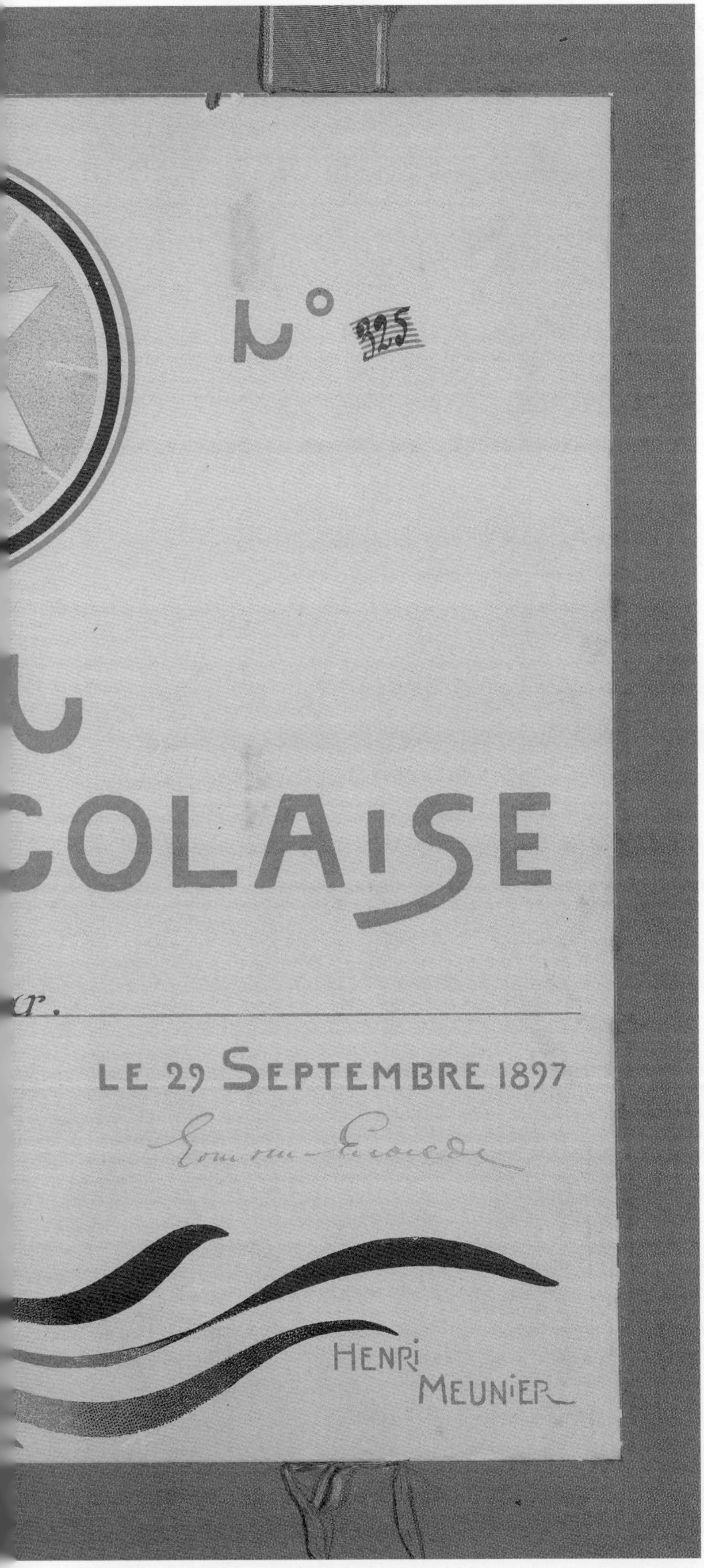
N° 325
COLAISE
LE 29 SEPTEMBRE 1897
HENRI
MEUNIER

1897 fig. 12, 13

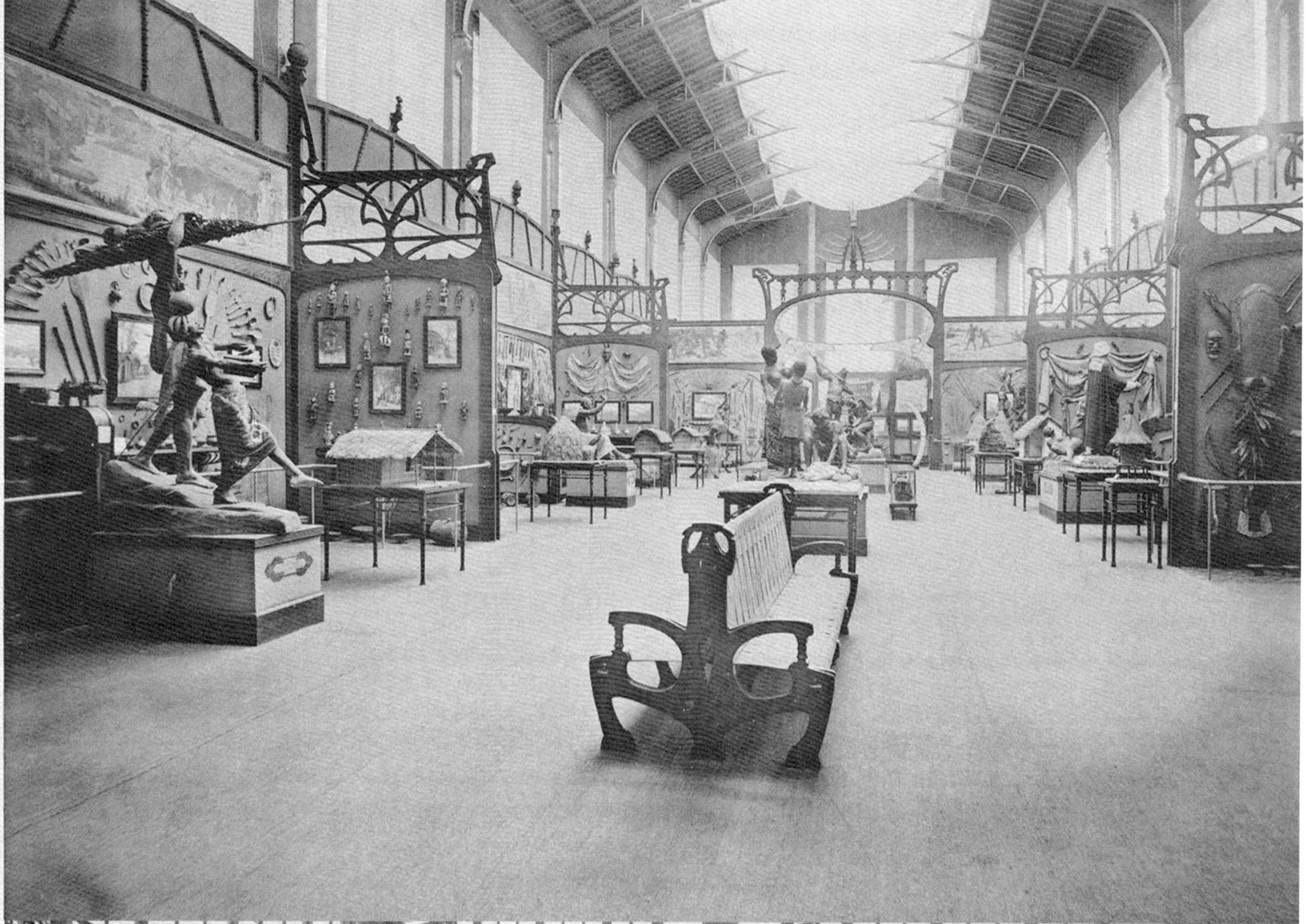

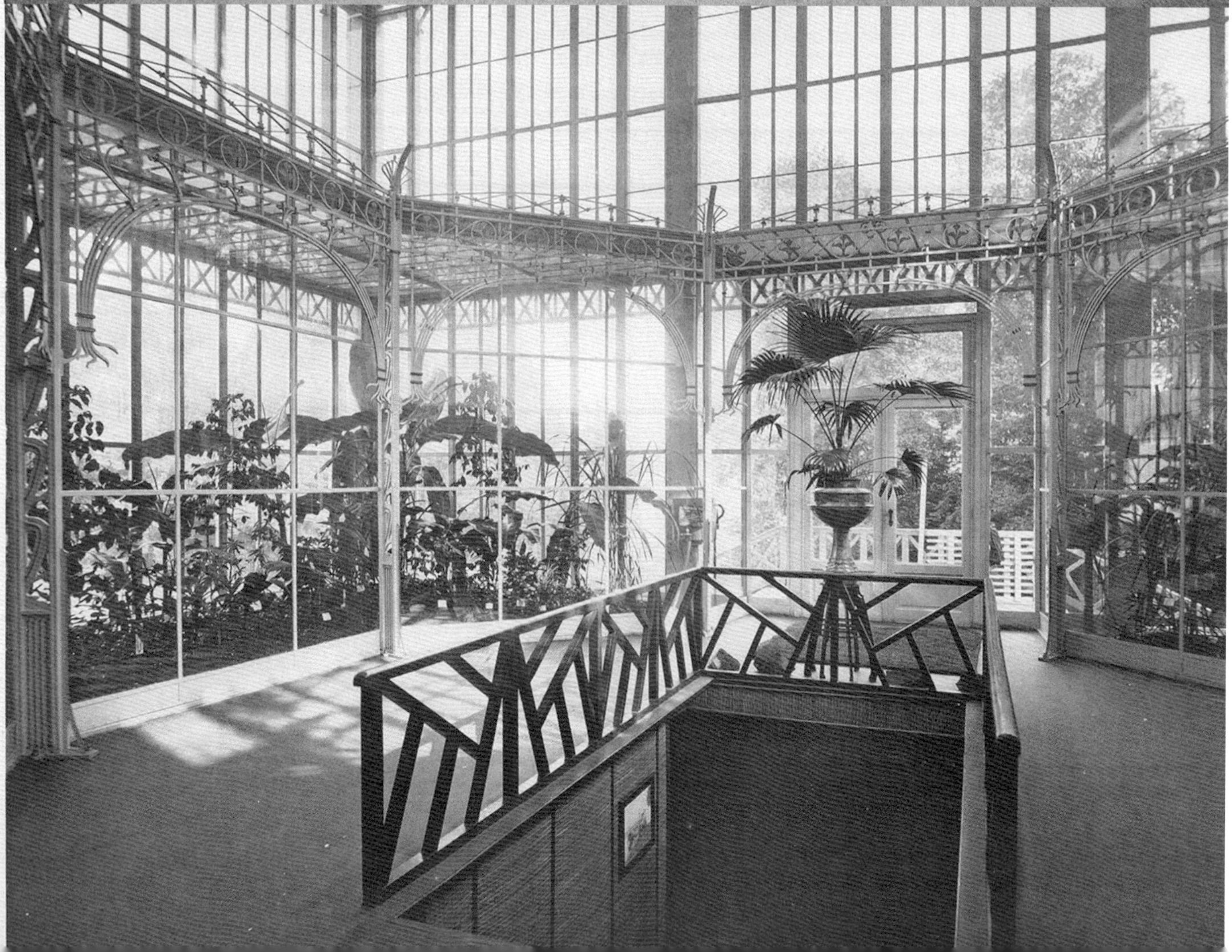

fig. 14

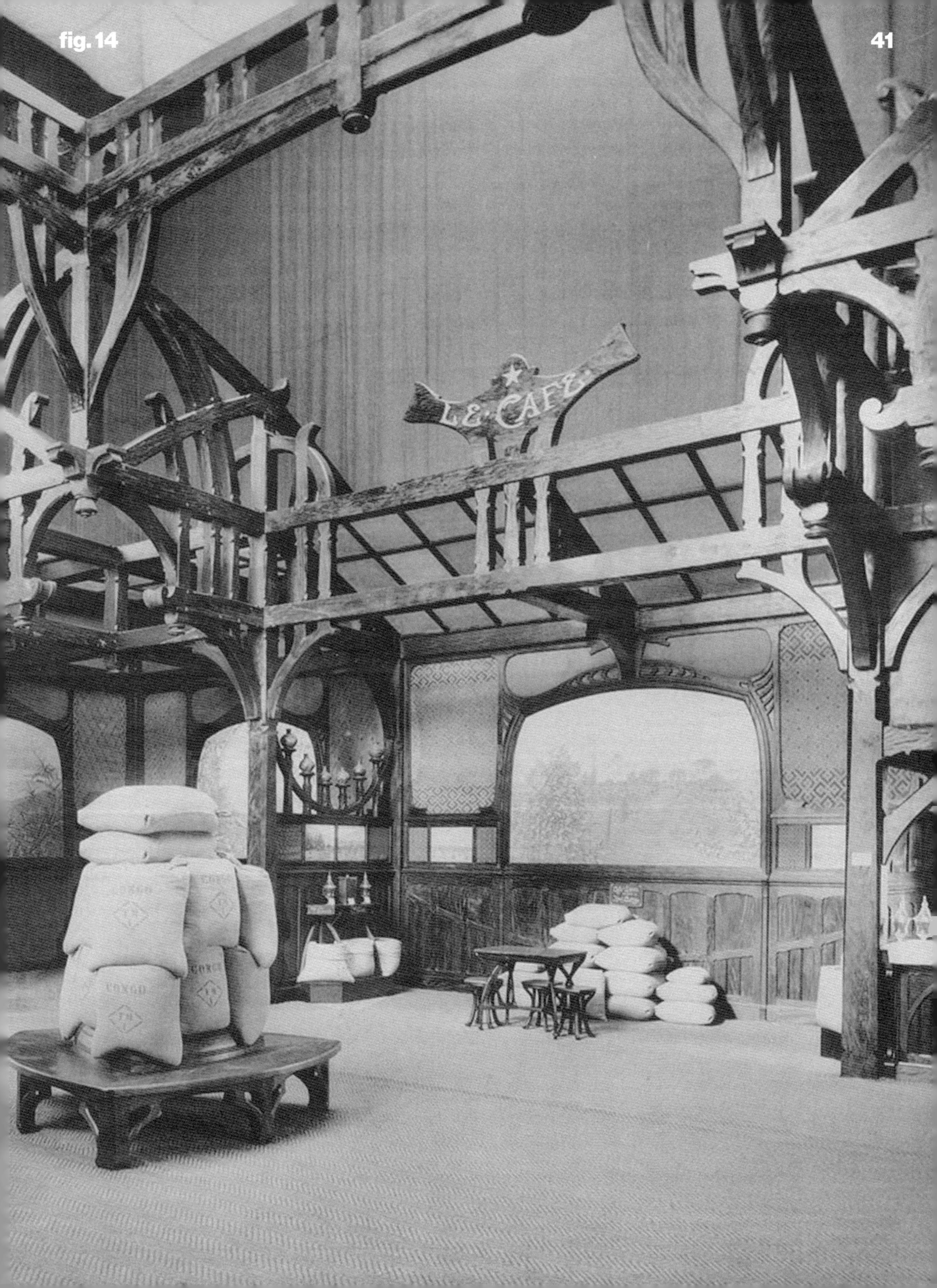

1897 fig. 15

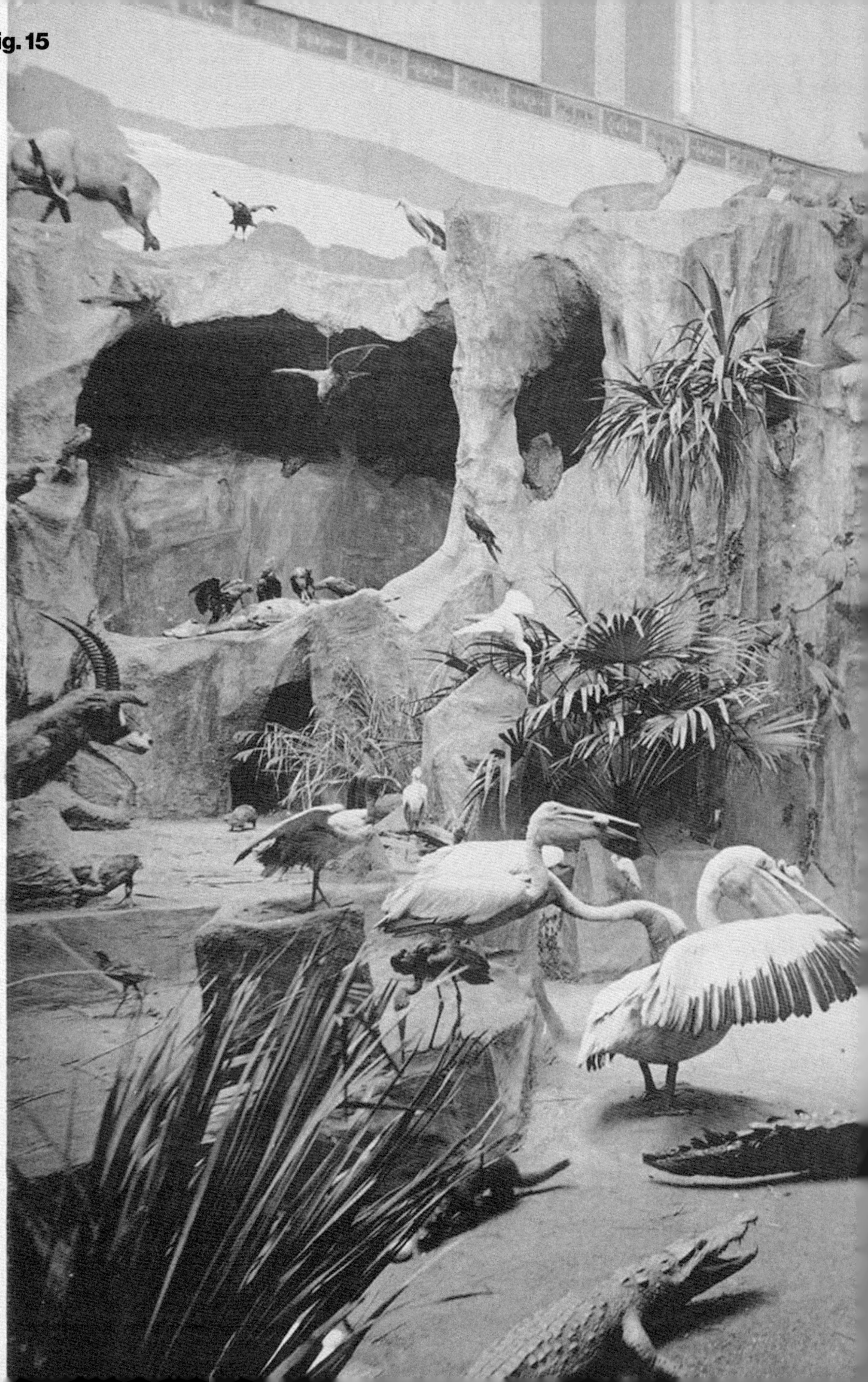

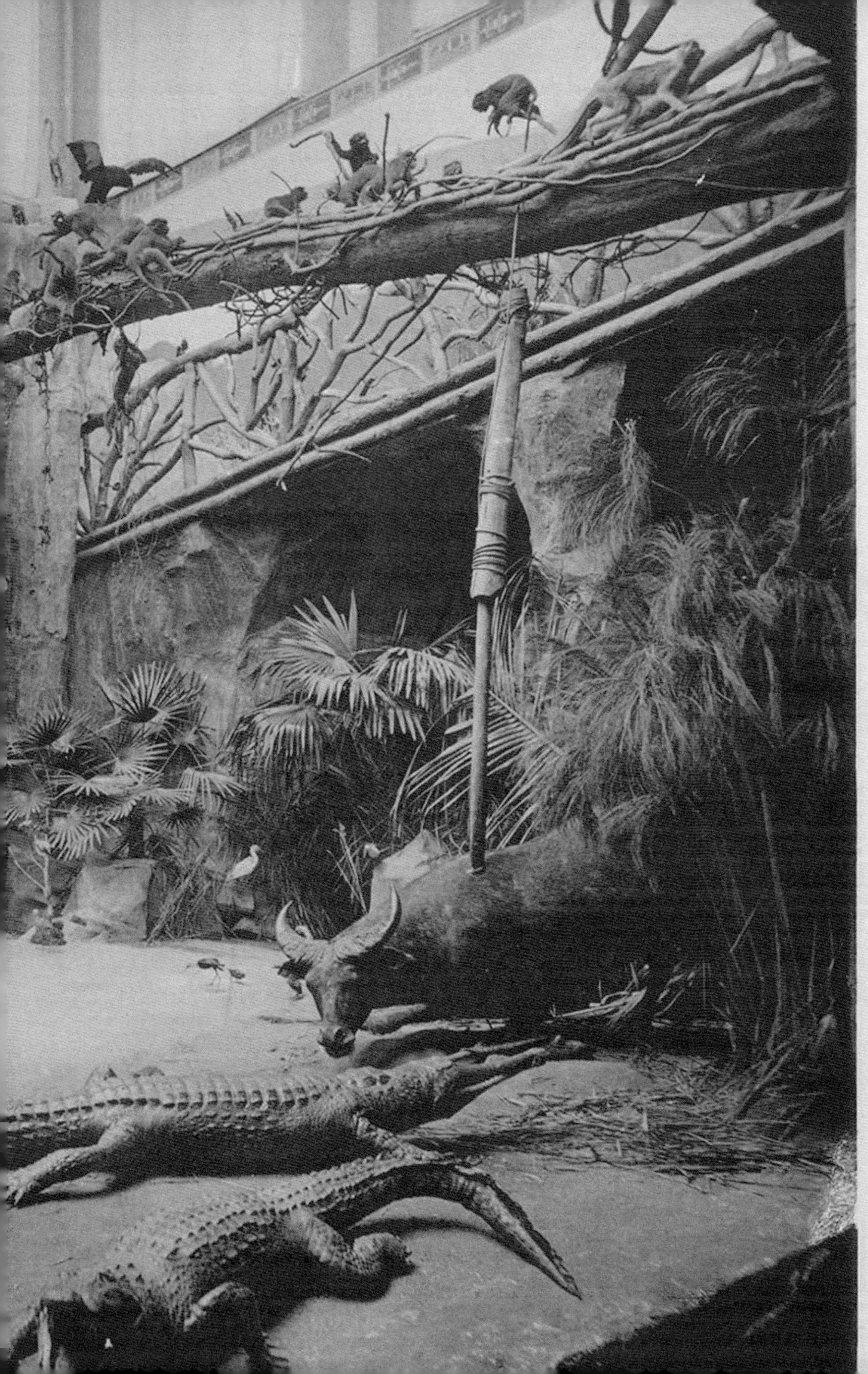

1897 fig. 16

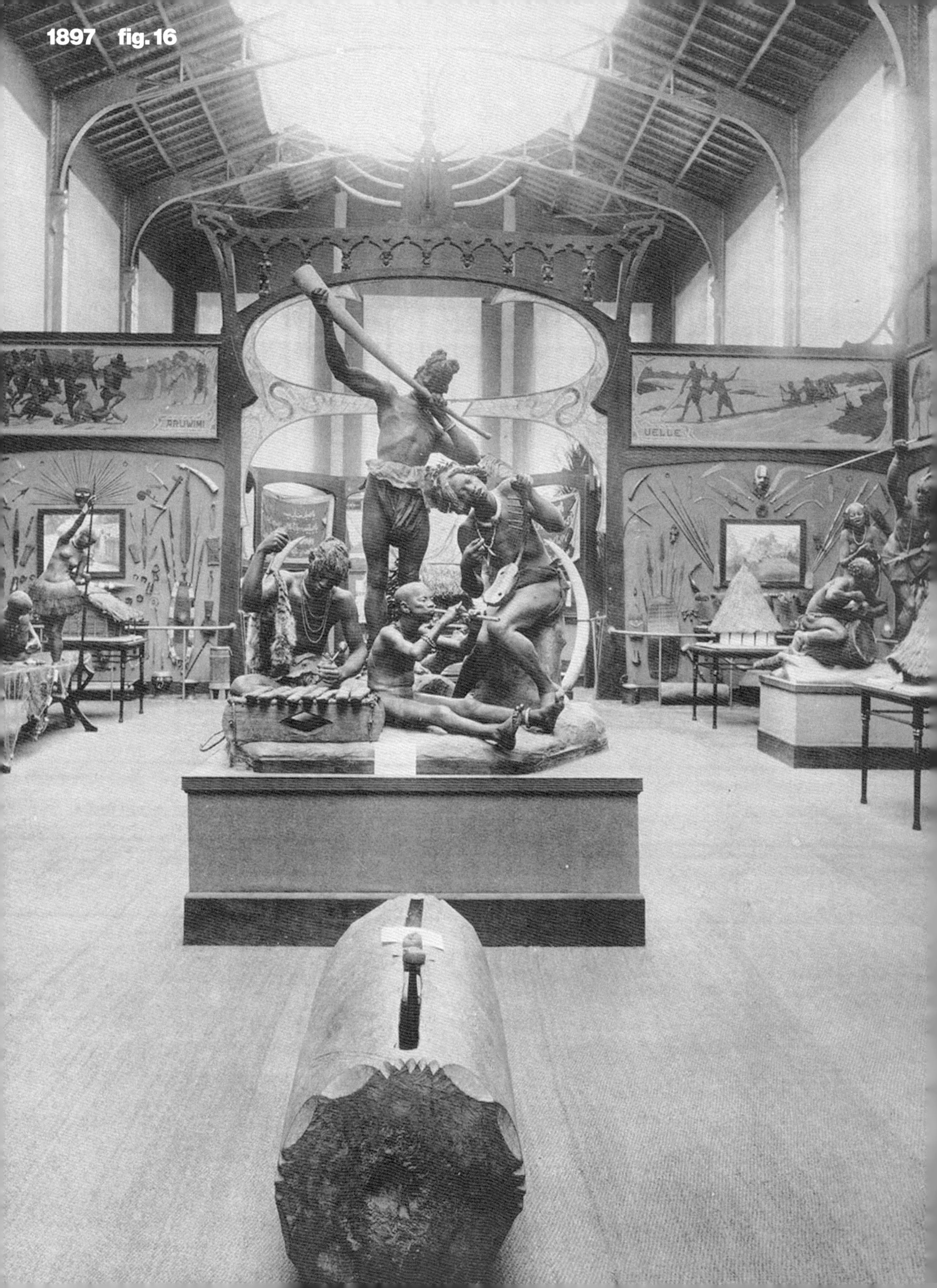

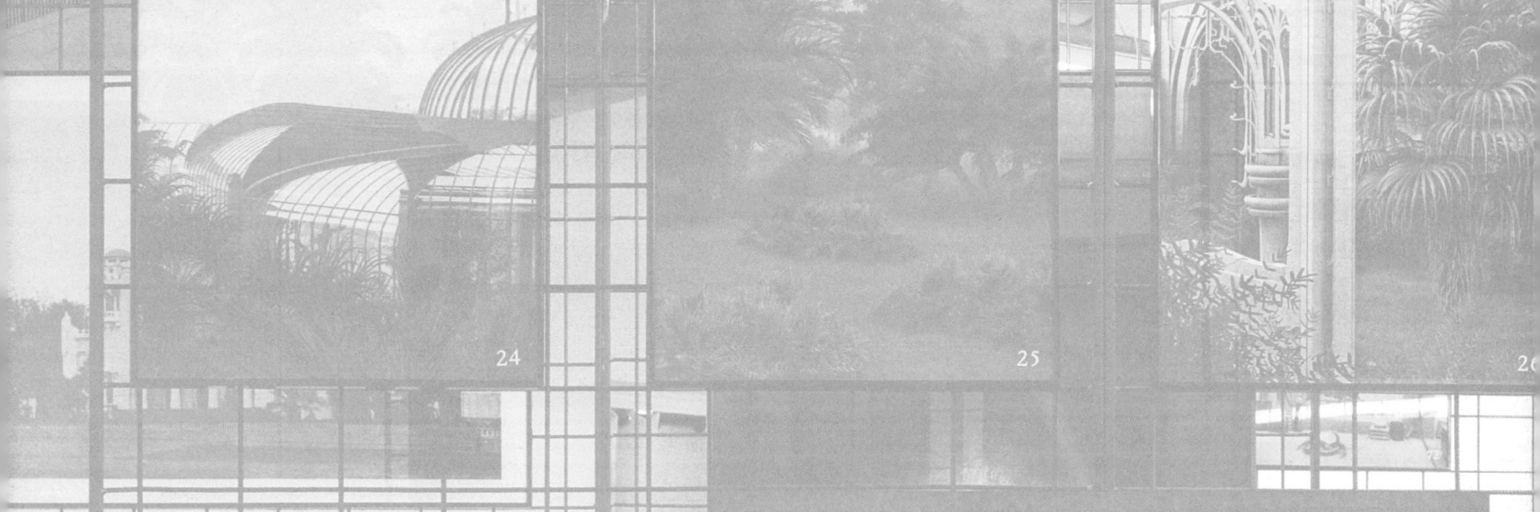

Horta's Paper Project for a Congo Palace

If the 1889 Exposition Universelle in Paris had heralded a novel architecture for a new era, the 1900 exhibition has been described by (architectural) historians as a disappointing return to Beaux Arts and eclecticism, embodied by the Grand Palais and the Petit Palais, as well as an event marked by the profusion of regionalist tendencies in the national pavilions. The Belgian Pavilion, for instance, was a tribute to the town hall in Oudenaarde. Edmond van Eetvelde, at the time still a key figure within powerful circles of the Congo Free State administration, commissioned his favorite architect, Victor Horta, to design the Congo Pavilion. A presentation of tropical wood from Congo was to be the key feature of the display. Horta conceived an elegant glass and metal structure. While reminiscent of the impressive greenhouses of Laeken, including one for plants from Congo, designed by architect Alphonse Balat for King Leopold II in the previous decades, Horta's project was much more dynamic in its spatial experience than Balat's symmetrical project. The Congo Pavilion would remain a paper project, however. That van Eetvelde fell ill during the early stages of the project's construction no doubt hampered the crucial negotiations necessary to solve a growing conflict with the building contractor. But the decision to finally withdraw the Congo section from the 1900 exhibition altogether should also be understood in the geopolitical context of the time, as King Leopold II's colonial enterprise was becoming a highly contested affair. Keeping the colonial enterprise in Congo "off the radar" was thus strategic.

Johan Lagae

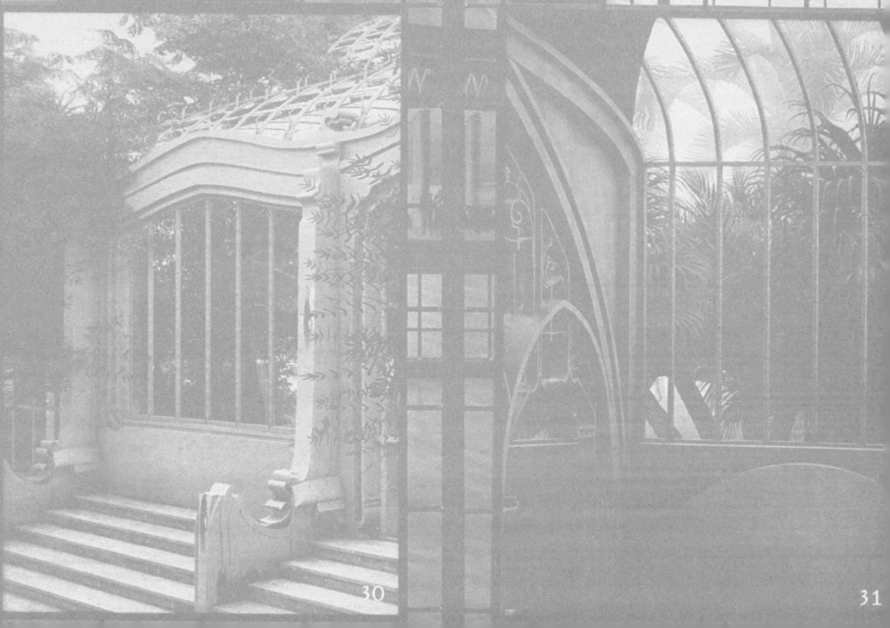

1900 fig. 17

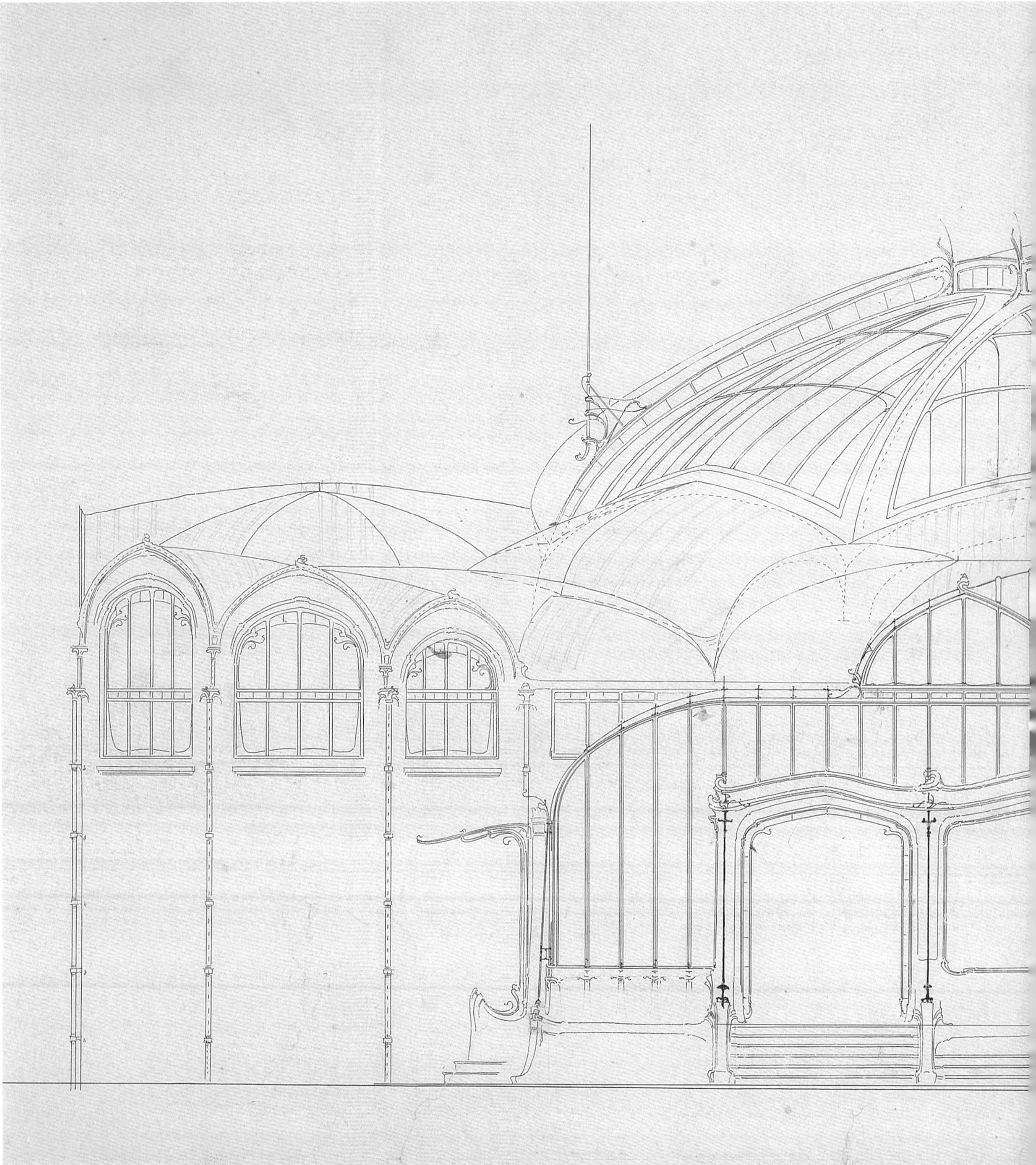

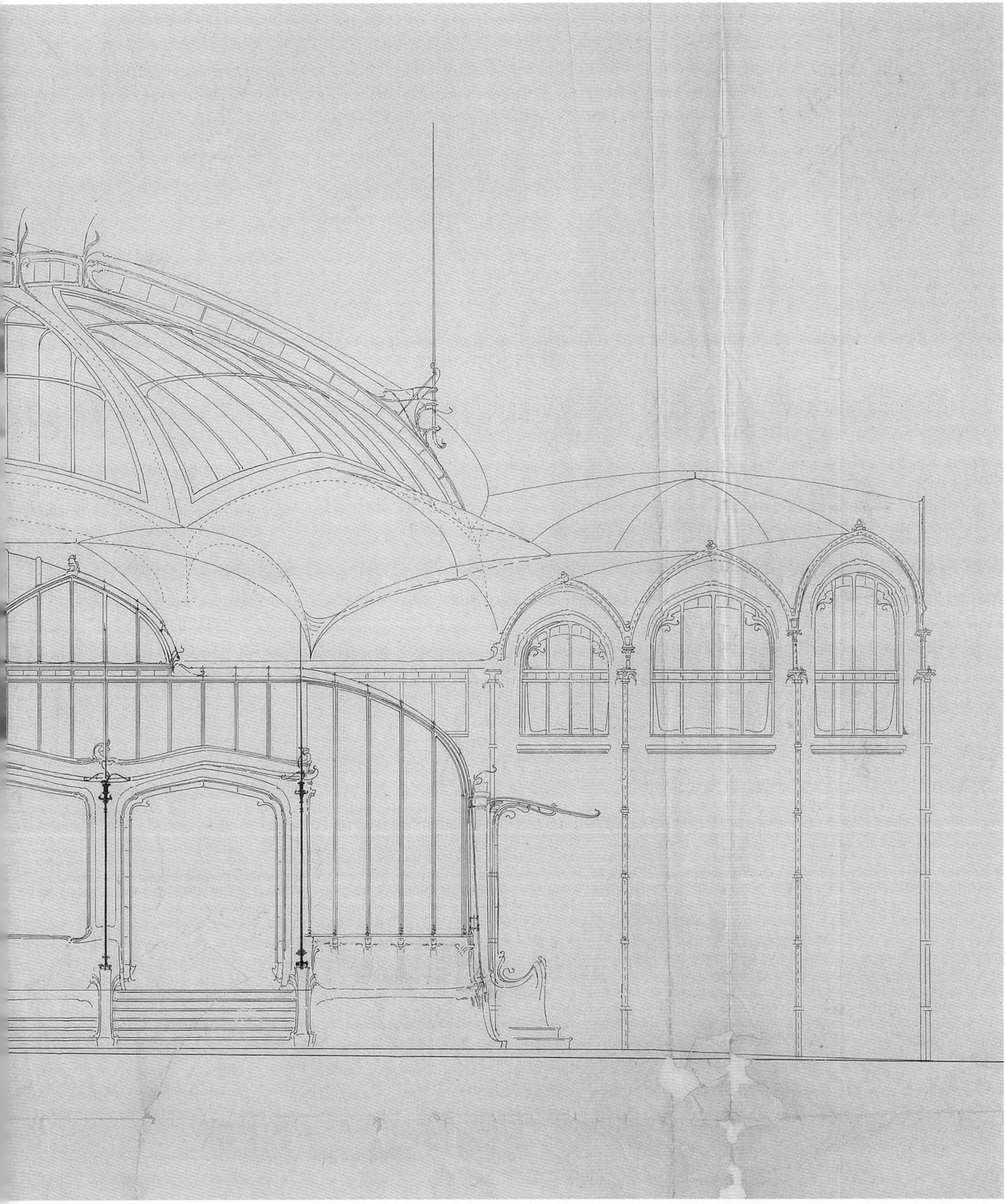

Pavillon du Congo (1898-1899)

Autour du Congo, on commençait à s'enrichir pour peu qu'on fût dans les secrets des lieux, car à ce moment il n'y avait pas encore de dieux... Le Roi ayant trop sacrifié de lui-même, non pas pour lui-même, mais pour la nation contre la volonté de celle-ci, donc à l'encontre de toute reconnaissance. Dire que cette opposition satisfaisait Léopold et n'indignait pas son Secrétaire d'Etat serait probablement exagéré, mais ce que l'on peut affirmer, c'est que le Souverain ne s'y arrêta pas un instant.

Si, en ce moment, il eut quelque ennui de ce qui arrivait, ce fut du congé définitif que la neurasthénie l'avait obligé de donner à van Eetvelde. Aussi, après quelque repos, van Eetvelde fut rappelé pour s'occuper, sans fatigue, de la participation de l'Etat du Congo à l'Exposition Universelle de Paris de [1900]. Comment cette participation fut-elle décidée contre toute prudence? Comment l'habile souverain risqua-t-il de faire connaître aux nations avides et jalouses la valeur réelle que le Congo représentait? Je n'étais pas dans les secrets pour le savoir, mais ce n'était pas à l'égard d'une enclave à obtenir qu'on se disputait. Plus difficile à deviner qu'à comprendre la raison pour laquelle il s'aboucha (pour le public, il s'amouracha) avec la belle Cléo pour s'offrir en couple cascadeur! De ce gâtisme relatif, j'ai toujours pensé que, colosse politique, sa seule et unique pensée était de démontrer combien il avait eu raison d'aborder au centre de l'Afrique, quitte à se ruiner avec l'idée ou à réussir et tout en récupérant ses biens si généreusement exposés, de doter le monde d'un bienfait inestimable le jour où l'accord entre les nations serait obtenu.

Fig. 71 Projet pour le pavillon du Congo (Archives du musée Horta)

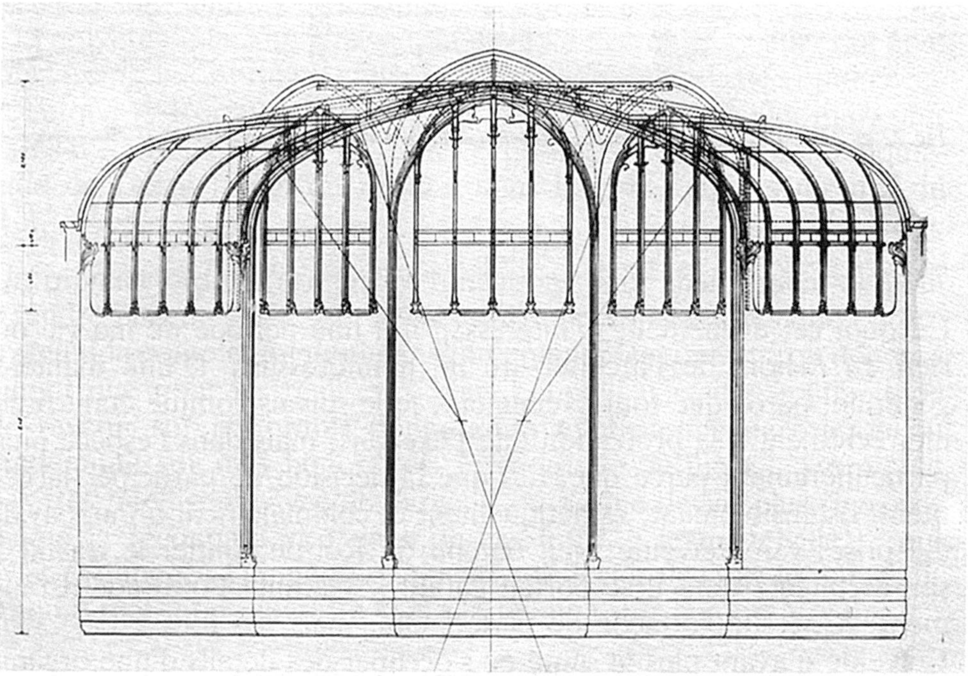

fig. 19

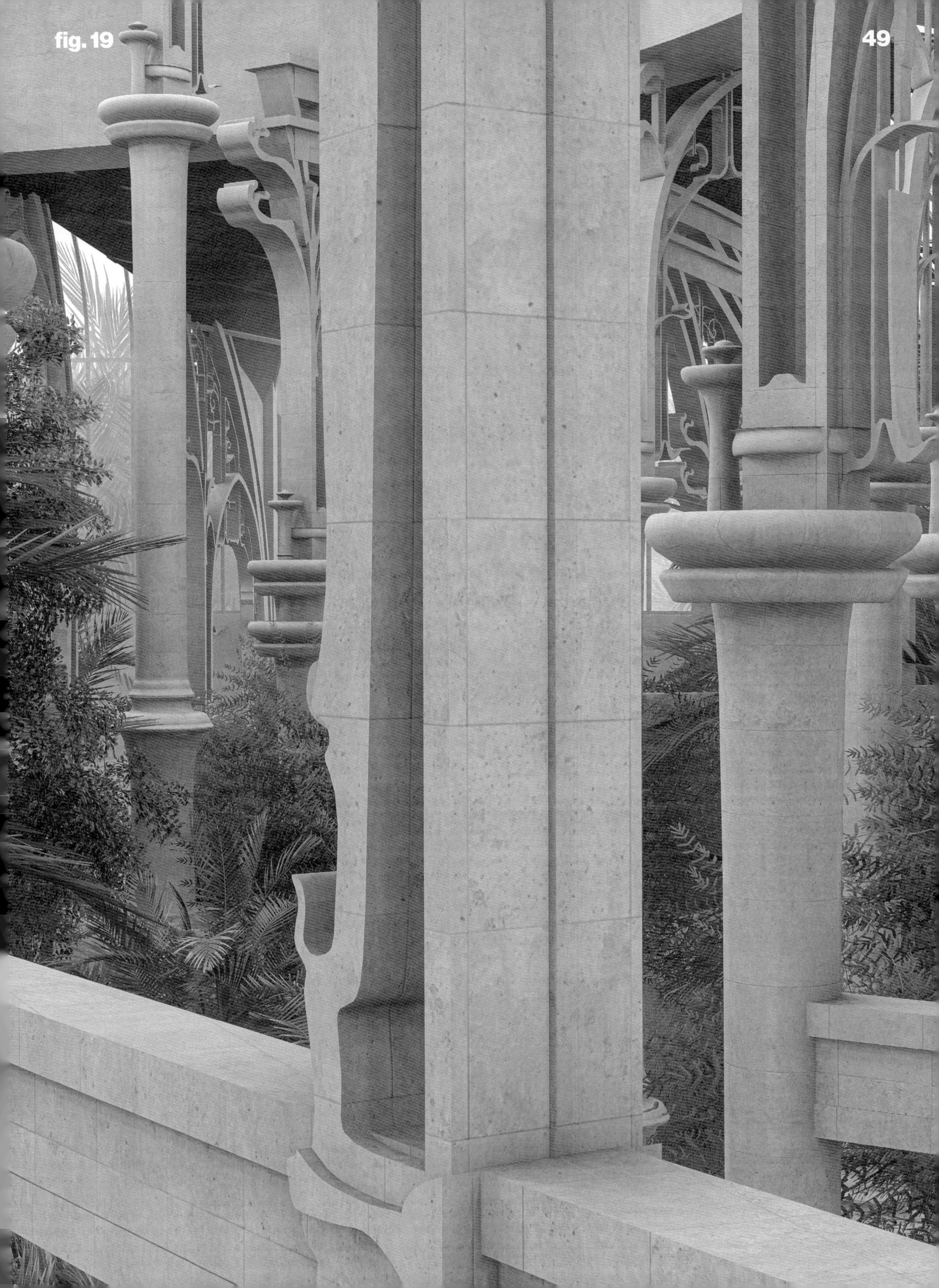

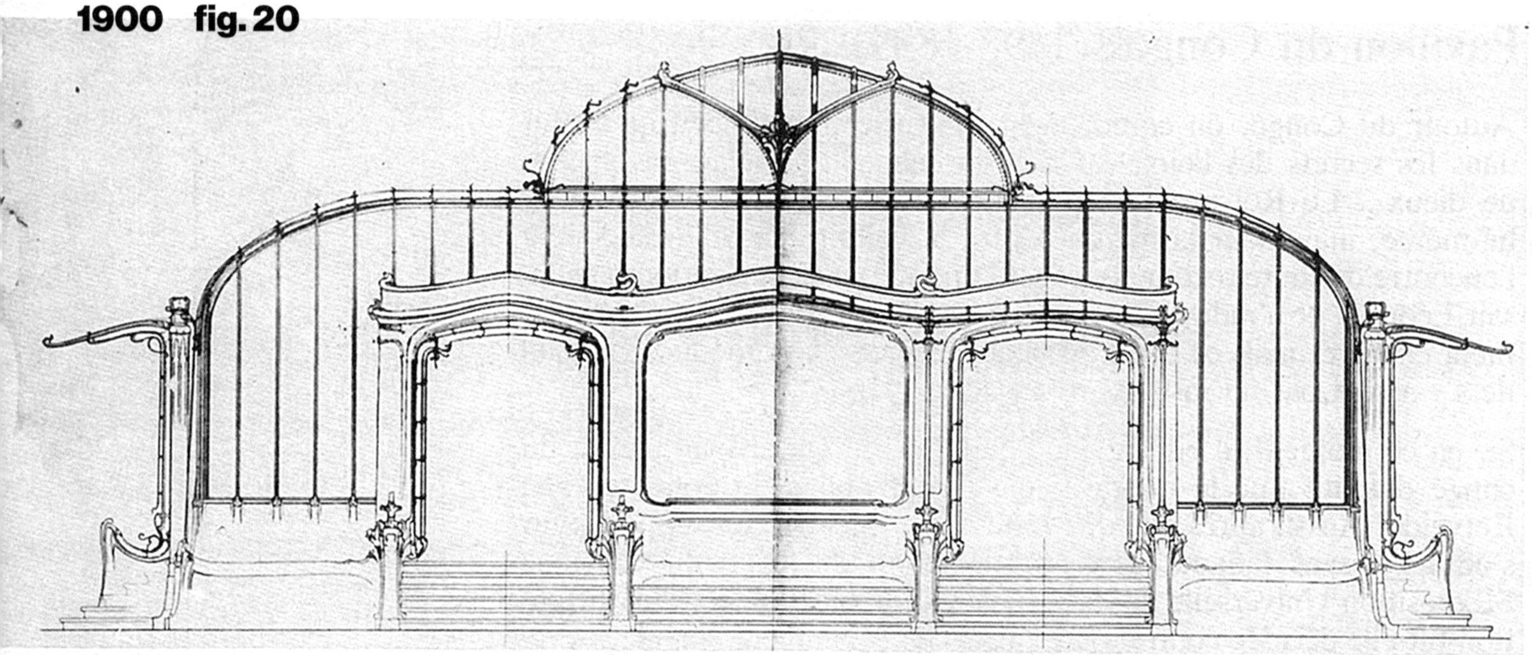

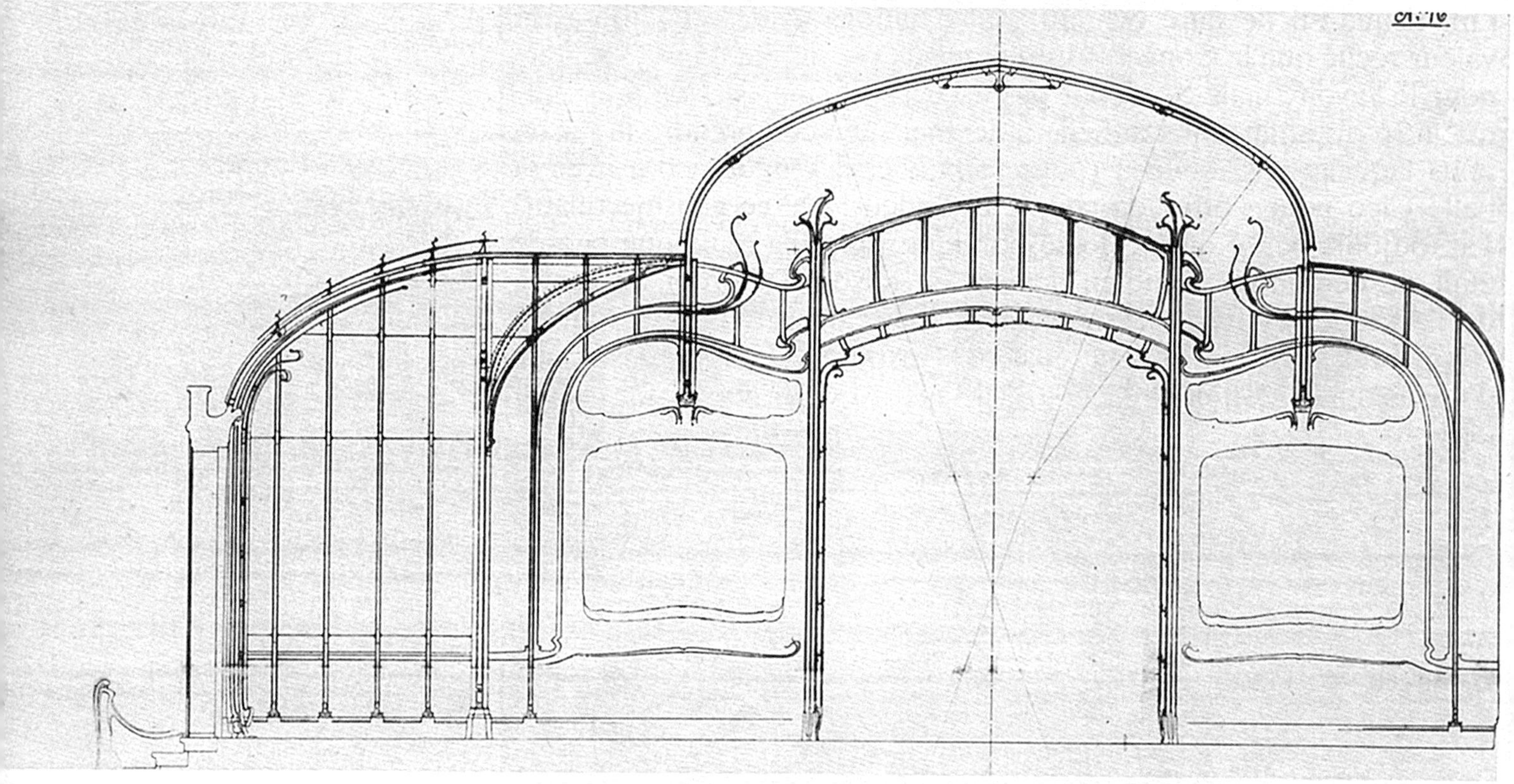

Fig. 72 et 73   Pavillon du Congo. Projets (Archives du musée Horta)

En quoi cet événement m'intéressait-il à une période de ma vie où rien en dehors de l'architecture ne m'intéressait? D'une manière générale, parce que tout événement, je le suivais comme étant utile indirectement à la profession que j'exerçais, mais dans l'espèce plus particulièrement parce que, dès que la décision de participer largement, ostensiblement, esthétiquement et colonialement à Paris avait été prise, van Eetvelde avait obtenu du Roi de confier le travail à son architecte dont il se portait garant... Garant? Pourquoi? Comment? Une simple façon de parler! Oui, mais pas tout à fait. Van Eetvelde n'ayant plus la santé de s'occuper des détails d'une organi-

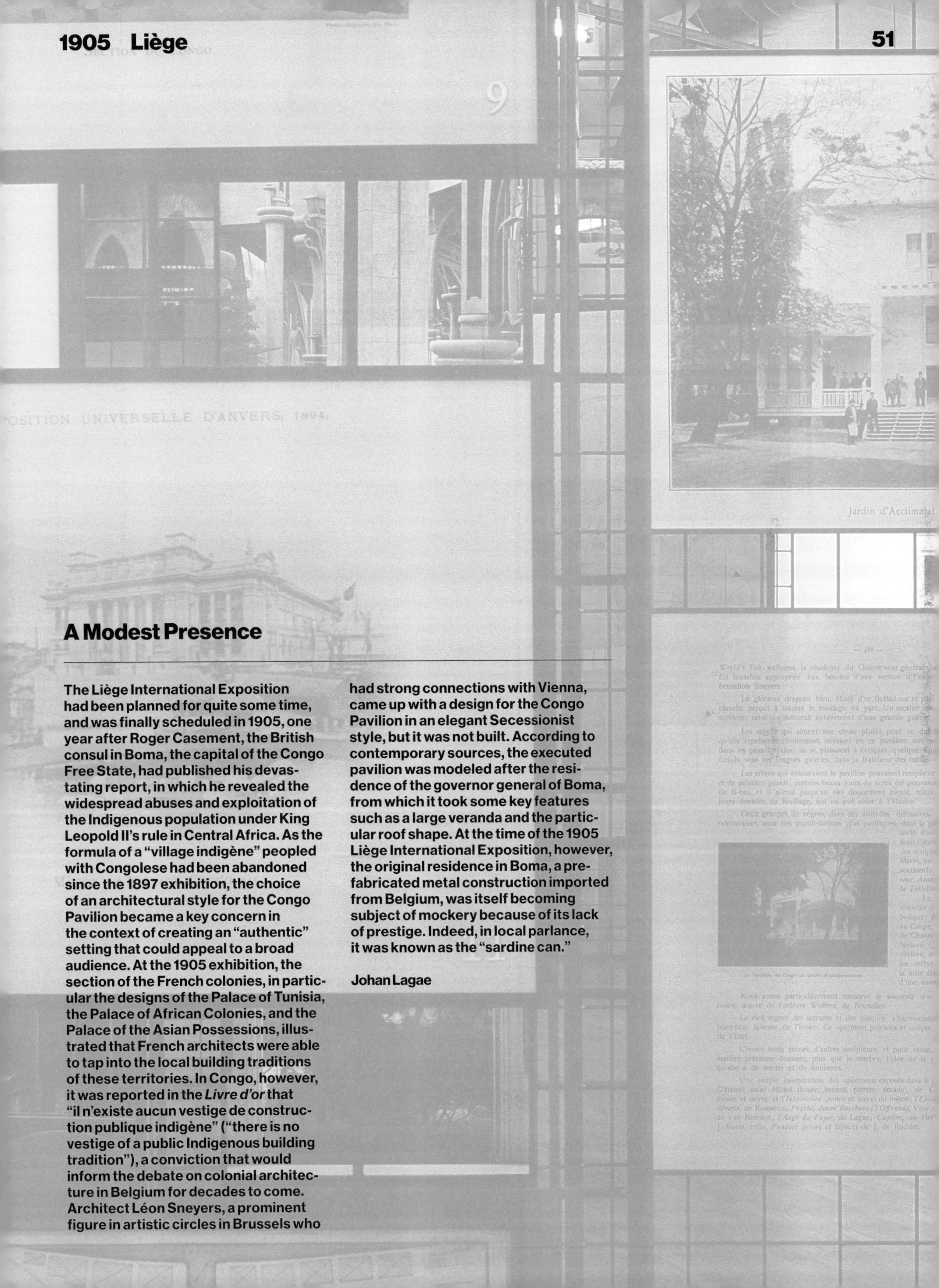

A Modest Presence

The Liège International Exposition had been planned for quite some time, and was finally scheduled in 1905, one year after Roger Casement, the British consul in Boma, the capital of the Congo Free State, had published his devastating report, in which he revealed the widespread abuses and exploitation of the Indigenous population under King Leopold II's rule in Central Africa. As the formula of a "village indigène" peopled with Congolese had been abandoned since the 1897 exhibition, the choice of an architectural style for the Congo Pavilion became a key concern in the context of creating an "authentic" setting that could appeal to a broad audience. At the 1905 exhibition, the section of the French colonies, in particular the designs of the Palace of Tunisia, the Palace of African Colonies, and the Palace of the Asian Possessions, illustrated that French architects were able to tap into the local building traditions of these territories. In Congo, however, it was reported in the *Livre d'or* that "il n'existe aucun vestige de construction publique indigène" ("there is no vestige of a public Indigenous building tradition"), a conviction that would inform the debate on colonial architecture in Belgium for decades to come. Architect Léon Sneyers, a prominent figure in artistic circles in Brussels who had strong connections with Vienna, came up with a design for the Congo Pavilion in an elegant Secessionist style, but it was not built. According to contemporary sources, the executed pavilion was modeled after the residence of the governor general of Boma, from which it took some key features such as a large veranda and the particular roof shape. At the time of the 1905 Liège International Exposition, however, the original residence in Boma, a prefabricated metal construction imported from Belgium, was itself becoming subject of mockery because of its lack of prestige. Indeed, in local parlance, it was known as the "sardine can."

Johan Lagae

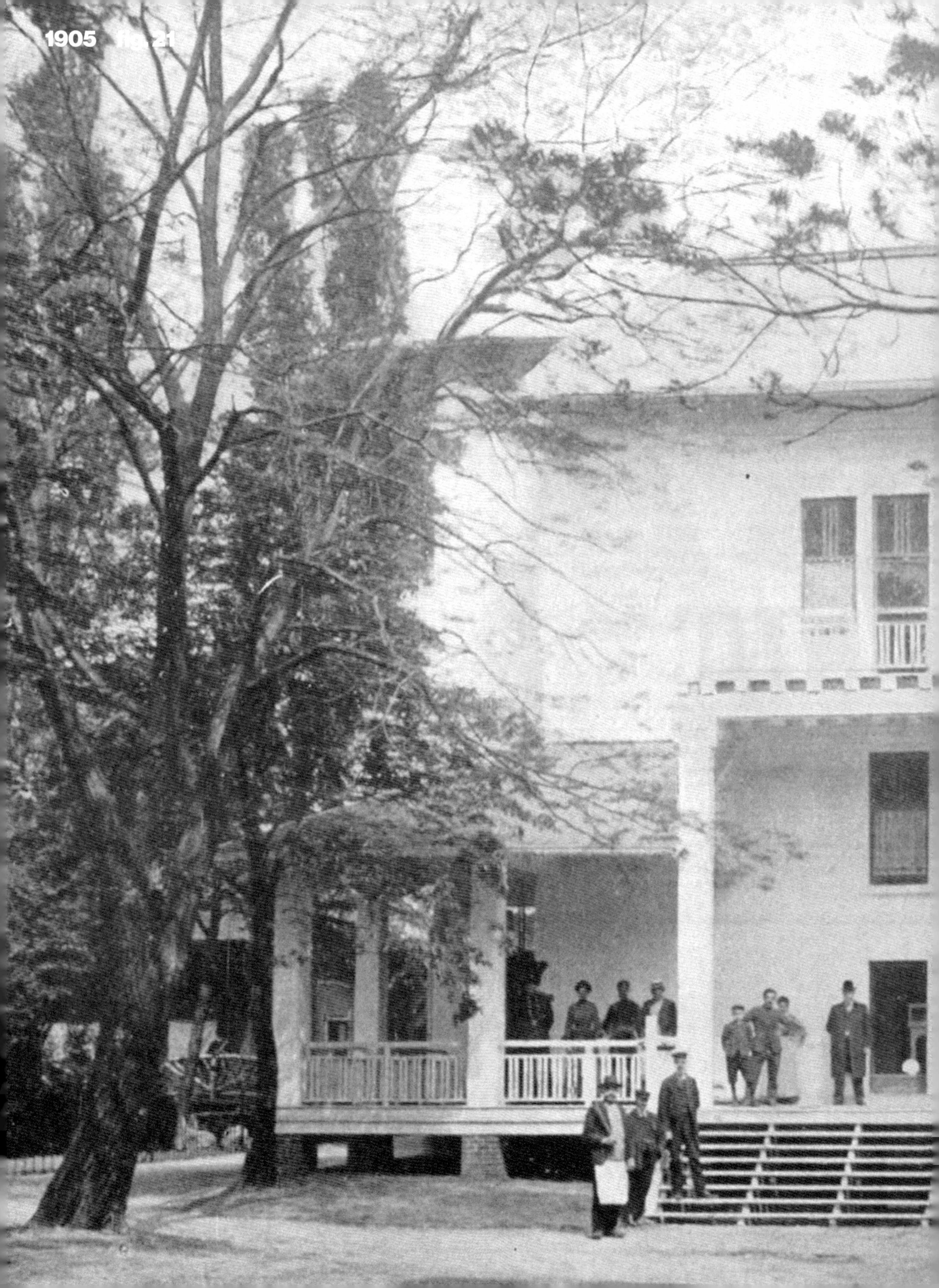

1905 fig. 21

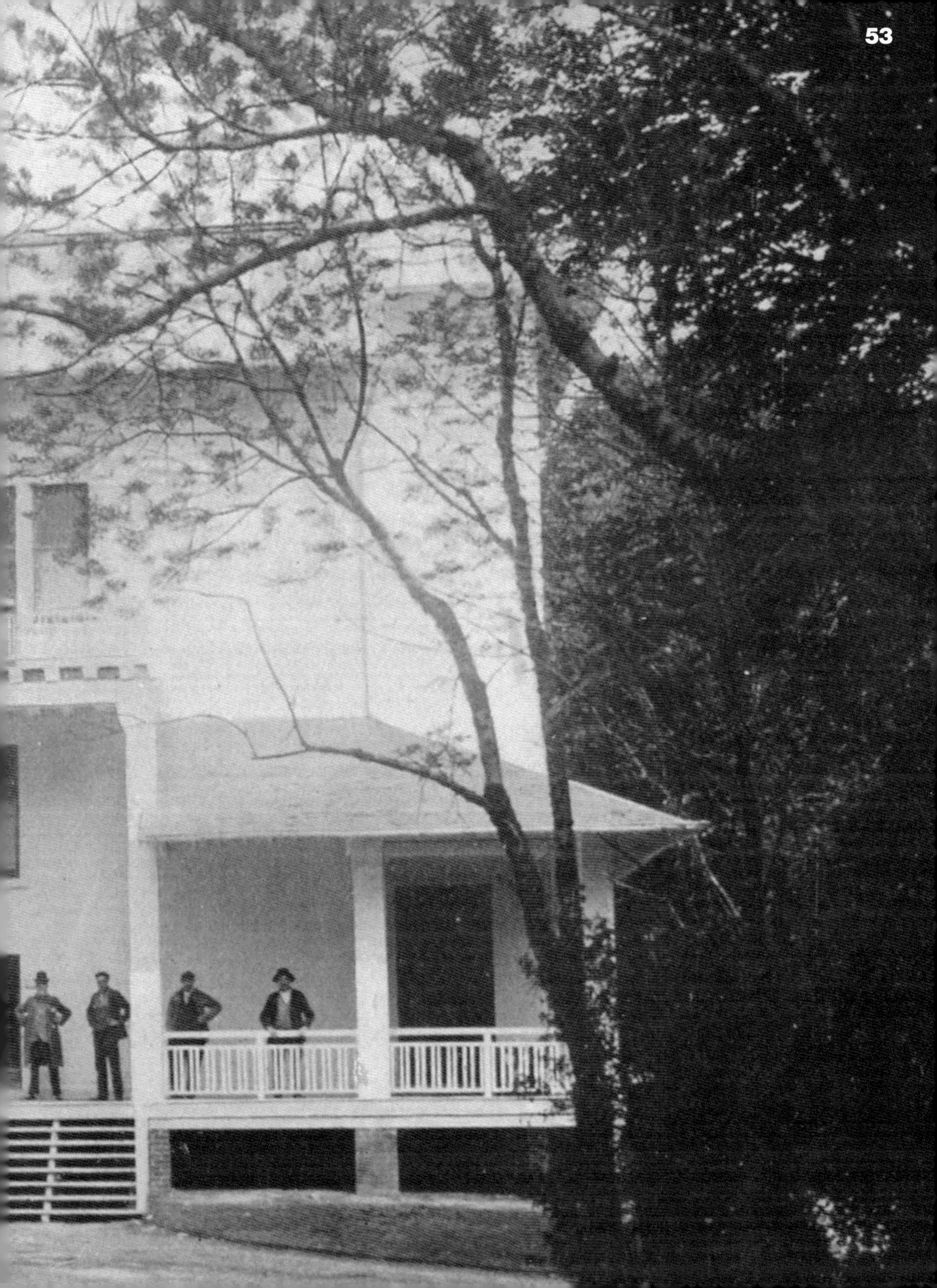

1905 fig. 22

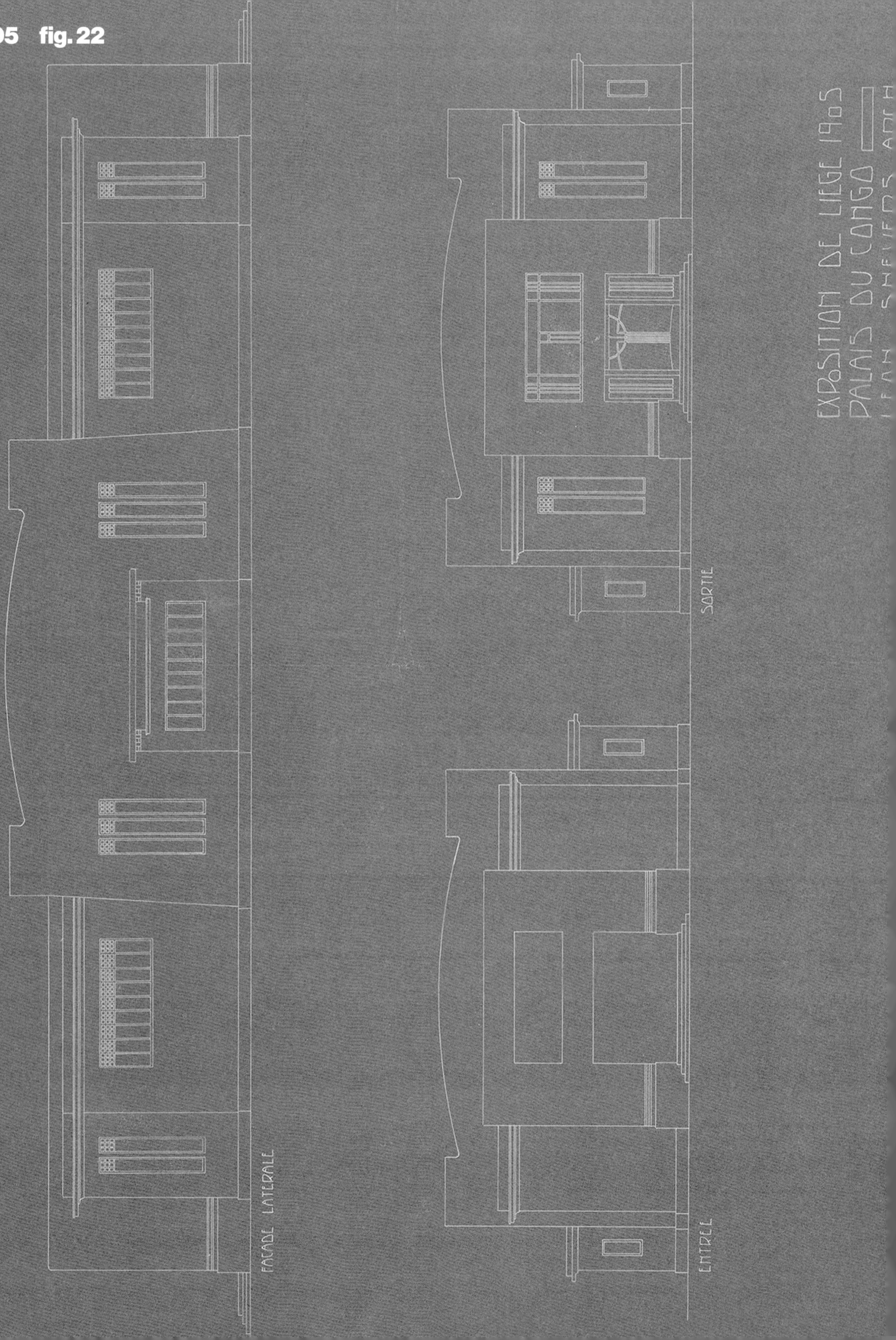
EXPOSITION DE LIEGE 1905
PALAIS DU CONGO
FACADE LATERALE
SORTIE
ENTREE

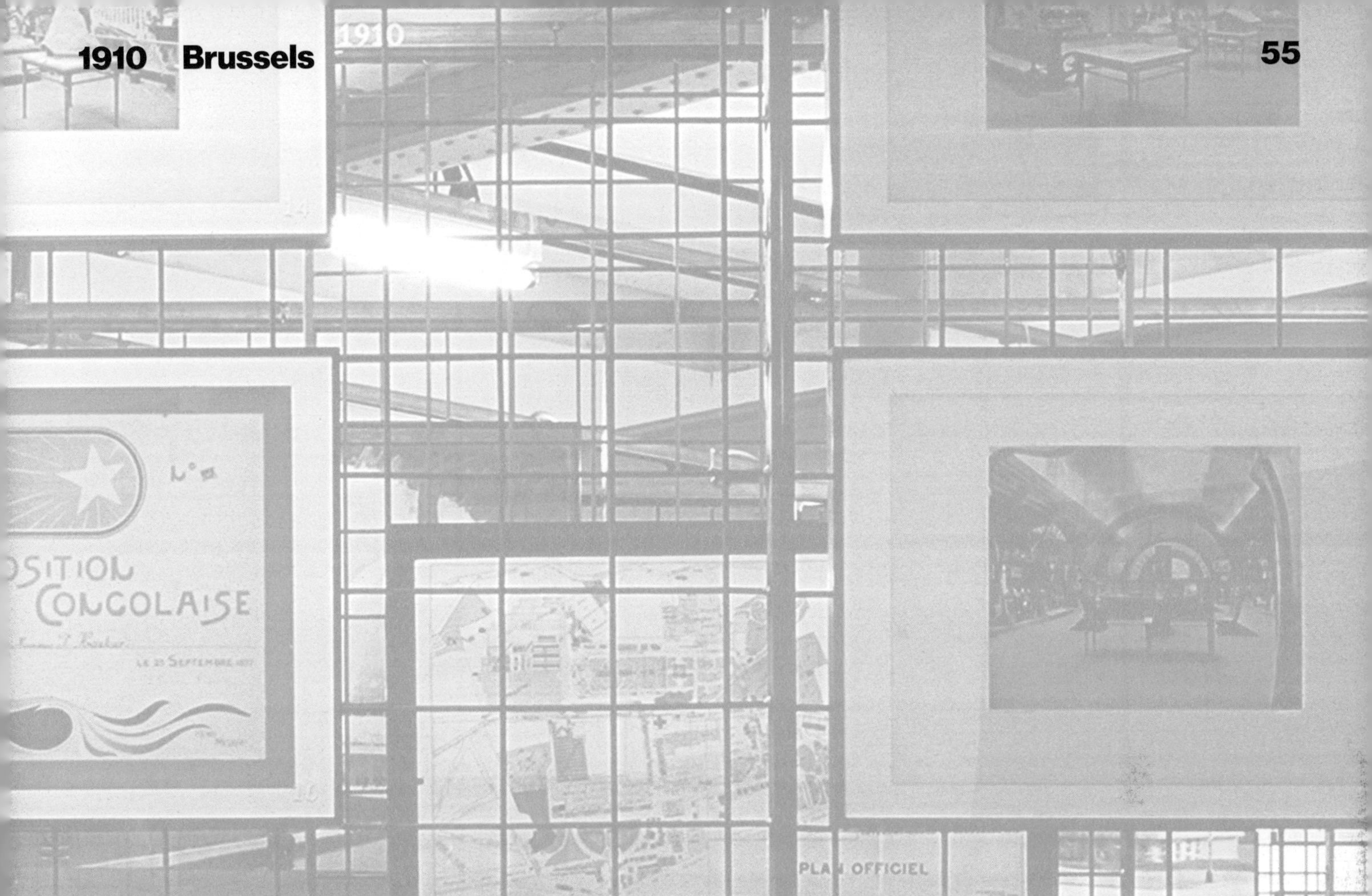

An Incomplete Educational Project

After the 1897 exhibition, the Palais des Colonies was turned into a permanent museum to propagate King Leopold II's colonial enterprise. In 1901, the king tasked the French architect Charles Girault, whose Petit Palais at the Paris 1900 fair he greatly admired, to design the new Musée du Congo as part of a larger project for what he called Cité Coloniale. The king would not live to see the inauguration of the museum, which opened on the occasion of the 1910 Brussels International Exposition, having passed away the previous year. The king's death also marked the end of the ambitious scheme of Cité Coloniale, which prefigured a series of projects for a Mundaneum conceived during the 1920s that would have encompassed a colonial university (École mondiale), a library, a conference center, museums for Chinese and Japanese art, and large sports facilities. If Cité Coloniale remained an incomplete project, the permanent trace of the museum signaled a shift in the presentation of Congo at the Brussels International Exposition: science and education became a strong part of the official narrative on colonial possession, complementing the previous dominant focus on commerce and exploitation. Simultaneously, in 1908 the Congo Free State had come to an end, when, after long and troublesome negotiations, King Leopold II finally ceded his territory in Central Africa to the Belgian state, turning it into a colony in the true sense of the word. A ministry of colonies was founded immediately. In order to create efficient governance and to develop the overseas territory, a large body of knowledge in different domains was required. At the 1910 expo, the Association pour le perfectionnement du matérial colonial tellingly organized an international conference, focusing on all kinds of novel products and technologies that could help the colonial enterprise thrive.

Johan Lagae

1910 fig. 23

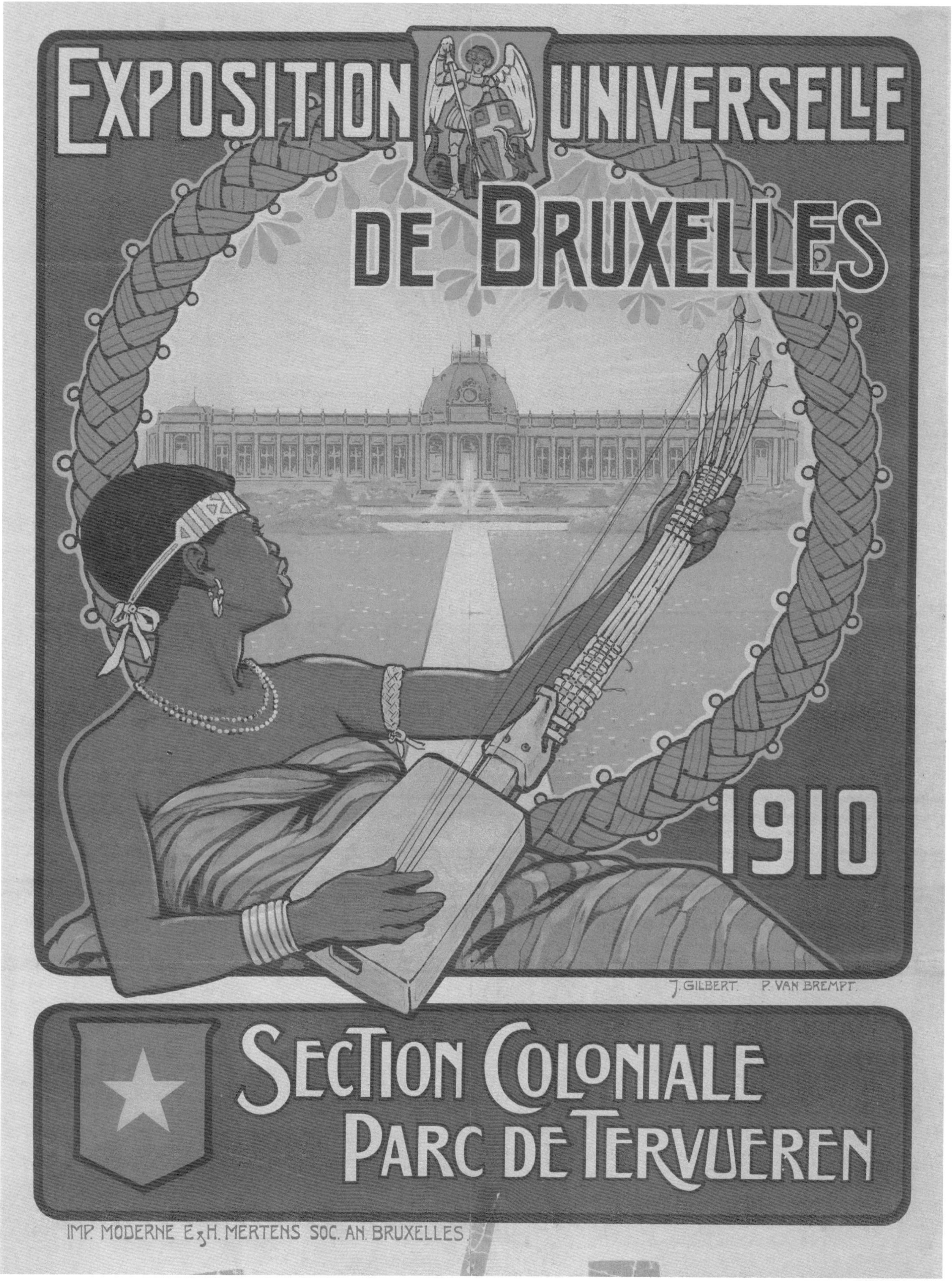
EXPOSITION UNIVERSELLE
DE BRUXELLES
1910
J. GILBERT. P. VAN BREMPT.
SECTION COLONIALE
PARC DE TERVUEREN
IMP. MODERNE E. & H. MERTENS SOC. AN. BRUXELLES

Celebrating the Belgian Nation as a Strong Colonial Power

If the 1910 exhibition was an important event to mark the shift from the Congo Free State to a Belgian colony, the Ghent exhibition of 1913 is often described as "la première exposition coloniale belge." Its main agenda was to portray Belgium to other European countries as a strong colonial power, able to govern an immense territory in the center of the African continent. Five years had passed since King Leopold II's death, and the event thus marked the beginning of an explicit rehabilitation of the king as the *père fondateur* of the Belgian colony. The modesty of the 1905 exhibition was replaced by an impressive Congo Palace, with a floor surface of 6,000 square meters, prominently located at the crossroads of two important axes of the exhibition grounds. Architect Joseph Caluwaers authored its Neo-Byzantine design, applying decorative geometric patterns that were inspired by Congolese textiles and displaying spears, knives, and shields on strategic wall surfaces. After passing the *Salon d'honneur* where tribute was paid to the Belgian monarchy, visitors would enter a circular gallery with presentations on topics such as colonial education, cartography, mining, hygiene, and the rapidly expanding Catholic missionary efforts in Congo. As in previous exhibitions, ethnographic artifacts were displayed within a larger framework of nineteenth-century racial theories claiming Europe's civilizational superiority. The centerpiece of the Congo Palace was the immense *Panorama du Congo*, installed in the main circular hall. Measuring 115 by 14 meters, this colorful canvas depicted the port city of Matadi in eight tableaux, including, among others, the railway and harbor infrastructures, a market scene, and "traditional dances." The *Panorama* illustrated, in the words of the organizers, "le Congo tel que les Belges l'ont trouvé et le Congo tel qu'ils l'ont outillé" (the Congo as found by the Belgians and how they have developed it).

Johan Lagae

1913 fig. 24

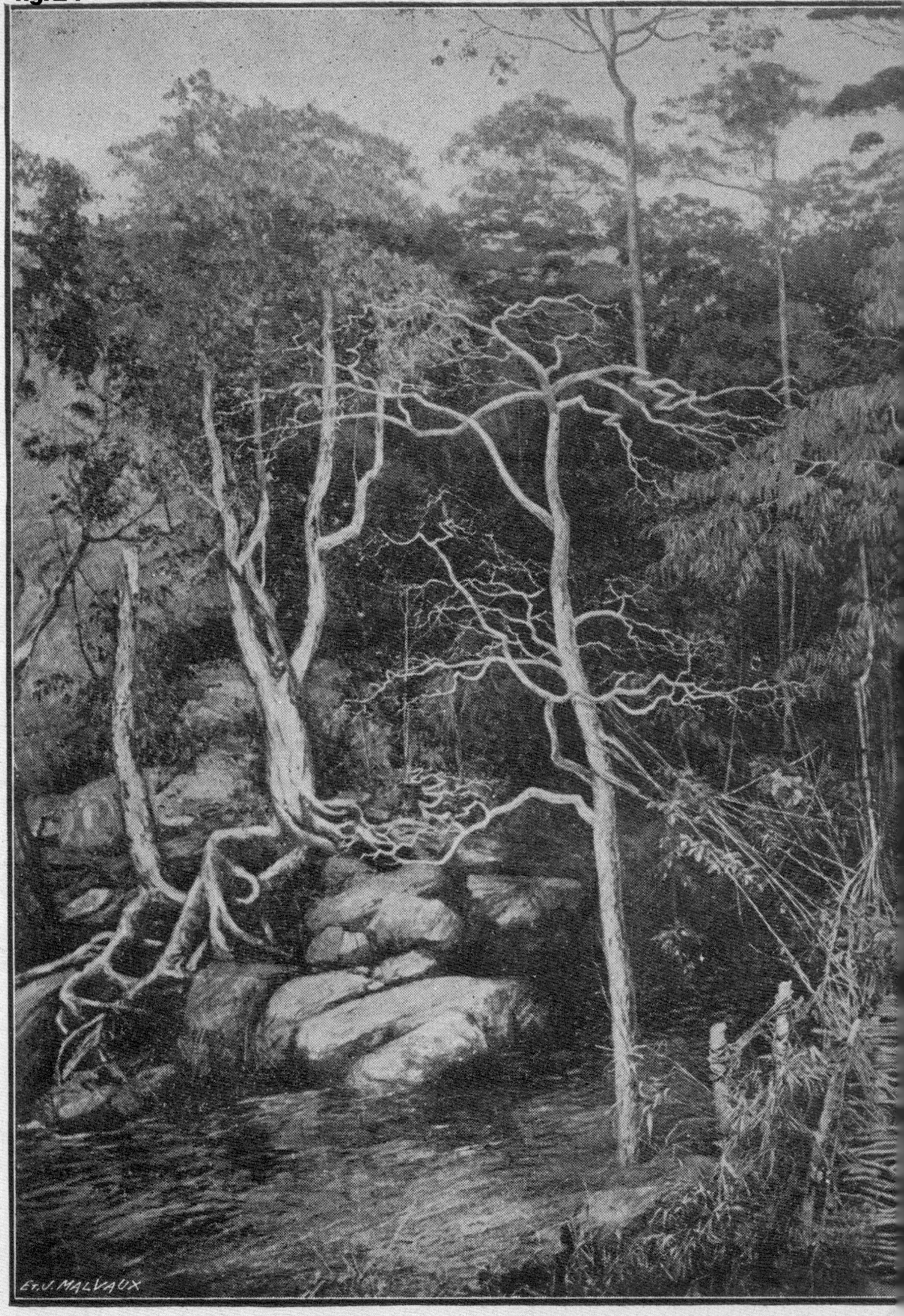

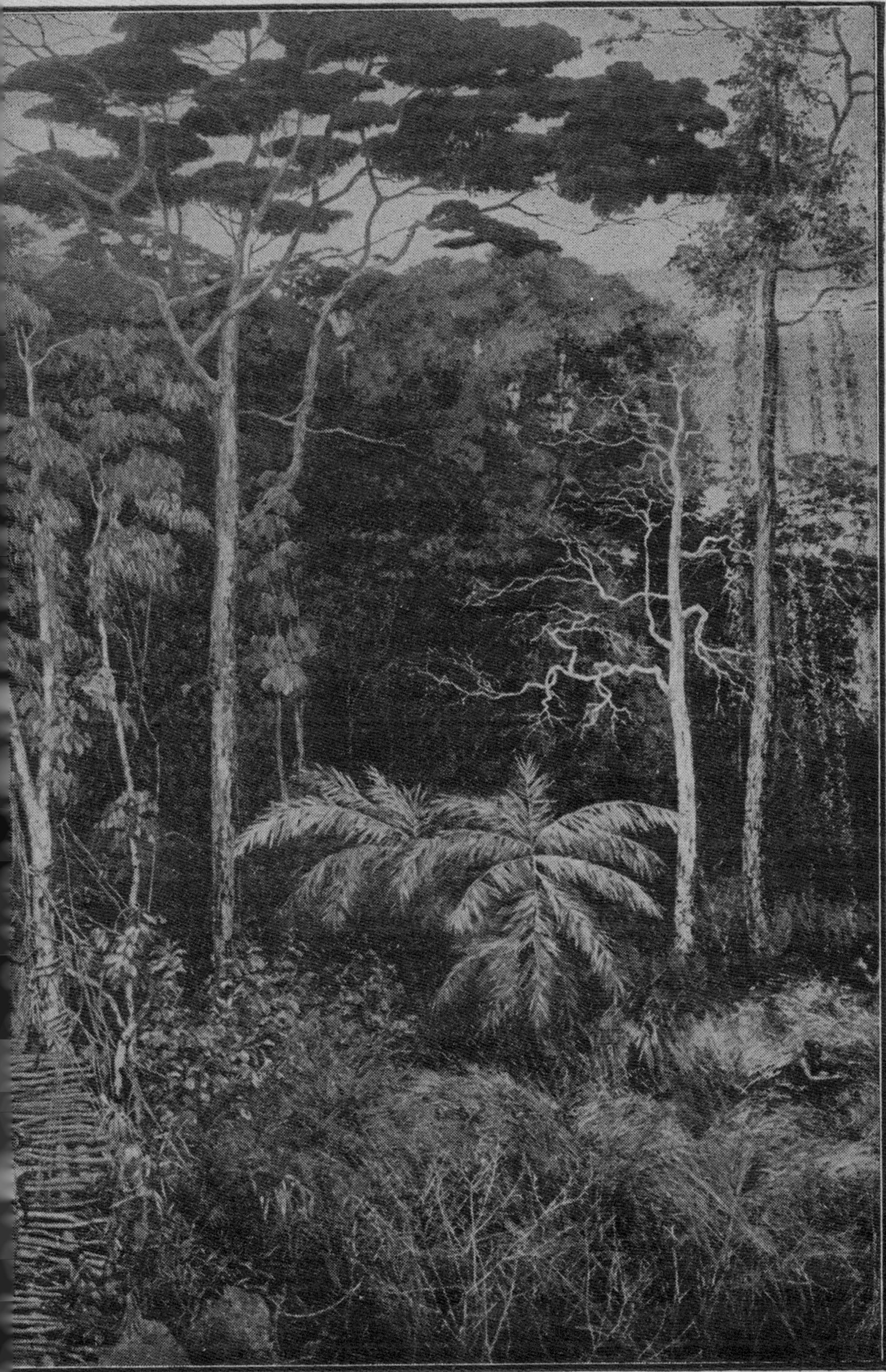

Panorama du Congo de PAUL MATHIEU et ALFRED BASTIEN.
II. — Forêt. Pont de lianes. — Het woud. Lianenbrug.

1913 fig. 25

Le Congo à l'Exposition de Gand

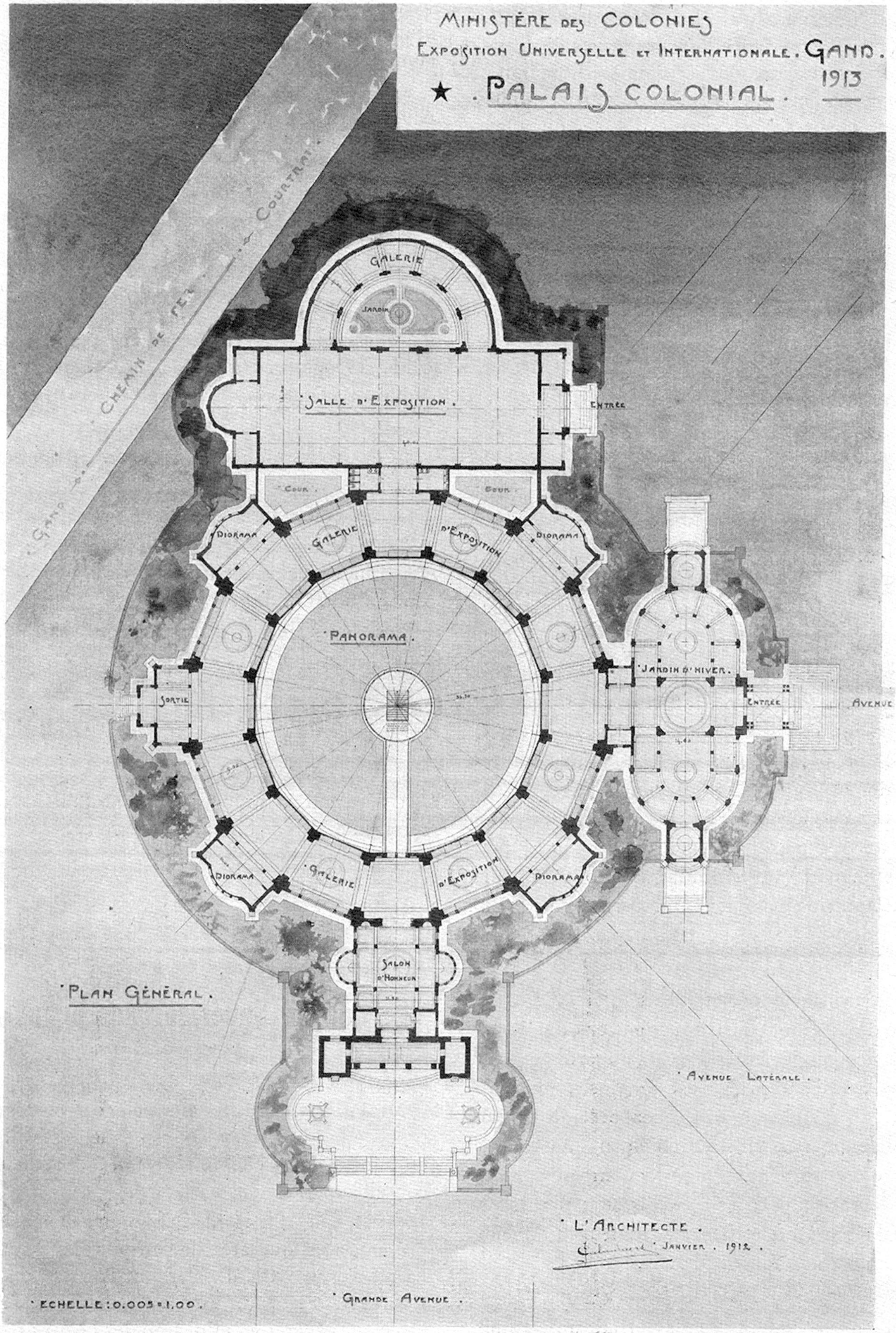

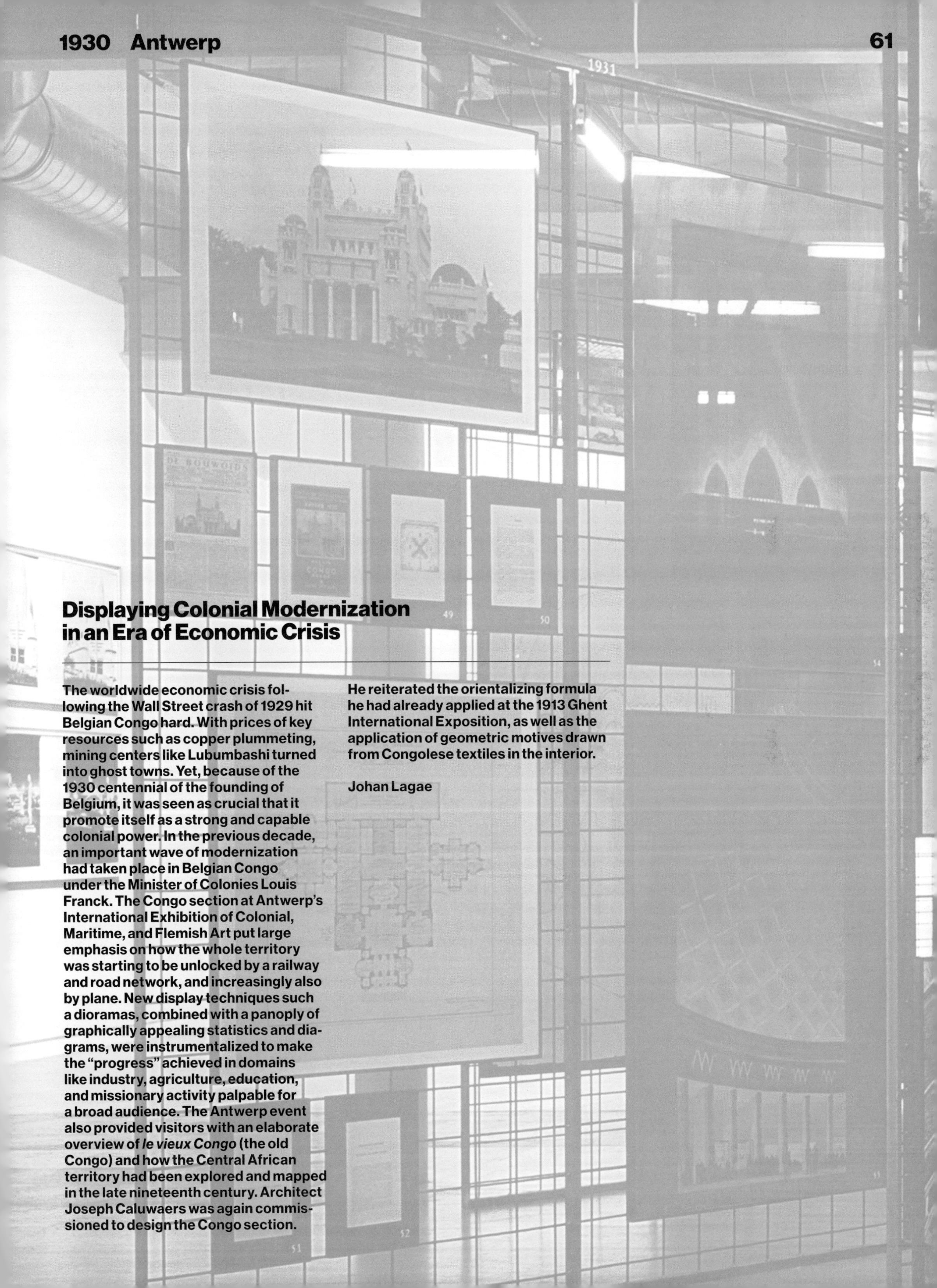

Displaying Colonial Modernization in an Era of Economic Crisis

The worldwide economic crisis following the Wall Street crash of 1929 hit Belgian Congo hard. With prices of key resources such as copper plummeting, mining centers like Lubumbashi turned into ghost towns. Yet, because of the 1930 centennial of the founding of Belgium, it was seen as crucial that it promote itself as a strong and capable colonial power. In the previous decade, an important wave of modernization had taken place in Belgian Congo under the Minister of Colonies Louis Franck. The Congo section at Antwerp's International Exhibition of Colonial, Maritime, and Flemish Art put large emphasis on how the whole territory was starting to be unlocked by a railway and road network, and increasingly also by plane. New display techniques such a dioramas, combined with a panoply of graphically appealing statistics and diagrams, were instrumentalized to make the "progress" achieved in domains like industry, agriculture, education, and missionary activity palpable for a broad audience. The Antwerp event also provided visitors with an elaborate overview of *le vieux Congo* (the old Congo) and how the Central African territory had been explored and mapped in the late nineteenth century. Architect Joseph Caluwaers was again commissioned to design the Congo section. He reiterated the orientalizing formula he had already applied at the 1913 Ghent International Exposition, as well as the application of geometric motives drawn from Congolese textiles in the interior.

Johan Lagae

1930 fig. 26

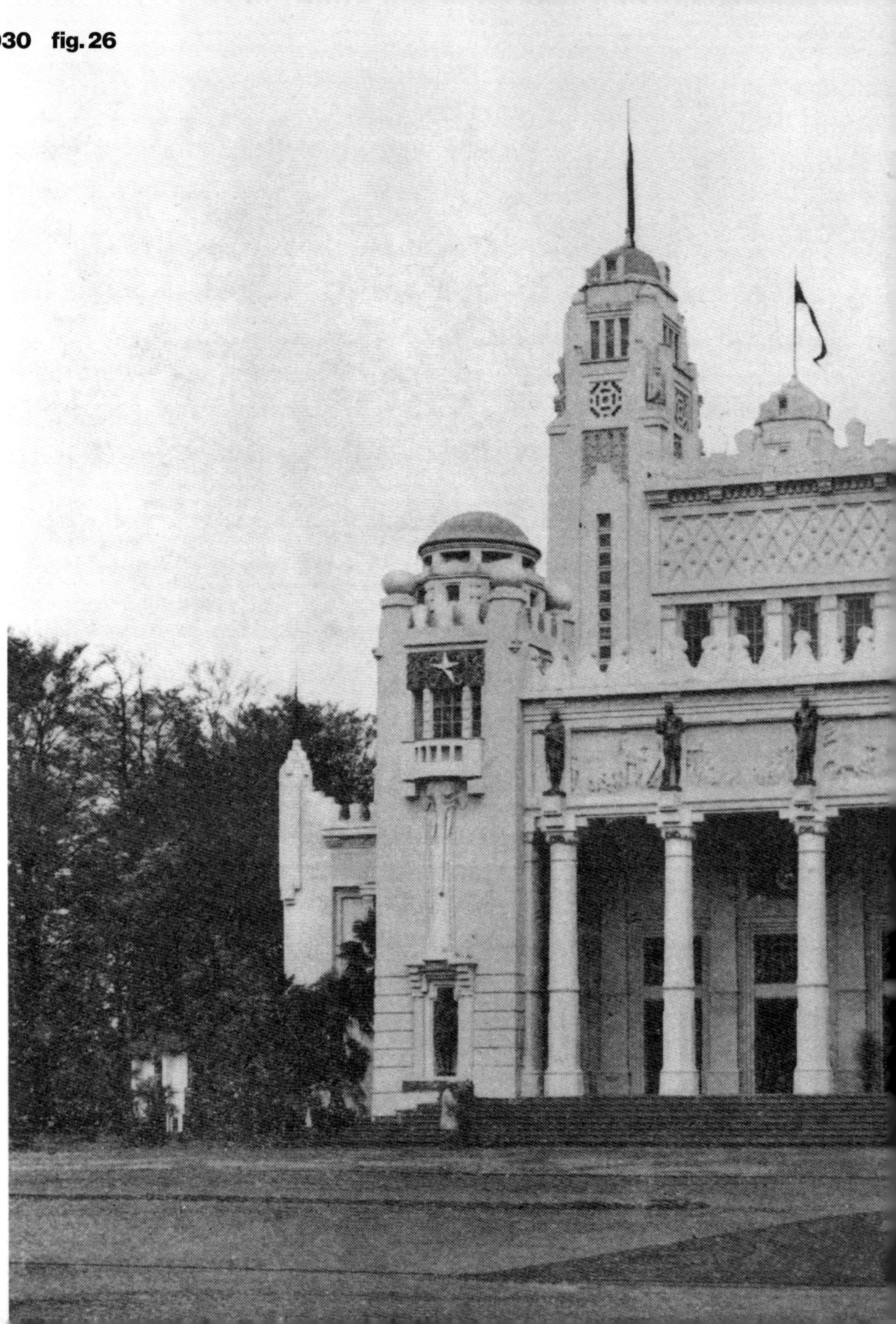

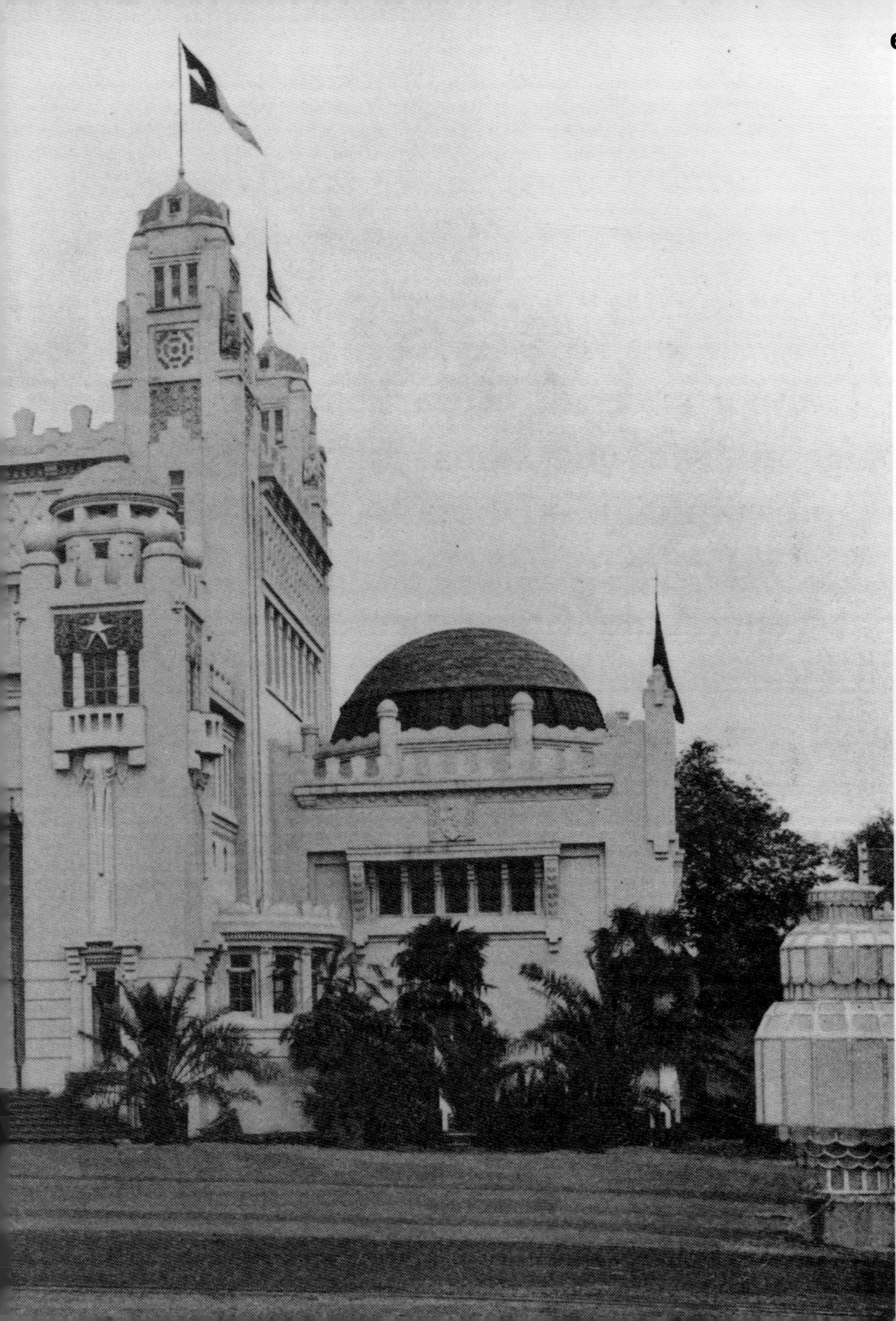

1930 fig. 27

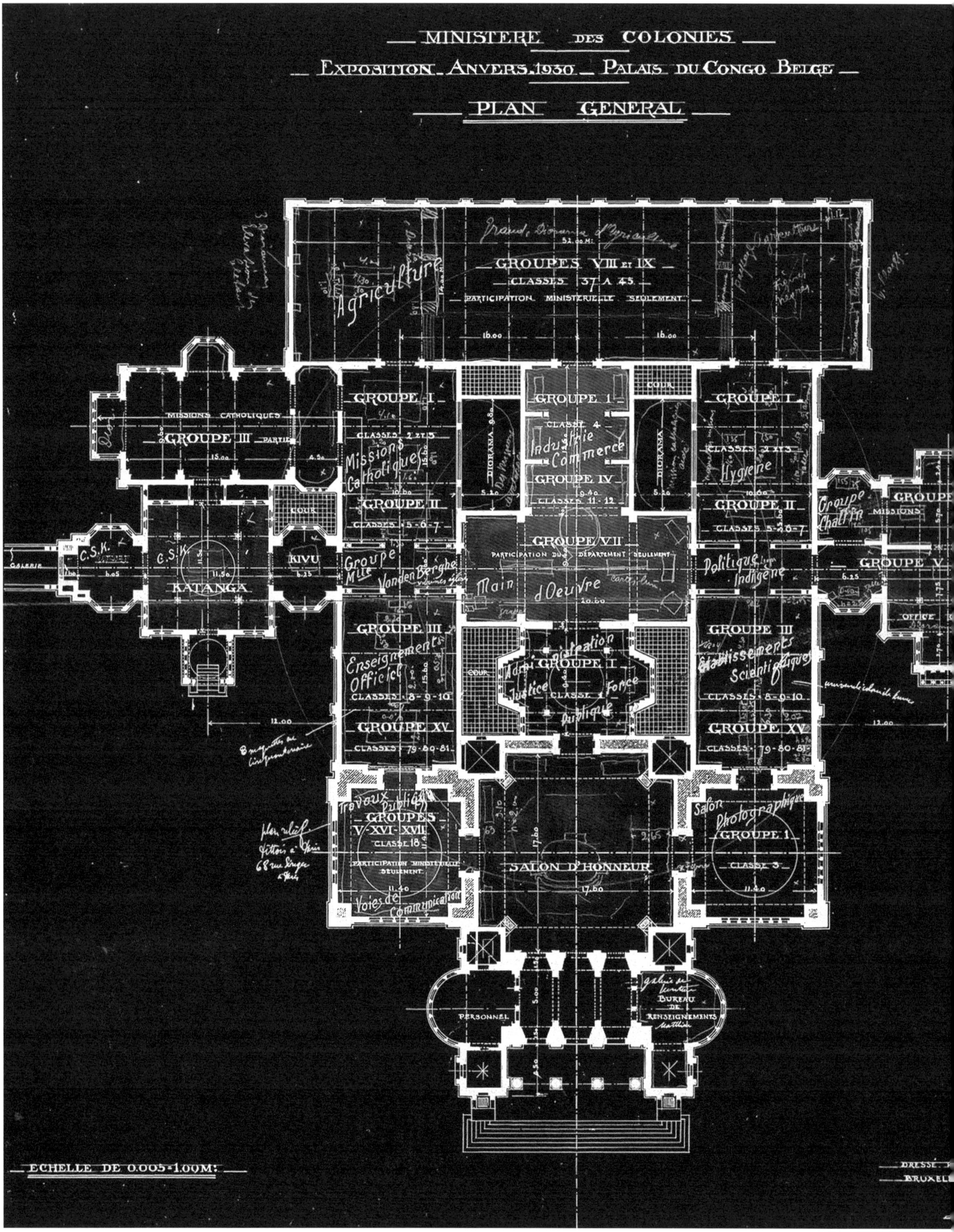
MINISTERE DES COLONIES
EXPOSITION ANVERS 1930 – PALAIS DU CONGO BELGE
PLAN GENERAL
GROUPES VIII ET IX
CLASSES 37 A 45
PARTICIPATION MINISTERIELLE SEULEMENT
Agriculture
MISSIONS CATHOLIQUES
GROUPE III
GROUPE I
CLASSES 2 ET 3
GROUPE II
CLASSES 5-6-7
GROUPE IV
CLASSES 11-12
DIORAMA
COUR
GROUPE VII
PARTICIPATION DU DEPARTEMENT SEULEMENT
Main d'Oeuvre
C.S.K.
KATANGA
KIVU
GALERIE
GROUPE V
MISSIONS
OFFICE
Politique Indigène
Hygiène
Missions Catholiques
Industrie Commerce
Enseignement Officiel
CLASSES 8-9-10
GROUPE XV
CLASSES 79-80-81
Administration Justice Force Publique
Etablissements Scientifiques
GROUPES V-XVI-XVII
CLASSE 18
PARTICIPATION MINISTERIELLE SEULEMENT
Travaux Publics
Voies de Communication
SALON D'HONNEUR
Salon Photographique
CLASSE 3
PERSONNEL
BUREAU DE RENSEIGNEMENTS
ECHELLE DE 0.005=1.00M:

TANTES
LASSE 11
ECTE SOUSSIGNÉ
SEPTEMBRE 1929

1930 fig. 28

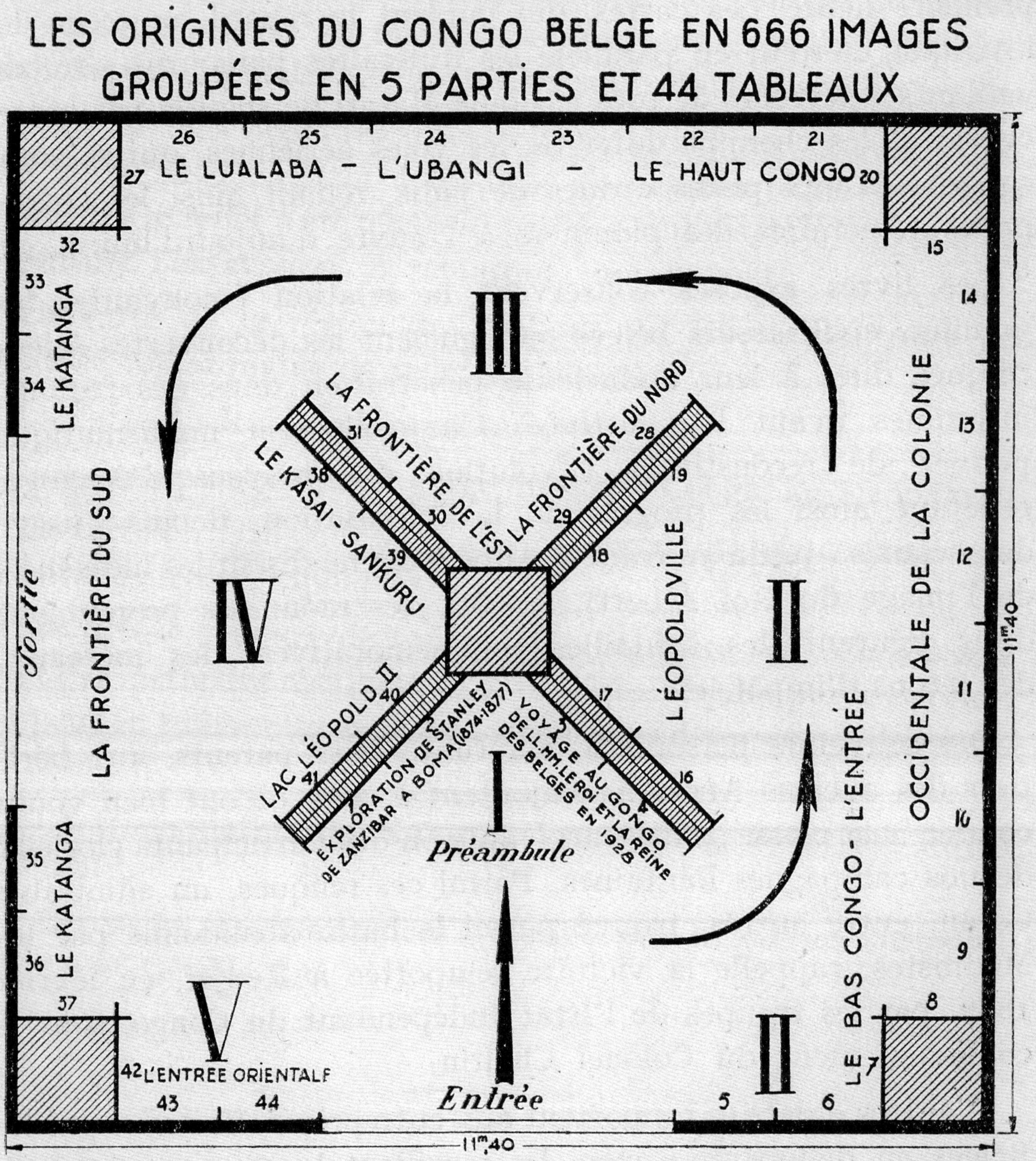

LES ORIGINES DU CONGO BELGE EN 666 IMAGES
GROUPÉES EN 5 PARTIES ET 44 TABLEAUX
LE LUALABA – L'UBANGI – LE HAUT CONGO
LE KATANGA
LA FRONTIÈRE DU SUD
Sortie
LE KATANGA
L'ENTREE ORIENTALE
OCCIDENTALE DE LA COLONIE
LE BAS CONGO - L'ENTRÉE
LÉOPOLDVILLE
LA FRONTIÈRE DE L'EST
LE KASAI - SANKURU
LA FRONTIÈRE DU NORD
LAC LÉOPOLD II
EXPLORATION DE STANLEY DE ZANZIBAR A BOMA (1874-1877)
VOYAGE AU CONGO DE LL.MM. LE ROI ET LA REINE DES BELGES EN 1928
I
II
III
IV
V
Préambule
Entrée
11m.40

Salon du Vieux Congo.

Cette évocation du Congo, des explorateurs et des pionniers, se trouve à l'entrée du Palais du Congo, emplacement tout indiqué pour une reconstitution de ce genre. Il est logique en effet que le visiteur, avant de voir dans le restant du Palais ce qu'est le Congo de 1930, reçoive d'abord une impression de ce qu'était le Congo en 1885 et de sa première croissance. Ainsi pourra-t-il, par ce contraste, mieux percevoir les progrès réalisés au cours d'un demi-siècle de colonisation.

L'auteur a eu à choisir entre deux modes d'exécution.

Il pouvait classer les clichés et gravures par grands sujets généraux : transports — centres urbains — agriculture, — élevage — industrie — commerce — hygiène — instruction — types indigènes — paysages — et ce fut le premier projet, mais la valeur très inégale des collections anciennes suivant les sujets et aussi la préoccupation de donner une leçon d'histoire dans le milieu géographique exact firent abandonner cette méthode. Le Congo, pays vaste comme 80 fois la Belgique, ne peut être présenté comme une entité absolue, mais plutôt comme un ensemble de régions qui ont eu, à l'origine, des caractéristiques propres à tous égards.

Ce sont ces caractéristiques qu'il importait de faire ressortir. A cette fin, le sujet a été divisé en cinq parties correspondant à des régions bien déterminées et aux faits marquants de l'histoire de ces contrées.

L'évocation est réalisée par 640 photographies lumineuses reproduites sur verres (diapositifs mesurant de 18×24 cm. à 30×40 cm.) et par 26 agrandissements sur papier d'un format allant de 0.60×0.90 à 1.15×2 mètres. L'exposé est réparti entre 44 tableaux comprenant chacun de 12 à 20 images lumineuses, datées et groupées dans le milieu géographique.

Au-dessus des tableaux sont déployés les agrandissements photographiques, dont les sujets résument la matière traitée en dessous.

1930 fig. 30

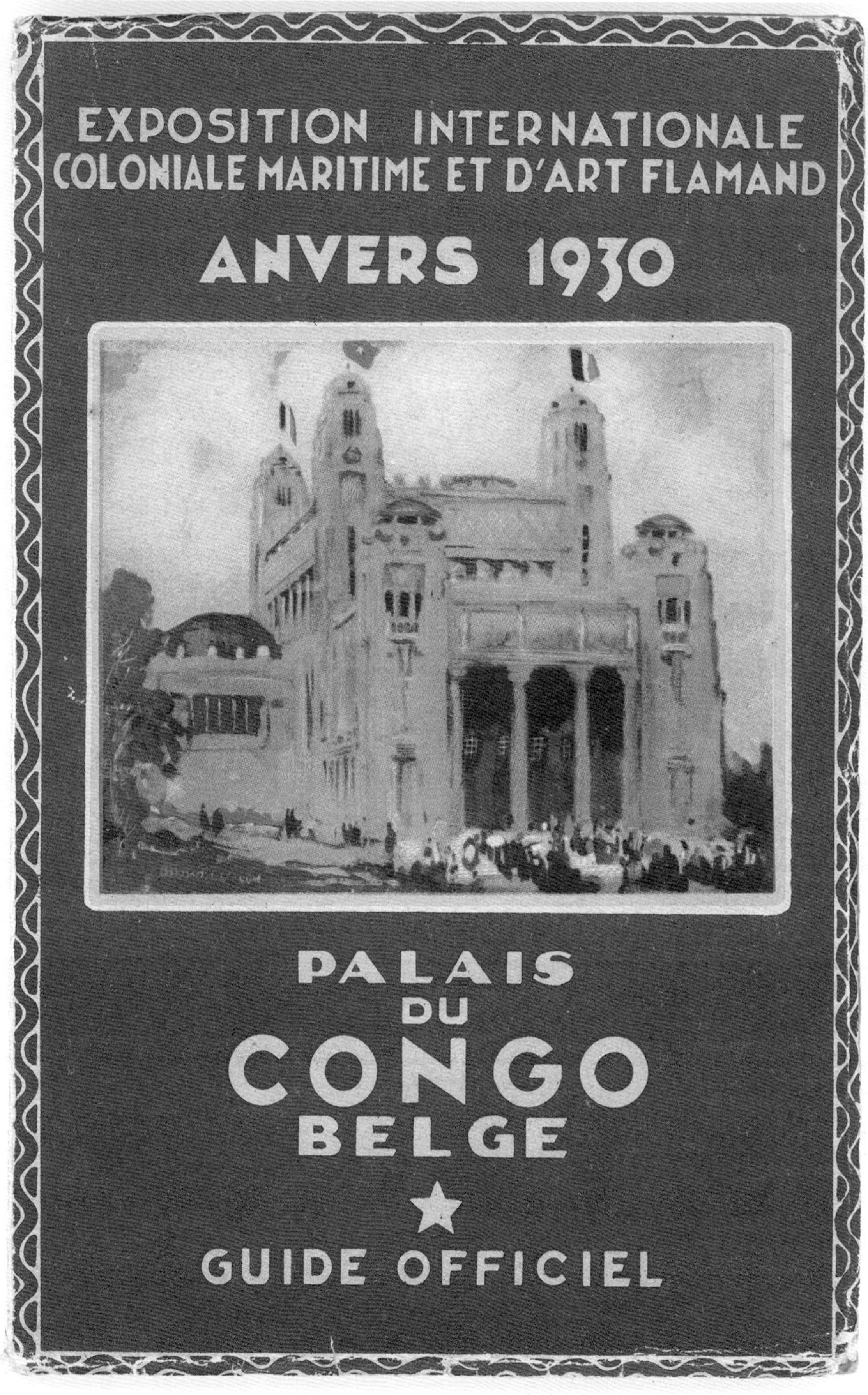
EXPOSITION INTERNATIONALE
COLONIALE MARITIME ET D'ART FLAMAND
ANVERS 1930
PALAIS
DU
CONGO
BELGE
GUIDE OFFICIEL

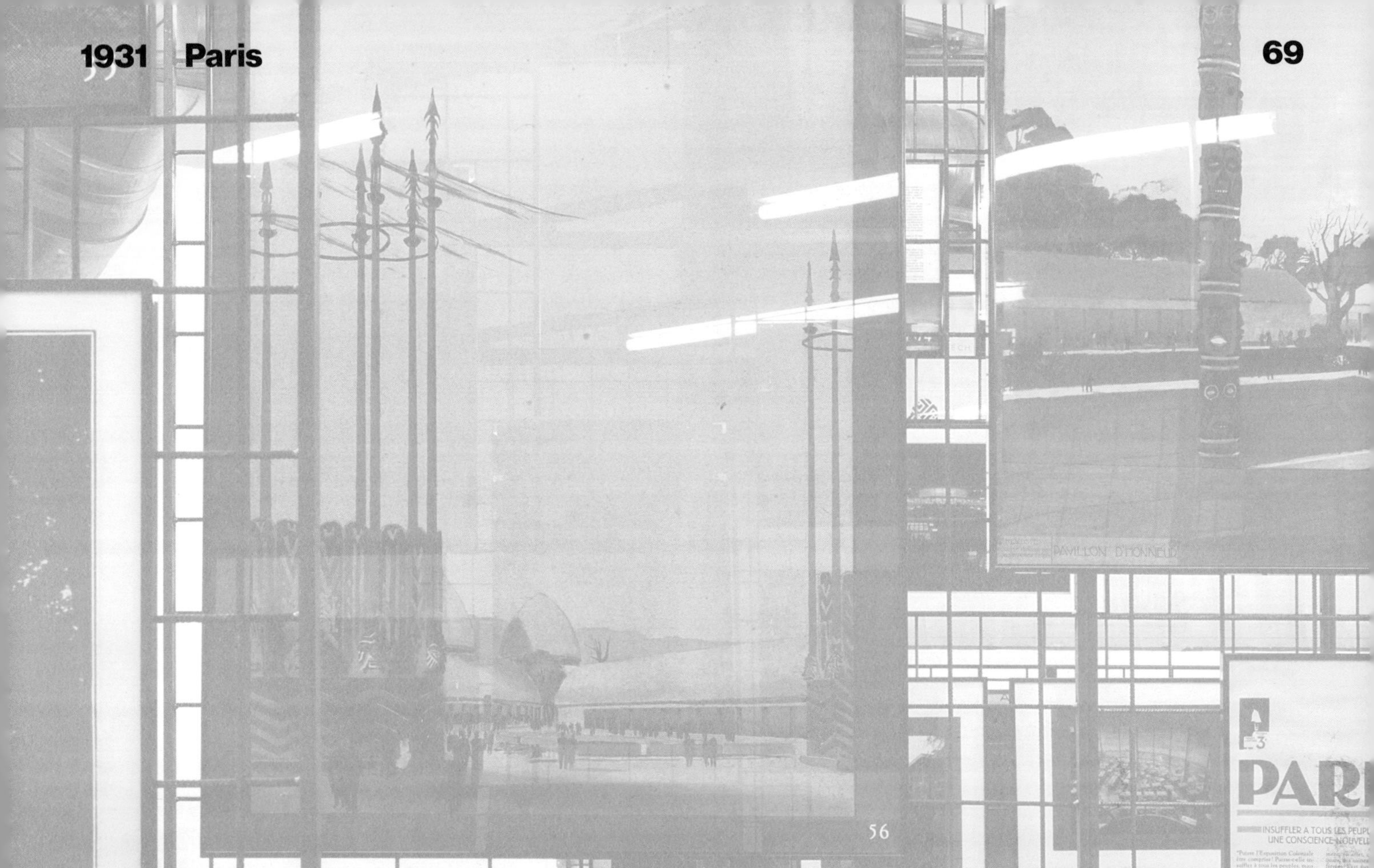

A Phantasmagoric, yet Erudite and Functional Architectural Response

The dichotomy between an interior display of colonial modernization and an exterior architectural evocation of an "authentic" Central African culture, which was already present in previous exhibitions, reached its apogee in the presentation of Belgian Congo at the 1931 International Colonial Exhibition in Paris, the ultimate "théâtre des colonies," as architectural historian Sylviane Leprun dubbed the event. Designed by architect Henry Lacoste, the section was large, consisting of three spaces that were arranged in such a way as to produce an imposing symmetrical vista onto the central space, with its three conical domes. The temporary and somewhat rudimentary exhibition halls, constructed mainly out of industrial building components, topped with thatched roofs and lined with a long row of columns whose capitals were formed by masks of an unabashed, invented Africanizing design. As numerous archival drawings demonstrate, Lacoste based the decorative repertoire of his project on meticulous research on Congolese and African artifacts and textiles that he had conducted—primarily via publications and in the collections of the Musée du Congo in Tervuren. In the 1980s, art and architectural historians such as Paul Greenhalgh and Jean-Claude Vigato denounced Lacoste's project as "mock African architecture," arguing that the "vocabulary of exotic architecture was colonized through the architectural principles of the École des Beaux-Arts." In 1931, however, critics praised the design as an apt response to the architectural challenge of colonial display, emphasizing in particular the functional logic of Lacoste's project. This ambivalence between exoticism and functionalism most strikingly appears in the use of a *charpente à lamelles* (a diamond grid, timber lamella roof) for the three domes: while it immediately evokes the roof construction of vernacular architectures, the building method was, in fact, a cost-efficient solution that Lacoste had borrowed from the so-called Zollinger roof system applied in the previous decade in social housing schemes in Germany.

Johan Lagae

1931 fig. 31, 32, 33, 34

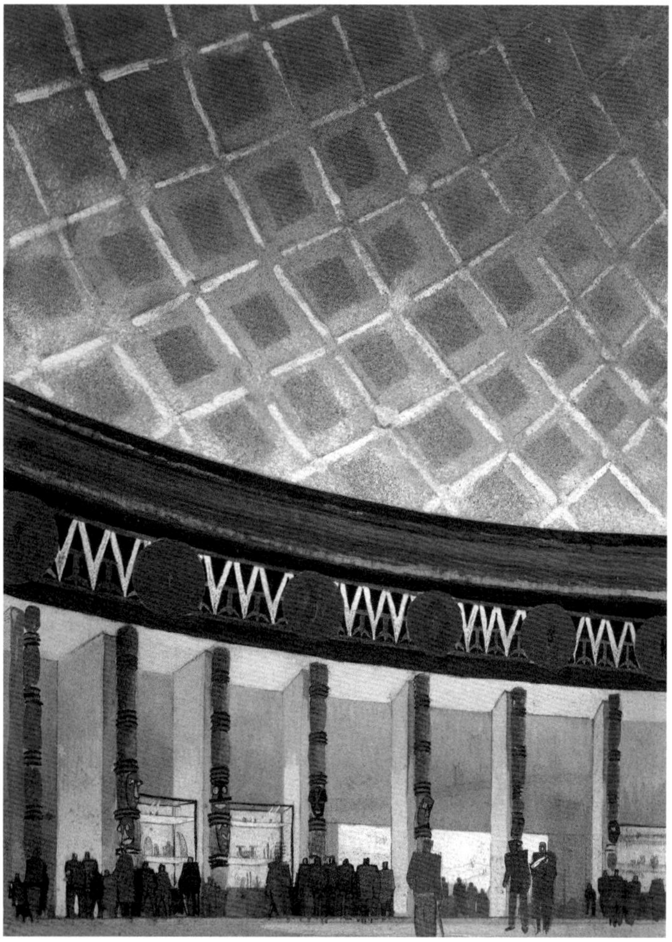

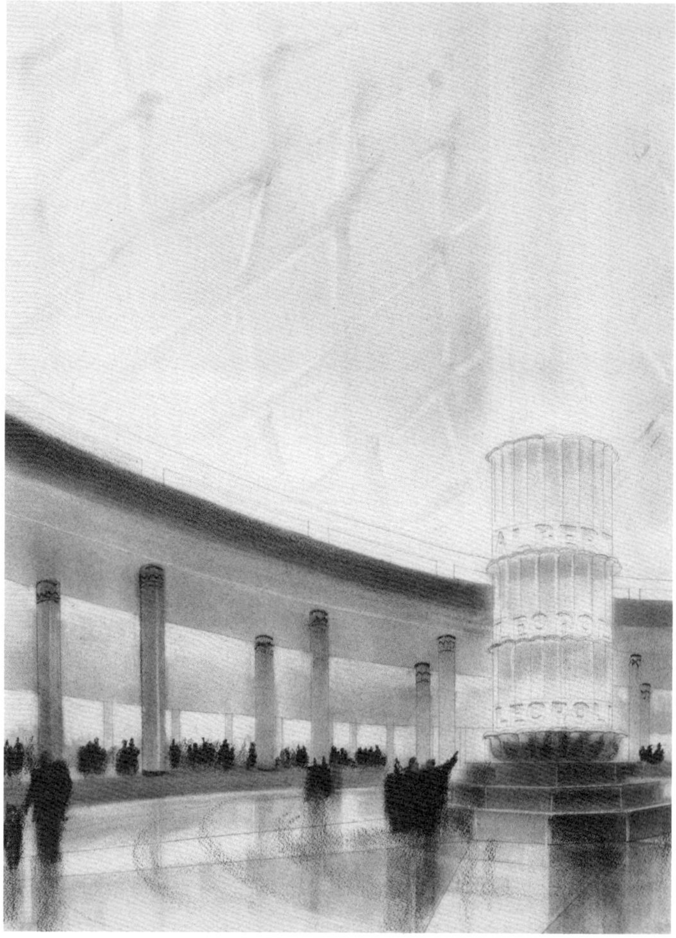

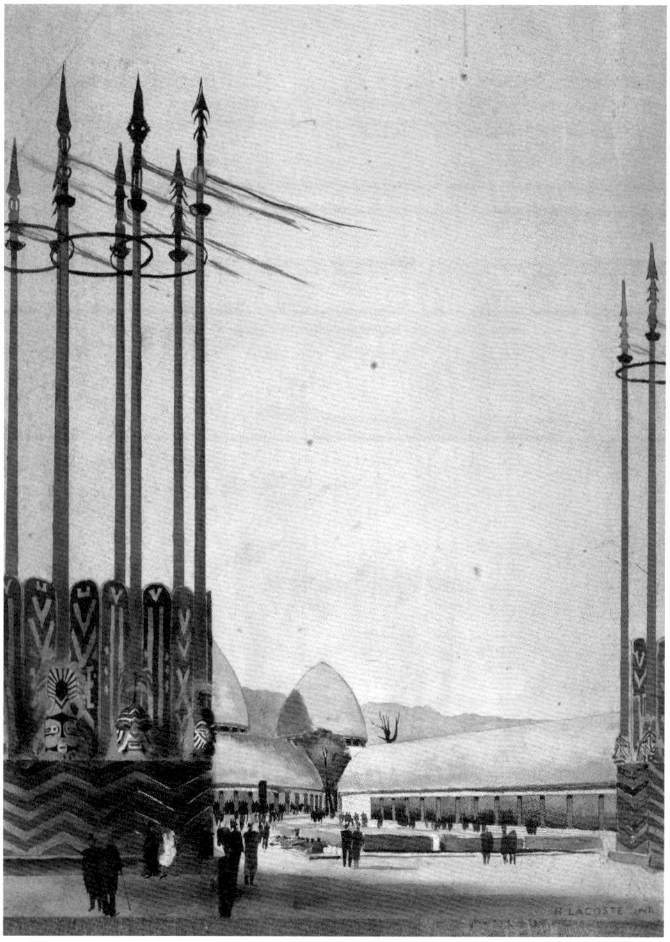

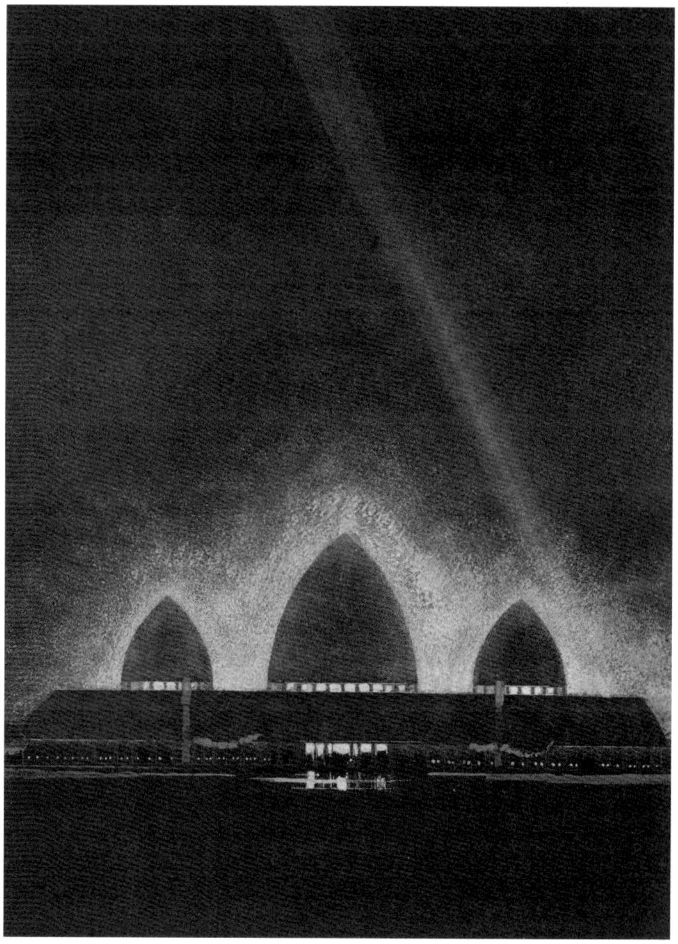

fig. 35

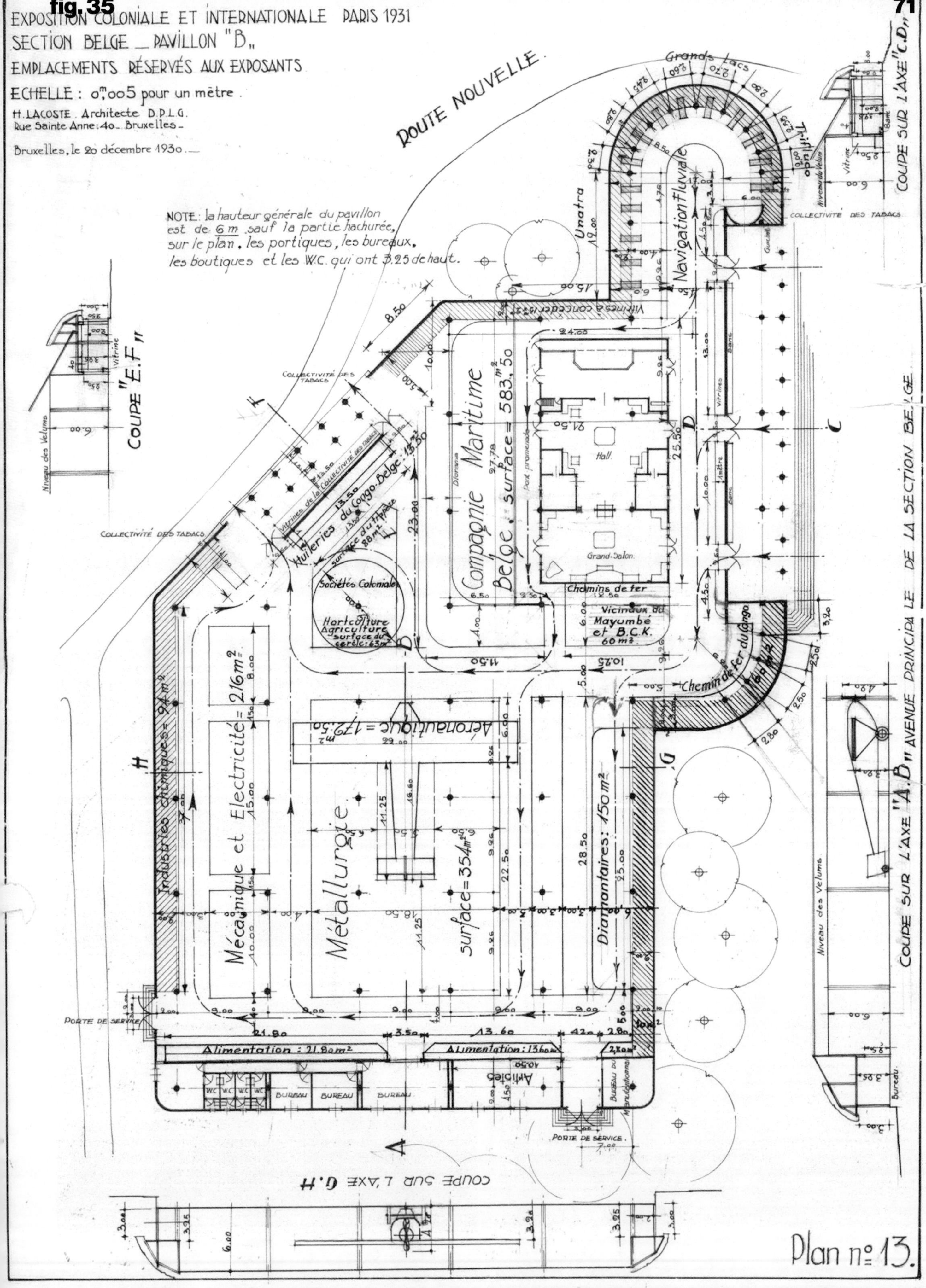

EXPOSITION COLONIALE ET INTERNATIONALE PARIS 1931
SECTION BELGE _ PAVILLON "B"
EMPLACEMENTS RÉSERVÉS AUX EXPOSANTS
ECHELLE : 0m,005 pour un mètre.
H. LACOSTE. Architecte D.P.L.G.
Rue Sainte Anne: 40 _ Bruxelles _
Bruxelles, le 20 décembre 1930.
ROUTE NOUVELLE
Grands Lacs
NOTE: la hauteur générale du pavillon est de 6 m sauf la partie hachurée, sur le plan, les portiques, les bureaux, les boutiques et les W.C. qui ont 3.25 de haut.
Unatra
Navigation fluviale
Collectivité des Tabacs
Vitrines à concéder
Compagnie Maritime Belge. Surface = 583m² 50
Hall
Grand-Salon
Huileries du Congo Belge
Sociétés Coloniales
Horticulture Agriculture
Chemins de fer Vicinaux du Mayumbé et B.C.K. 60 m²
Chemin de fer du Congo
Industries chimiques = 94 m²
Mécanique et Electricité = 216 m²
Aéronautique = 172.5 m²
Métallurgie
surface = 354 m²
Diamantaires: 150 m²
Alimentation: 21.80 m²
Alimentation: 13.60 m²
Artistes
BUREAU
W.C.
PORTE DE SERVICE
COUPE "E.F"
COUPE SUR L'AXE "C.D"
COUPE SUR L'AXE "A.B" AVENUE PRINCIPALE DE LA SECTION BELGE
COUPE SUR L'AXE G.H
Niveau des Velums
Vitrine
Bureau
Plan n° 13.

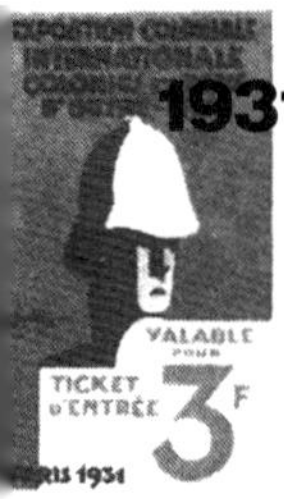

1931 fig. 36

Colonisér, ce n'est pas uniquement, en effet, construire des quais, des usines, ou des voie ferrées ; c'est aussi gagner à la douceur humaine les cœurs farouches de la savane o du désert. (2)

PARIS 1931

INSUFFLER A TOUS LES PEUPLES UNE CONSCIENCE NOUVELLE

›uisse l'Exposition Coloniale re comprise! Puisse-t-elle in- ıffler à tous les peuples, mais abord aux peuples aînés, un es- ›it nouveau, une conscience ›uvelle!
olonisér, ce n'est pas unique- ment, en effet, construire des quais, des usines, ou des voies ferrées; c'est aussi gagner à la douceur humaine les cœurs farouches de la savane ou du désert." (2)

UNE ŒUVRE DE PAIX ET DE PROGRÈS

En décidant cette Exposition, le parlement a voulu montrer, au lendemain de la période meurtrière et fratricide qui a couvert le monde de ruines, qu'il y a, pour notre civilisation, d'autres champs d'act que les champs de bataille que les nations du XXe siè peuvent rivaliser loyalem généreusement, dans les vres de paix et de progrès.

NE VISITEZ PAS L'EXPOSITION COLONIALE

la veille du 1er Mai 1931 et à ıvant-veille de l'inauguration : l'Exposition Coloniale, :tudiant indochinois Tao est ılevé par la police française.)
opinion mondiale s'est émue ı vain du sort des deux con- ımnés à mort Sacco et Van- tti. Tao, livré à l'arbitraire de justice militaire et de la justi- des mandarins, nous n'avons ıs aucune garantie pour sa e. Ce joli lever de rideau était bien celui qu'il fallait, en 1931, à l'Exposition de Vincennes.
L'idée du brigandage colonial (le mot était brillant et à peine assez fort), cette idée, qui date du XIXe siècle est de celles qui n'ont pas fait leur chemin. On s'est servi de l'argent qu'on avait en trop pour envoyer en Afrique, en Asie, des navires, des pelles, des pioches, grâce auxquels il y a enfin là-bas, de quoi travailler pour un salaire et cet argent, on le représente volontiers comme un don fait aux indigènes.
Il est donc naturel, prétend-t-on, que le travail de ces millions de nouveaux esclaves nous ait donné les monceaux d'or qui sont en réserve dans les caves de la Banque de France. Mais, que ces hommes dont nous distingue ne serait-ce que notre qualité de blancs, nous qui disons hommes de couleur, nous sommes sans couleur, aient été tenus, par la seule puissance de la métallurgie ropéenne, en 1914, de se fa crever la peau pour un très monument funéraire colle – c'était d'ailleurs, si nous nous trompons pas, une i française, cela répondait à calcul français – voilà qui n permet d'inaugurer, nous au à notre manière, l'Expositi Coloniale. (3)

André Breton, Paul Eluard, Arag Maxime Alexandre. (...)

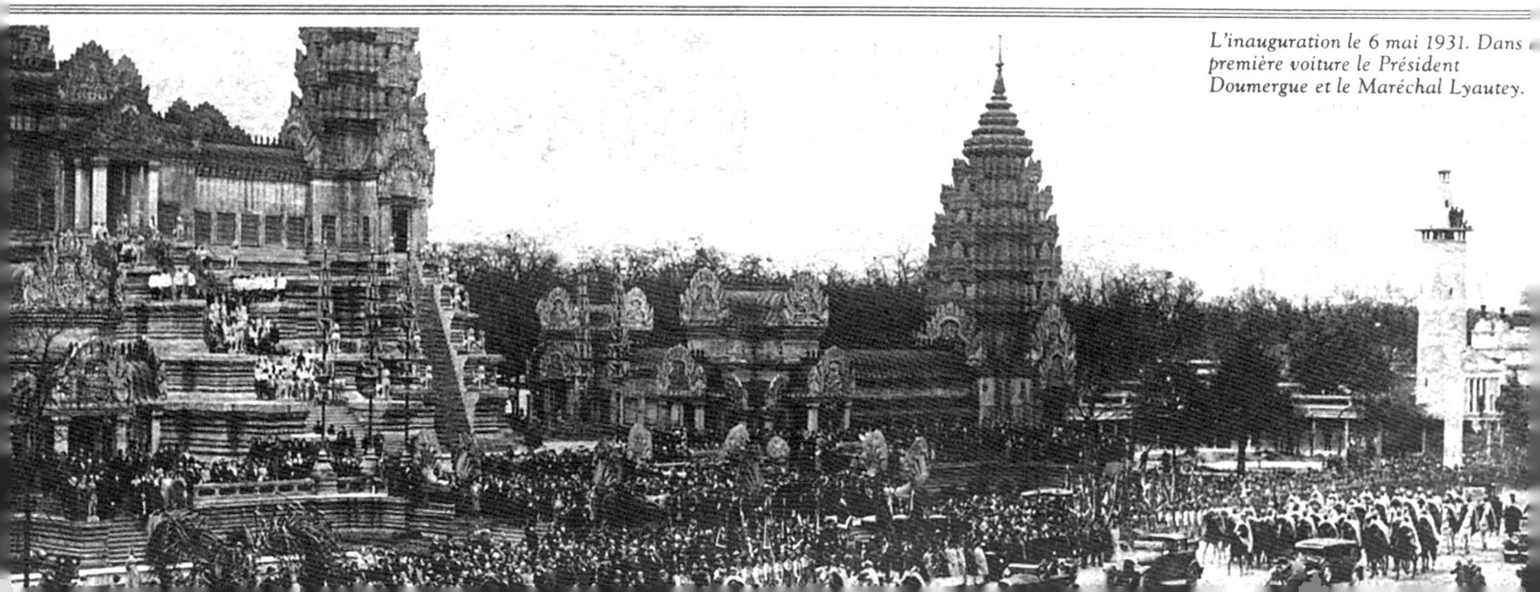

L'inauguration le 6 mai 1931. Dans première voiture le Président Doumergue et le Maréchal Lyautey.

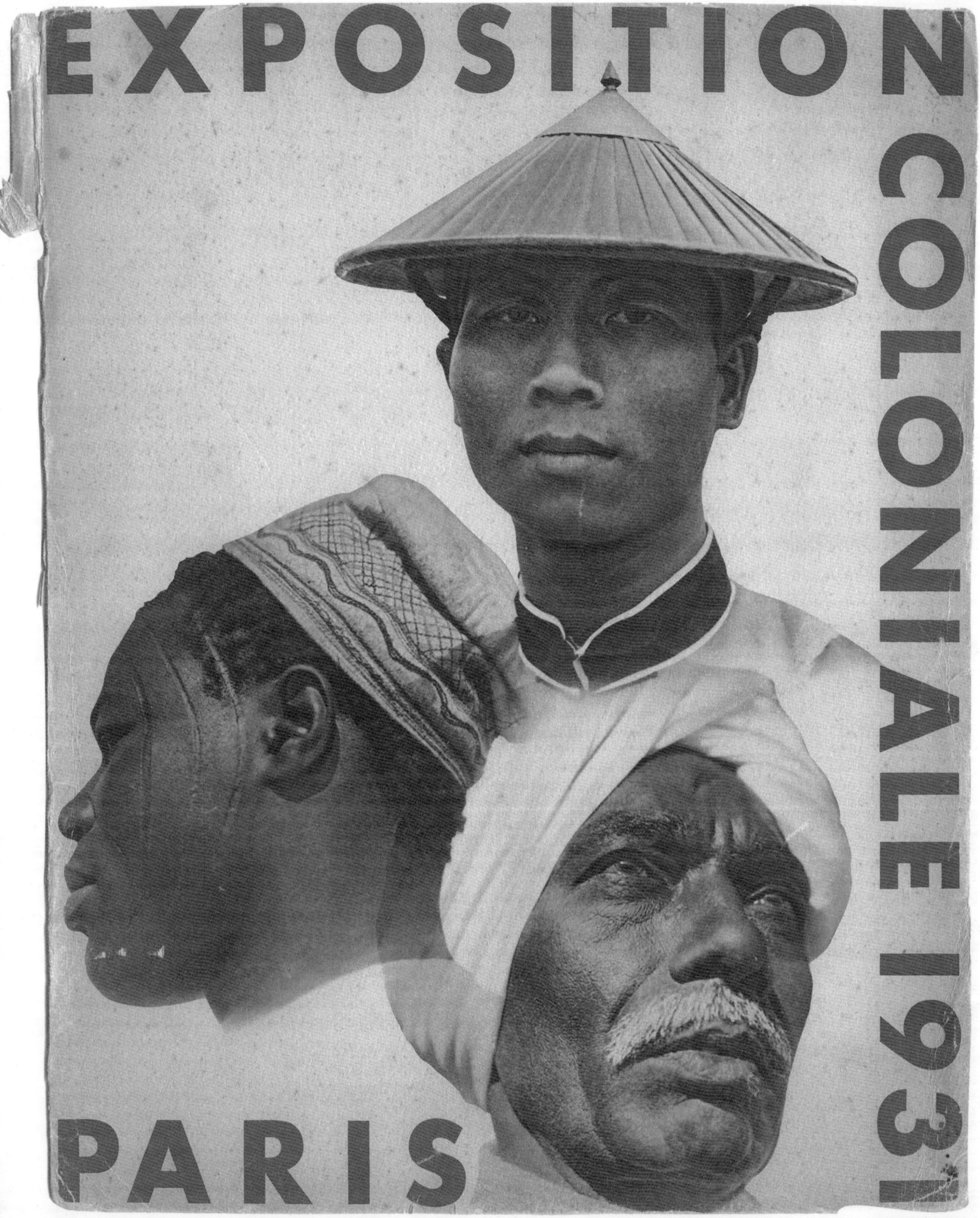
EXPOSITION
COLONIALE 1931
PARIS

1931 fig. 38

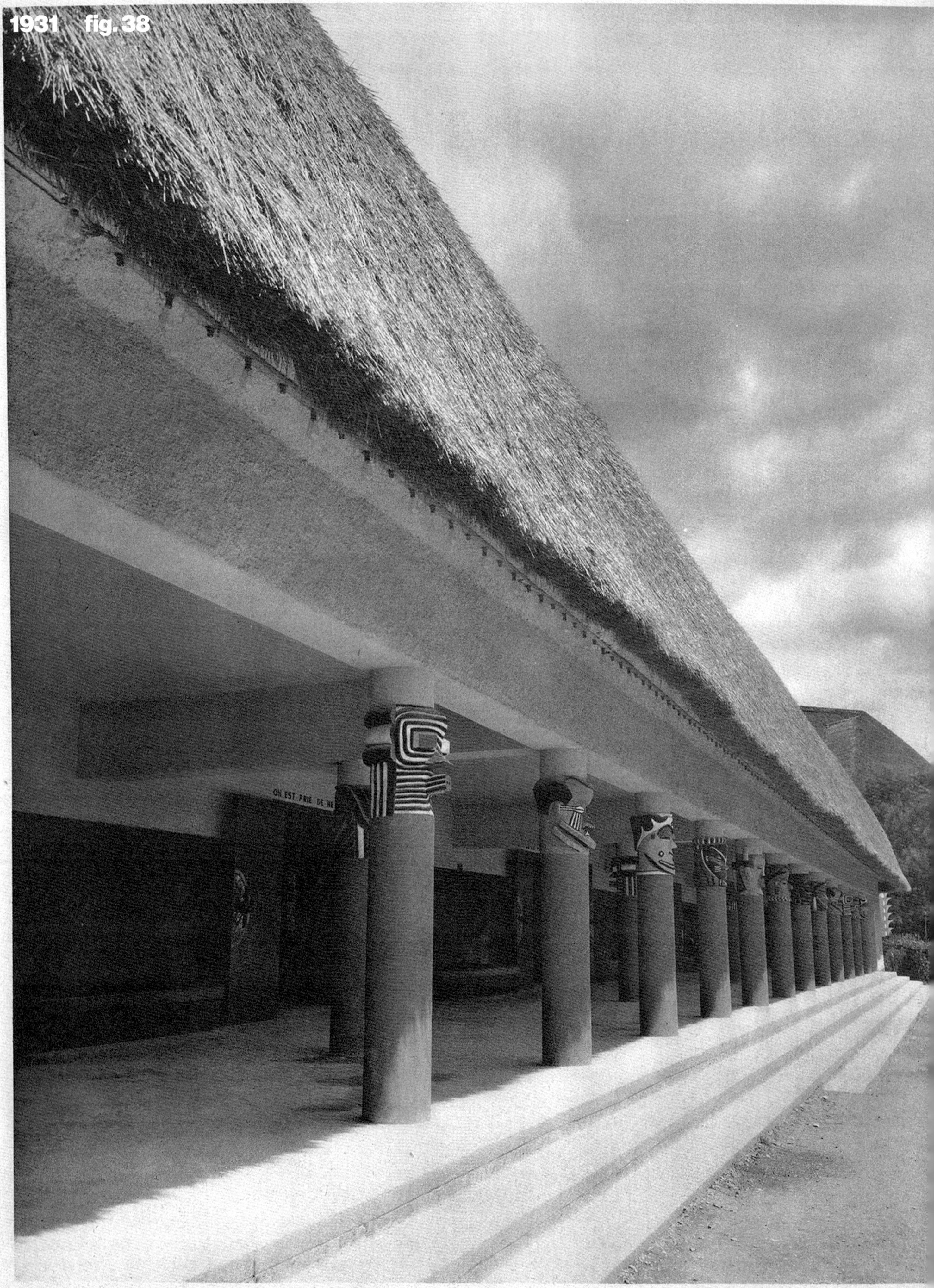

44 - Pavillon de la Belgique (Congo Belge)

Henri LACOSTE, Ar.

fig. 39

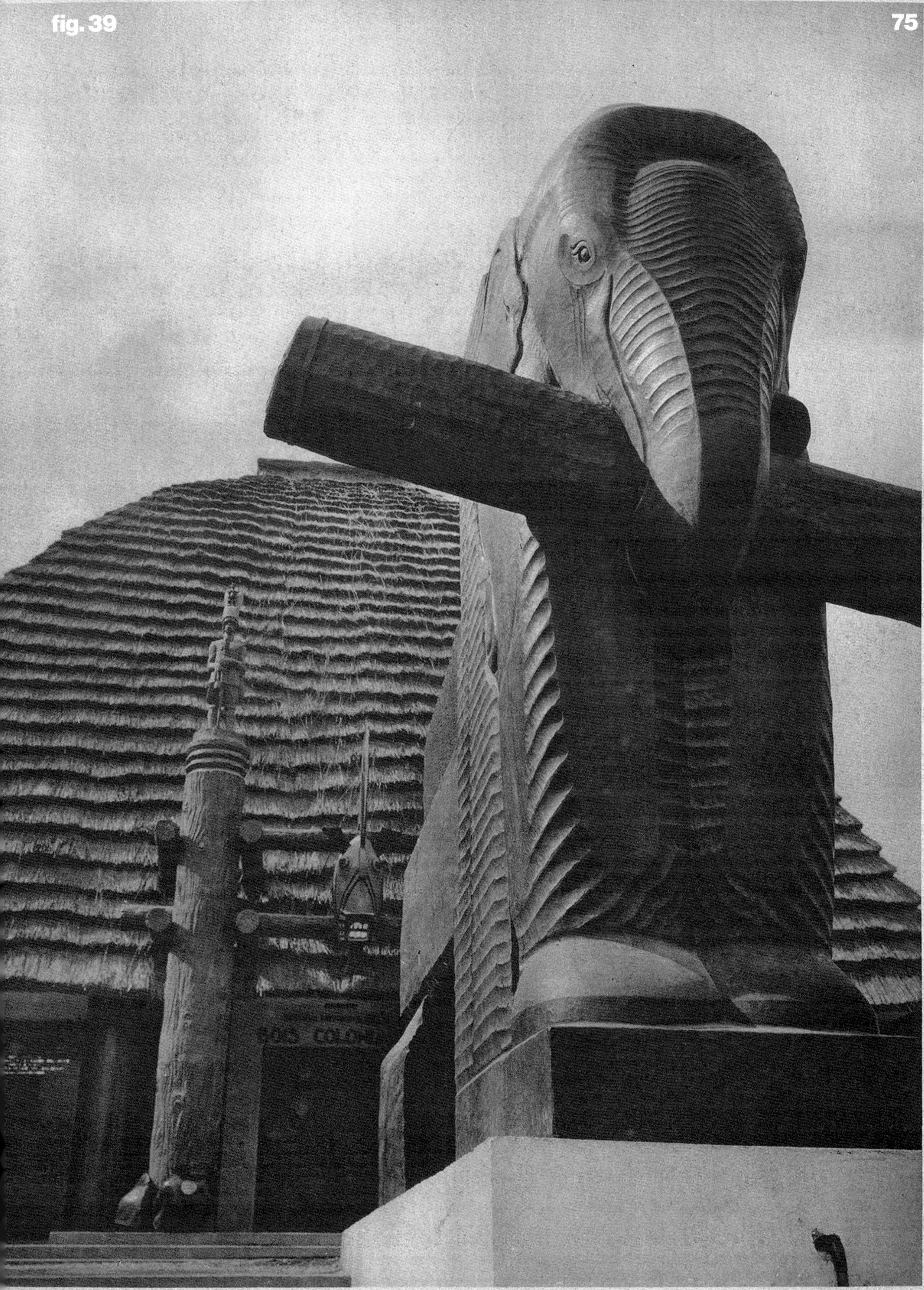

villon des Bois Coloniaux

LEROY et CURY, Architectes

1931 fig. 40

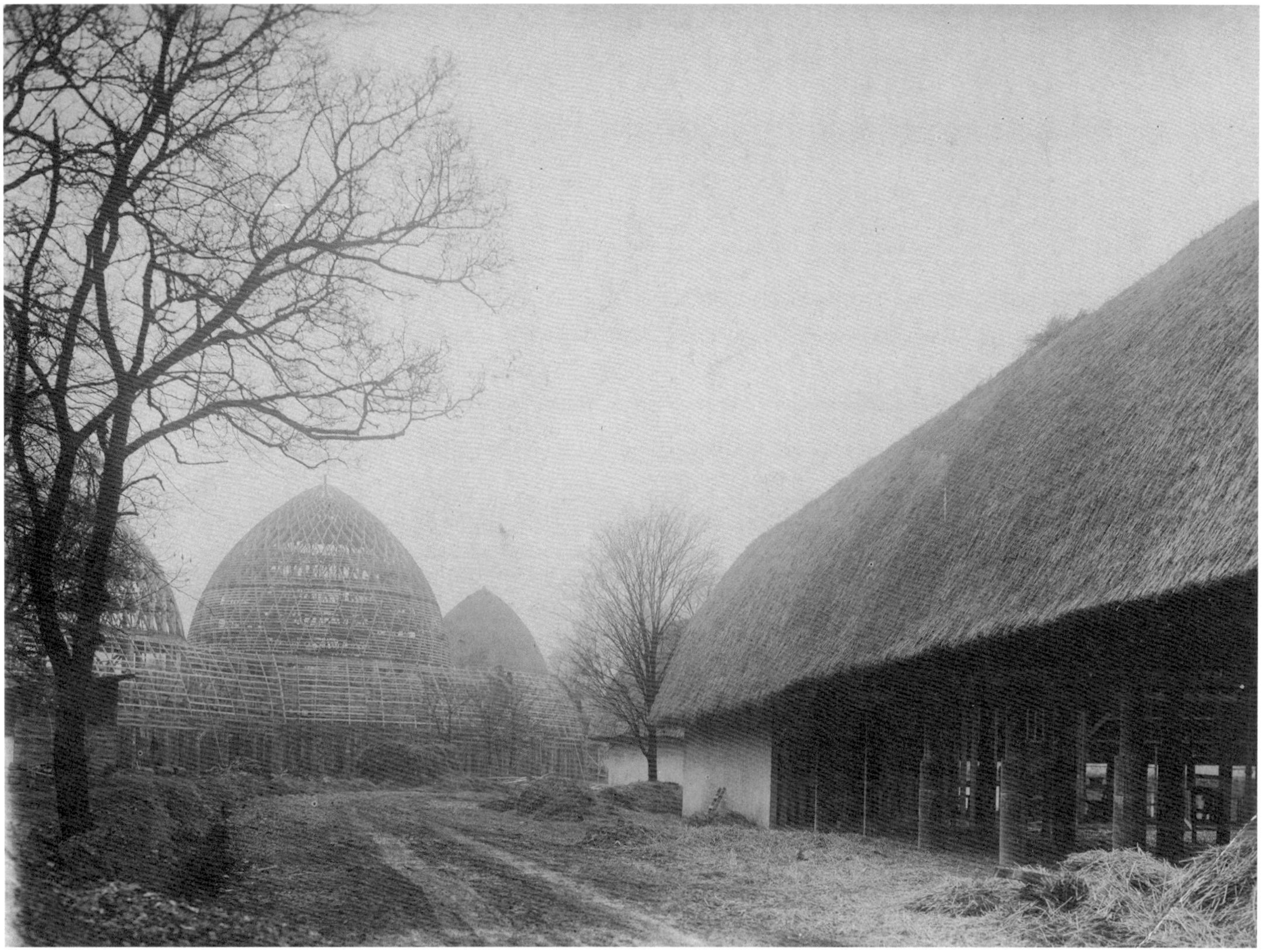

Celebrating a *Cinquantenaire* in Uncertain Times

Stakes were high for the Congo section of the 1935 Brussels International Exposition. It was the year of the *cinquentenaire* of the founding of the Congo Free State, but the worldwide economic situation was still dire and other European powers, Germany in particular, were eager to claim parts of Central Africa. The Belgian authorities proved quite reluctant to invest large sums in the event, however, and the 1935 Congo section was largely indebted to the initiative of private entrepreneurs. Architects showed a particular interest, and those with experience in Congo, such as Raymond Cloquet, made an explicit plea to use the event for the development of a truly contemporary colonial architecture. Henry Lacoste submitted a striking proposal, entitled "Reconstitution géohydraphique et climatérique d'un voyage d'exploration au Congo." Through an innovative and technologically daring immersive mise-en-scène that created a dynamic climatic (sub)tropical environment, including flows of rivers, waterfalls and clouds of fog through innovative hydraulic engineering, visitors were to be offered the sensory experience of traveling through Congo's three climatic zones: the savanna, the tropical forest, and the mountain ridge of Ruwenzori, which had been recently documented by a scientific expedition. In the end, the commission for the main pavilion was granted to René Schoentjes, an engineer-architect employed at the Ministry of Colonies. Like Lacoste's 1931 project, his design embodied an invented Congolese architecture. Schoentjes's project tapped into different registers, and was described in contemporary sources as drawing on "negro," "Muslim," and "Egyptian" references. The Congo section was completed with a pavilion for colonial enterprises in a similar Africanizing style, as well as two buildings authored by the prominent modernist architect Victor Bourgeois: the Société Auxiliaire de Propagande Coloniale Pavilion housing a display on tourism and coffee, while also re-presenting the 1913 *Panorama du Congo*, and the Leopold II Restaurant, housed in a modernist glass structure with striking interior decoration by contemporary Congolese artist Masalaï. Despite its significant size, the 1935 Congolese section spoke of Belgium's blurred imperial ambitions, and contemporary observers lamented the lack of enthusiasm in celebrating this *cinquantenaire*.

Johan Lagae

1935 fig. 41

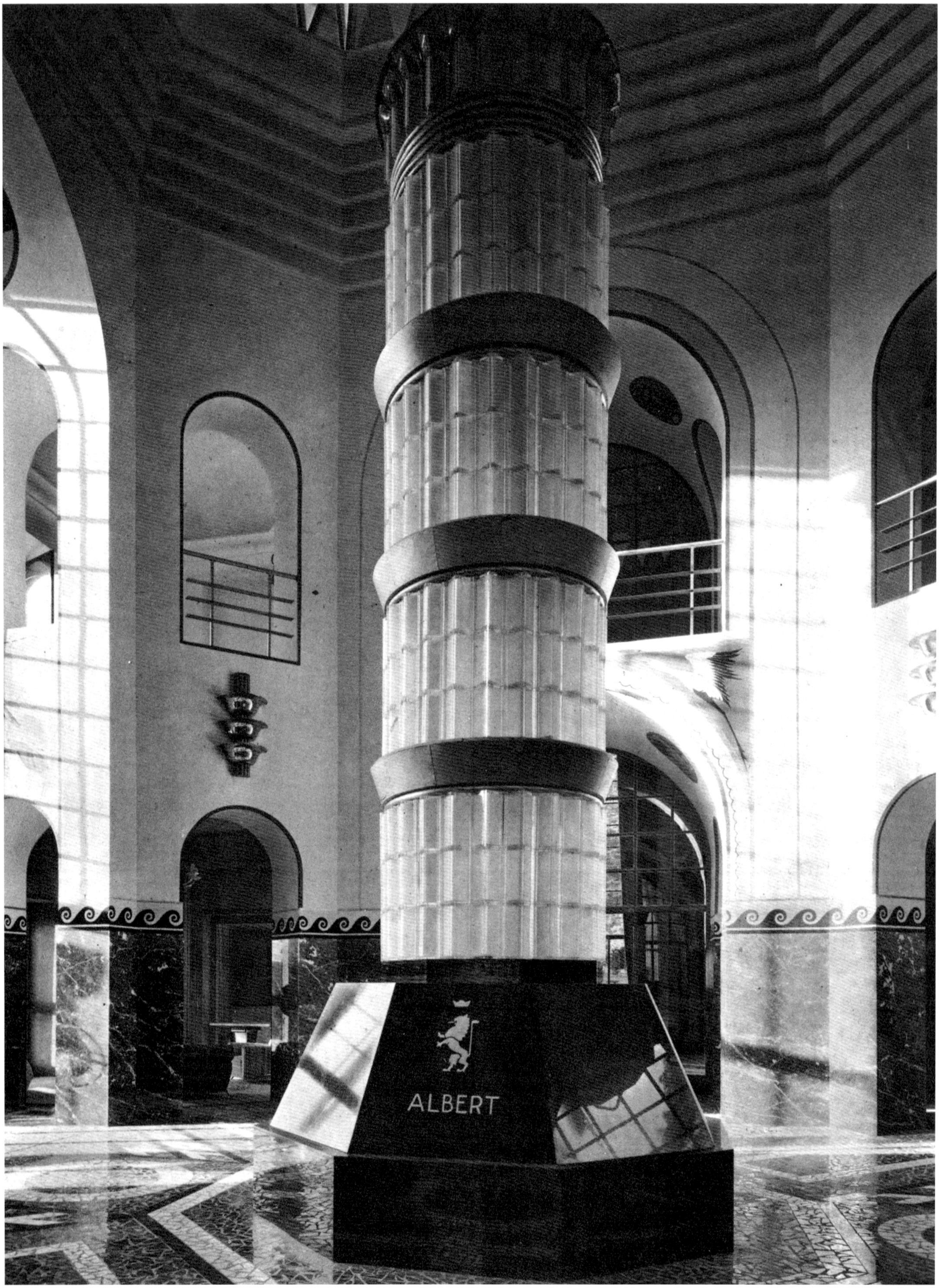

fig. 42

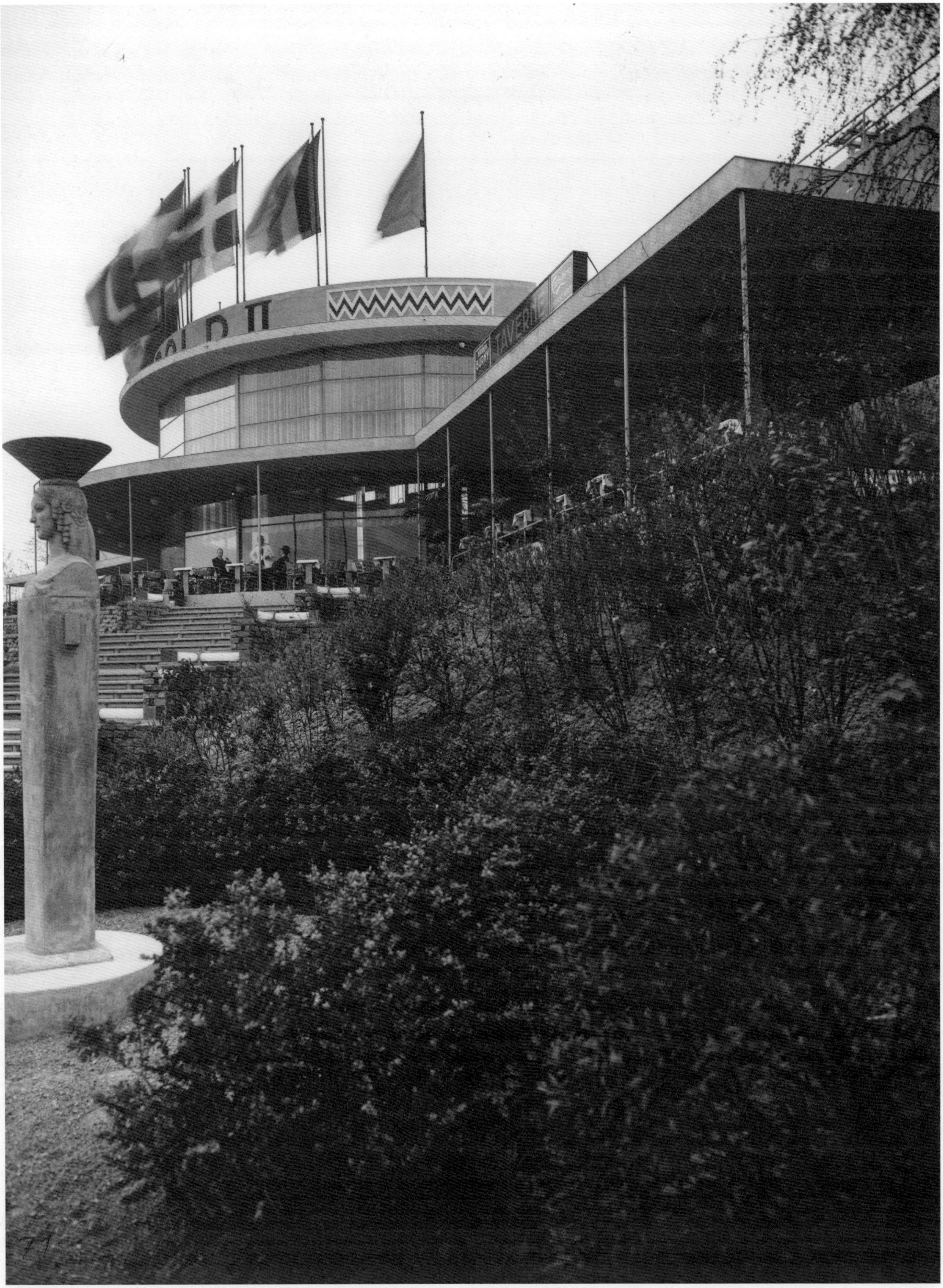

1935 fig. 43

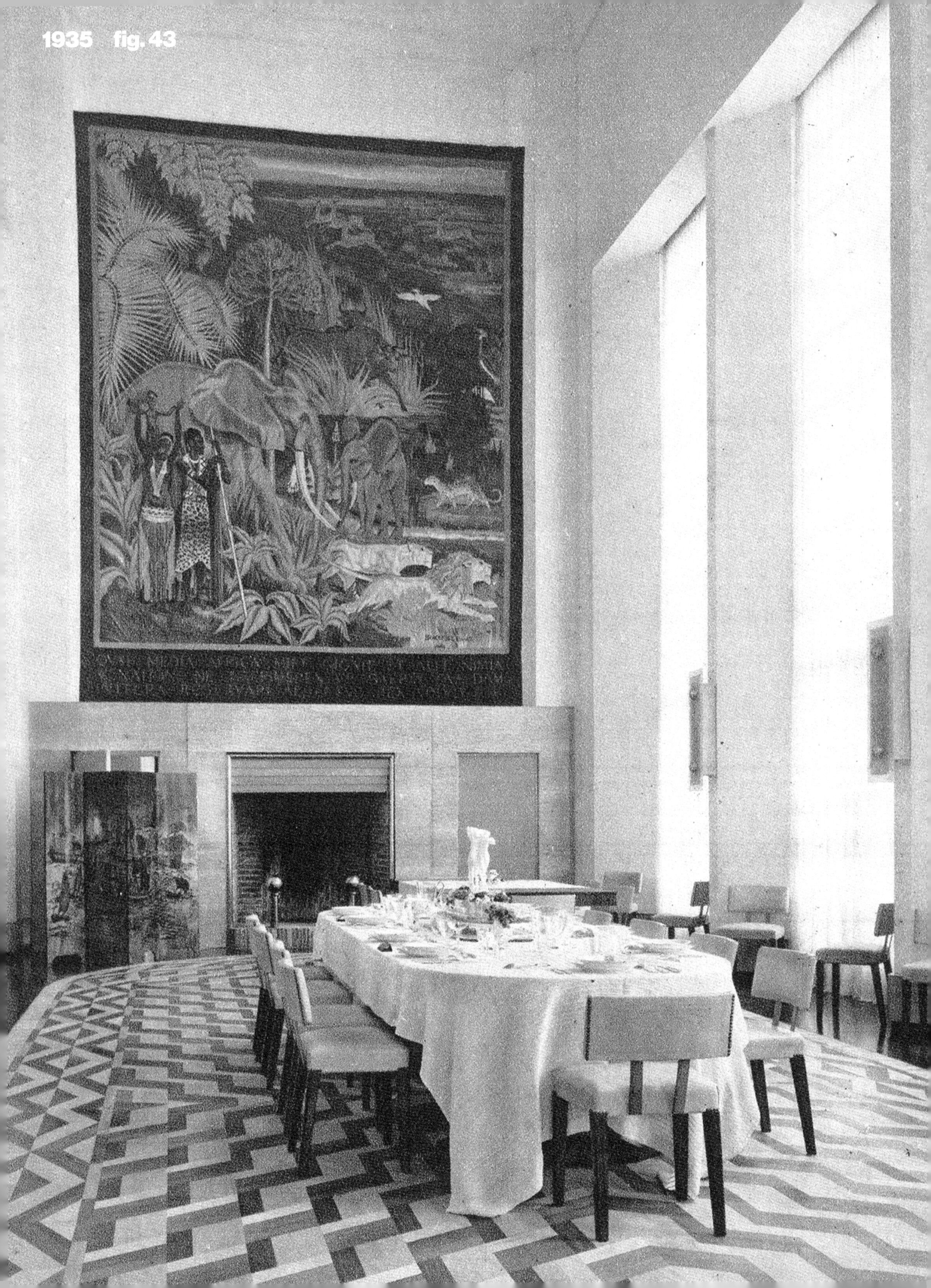

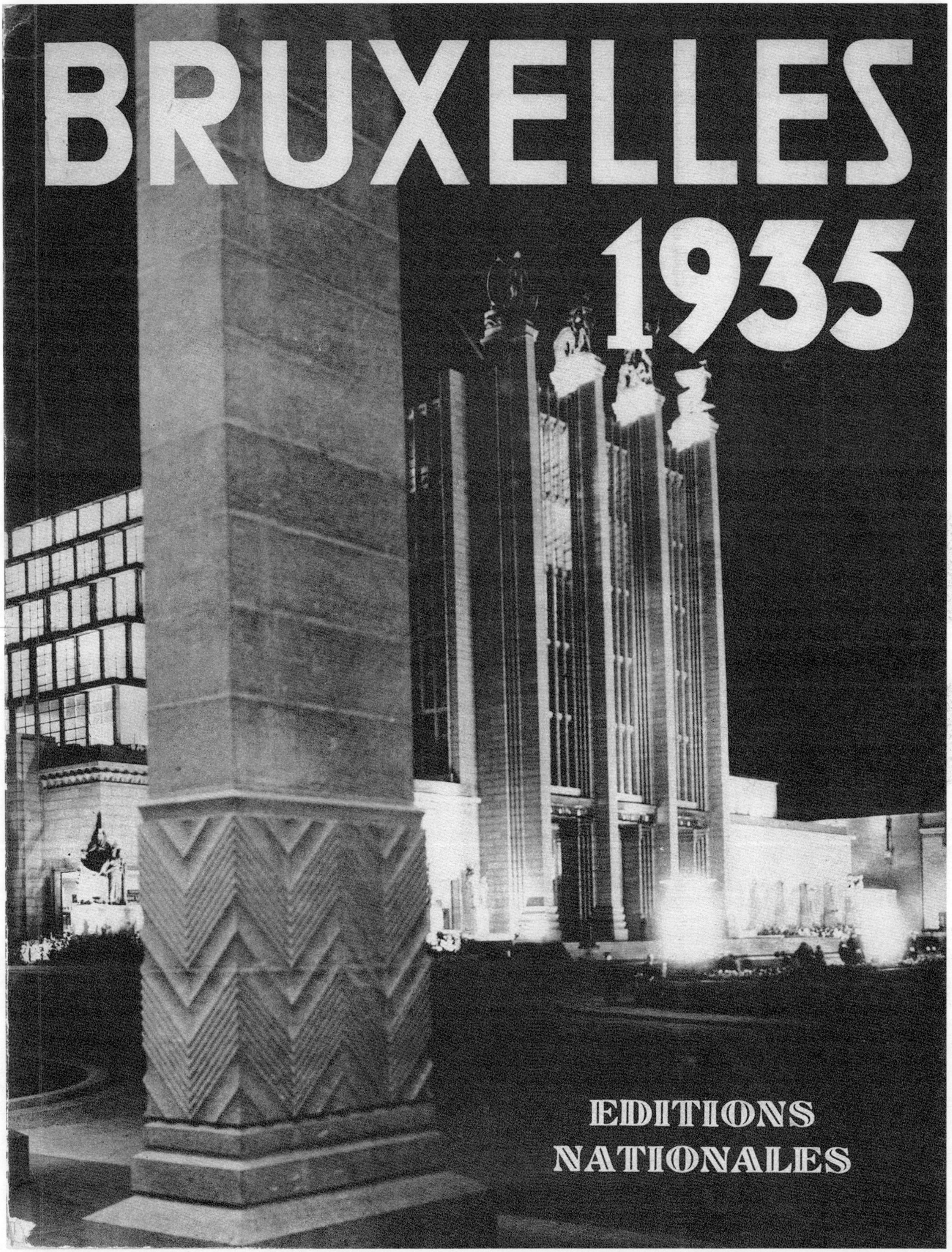
BRUXELLES
1935
EDITIONS
NATIONALES

Pavillon du Congo belge.
(Architecte Schoentjes.)
1935 fig. 45

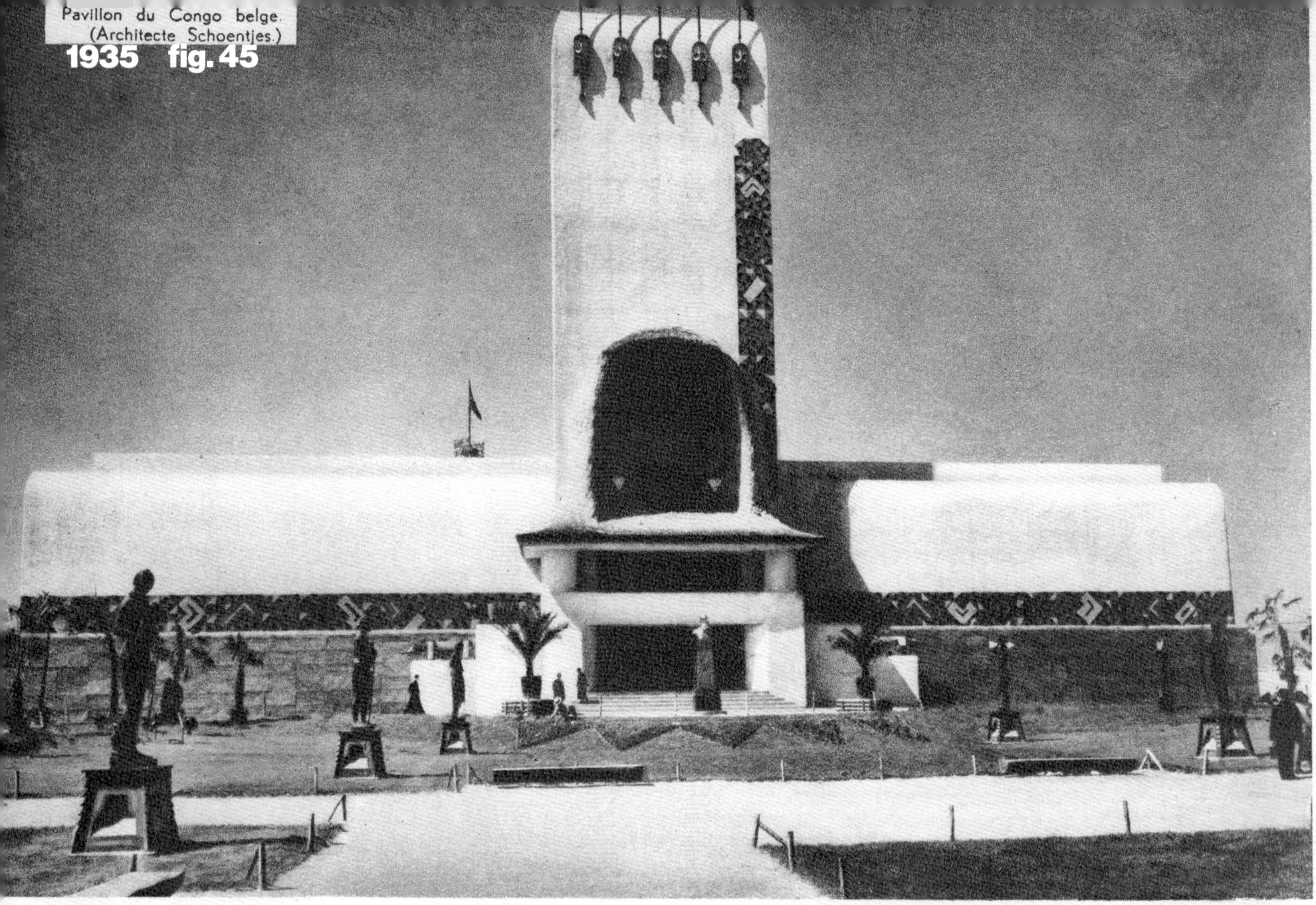

LE CONGO

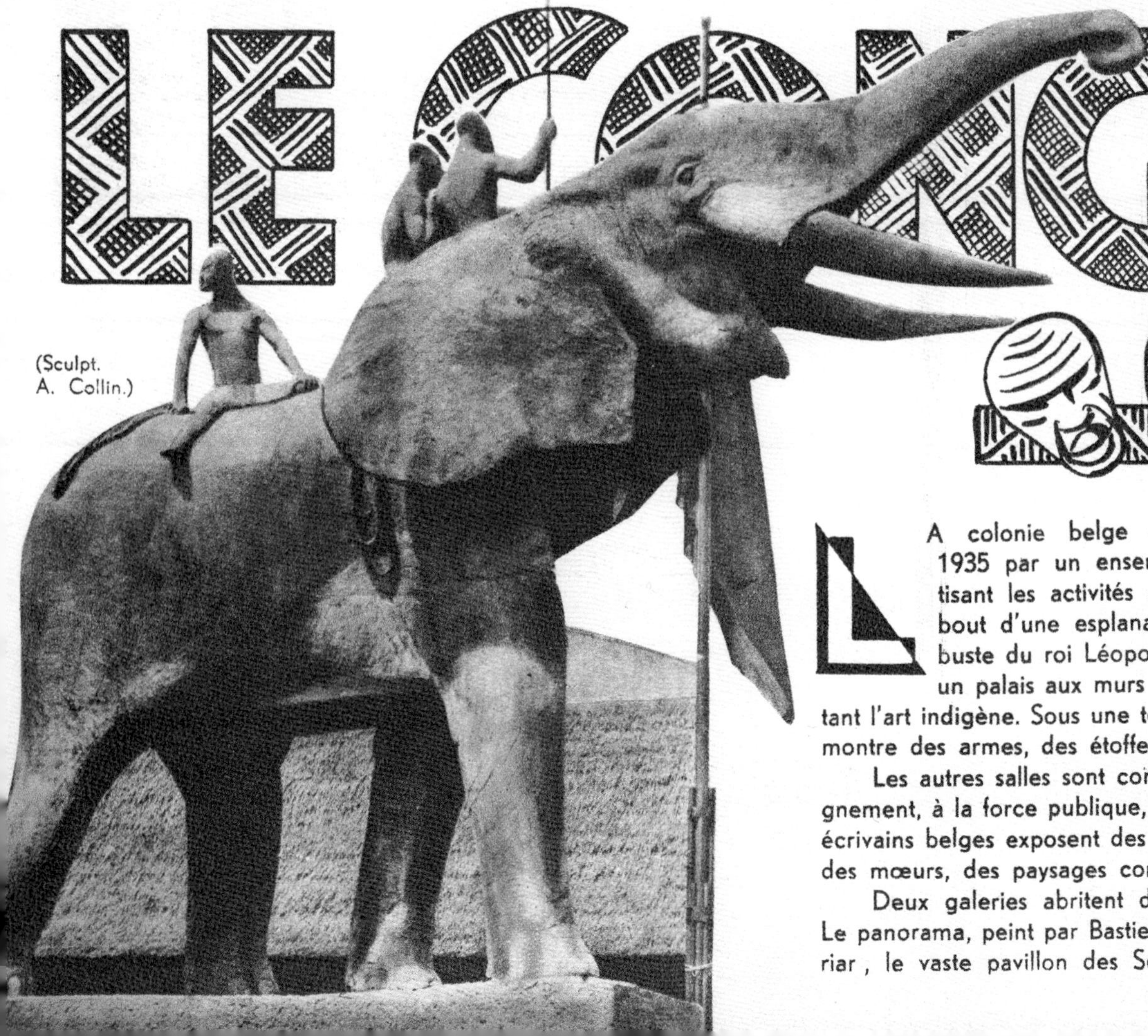

(Sculpt. A. Collin.)

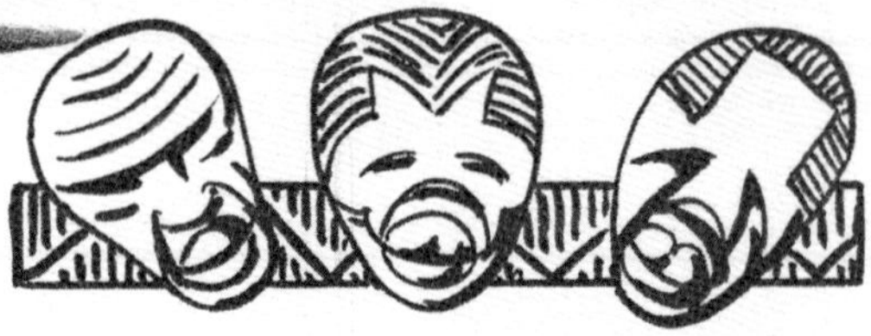

LA colonie belge est représentée à Bruxelles 1935 par un ensemble de constructions synthétisant les activités africaines de la Belgique. Au bout d'une esplanade fleurie que commande le buste du roi Léopold II, des degrés montent vers un palais aux murs clairs, ornés de fresques exaltant l'art indigène. Sous une tour carrée, le salon d'honneur montre des armes, des étoffes, un lumineux diorama.

Les autres salles sont consacrées à l'hygiène, à l'enseignement, à la force publique, aux missions. Des artistes, des écrivains belges exposent des œuvres inspirées de l'histoire, des mœurs, des paysages congolais.

Deux galeries abritent des artisans nègres au travail Le panorama, peint par Bastien , les dioramas de James Thiriar , le vaste pavillon des Sociétés coloniales (Soprocol)

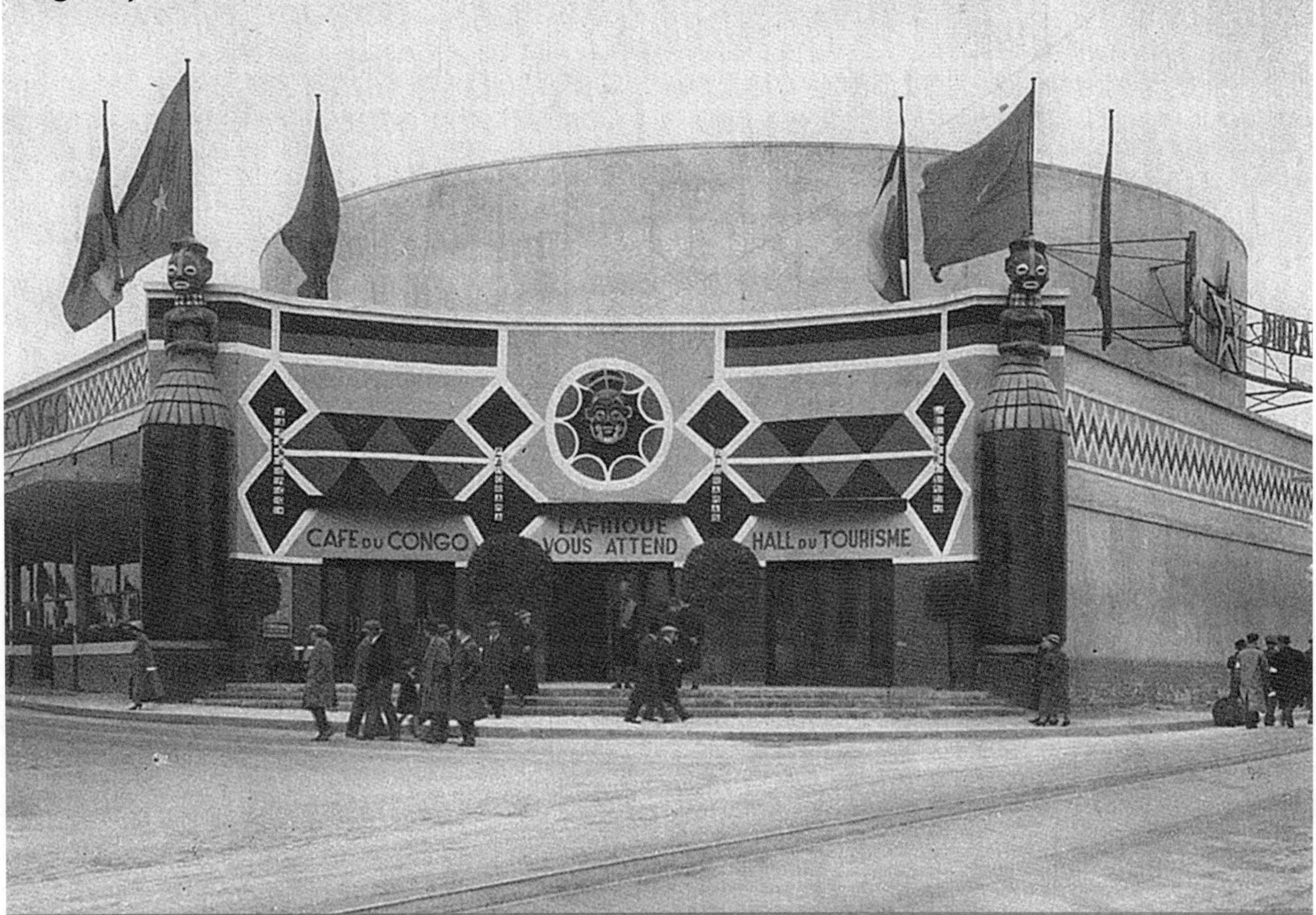
CAFE DU CONGO
L'AFRIQUE VOUS ATTEND
HALL DU TOURISME

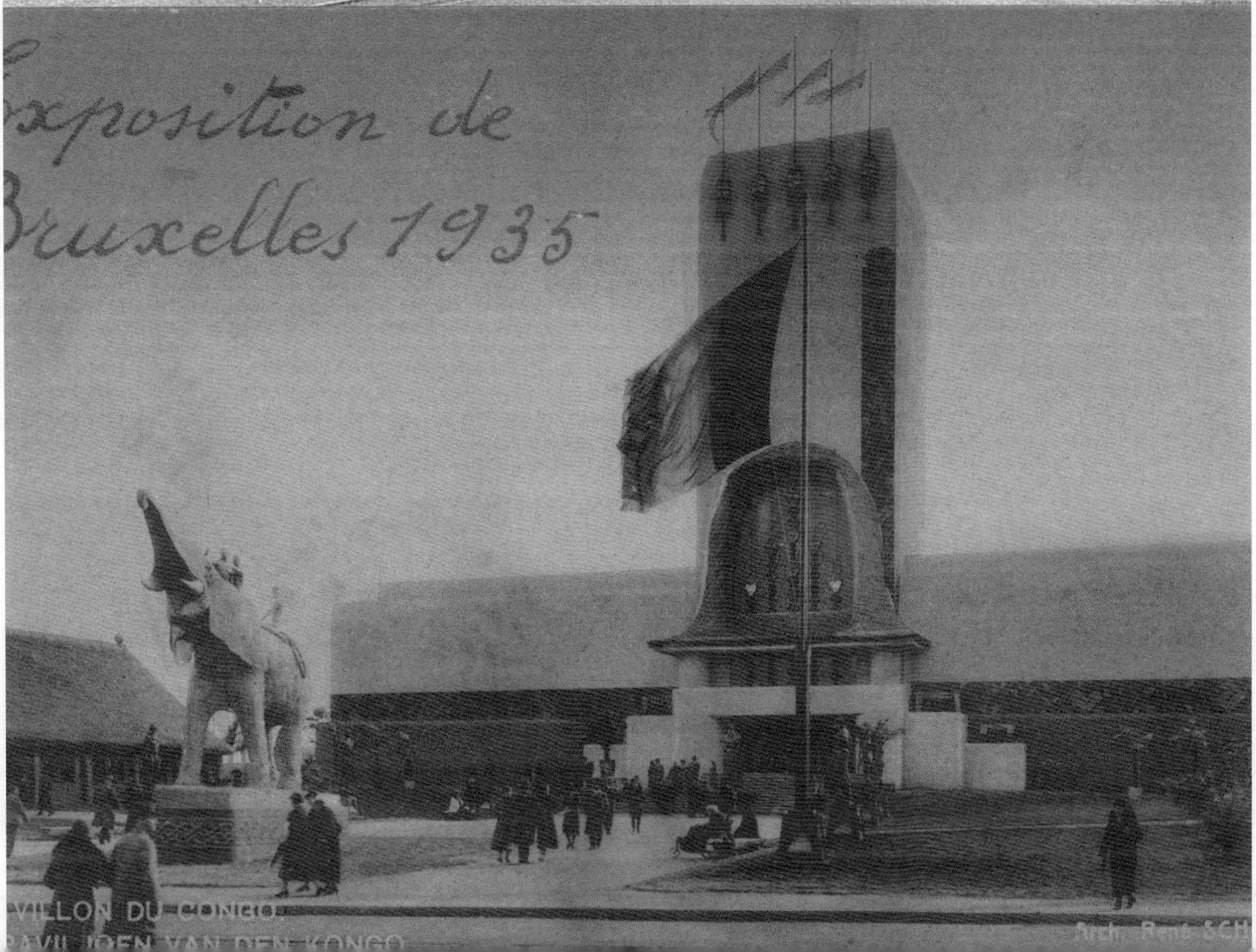
Exposition de Bruxelles 1935
VILLON DU CONGO.

1935 fig. 48

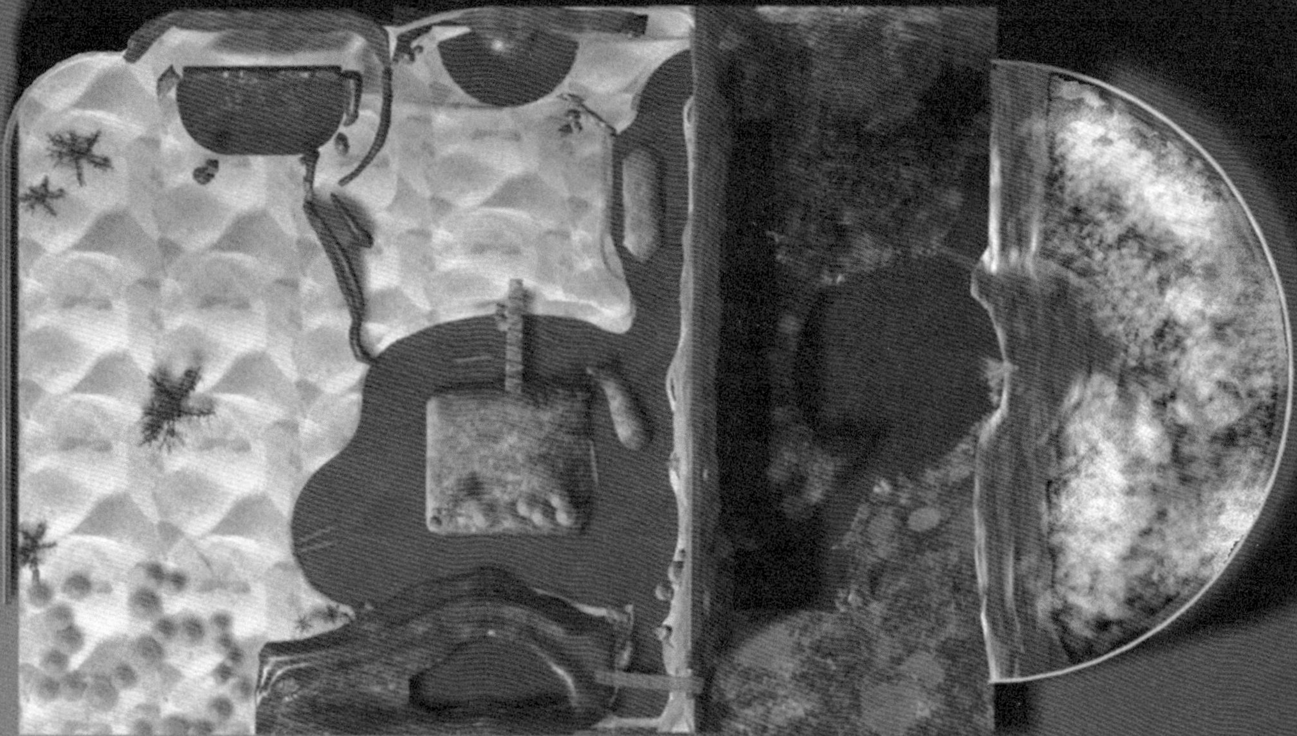

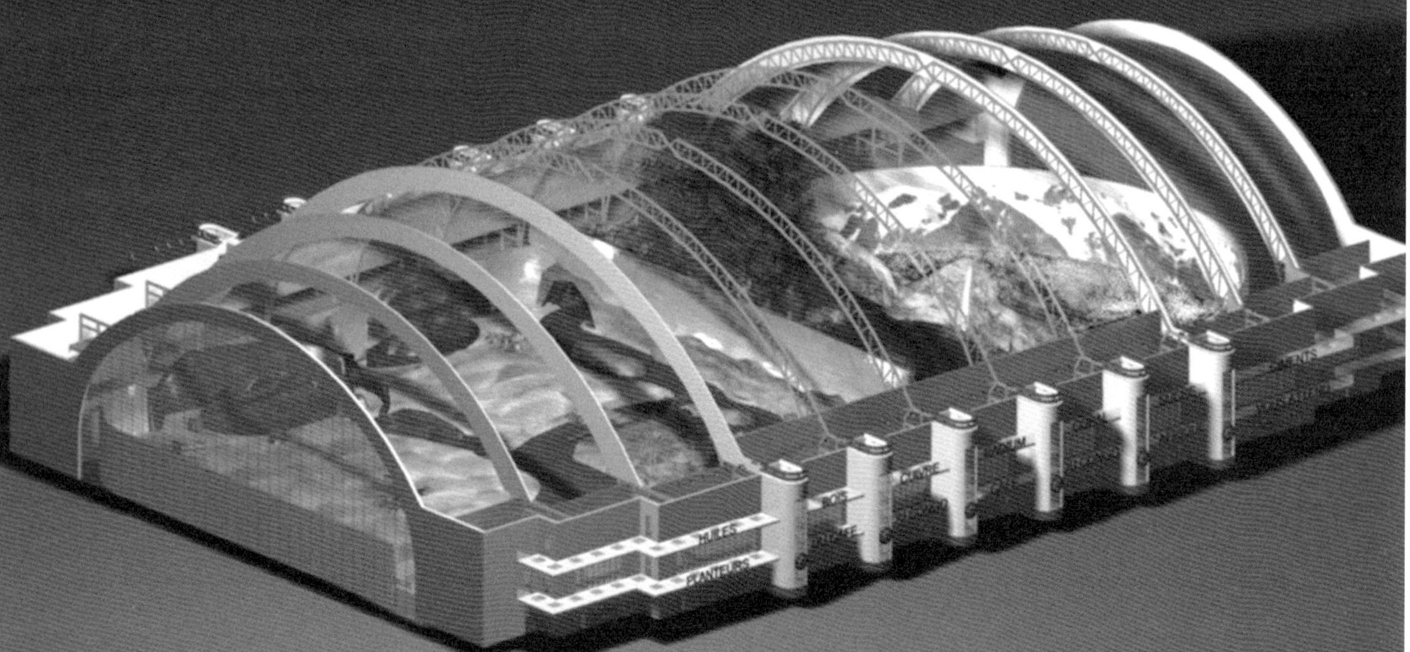

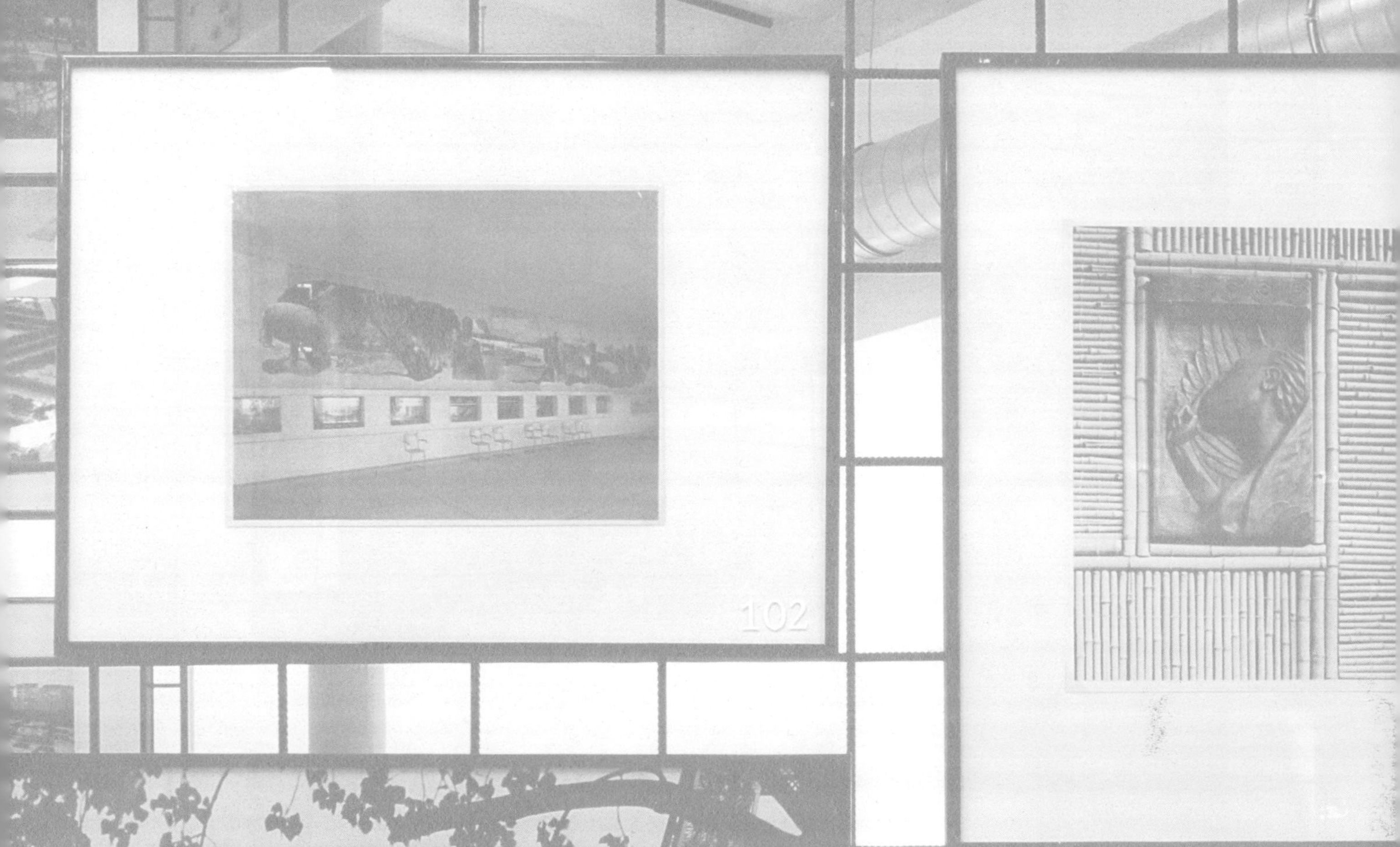

Romanticizing Colonial Life in Modern Congo

Situated in the garden behind the imposing modern classicist Belgian Pavilion, the Congo section at the Paris 1937 International Exposition of Art and Technology in Modern Life differed significantly from those at previous expos. Rather than reiterating the formula of an invented "authentic" Congolese palace, the section was now housed in a series of pavilions that were modeled on an idealized tropical bungalow, interconnected through covered walkways. Architect Fernand Petit understood the key features of this early colonial typology, including the wraparound veranda and its climate-responsive logic based on natural ventilation, and translated them into an elegant design. Apart from a series of ethnographic artifacts that were skillfully presented as delicate art objects to be valued in their own right (as was becoming a standard in those days), the section, in line with the general theme of the exhibition, presented an evocation of a comfortable life inside a colonizer's house in the tropics. The interior fittings and tubular furniture were in tune with progressive design tendencies of the day. But the section also explicitly suggested that one's interior should be conceived in relation to local context. For Gaston-Denys Périer, one of the most prominent contemporary promoters of African and Congolese art in Europe, the presentation spoke of a new way of life in Congo, and demonstrated that the contemporary colonizer "loved to surround himself with decorative objects in which the lyric spirit of the black race is embedded and which can perfectly harmonize with the atmosphere [within the colonizer's dwelling]." Yet by referring to the tropical bungalow typology and its adjacent lifestyle, the section also romanticized colonial life—everyday life in the urban centers of Congo most often proved quite different.

Johan Lagae

104

1937 fig. 49

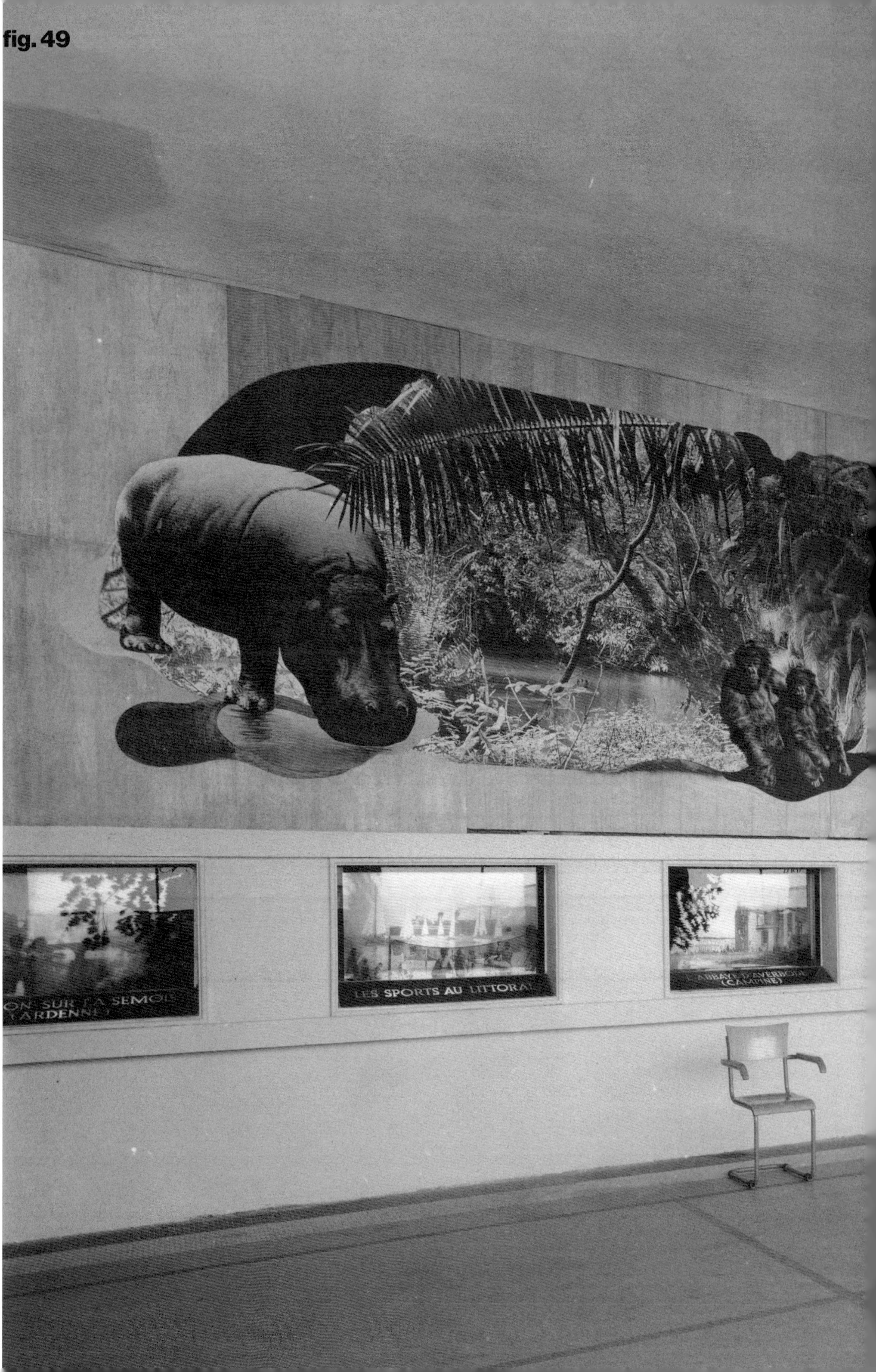

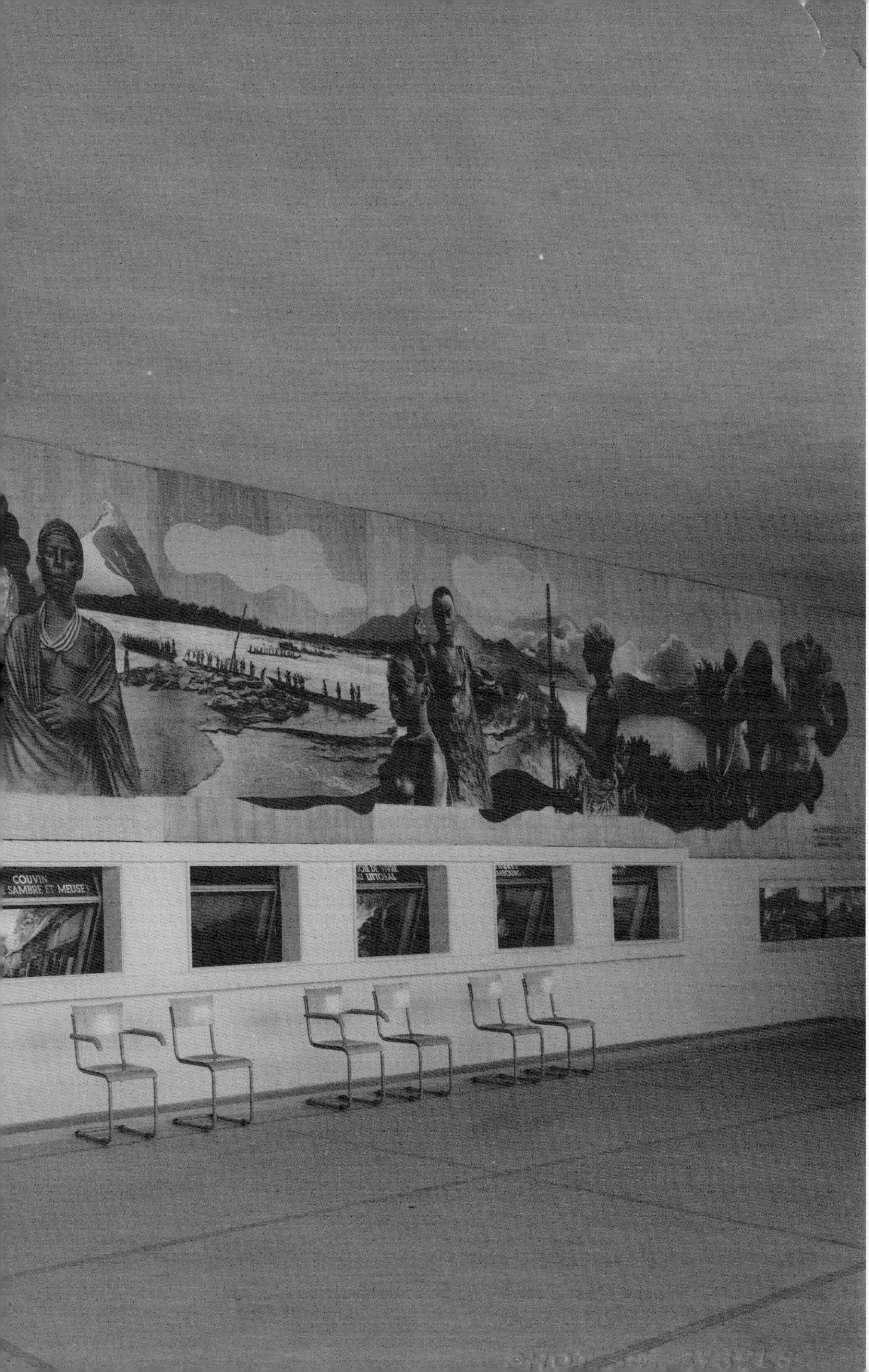
COUVIN
SAMBRE ET MEUSE)
LITTORAL

1937 fig. 50

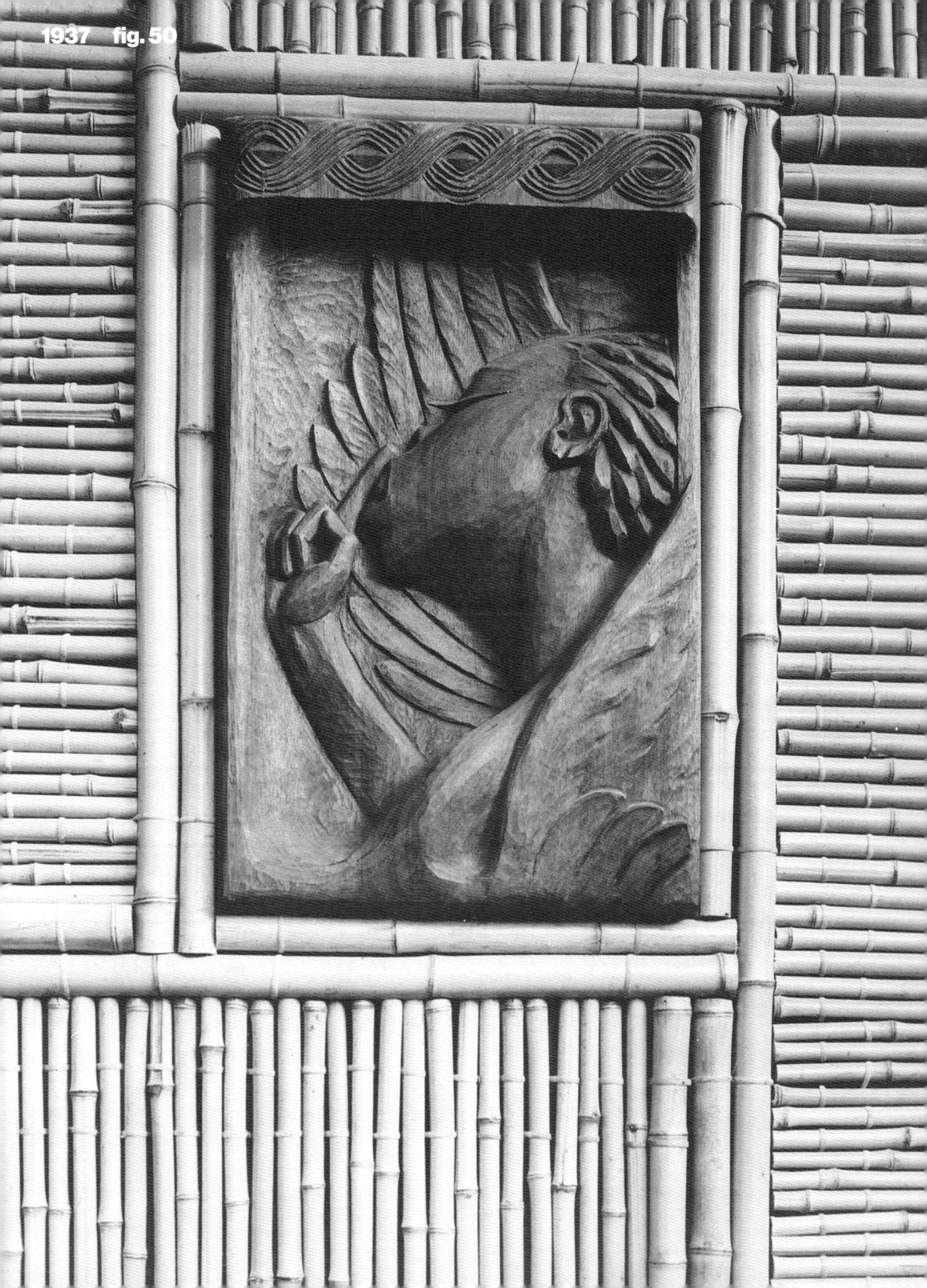

fig. 51

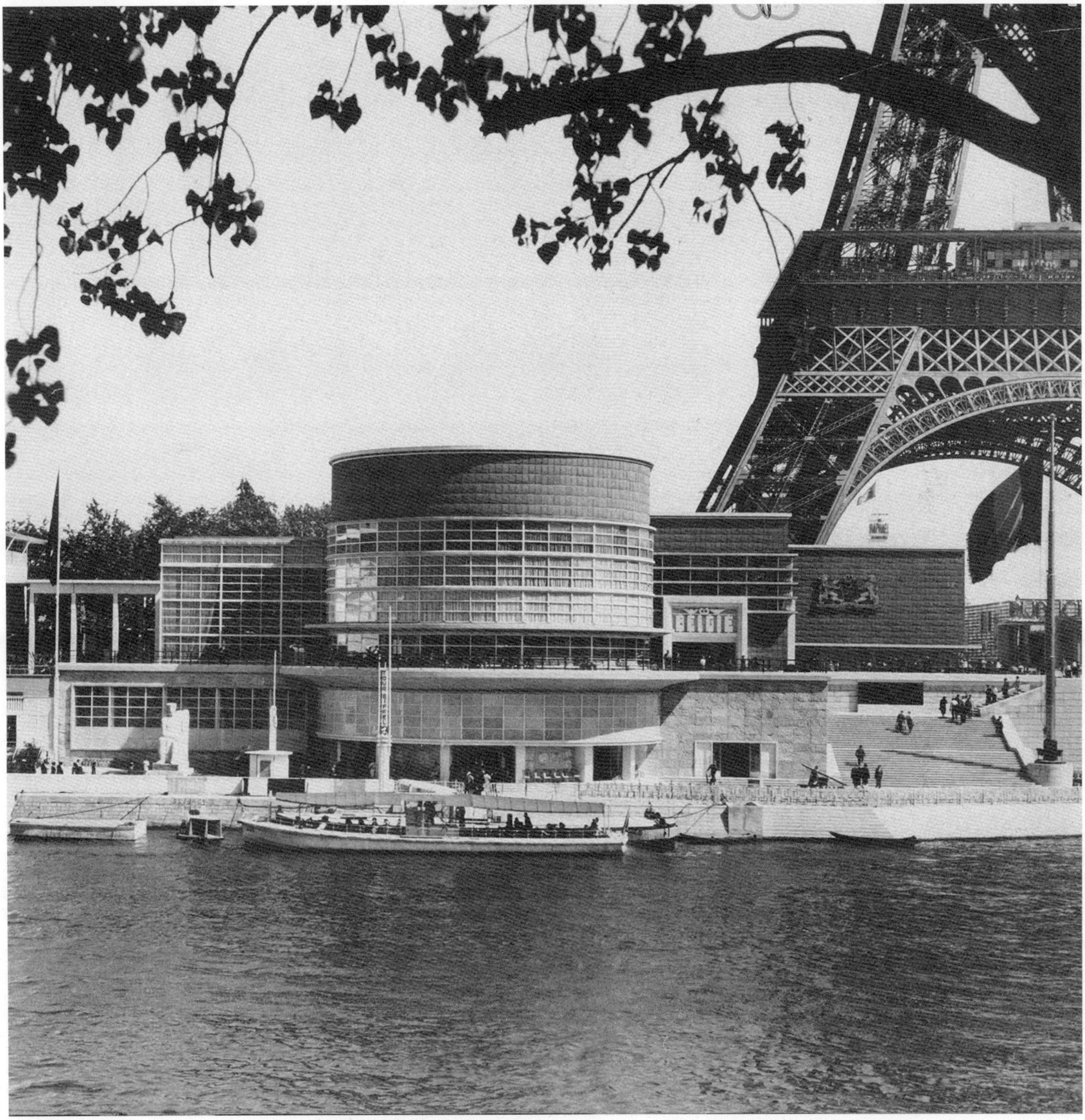

1937 fig. 52

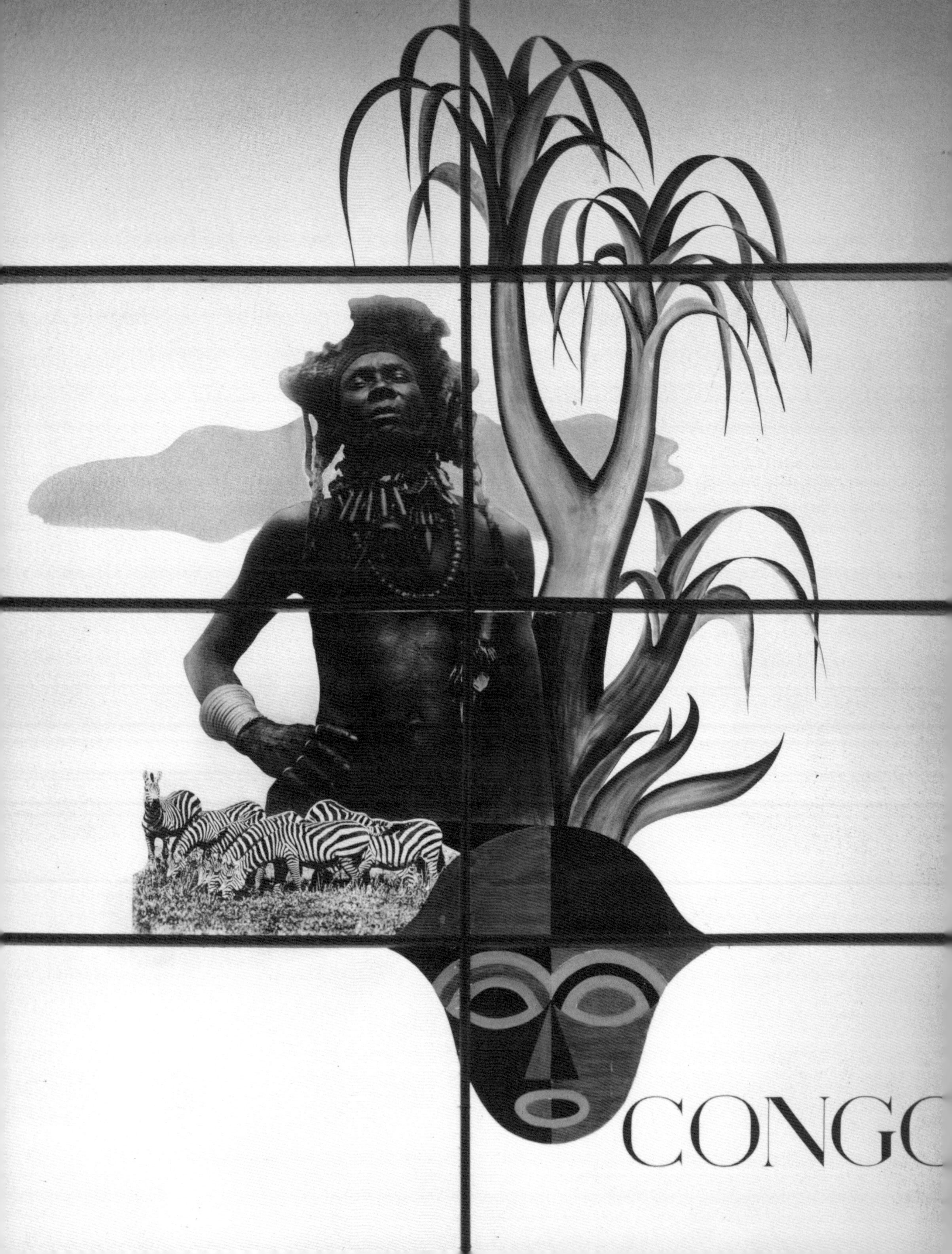

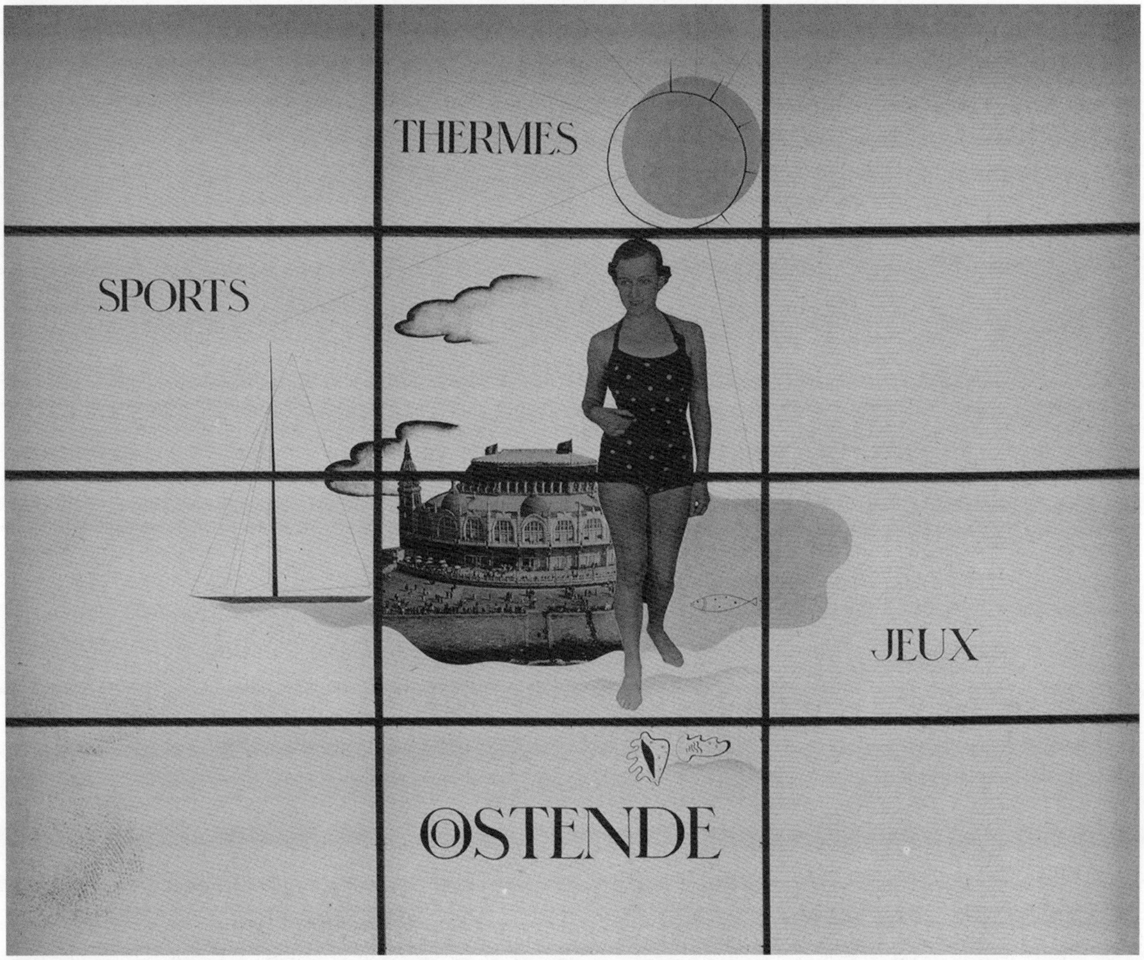
THERMES
SPORTS
JEUX
OSTENDE

1937 fig. 54

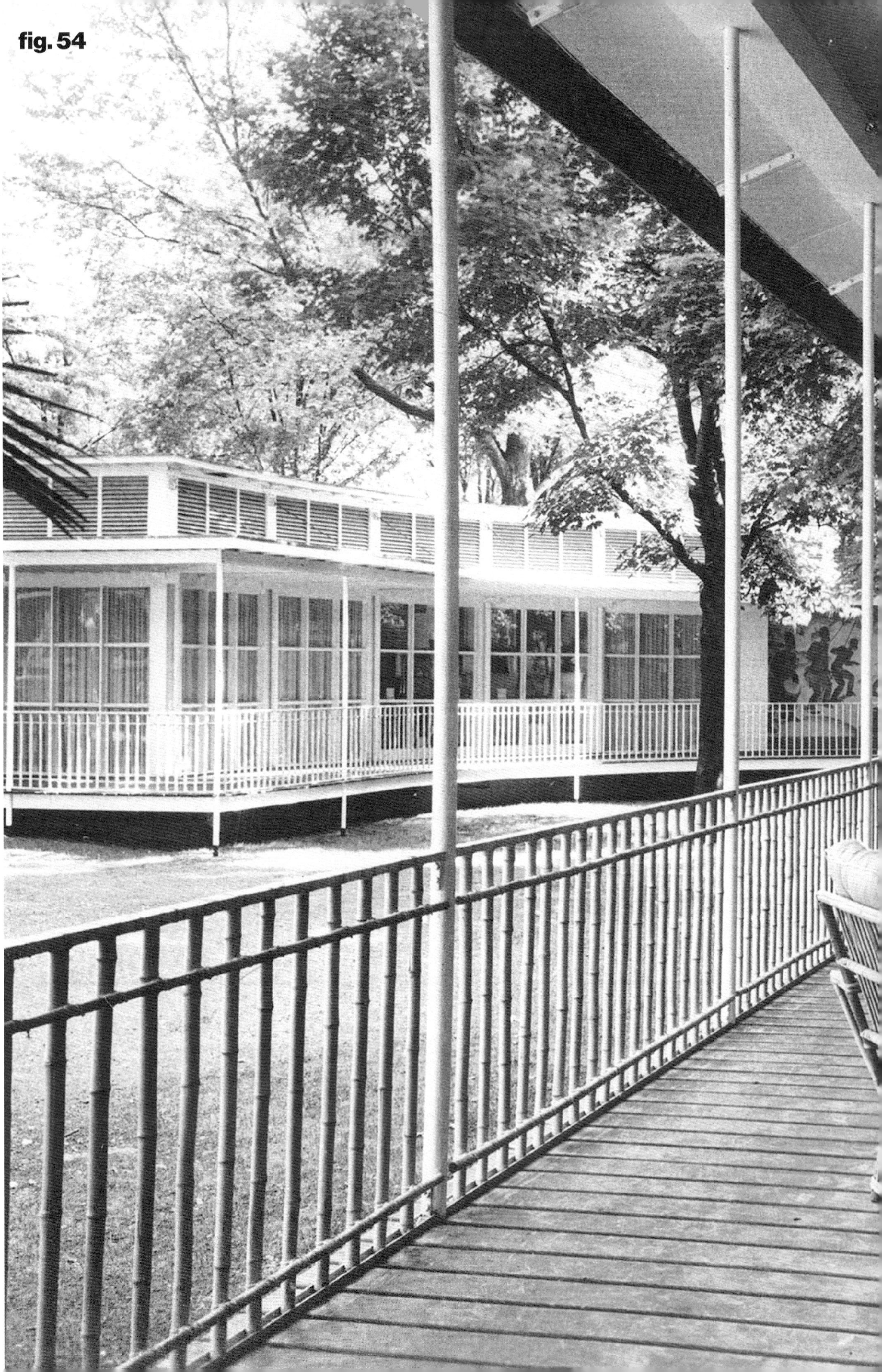

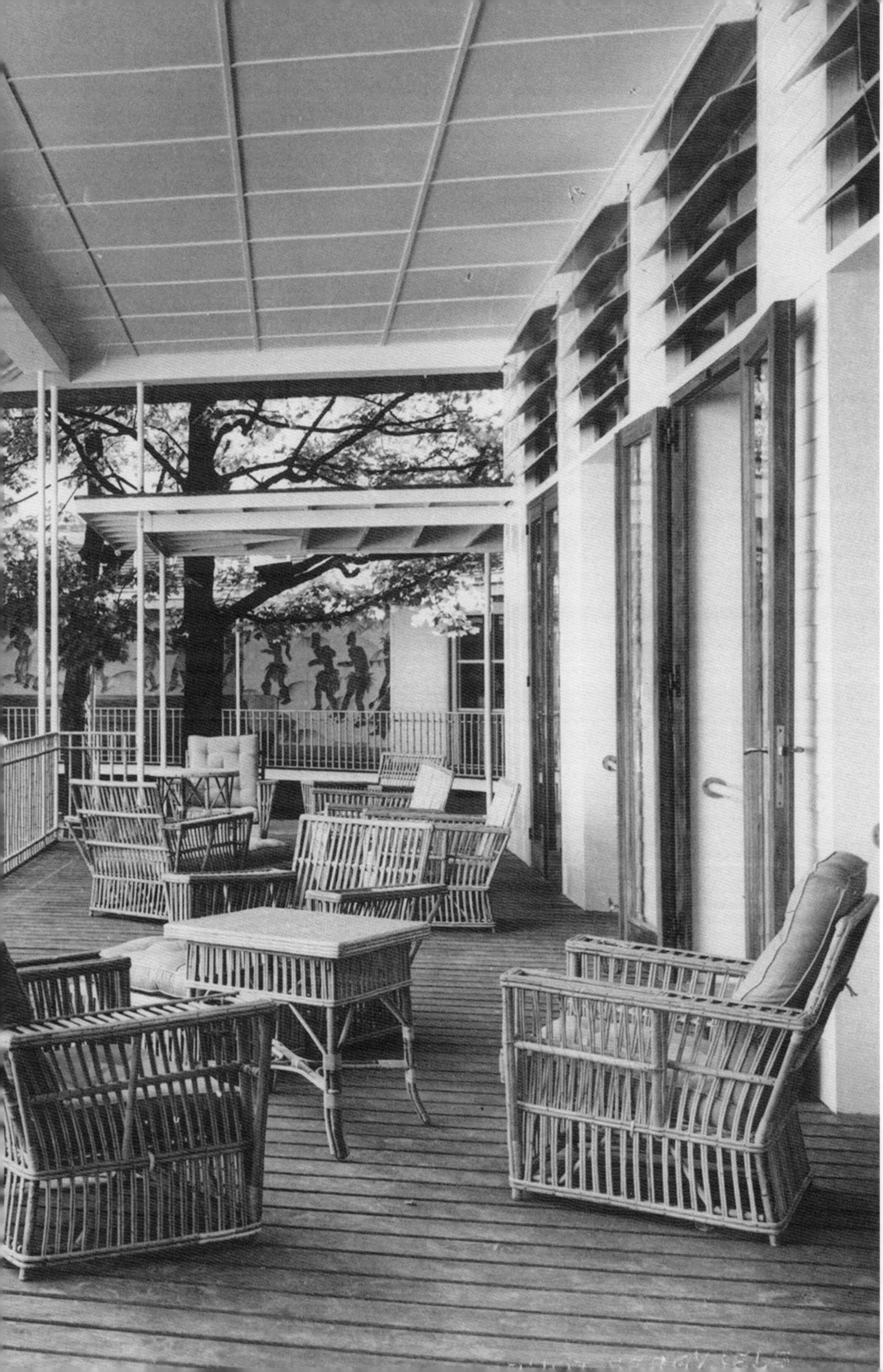

1937 fig. 55

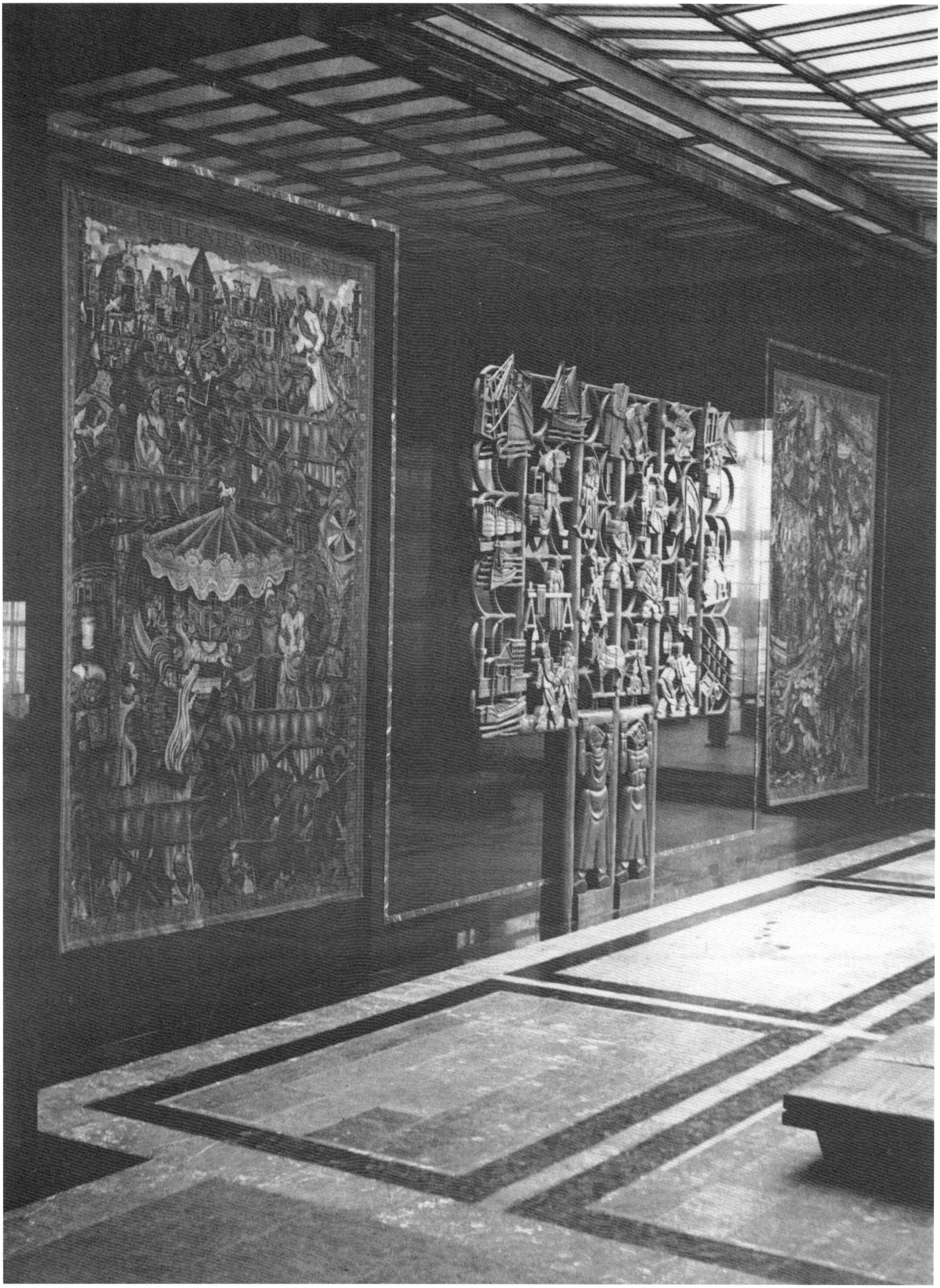

An Exoticizing Decorated Shed on the River's Edge

In 1939, the city of Liège was the site of the International Exhibition of the Art of Water. The exhibition grounds were located along the Meuse River, and the team of young and progressive architects who were commissioned to oversee the overall design of the event defined a series of guidelines, based on a functionalist doctrine, resulting in an overall modernist architectural language. Henry Lacoste, who was in charge of the Congo section, nevertheless deployed his unbridled imagination. In an initial design proposal, he sought to place four gigantic painted gold elephants in the river, in front of the colonial pavilion. The final design was a simplified version of the phantasmagoric proposal: a rather straightforward exhibition hall, its interior walls, floor tiling, and claustra elements in the facades decorated with geometric patterns evoking Congolese textiles, while in front of the building, in the water, stood a huge, totem pole–like construction, adorned with Congolese masks and armory. Considering that the Congolese section was supposed to demonstrate the progress in hydraulic works achieved in Congo, including several impressive concrete dam structures that had been realized in the previous decade, Lacoste's project was little more than an exoticizing decorated shed, lacking the ingenuity and hybrid ambivalence of his 1931 project.

Johan Lagae

1939 fig. 56

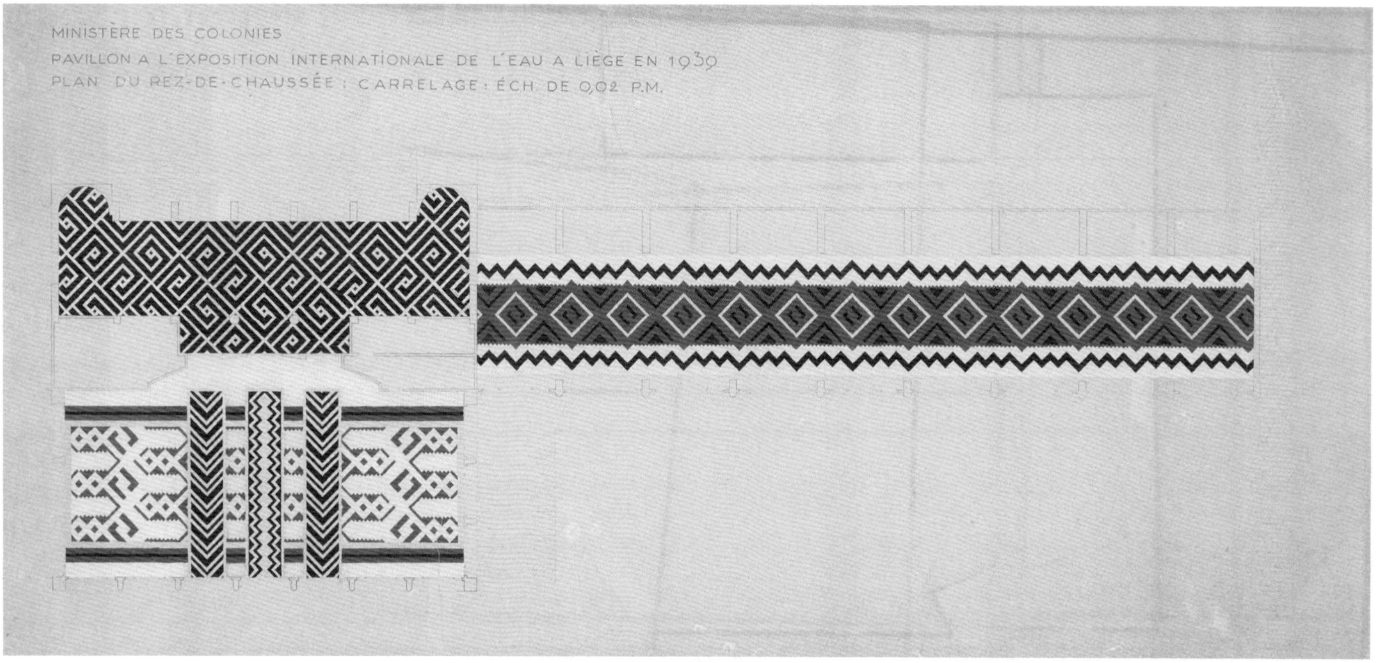
MINISTÈRE DES COLONIES
PAVILLON A L'EXPOSITION INTERNATIONALE DE L'EAU A LIÈGE EN 1939
PLAN DU REZ-DE-CHAUSSÉE : CARRELAGE : ÉCH DE 0,02 P.M.

fig. 57

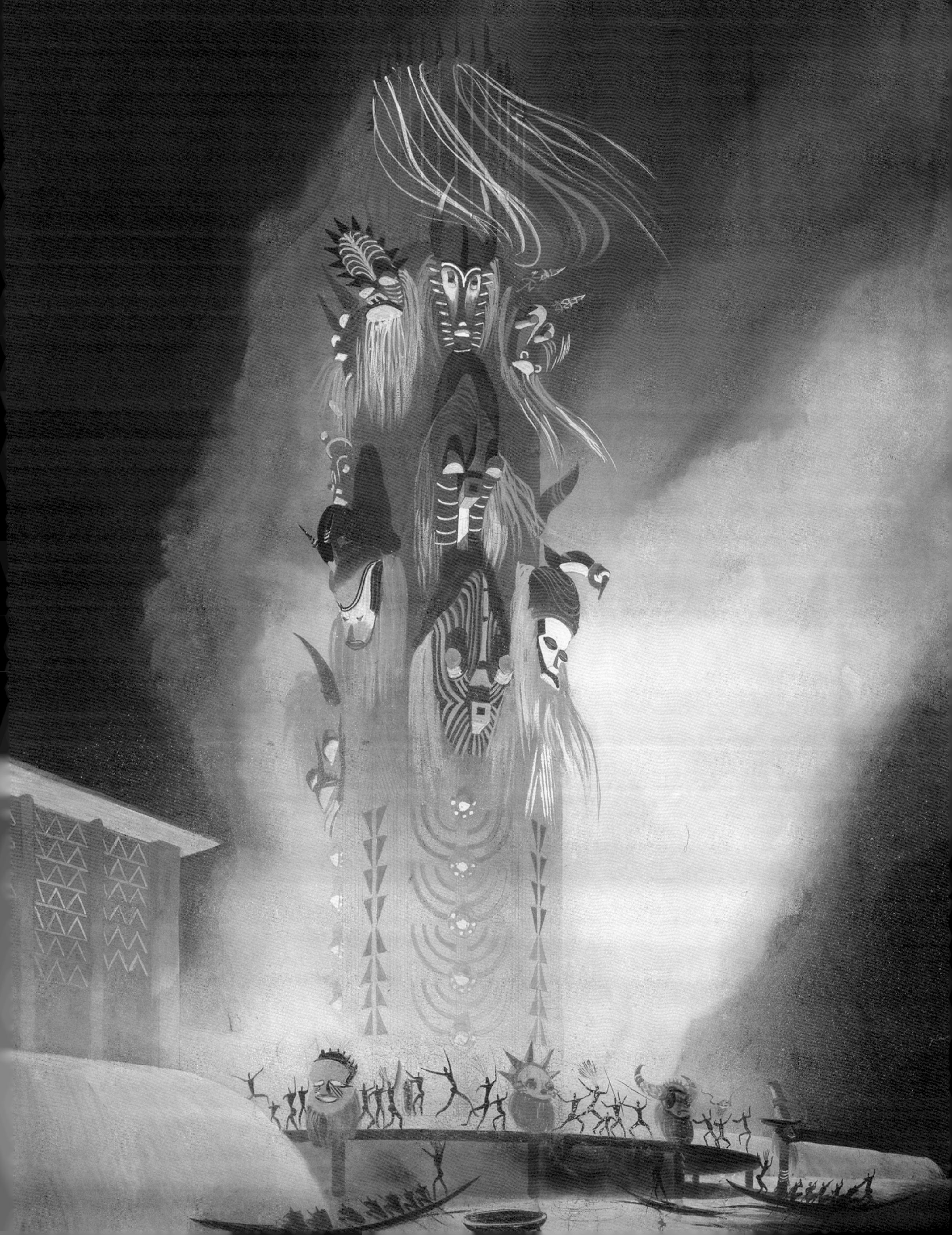

1939 fig. 58

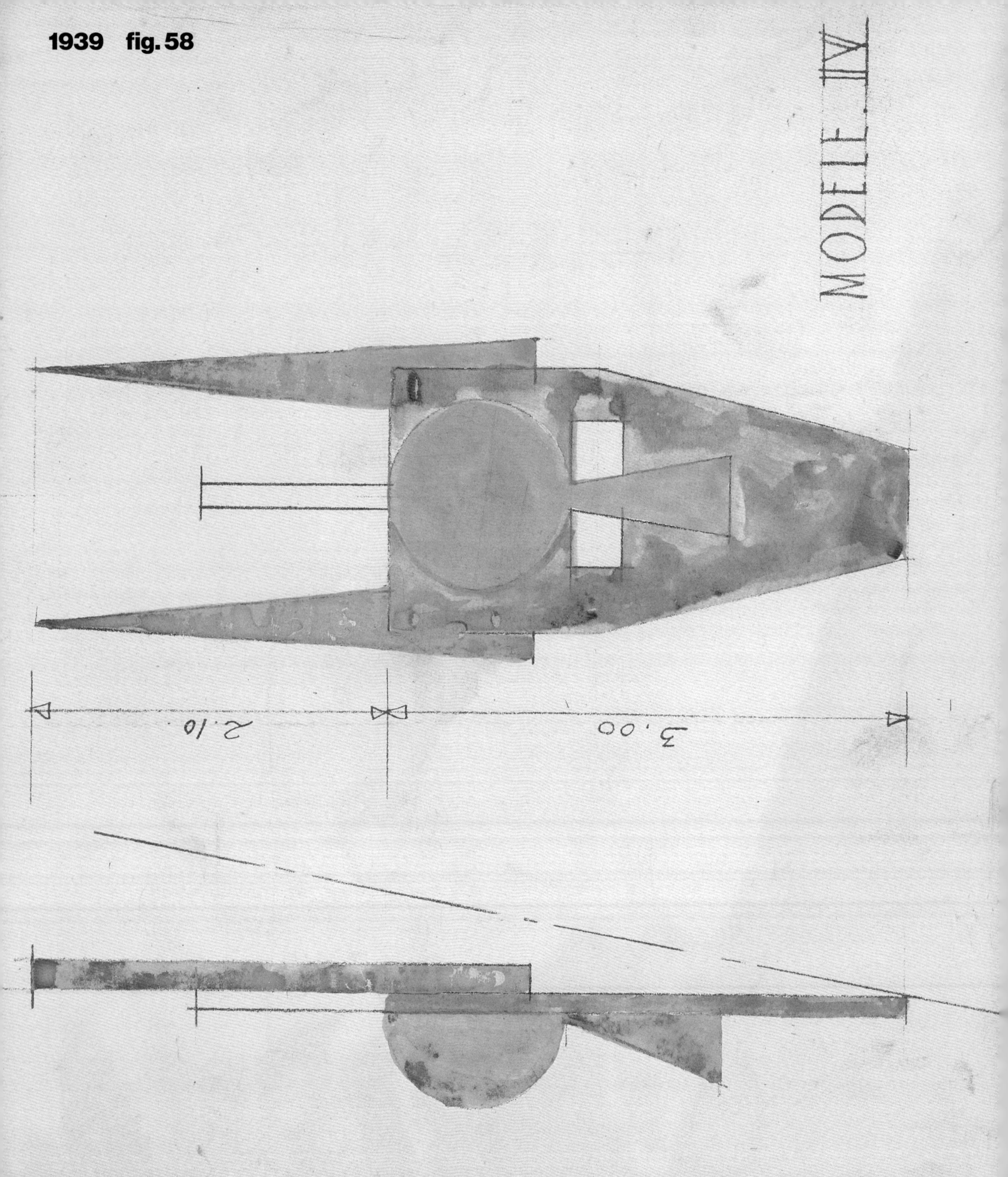

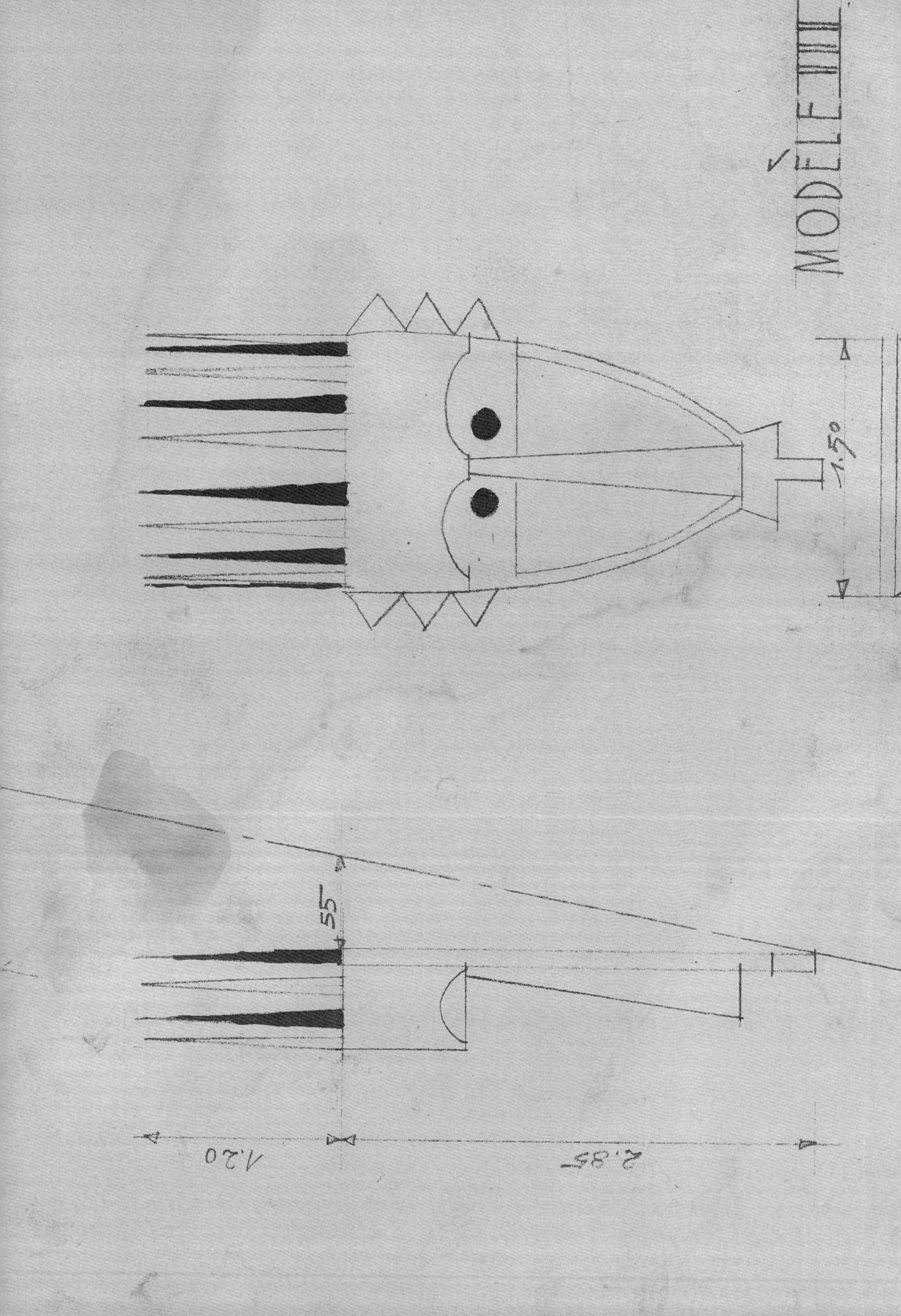
MODÈLE VIII
1.50
55
1.20
2.85

1939 fig. 59

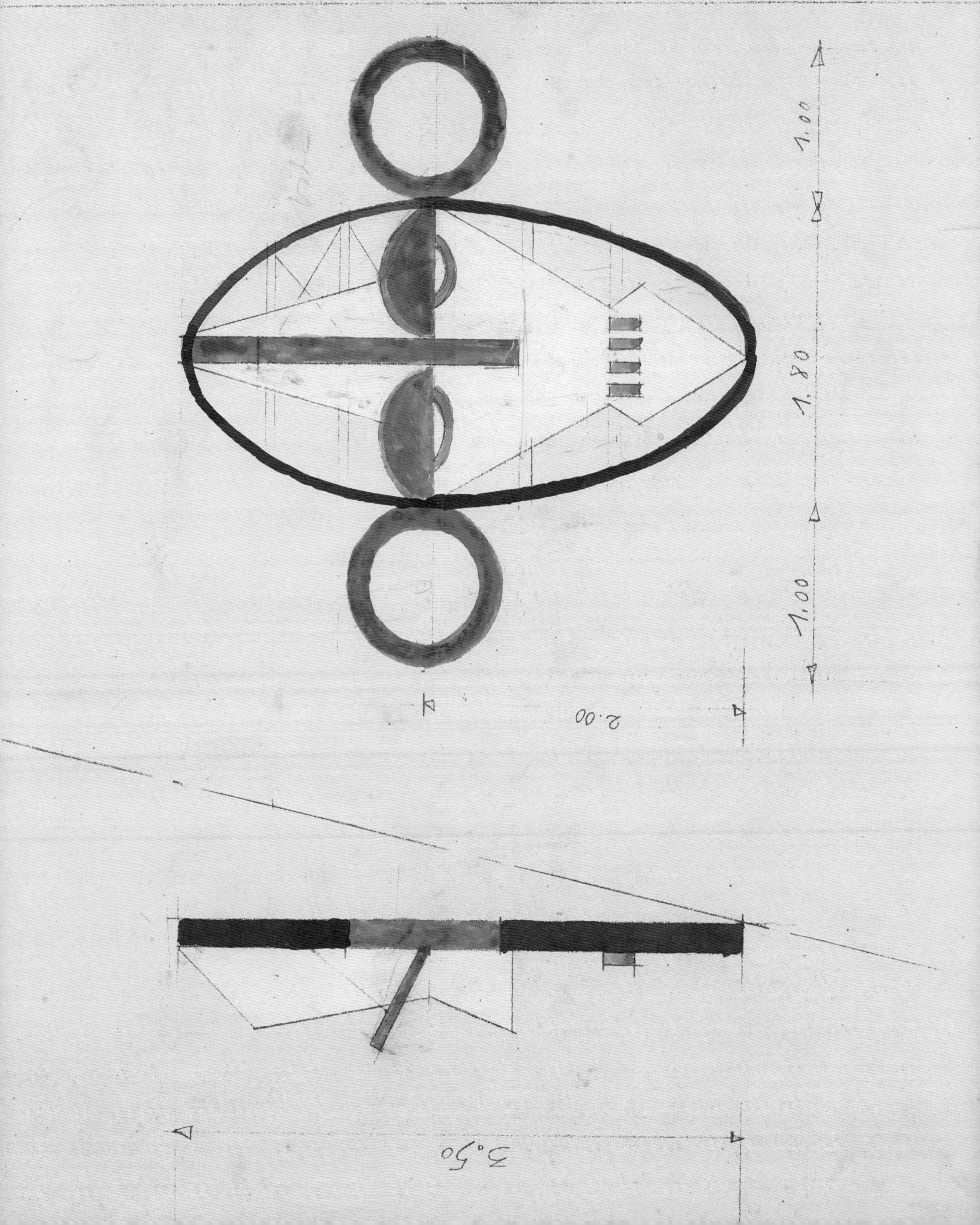

An Unanticipated Swan Song of Belgian Colonialism

In hindsight, one cannot but be puzzled by the celebratory framing of Belgian colonialism that pervaded the extensive Congo section at the Brussels World's Fair of 1958. The event took place only two years before Congo would gain its independence on June 30, 1960, after intense but hastily organized negotiations that were triggered by bloody riots in Kinshasa on January 4, 1959. The main Congo Pavilion, authored by Georges Ricquier, was grandiose in size and appearance, but a decorated shed much like previous pavilions. The Mining Pavilion, with its dazzling black-and-white motives, and as well as the Fauna Pavilion, designed by architect Constantin Brodzki, on the contrary, showed an ambition to define a new architectural language that could resonate with Congolese culture. Modern living was again a prominent theme, articulated this time through elaborate displays of the latest household utensils and appliances available on the colonial market, as well as a model house for colonizers, authored by architects Jean Van Doosselaere and André Noterman. The house was built mainly out of prefabricated aluminum components produced by the Belgian firm Chamebel, which was active in Congo and was seeking to expand its activities. It was situated in the Jardin Congolais, a park-like setting designed by the prominent landscape architect René Pechère. The layout of the Jardin Congolais was based largely on patterns reminiscent of the velours du Kasaï, a Congolese textile that had been a source of inspiration for colonial designers and architects since the interwar period. In this respect, the Jardin Congolais was a precise application of Pechère's own advice on how to conceive a colonial garden, which he had been publishing in the pages of the *Bulletin de l'Union des Femmes Coloniales* for several years. The colonial garden, Pechère argued in blatant racist terms, should be based on "the European's creative genius, which is more intellectual and advanced," yet adapted to African resources ("matériaux nègres" in the original text). Just like the architects and designers involved in previous Congo sections, Péchère failed in fully capturing the subtleties of the complex geometric compositions of the velours du Kasaï. It was also in the Jardin Congolais that the earlier practice of displaying Congolese people in village-like settings, so prevalent in the turn of the century, was taken up again. Times had changed, however. By now, African voices were speaking up and contesting colonial order. In that respect, the most emblematic space of colonial reality at the 1958 World's Fair was perhaps not the Congolese section itself, but the Centre d'accueil du personnel africain (CAPA), a temporary accommodation for the large Congolese staff of the expo, located on the current site of the Royal Museum of Central Africa. It took the form of a series of demountable, single-story houses, initially planned to be shipped to Congo after the World's Fair. These houses were stacked on floors of the multistory concrete skeleton structure of the under-construction science building of the museum (today known as the CAPA Building), the whole masked behind a Africanizing facade. This temporary accommodation indeed became the place where, albeit only occasionally, critical encounters took place between Congolese yearning for independence and young white progressive intellectuals willing to support their struggle. While demonstrating the uncanny continuation of (design) strategies of colonial displays, already present in late nineteenth-century expos, the Brussels World's Fair, also known as Expo 58, was the ultimate swan song of Belgian colonialism, even if it was unanticipated by the ruling powers.

Johan Lagae

1958 fig. 60

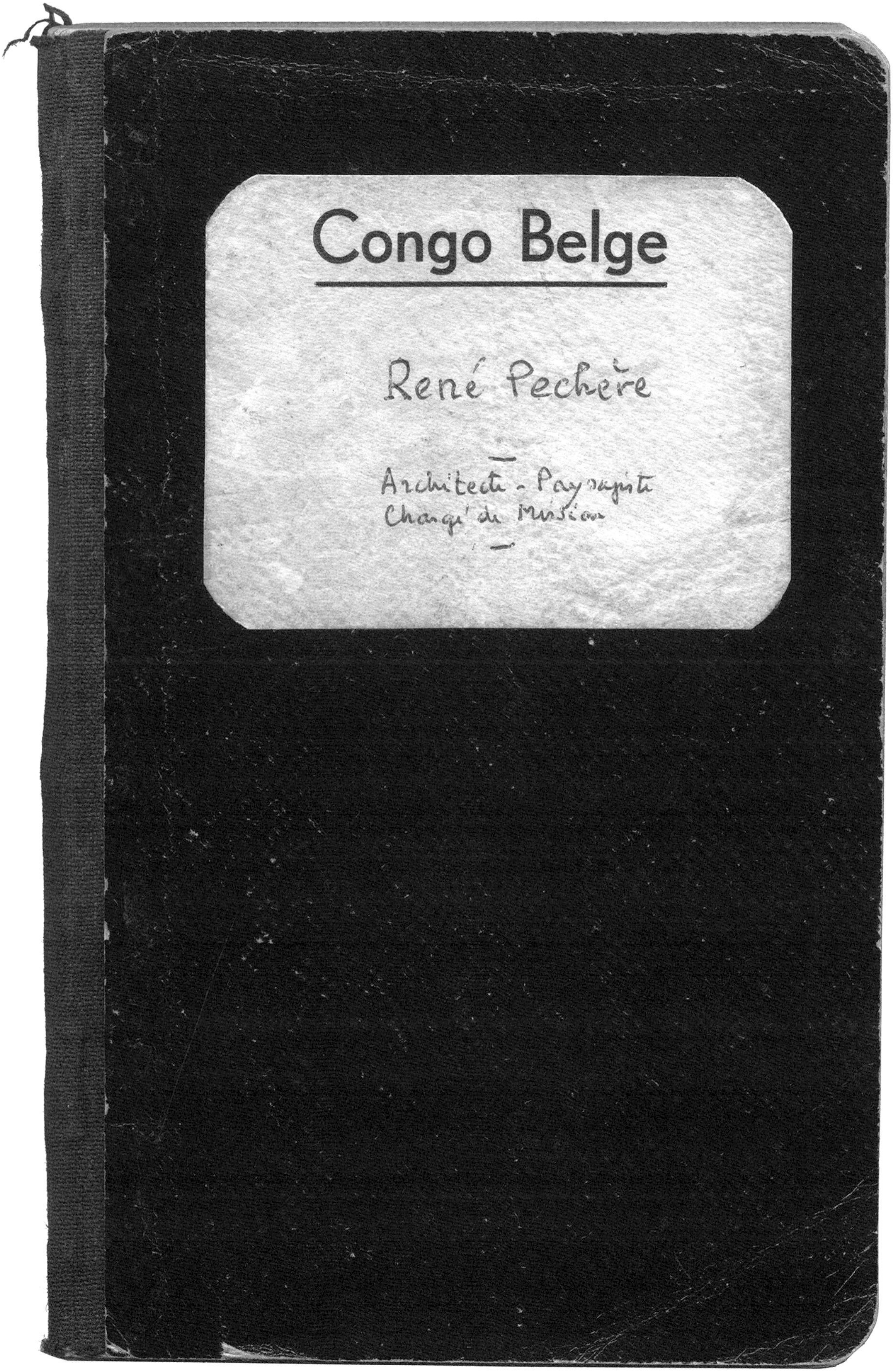
Congo Belge
René Pechère
Architecte - Paysagiste
Chargé de Mission

TRIPOCHITON . SCLEROXYLON.

- feuille ressemble à celle de l'érable
- essence du Bas-Congo
- croissance très rapide - en 3 ans
- peut atteindre 10 m au départ de la semence
- peut remplacer rapidement un vide. A conseiller uniquement comme intercalaire.
- bois de chauffage excellent
- terrain humide
- age maximum : 30 ans
- peut être taillé et limité en hauteur la forme générale est celle en pointillé

essence recommandée comme intercalaire
- ne fructifie pas à Yang. graines à demander au Mayumbe.

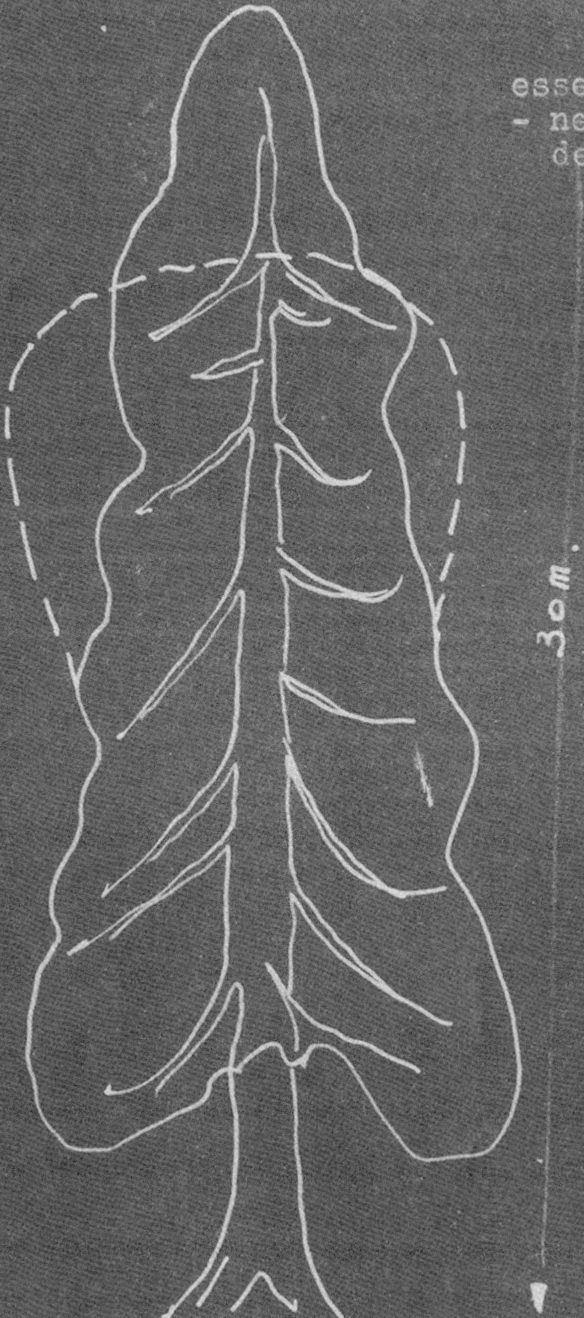

1958 fig. 62

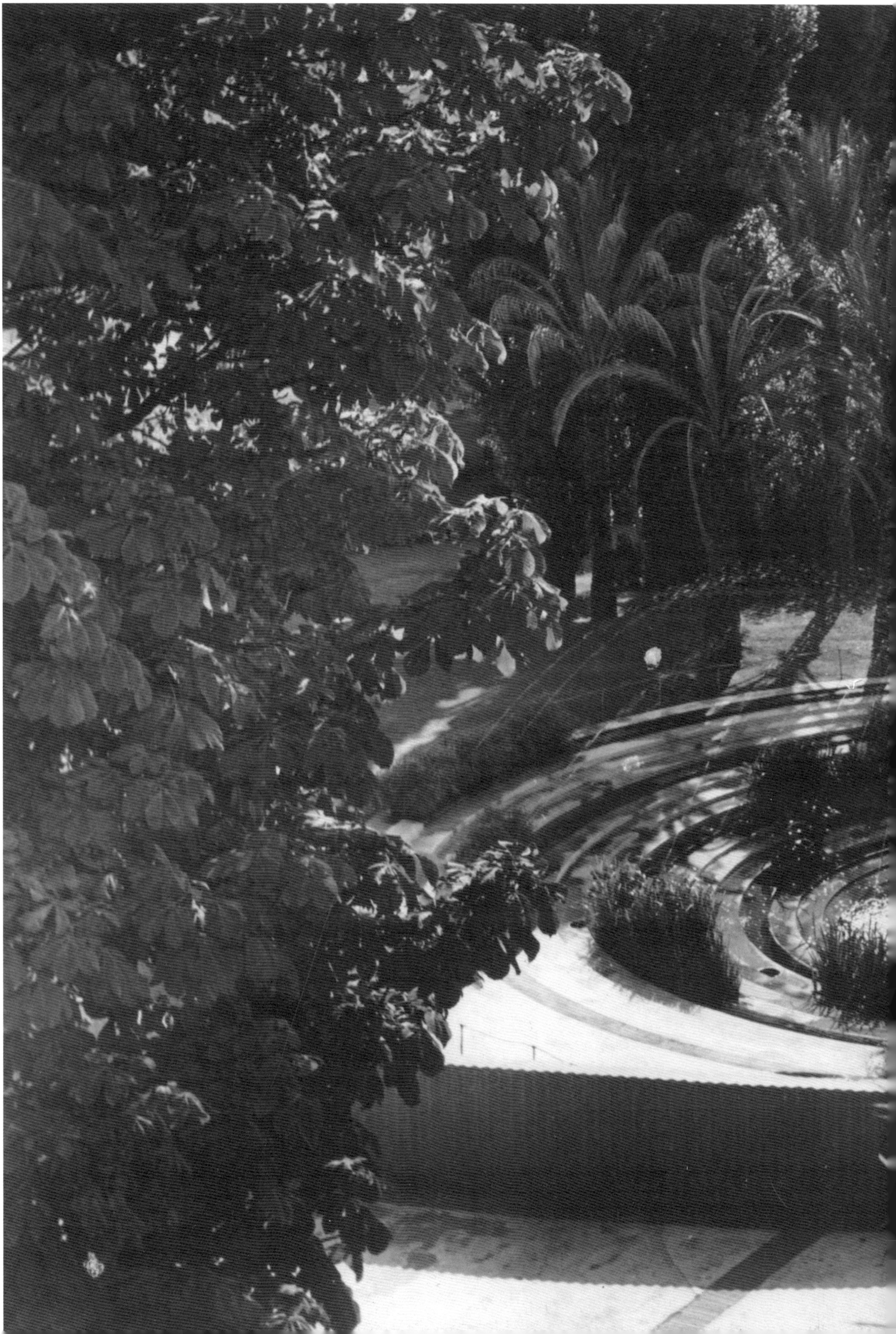

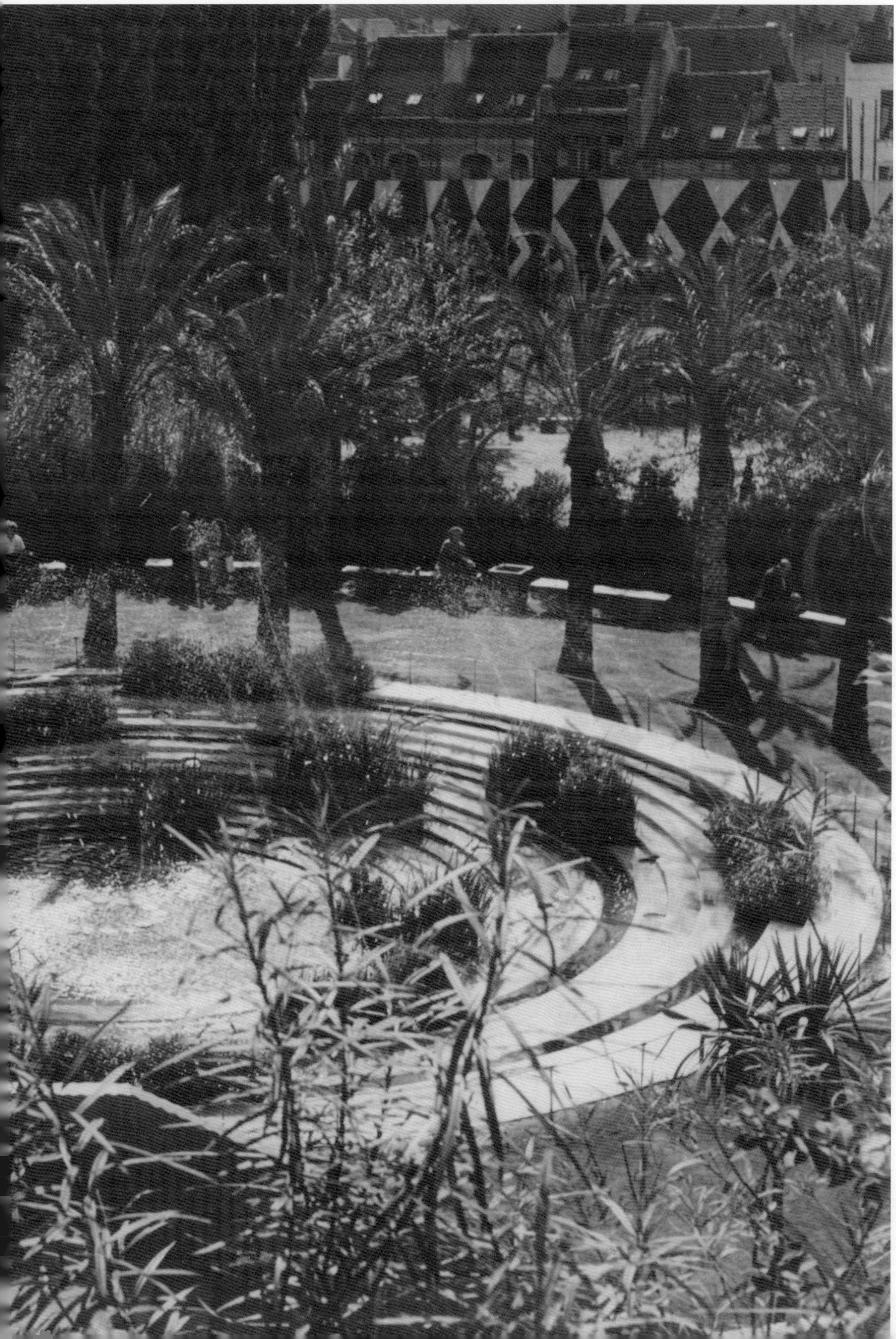

1958 fig. 63

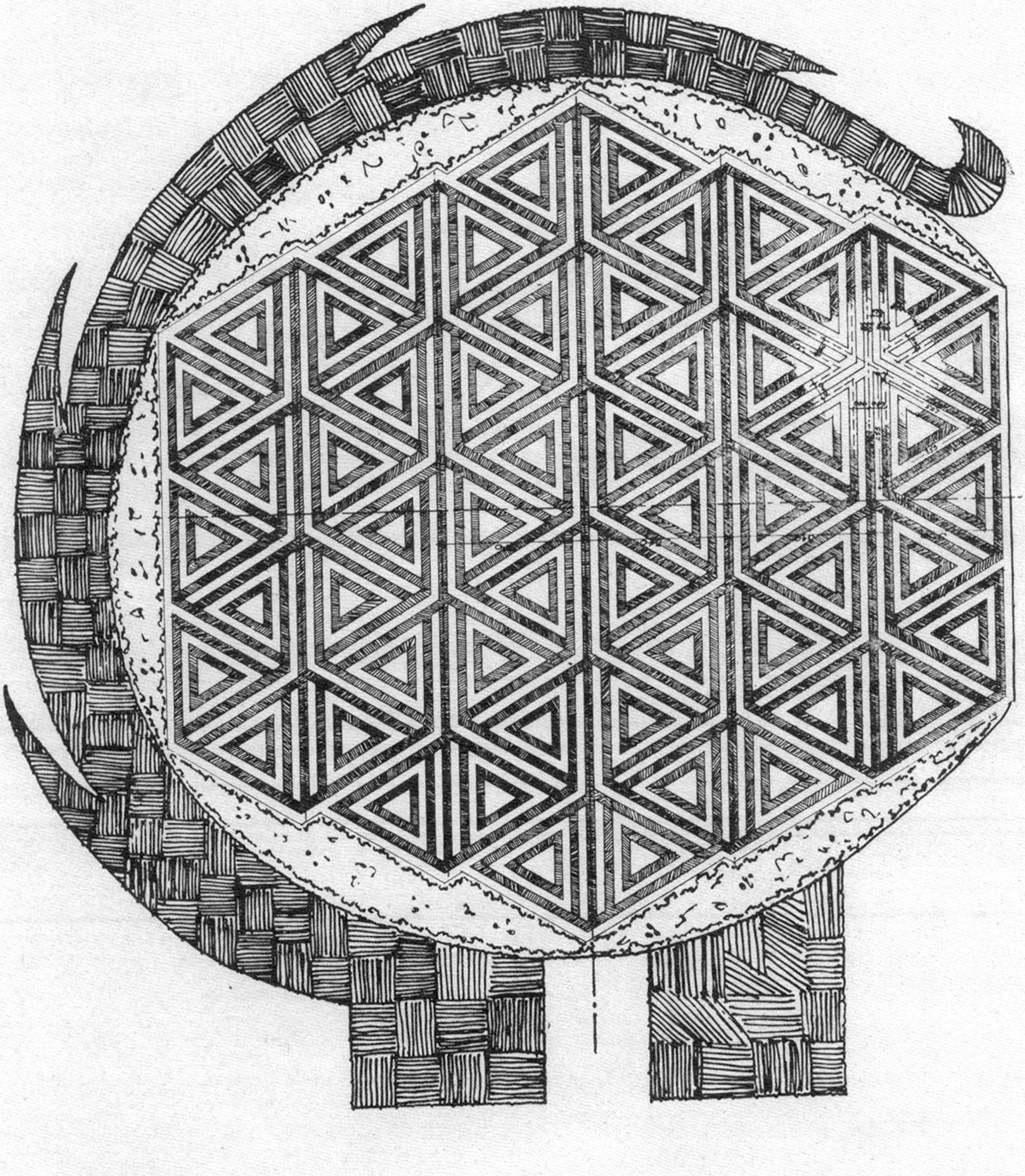

fig. 64

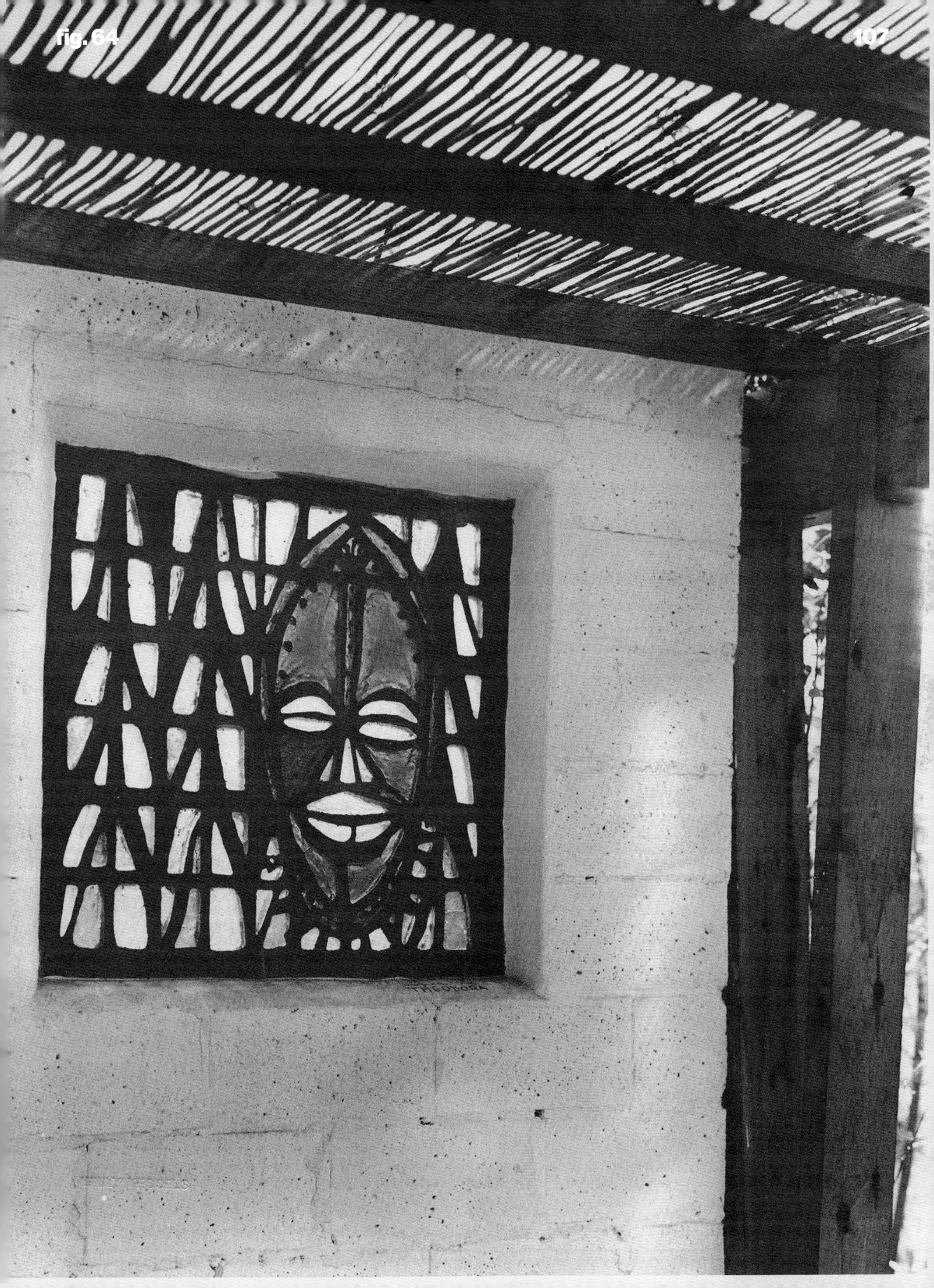

1958 fig. 65, 66

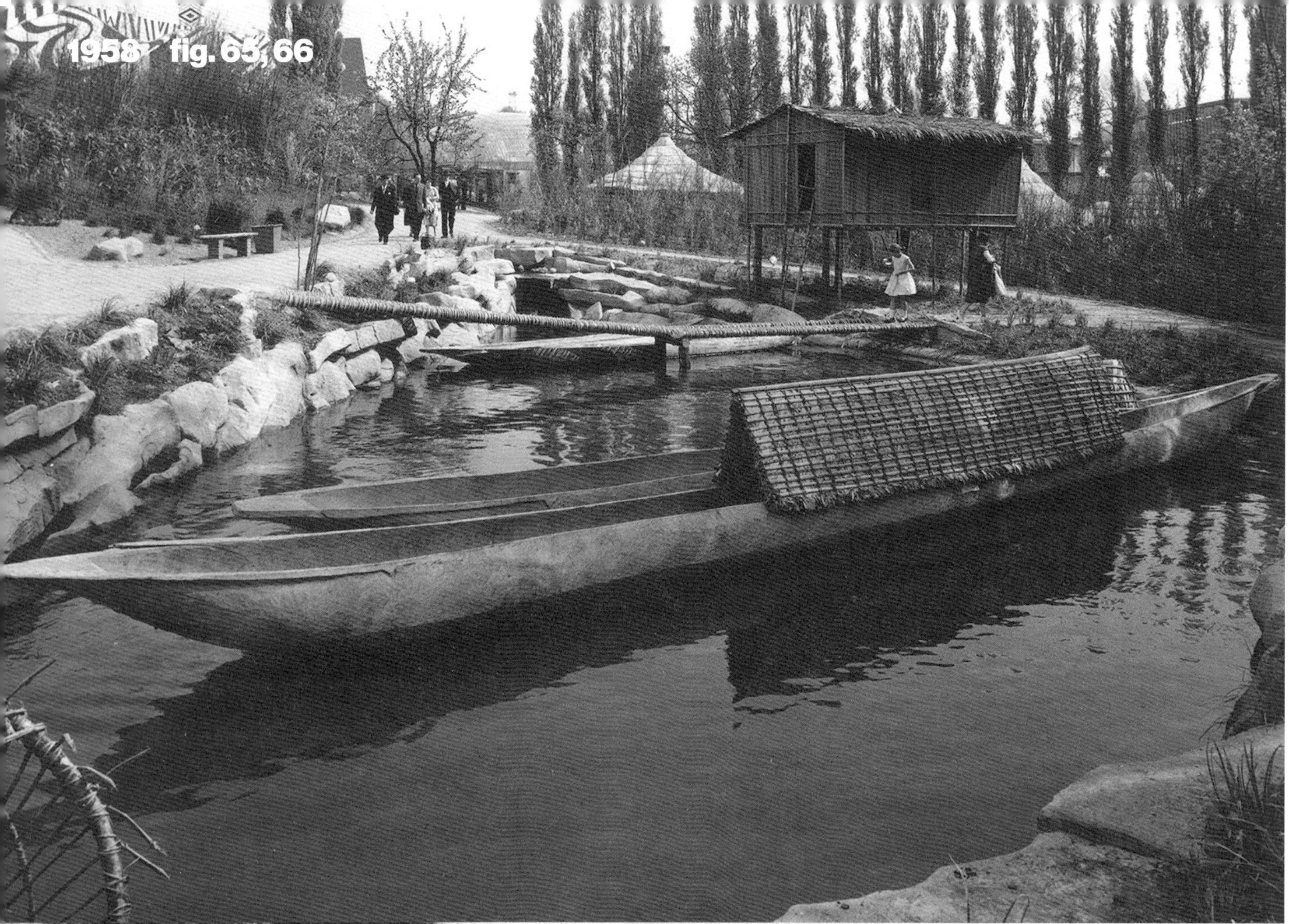

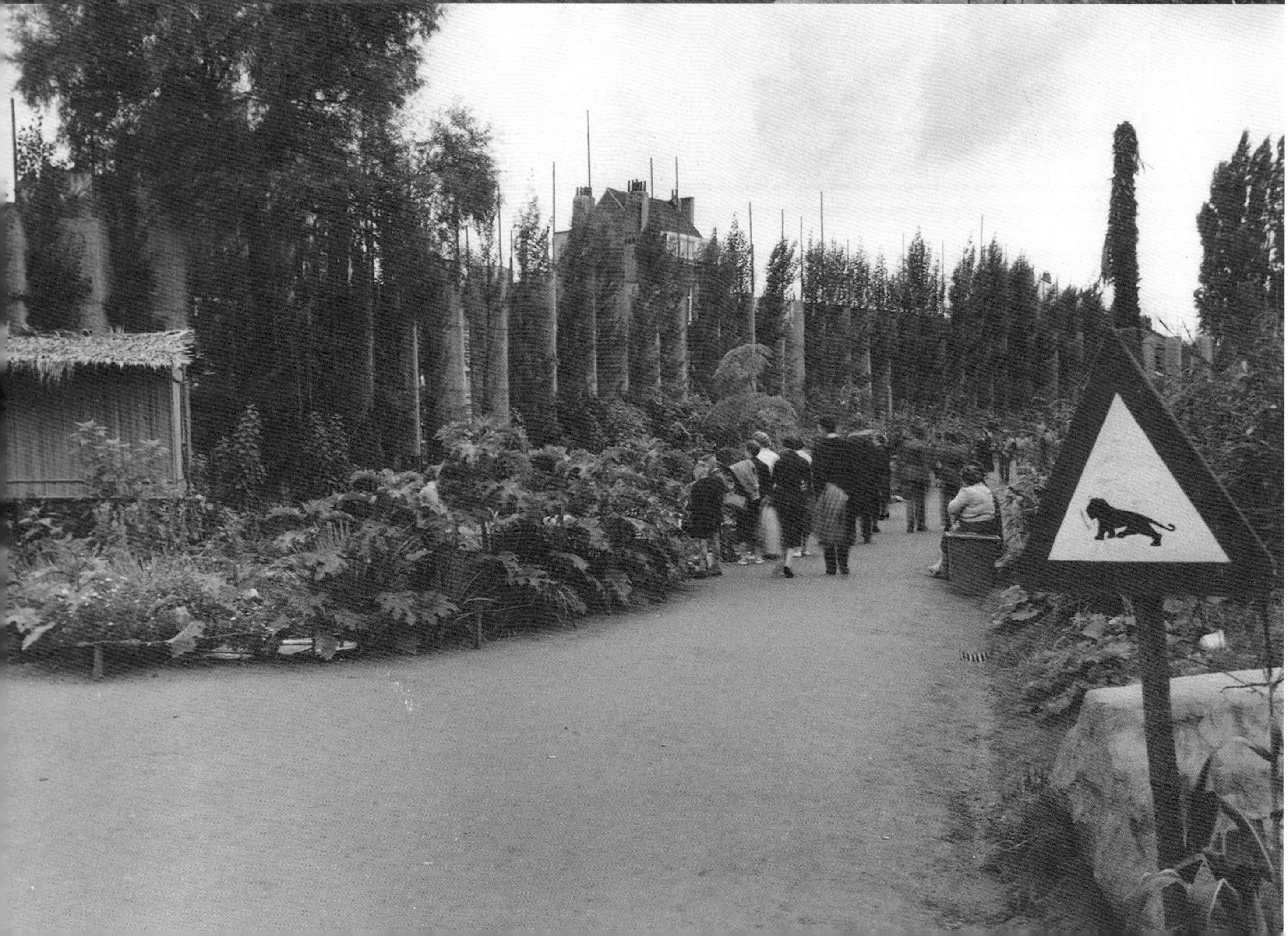

fig. 67

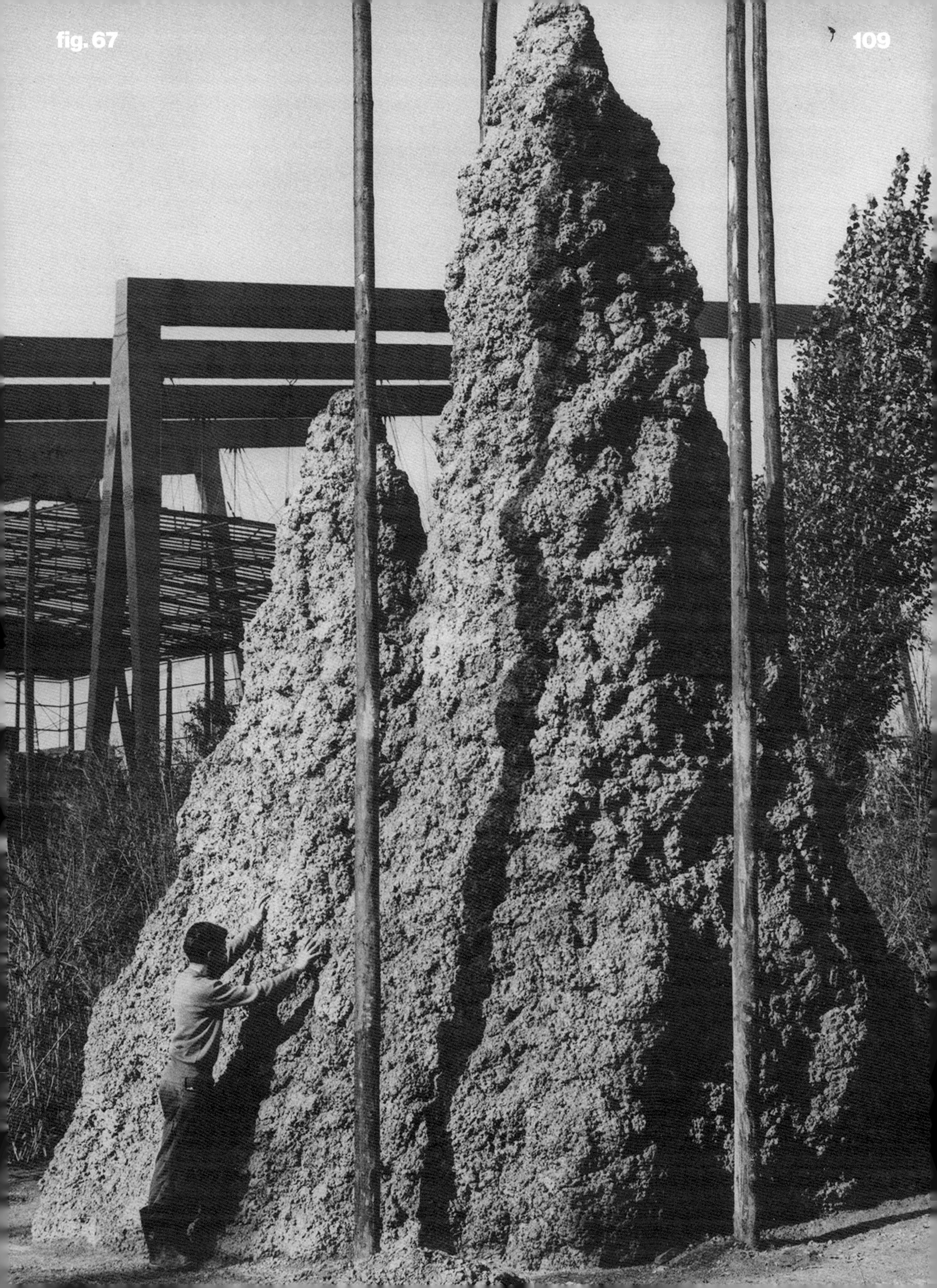

1958 fig. 68

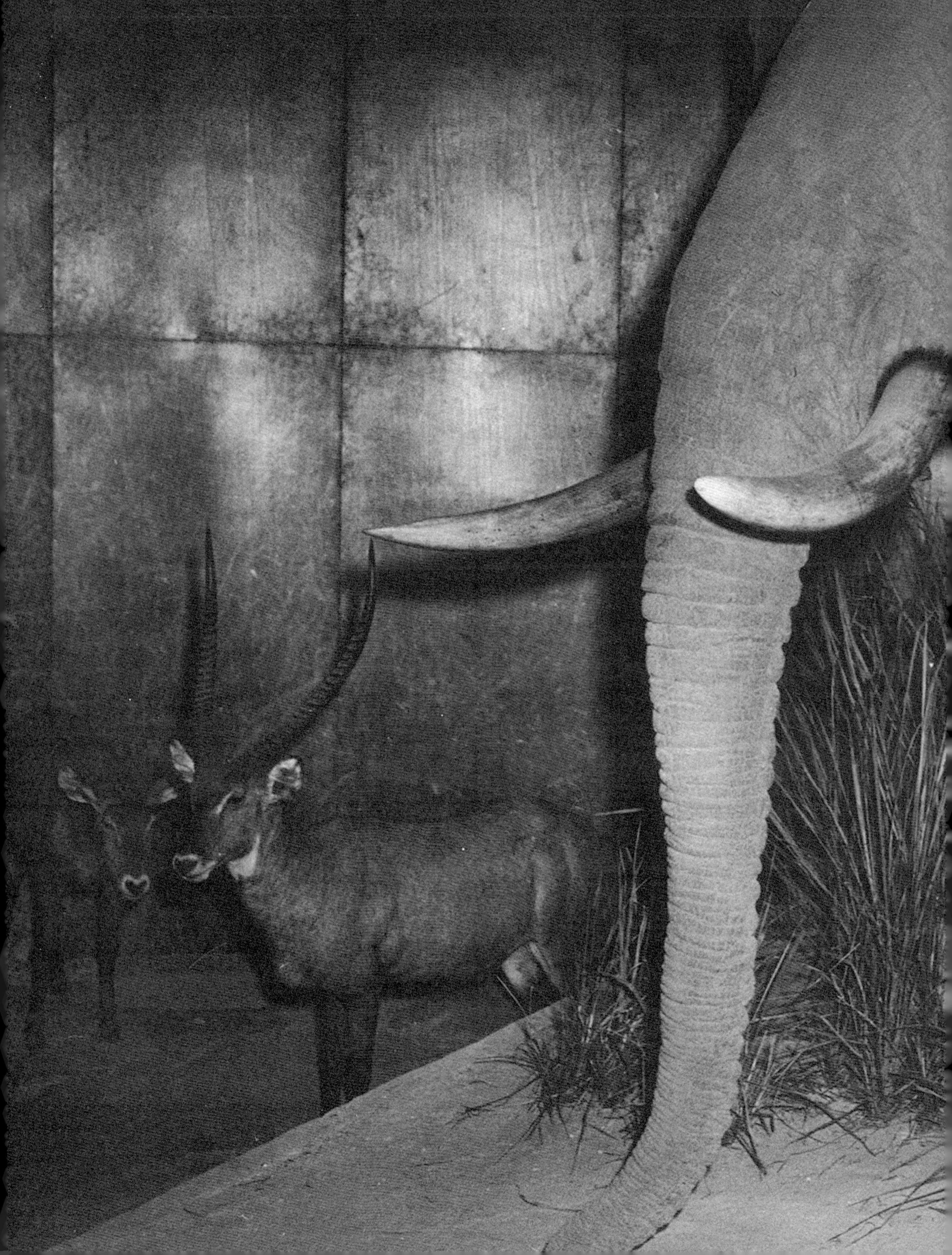

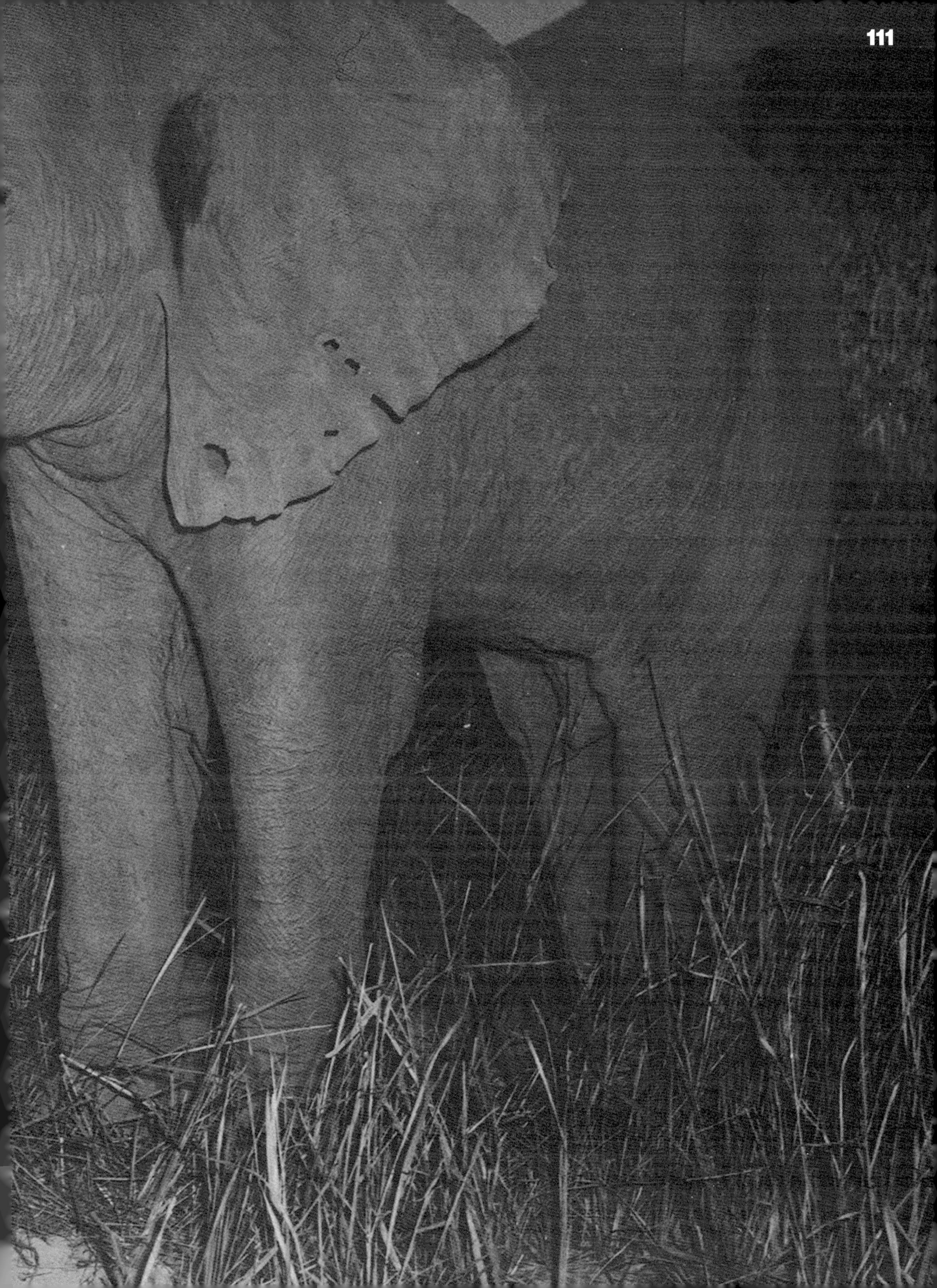

1958 fig. 69

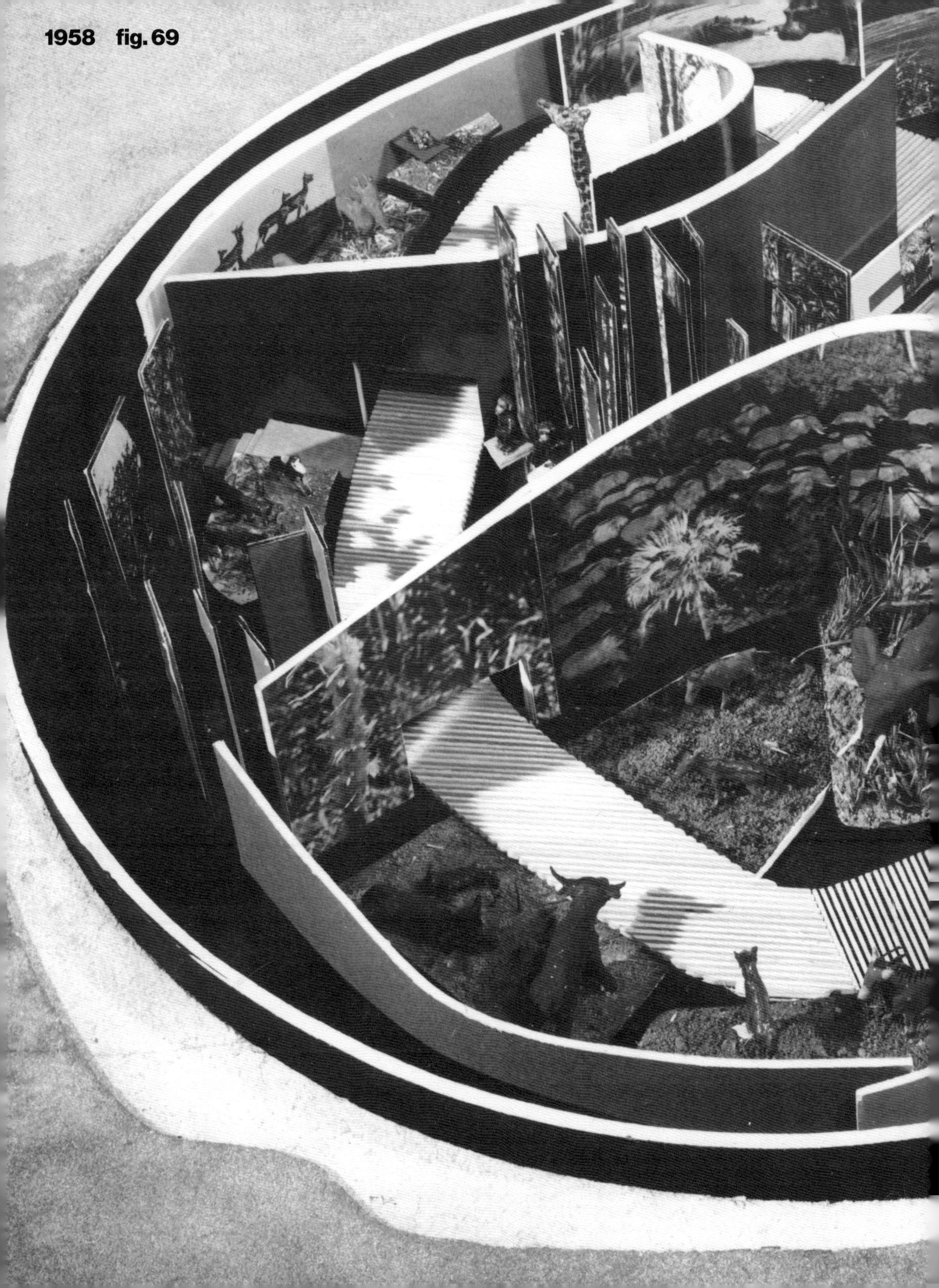

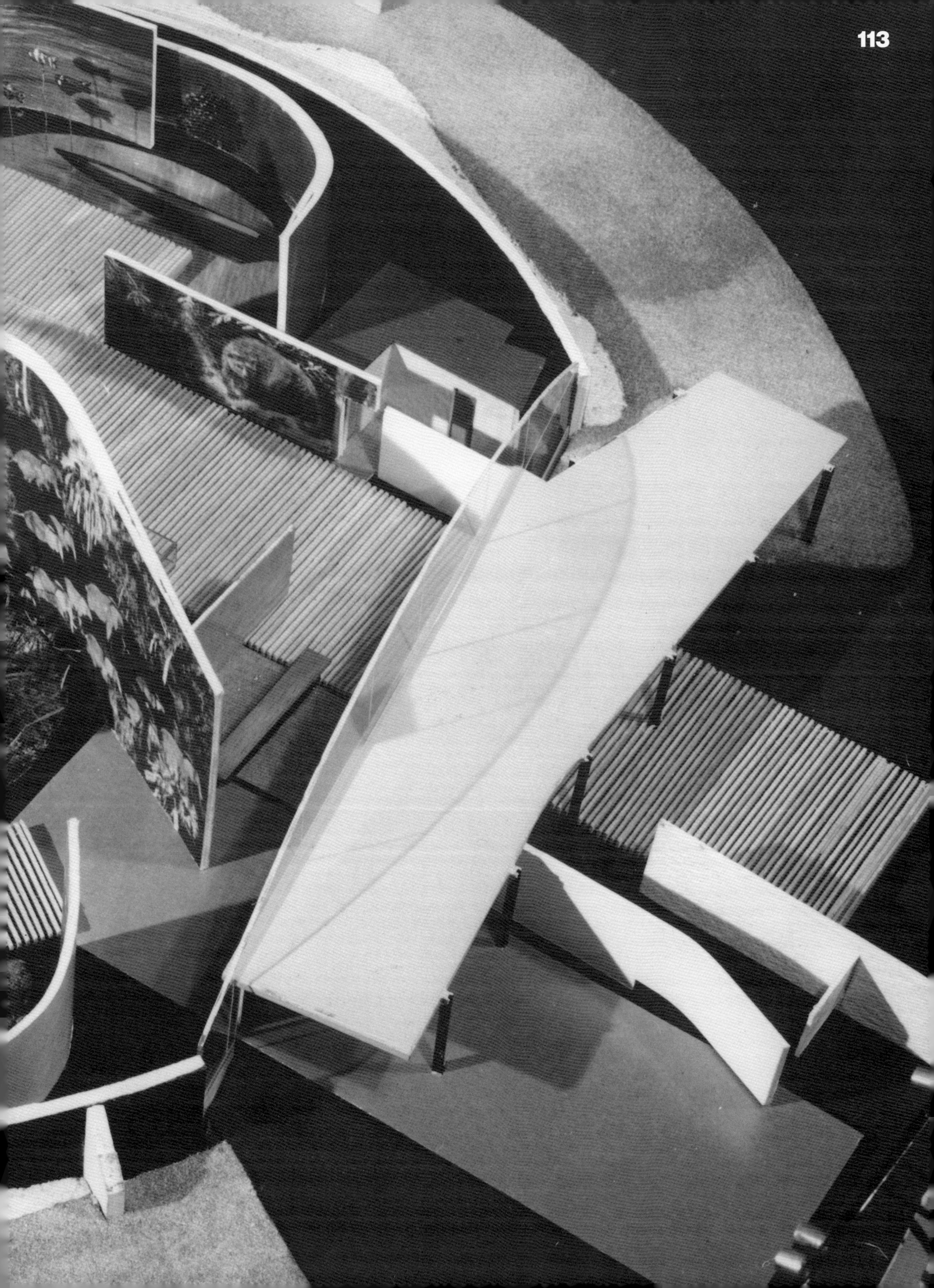

1958 fig. 70

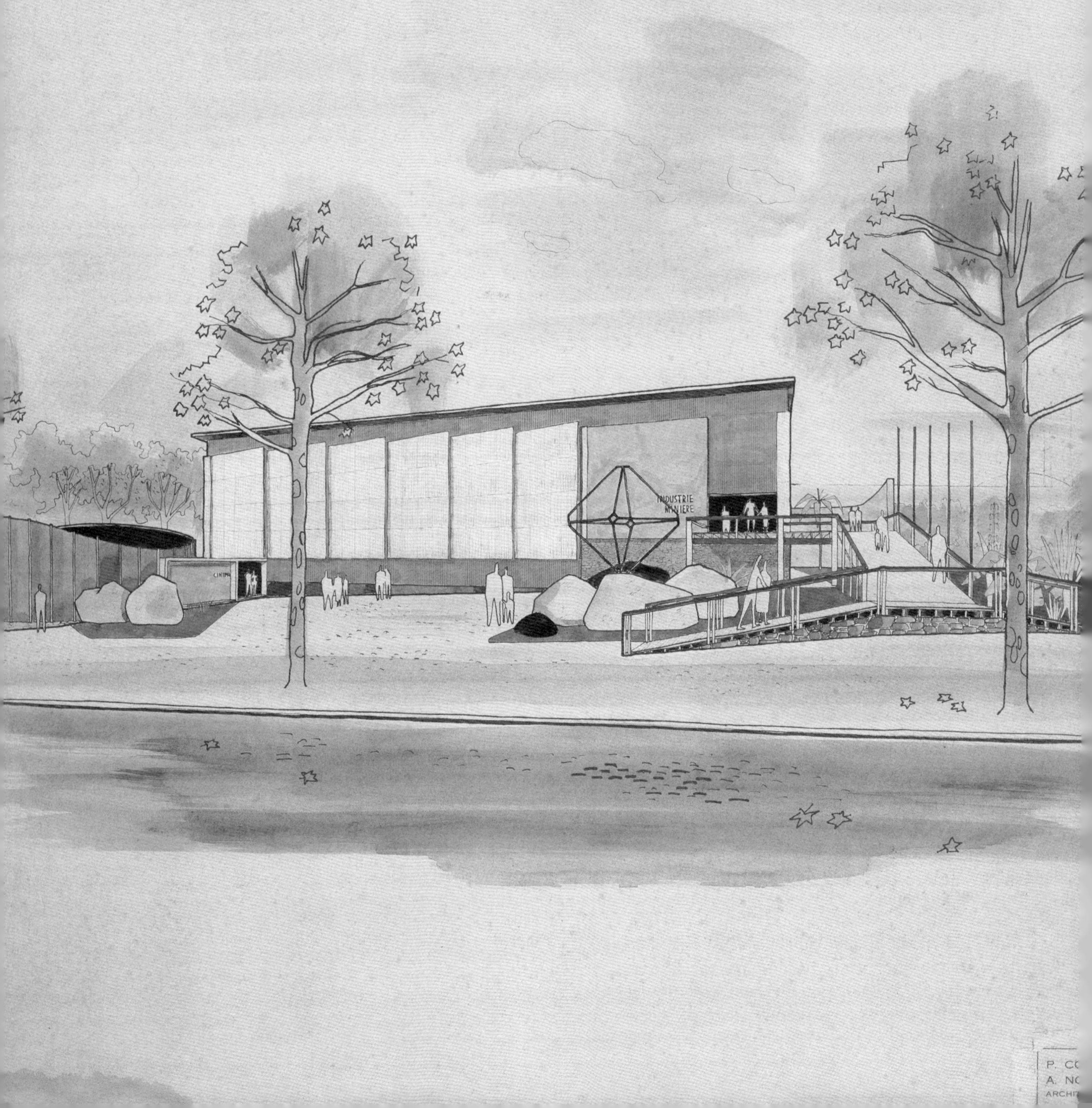

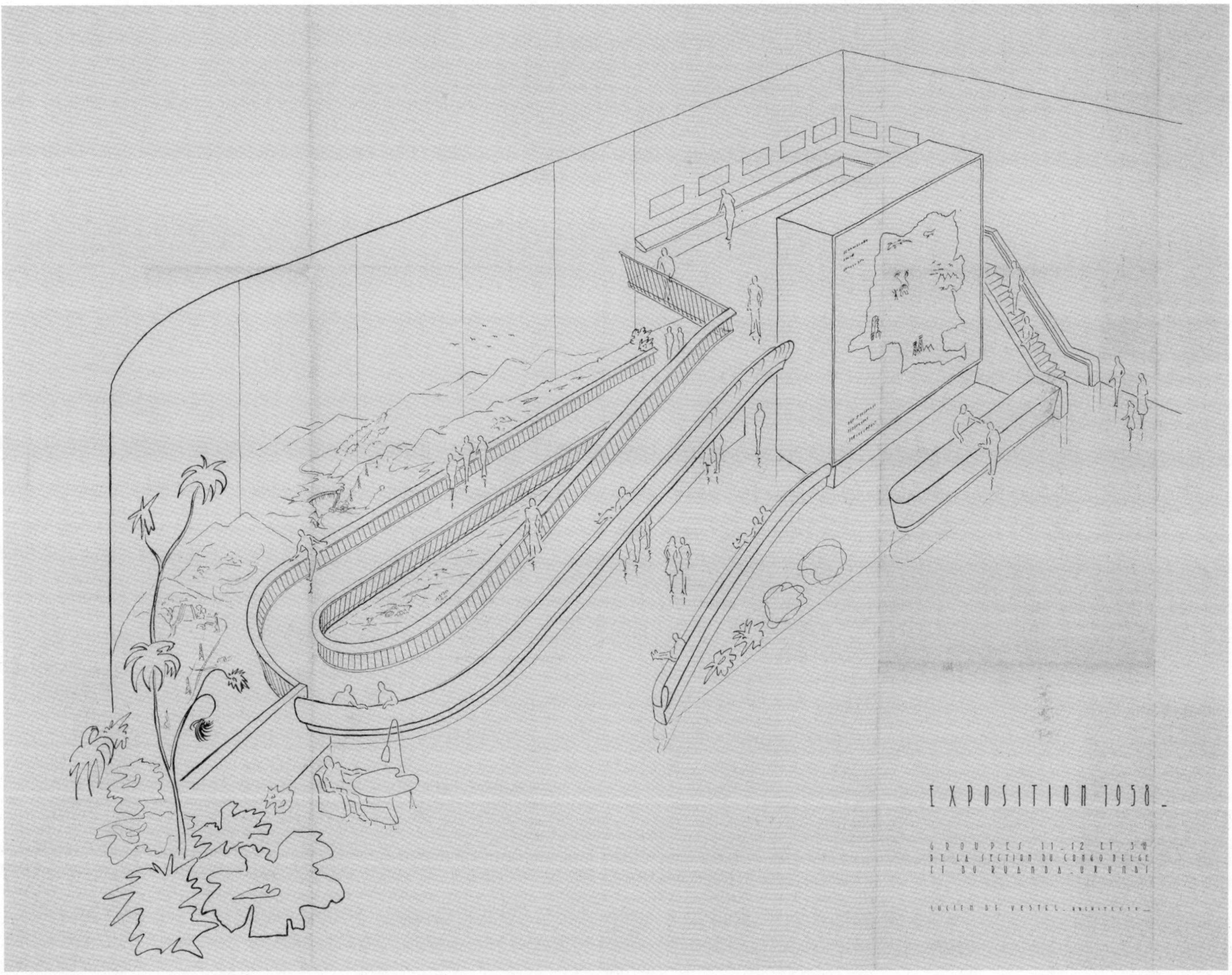
EXPOSITION 1958_
DE LA SECTION DU CONGO BELGE
ET DU RUANDA_URUNDI
LUCIEN DE VESTEL_ARCHITECTE_

1958 fig. 72

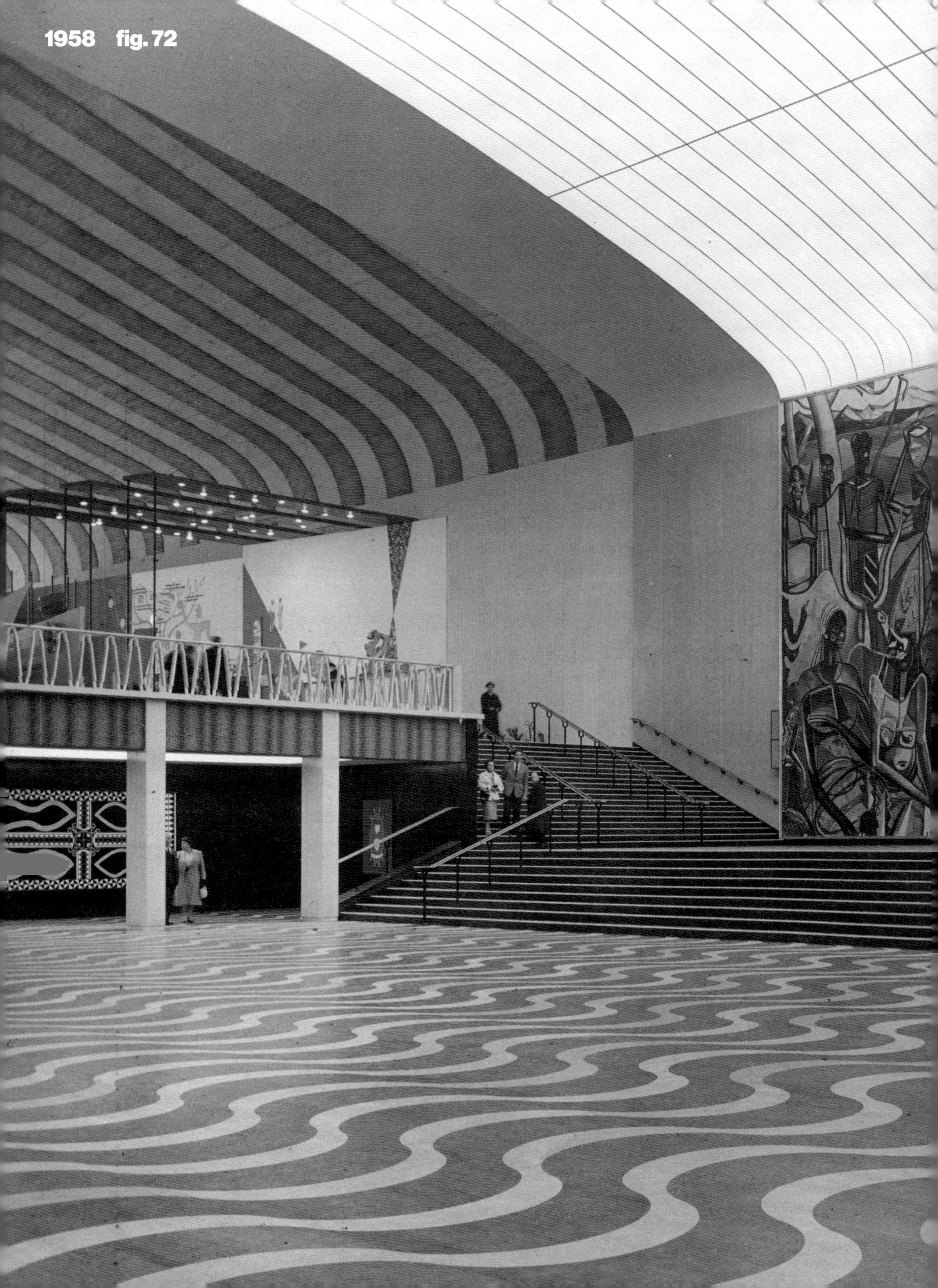

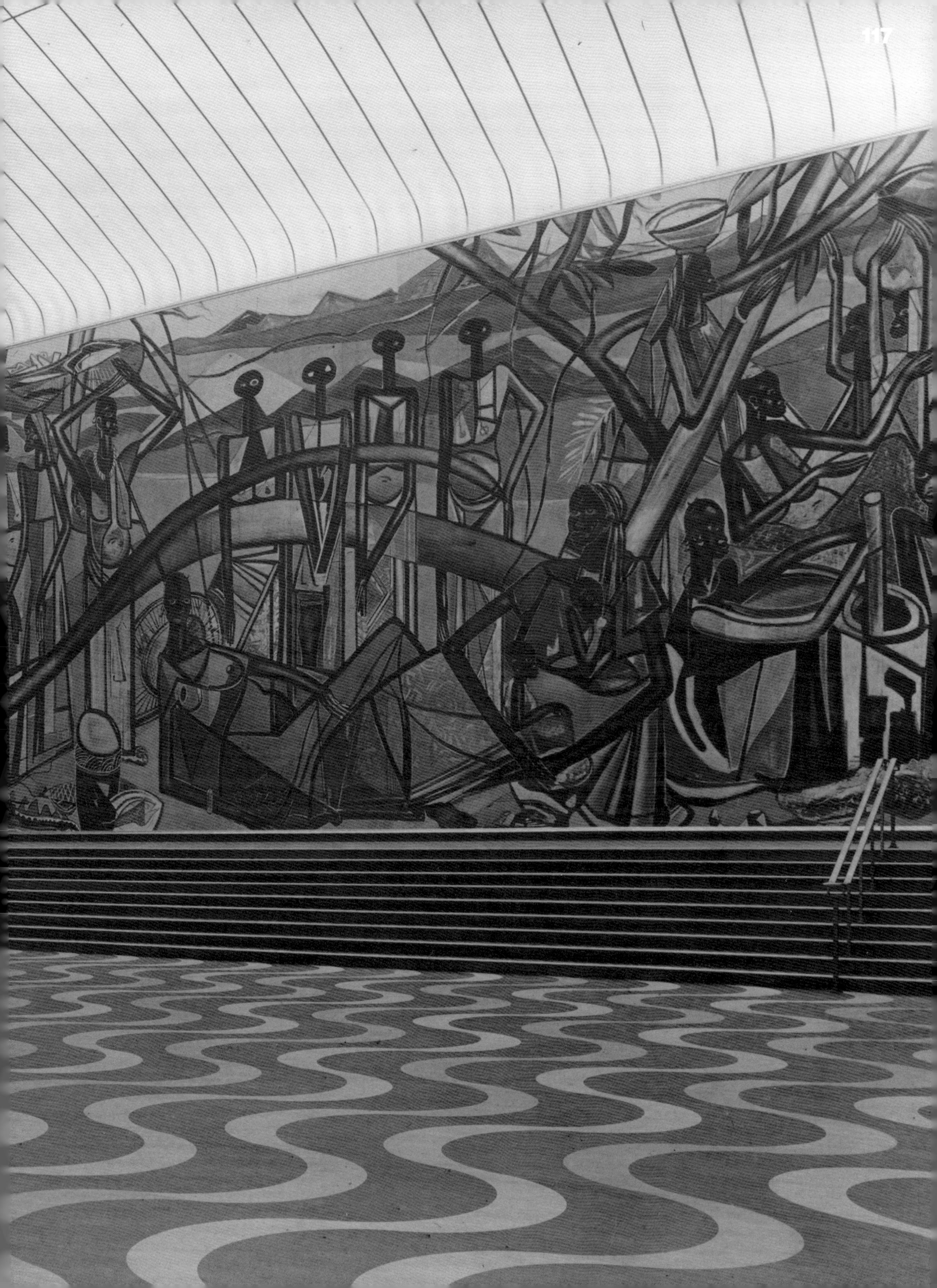

1958 fig. 73

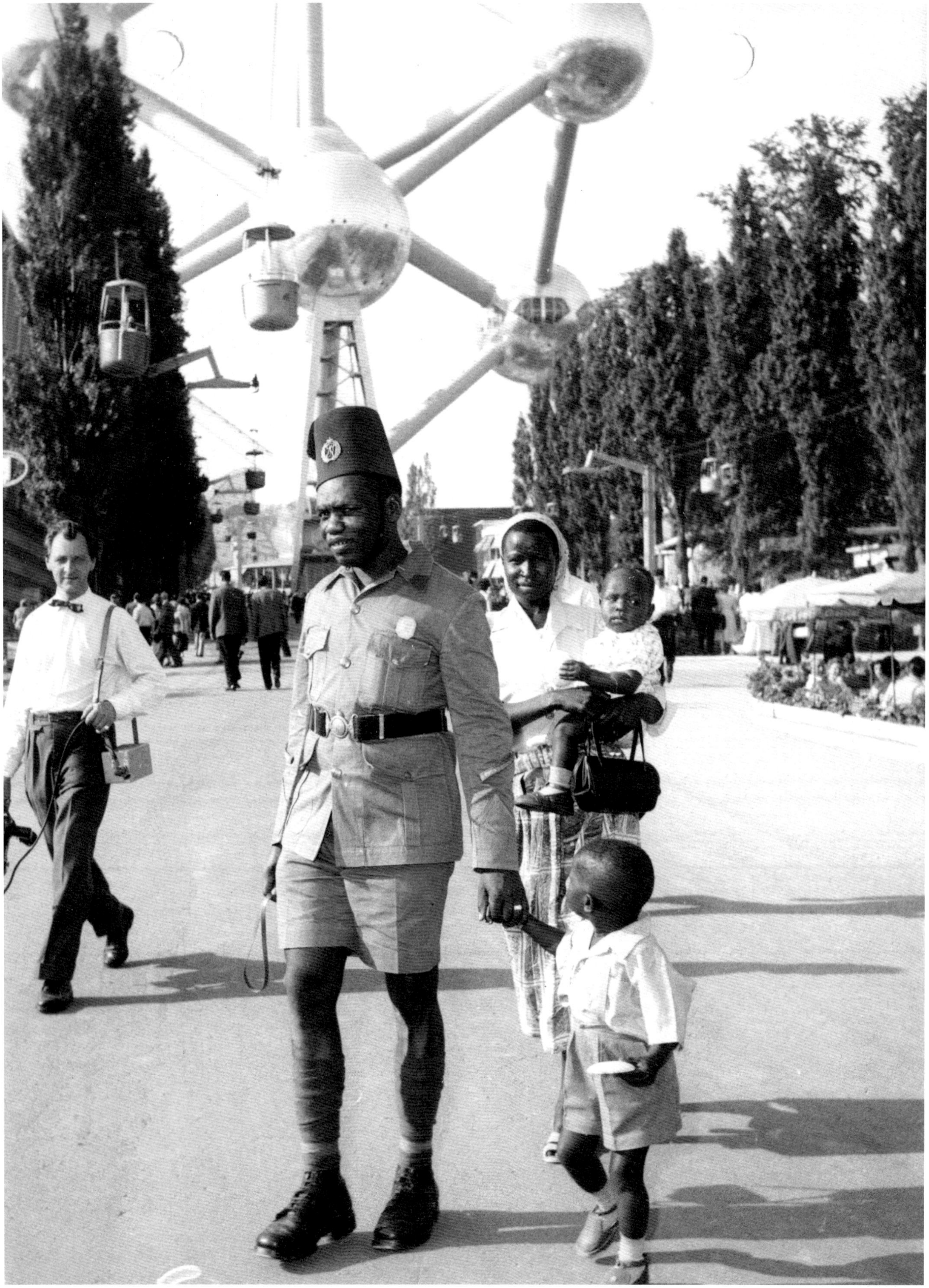

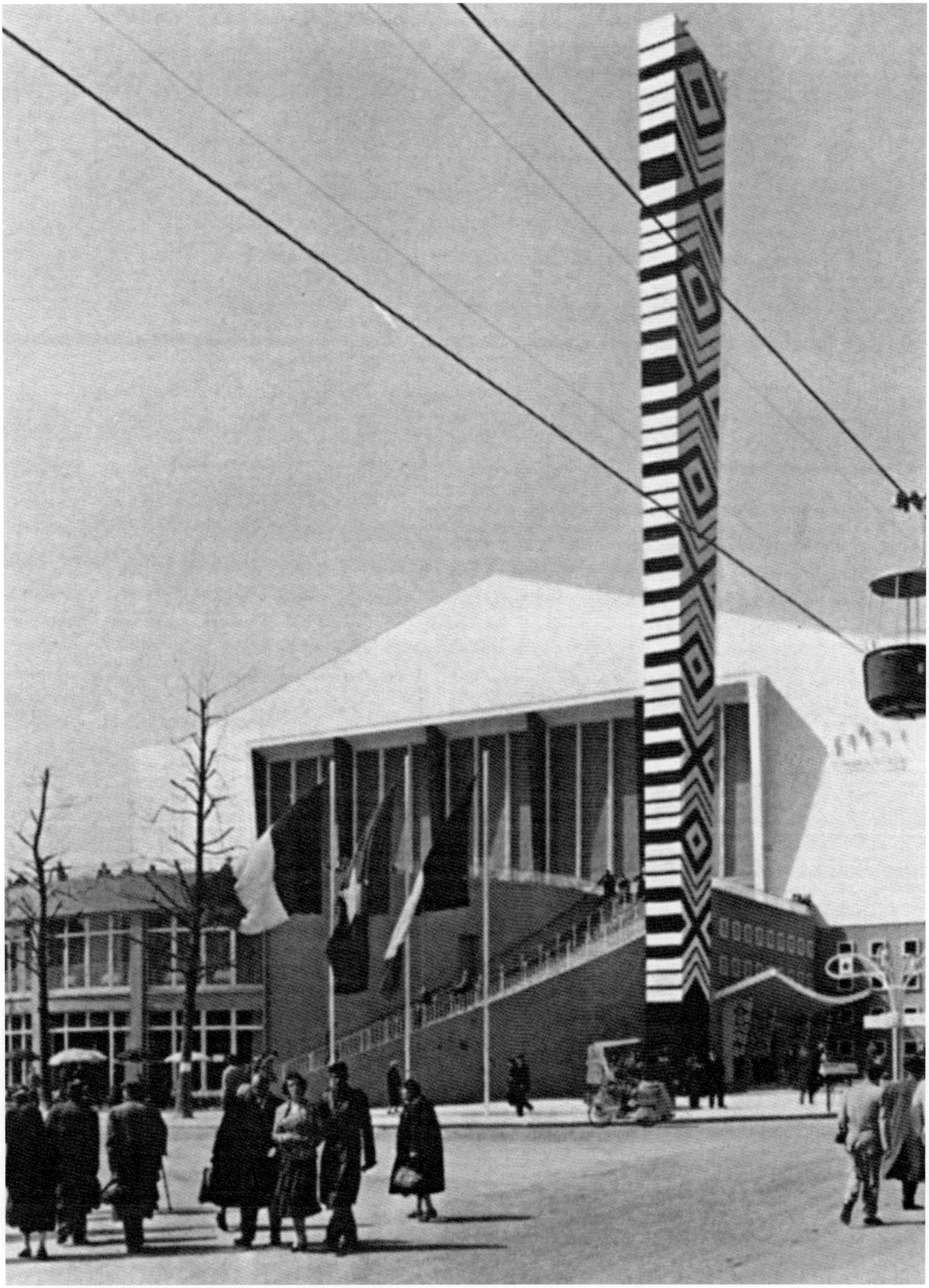

1958 fig. 75

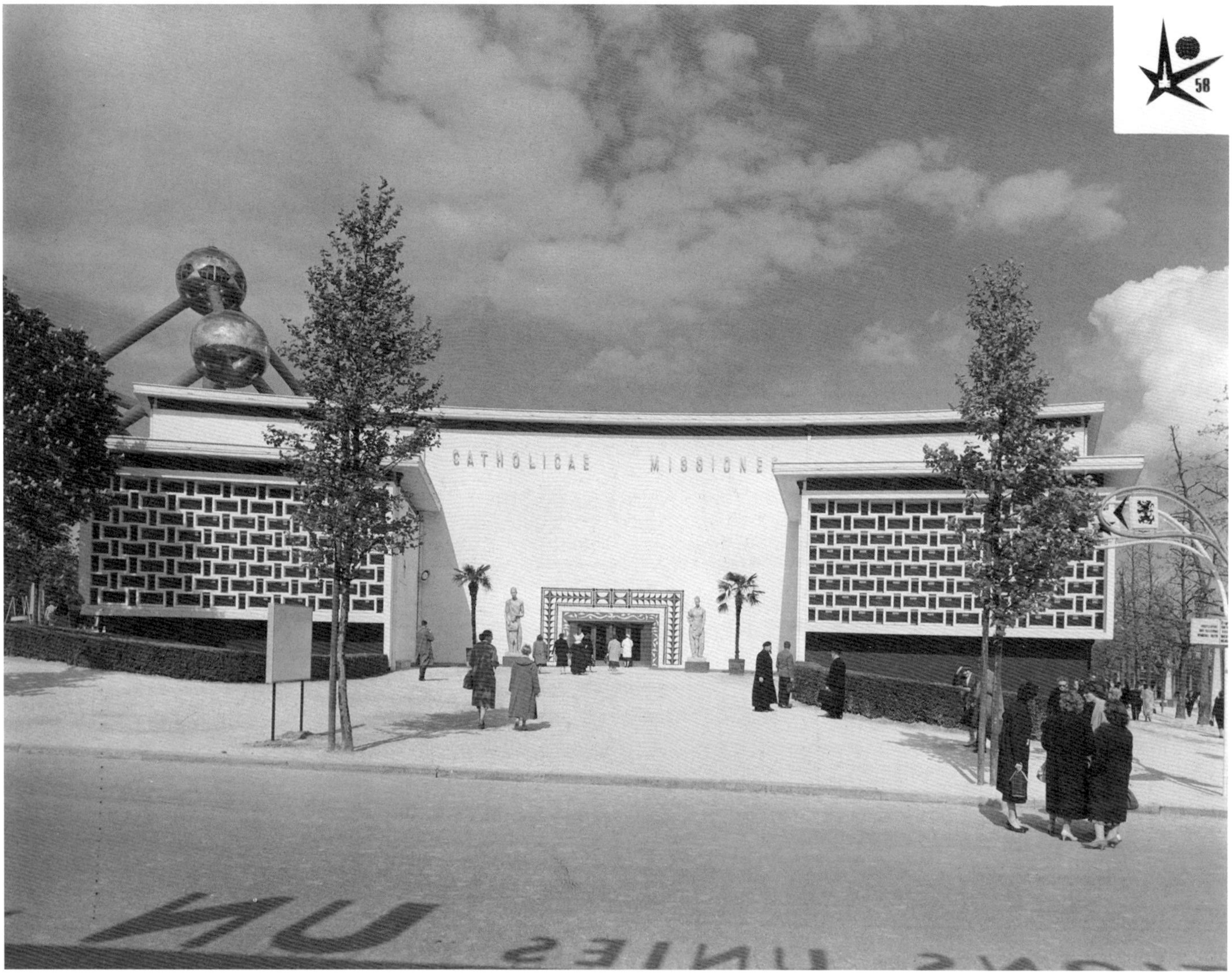

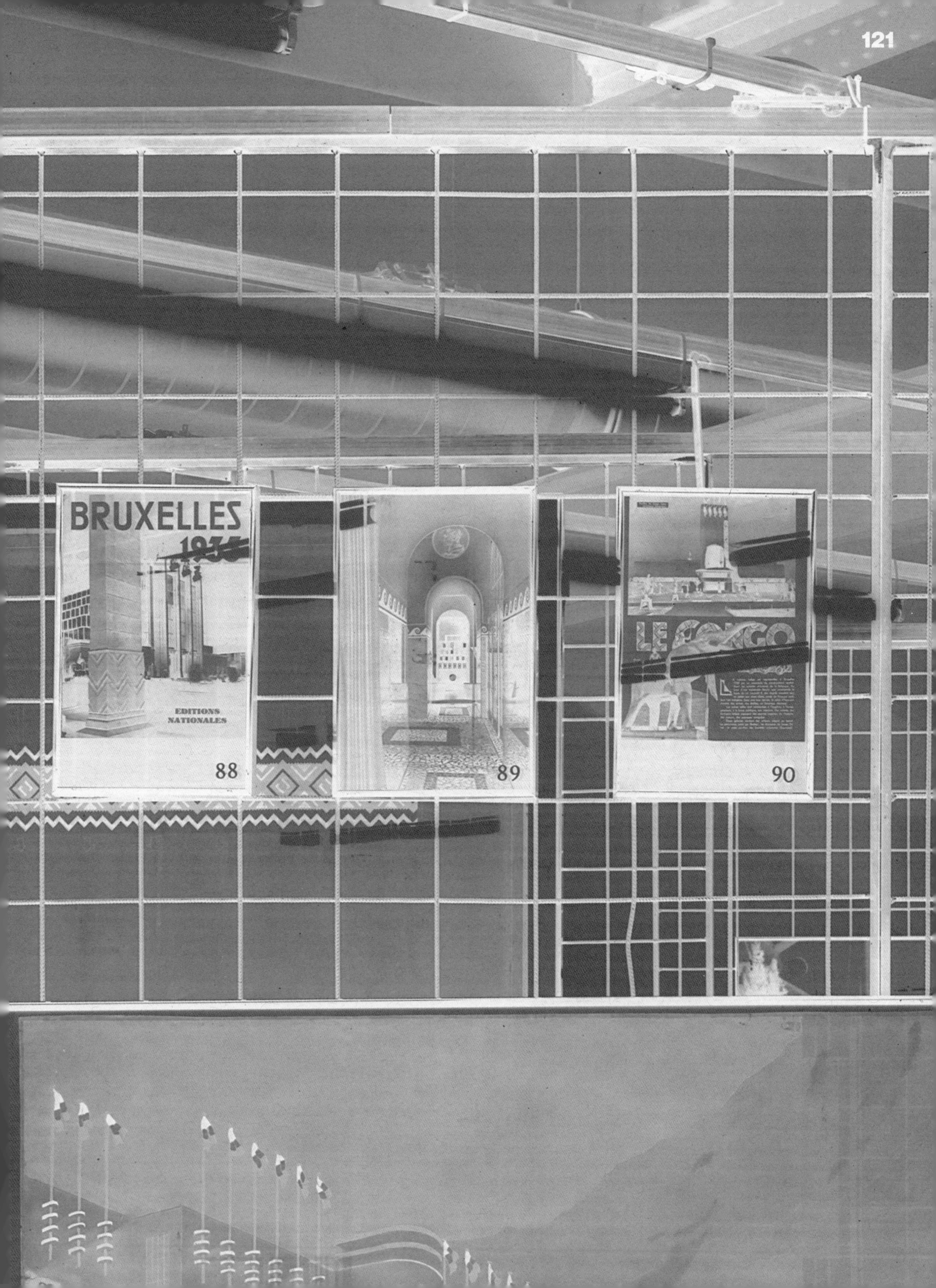
BRUXELLES
EDITIONS
NATIONALES
88
89
LE CONGO
90

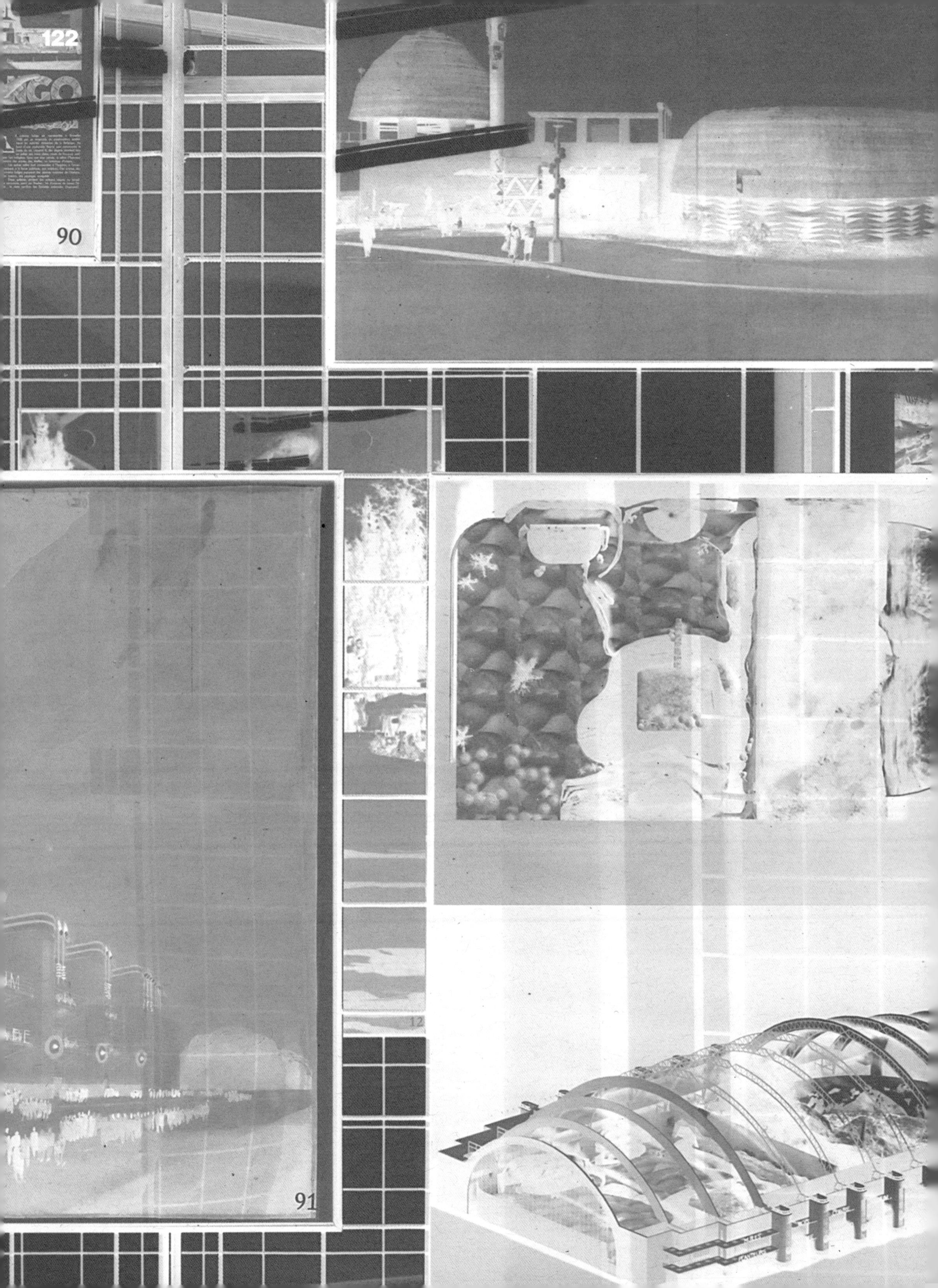

Johan Lagae, *Displaying Authenticity and Progress: Architectural Representation of the Belgian Congo at International Exhibitions in the 1930s*, Published at Third Text, Vol. 14, Issue 50, March 1, 2000.

Displaying *Authenticity* and *Progress*

Architectural Representation of the Belgian Congo at International Exhibitions in the 1930s

Johan Lagae

AUTHENTICITY AND PROGRESS IN THE DISPLAY OF COLONIES

The representation of colonies was an intrinsic part of international exhibitions since their inception. The Universal Exhibition of 1867, however, introduced a change in these displays and sought to present a new spatial concept for the exhibition grounds. For the first time, separate pavilions were now also erected outside the main exhibition hall, and henceforth, the participants would present themselves increasingly by means of an individual section or pavilion, using its design to evoke their own identities. Consequently, a visit to the exhibition became an architectural tour du monde, in which colonial pavilions brought distant and exotic cultures into view. This tour du monde and the evocation of identity in these colonial sections were, of course, highly ambiguous and eurocentric.[1] The display of colonies was, in fact, determined by a duality. The organisers of these settings claimed to offer an accurate, realistic representation of the colony's environment, the key notion in their discourse being the 'authenticity' of the display. Such 'authentic displays' are to be understood as architectural displays that refer, in one way or another, to the native architecture or material culture of the colony: colonial pavilions were sometimes designed as replicas of existing colonial buildings, but more often these so-called 'authentic displays' were hybrid mixtures of European and indigenous architectural languages, in which morphological elements selected from the native built environment were recombined according to western design rules. Often the section's claim of authenticity was enhanced by informal mise-en-scènes, like the 'Rue du Caire' (1889) or the 'Village Sénégalais' (1913). The presence of indigenous peoples, temporarily brought over for these events, was to secure the realistic character of the colonial setting in which the visitor was immersed. Because these authentic displays underscored precise

1 In recent years, a growing literature has appeared on the topic of colonial exhibitions, propaganda and iconography. Discussions on (the ambiguity of) the colonial sections's architecture, however, are rare: see Sylvianne Leprun, *Le Théâtre des Colonies. Scénographie, acteurs et discours de l'imaginaire dans les expositions 1855-1937*, Editions l'Harmattan, Paris, 1986; and Zeynep Celik, *Displaying the Orient. Architecture of Islam at Nineteenth-Century World's Fairs*, University of California Press, Berkeley / Los Angeles / Oxford, 1992.

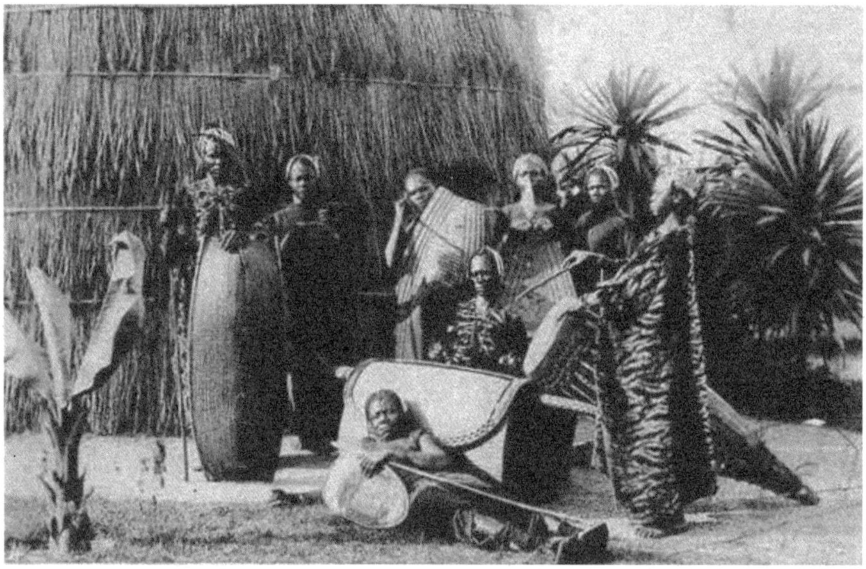

The 'African village' at the Congolese section in Tervuren, built for the Brussels *Exposition Universelle of 1897*. Photo courtesy of the Africa Museum, Tervuren, Belgium

ideological goals, they can be regarded as a translation into architecture of what Eric Hobsbawm has called the 'invention of tradilion'.[2]

The colonial sections were also, of course, essentially a legitimisation of colonialism itself. To convince visitors of the civilising mission of colonialism, a large emphasis was placed in the presentation on 'progress', progress as imported into the colonies. Progress, as defined in the discourse accompanying the colonial sections, encompassed the religious, educational and cultural upheaval of the indigenous population, as was particularly emphasisedin the presentations of missionary congregations. But progress also stood for modernisation as implemented through technology, that mirrored, or even represented, the advance of the western world itself. It is in this particular sense that I will refer to progress here, because the display of this modernisation became increasingly important in colonial sections from World War I onwards. An exotic setting, however, remained crucial for appealing to the general public. One can thus argue that at international exhibitions of the 1920s and '30s the main characteristic of colonial sections, and of the architecture of their main pavilions in particular, was the simultaneous display of authenticity and progress.

Such a simultaneity profoundly marked the representation of the Belgian Congo during the 1930s. In comparison to earlier exhibitions, the Congolese sections of this era are particular for two reasons: firstly, the large emphasis put on progress was stimulated by specific economic and political conditions. In answer to the world-wide economic crisis that left its mark on both Belgium and the Congo, trade possibilities with the colony were presented in Belgian colonial propaganda as a solution to Belgium's financial difficulties as late as 1939, as politicians and industrialists had never been eager to invest in the colonial project. During this decade, moreover, several other nations also tried to claim parts of the immense territory in the Belgian colony, while in the European political forum voices were raised in favour of a general international control that would substitute the authority of all colonial powers. Within such a context, the Belgian government was forced to present convincing demonstrations of its 'civilising mission' in the Congo if it wanted to maintain its absolute rule there. Therefore, technological progress in the Congo was given due attention in the presentations at international events, albeit accompanied by a philanthropic discourse emphasising the efforts made in the realm of education and medical services.[3]

Secondly, designing an authentic setting to represent the Belgian colony had proven to be a problematic undertaking for Belgian architects, and it was not until 1931 that a Congo pavilion was built that was unmistakably inspired

2 See E Hobsbawm, *The Invention of Tradition*, Cambridge University Press, Cambridge/New York/ Melbourne, 1983.

3 The economic and political goals of the 1931 Congolese section have been analysed in detail by Etienne Deschamps in 'La Participation de la Belgique à l'Exposition Coloniale Internationale de Paris/Vincennes 1931. L'affirmation d'une politique coloniale sur le scene internationale', unpublished thesis, Université Catholique de Louvain, 1994.

by the built forms of central Africa. Combining a convincing representation of Congolese culture with a display that evoked the modernised colony presented a specific architectural challenge. From 1930 onwards, architects addressed this challenge and proposed a wide range of divergent design solutions. A consideration of the Congolese sections from the 1930s sheds light not only on shifting interpretations of authenticity within the colonial milieu, but also on issues closely linked with architectural practices at the time.

THE PROBLEMATIC DISPLAY OF AUTHENTICITY

Although the Congo only became a colony in the true sense of the word in 1908, there had been Congolese sections at international exhibitions since the 1885 Antwerp Universal Exhibition. The last event in which the Congo was presented as a colony was the Brussels World's Fair of 1958. Even though ethnographic research on Congolese peoples had received a great deal of attention in the colonial milieu as early as the end of the nineteenth century, colonial officials, architects and critics all agreed that the Congo lacked a proper native architecture worthy of attention. Central African building forms were considered unsuitable sources of inspiration for the design of the Belgian Congo exhibition pavilions at World's Fairs, as well as for the elaboration of a contemporary colonial architecture. The *Livre d'Or* of the 1905 Liège Universal Exhibition, declaring why the Congo pavilion bore no reference to African built forms, gives us a telling example of the mainstream argument: 'Because no relic of an indigenous public building of importance is to be found anywhere in the Congo, it is meaningless to search for representative [morphological] elements amenable to transformation in a stylistic manner.'[4] As illustrated by Emile Bayard's popularising book *l'Art de reconnaîtreles styles coloniaux de la France* of 1931, published as a kind of guidebook for the 'Exposition Coloniale Internationale', this argument applied to the whole of *l'Afrique Noire*: its native built forms, *'les paillotes'*, could not be described in terms of contemporary western architectural conceptions such as 'monumentality', 'durability', and 'history'.[5]

Not surprisingly, in the first Congolese sections, the authentic atmosphere had depended less on the architectural image of the pavilion itself than on the informal reconstructions of Congolese villages, crowded with natives in indigenous garb. Due to their difficult acclimatisation to the Belgian weather, several of these Congolese died during the 1897 Universal Exhibition in Tervuren - an incident which put an end to this practice at future exhibitions. As a result, the representation of the Belgian colony became wholly dependent on the architectural design of the section. Yet, precisely because of the preconception that the Congo did not possess a built environment that could qualify as architecture, there was no clear answer to the question as to what the nature of an exhibition architecture for representing the colony was to be. This was not so for the architects commissioned to design authentic displays for the north or west African colonies. The former could be inspired by the Islamic architectural tradition, resulting in what Frarnçois Beguin has called *arabisances*[6] the latter were most often modelled on the mosque architecture of Djenne and Tombouctou. A similar design strategy — inventing a native architecture by mixing indigenous and European architectural forms —was initially considered inapplicable for the representation of the Belgian colony. As a result, several formal approaches had been followed or proposed for the design of the Congo pavillons since 1885, ranging from Beaux-Arts classicism

4 Gustave Dreze, *Le Livre d'Or de l'Exposilion Universelle et Internationale de 1905*, Tome I, lmprimerie Aug. Bénard, Liège, 1905, p 487.

5 It is significant, for instance, that Emile Bayard, apart from focusing mainly on those colonies with a monumental heritage – the built environment of *l'Afrique noire* is treated only marginally – also repeatedly tries to link impressive architectural ensembles, like the mosques of Djcnne, to stages of western civilisation. See Emile Bayard, *l'Art de reconnaître les styles coloniaux de la France*, Librairie Gamier, Paris, 1931, pp 118, 125.

6 See François Beguin & Gildas Baudez, '"Arabisances". Observations on French colonial architecture in North Africa between 1900 and 1950', *Lotus International*, 1980, no 26, pp 41-52; & François Beguin, *Arabaisances. Décor architectural et tracé urbain en Afrique du Nord 1830-1950*, Dunod/Bordas, Paris, 1983.

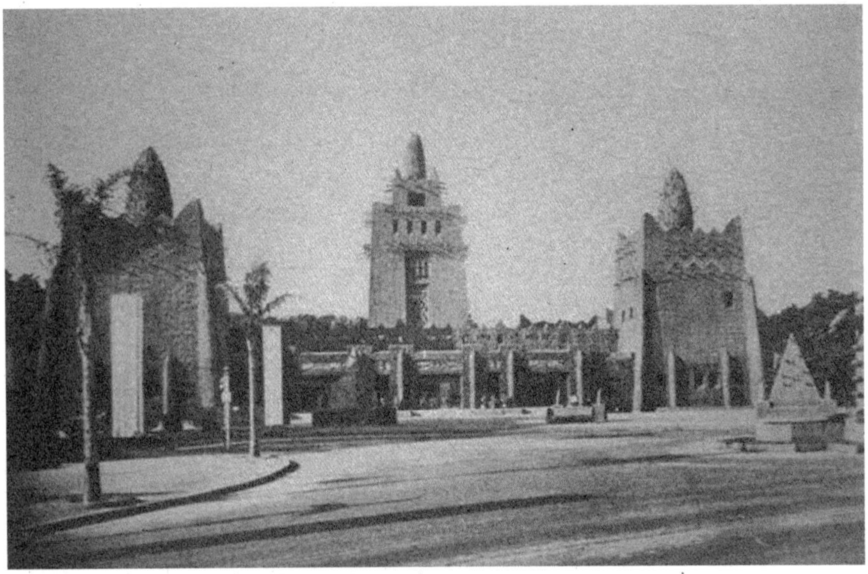

The French West Africa pavilion at the *Exposition Coloniale Internationale* in Vincennes, 1931.

(Antwerp 1894, Brussels 1897, Brussels 1910) and Art Nouveau (Brussels 1897, Paris 1900*), to Vienna Secession (Liege 1905*) and a bizarre form of classicist orientalism (Ghent 1913, Antwerp 1930).[7] Twice, the main pavilion was a replica of a building in the Congo, but significantly in both cases its source was not indigenous but Belgian/colonial in origin: at the 1885 Antwerp Exhibition, the sanatorium in Boma was reconstructed, while the pavilion at the 1905 World's Fair in Liège was modelled on the governor general's residence in Boma, a prefabricated metal construction erected in 1888. Of all these design solutions, only Art Nouveau offered an evocation of the native culture that was truly successful among the visitors: due to the interior decoration of the 1897 Congolese section in Tervuren (a design by Paul Hankar, Henry Van de Velde and other represen- tatives of the Art Nouveau movement) this style became popularly known as the '*style Congo*'. The Congo pavilion built at the 1930 'Exposition Coloniale, Maritime et d'Art Flamand' in Antwerp, however, leaves no doubt that until then the Congo was still not credited with an architecture of its own. Even in the *Rapport Général*, it was admitted that the pavilion was oriental, rather than Congolese, in appearance. The organisers relied on the architect's use of decorations based on indigenous patterns for their defence of the design; close analysis reveals this decoration to be superficial and mediocre.

THE PROBLEMATIC DISPLAY OF AUTHENTICITY

In 1931, just one year after the Antwerp World's Fair, France organised the 'Exposition Coloniale Internationale' in Paris (Vincennes). This event marked a turning point: for the first time (as was noticed in several contemporary commentaries) the visitor was confronted with an authentic architectural representation of the 'traditional Congo'. The architect Henri Lacoste had succeeded in inventing a native architecture by integrating a large number of elements from the Congo's material culture in the building's design. In the contemporary architectural and colonial press, the project was praised unanimously for its powerful and realistic impression. A French critic compared its effect to the Cameroon section, suggesting that in both cases the architects 'proved that they had understood the plain and instinctive grandeur of *art nègre* and had succeeded in interpreting it without deforming its essence'.[8] In historical studies, however, the design has been harshly criticised. Jean-Claude Vigato writes of an 'overblown and regularised hut', while Peter Greenhalgh saw it as an example of a 'mock African' exhibition architecture only serving as a stage set 'in an attempt to mentally transport the visitor away from Europe' and lacking all 'serious architectural considerations'.[9] If there can

7 The asterix (*) indicates that the project in the indicated style was not executed. In 1897 the Congo pavilion was designed in a Beaux-Arts style, but had an Art Nouveau interior.

8 R Cogniat, 'L'Exposition Coloniale. Les Palais metropolitains, les colonies étrangères, les pays sous mandats', *l'Architecture*, vol XLIV no 9, 1931, p 332. If this quote seems to point at Cogniat's sympathy for *art nègre*, the word 'instinctive' reveals that his comment stays in tune with the ethnocentrism of the contemporary colonial discourse.

9 See Jean-Claude Vigato 'The Architecture of the Colonial Exhibitions in France', *Daidalos*, no 19, March 1986, p 30; and Peter Greenhalgh, *Ephemeral Vistas. The Expositions Universelles, Great Exhibitions and World's Fairs, 1851-1939*, Manchester University Press, Manchester, 1988, pp 71-72.

10 This quote from Louis Madeleine is taken from G Périer, 'LeCongo Belge à Vincennes', *L'illustration Congolaise*, no 117, June 1931, p 3555.

11 Vigato, op cit, p 26.

12 Marcel Temporal, 'De la lettre et de l'esprit de l'architecture dite 'moderne' à l'Exposition Coloniale Internationale de 1931', *l'Architecture d'Aujourd'hui*, nr. hors série 'Paris', June-July 1931, p 151.

be little doubt that the essence of Lacoste's design was precisely such mental transportation, I would like to counter some of these criticisms.

First of all, one has to remember that Henri Lacoste was the first architect who did not a priori reject African built forms as a source of inspiration. If he had not actually travelled in the Congo at the time he designed the project, he did make a conscientious effort to study African and Congolese culture. Extensive research in museums and contemporary publications enabled him to develop a profound knowledge of African art, as is proven by his use of rare Congolese sources. Instead of using geometric *velours de Kasaï* motifs (which had already become very popular in the decorative arts by the end of the 1920s), Lacoste inserted animal motifs inspired by little known Yombe textiles in the mosaic floors of the main pavilion. But he also used motifs of non-Congolese origin: references to the cave paintings recently discovered by Leo Frobenius in Rhodesia and South Africa, as well as to artefacts from the Ivory Coast and Gabon, can be traced in the decoration of the 1931 Congo pavilion, revealing the influence of the 1930 Brussels exhibition 'L'Art negre: Les arts anciens de l'Afrique noire' on its design. It is obvious that the artefacts used as sources of inspiration were chosen according to aesthetic, rather than ethnological, principles, but this predominance of aesthetic criteria reflects the reception of indigenous art in Europe at the time. Louis Madeleine, a French architect and close friend of Lacoste's, wrote of the design that 'all [its] details are based on authentic indigenous sources, but have been applied according to a knowledge and approach that belongs only to Europe'.[10] Within the French ethnographic milieu, moreover, it was only at the time of the 'Exposition Coloniale Internationale' that the aesthetic presentation of indigenous objects began to be questioned.

The Congolese section at the *Exposition Coloniale Internationale*, Vincennes, 1931 (architect: Henri Lacoste)

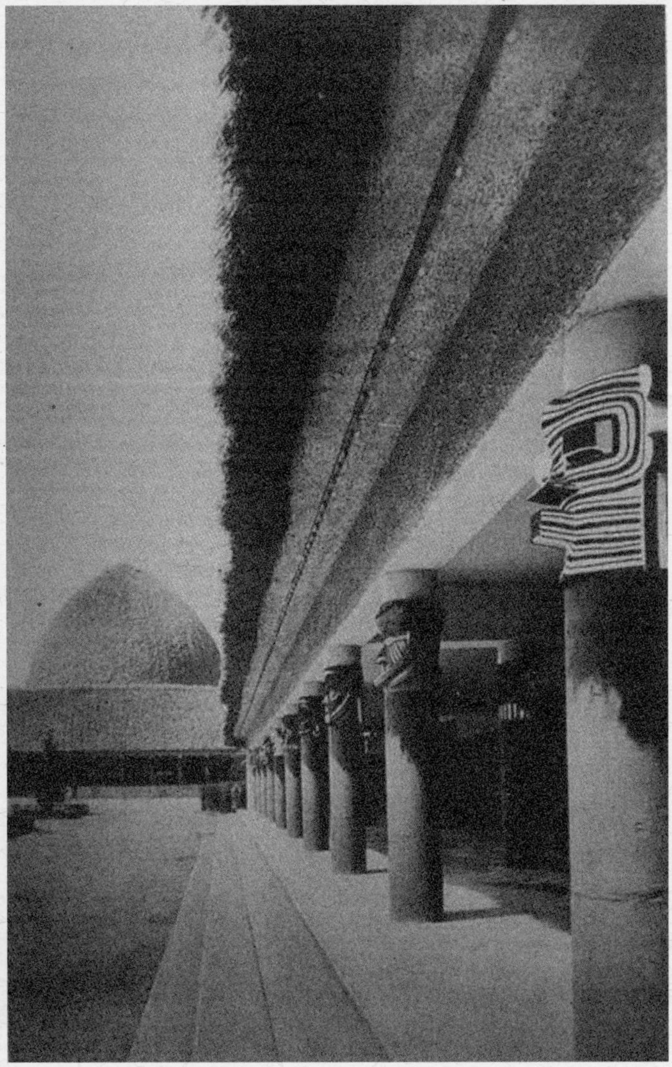

In its use of decoration, Henri Lacoste's design also sheds light on the role of ornament in architecture, a fundamental theme of contemporary architectural debate in Belgium at the time as well as elsewhere. Jean-Claude Vigato has argued that, since the 1925 'Exposition des Arts Decoratifs' in Paris, architects had been seeking to 'reinstate the architectural symbol at the peak of social signification'. In his view the 'Exposition Coloniale Internationale' of 1931, because of its particular ideological programme, offered an ideal context for implementing this ambition.[11] It is significant in this respect that Marcel Temporal, a critic who wrote a commentary on the exposition for *L'Architecture d'Aujourd'hui* in 1931, vehemently reacted against the empty formalism of many pavilions built in the 'modernist' style. The most contemporary designs, according to Temporal, were not the undecorated cubist constructions, but the pavilions 'uniting the spirit of the colonial style, which they should represent, with a formal logic resulting from functional demands'.[12] The examples he used to illustrate his statement were the pavilions of Madagascar, Togo / Cameroon, the Dutch Indies and the Belgian Congo — curiously enough all hybrid reinterpretations of native architectures. Within this selection, Lacoste's design is particularly interesting for its efficient combining of divergent design practices. On the one hand, through the accurate positioning of the three building parts, Lacoste created a visual symmetry from a privileged point of view, with cupolas marking the centre of the volumetric composition. This approach seems to coincide with what Jean-Claude Vigato has described as colonising the vocabulary of exotic architecture through the architectural principles of the *Ecole des Beaux-Arts.*[13] On the other hand, when one analyses the conception of the plans and structure of the pavilions, Lacoste's handling of the programme and the interior layout proves to be in tune with some of the major tenets of architectural functionalism, as suggested by Temporal.[14] Ingenious solutions for illuminating the pavilion were also applied, using new technologies for artificial, indirect lighting.

The apparent dichotomy between the interior and exterior of Lacoste's design — the stage set-like outer appearance versus the very functionally organised interior — is partly dissolved in the striking design of the cupolas, whichdearlyrefertonativearchitecture.Thesecupolasconsistofastructural wooden frame, left unconcealed on the inside and covered with straw on the outside. The frame is made of prefabricated elements, permitting easy assemblage on site and allowing large spans without secondary supports. At the time, this structural solution was regarded as highly innovative. In 1937, the leading periodical *l'Architecture d'Aujourd'hui* would still describe this charpentealamellesas a totally new concept offering promising prospects for future constructions. Yet, as was already noted in 1931 by several critics, the frame simultaneously refers to the construction of indigenous building forms of what were still considered 'primitive' cultures.[15] In its duality — being both 'modern' and 'primitive' — this structural solution of the cupolas blurs preconceived notions of colonial imagery, and embodies the intriguing hybridity of Lacoste's design.[16]

THE PROBLEMATIC DISPLAY OF AUTHENTICITY

If the Congo pavilion at the 1931 'Exposition Coloniale Internationale' was applauded as one of the most remarkable constructions of the event, it did not succeed in setting a standard for the representation of the Belgian colony in the years to come. Marcel Schmitz, an influential Belgian architect and critic, formulated a fundamental critique on this kind of 'authentic display'. In his opinion, colonial sections should function as laboratories for developing a contemporary colonial architecture, rather than as displays for evoking the native culture. Lacoste's design thus offered no solution for future events: 'The hut, used in a very pleasing decorative way indeed by the architect Lacoste in his design for the Belgian pavilion,' Schmitz argued, 'is for current [architectural] practice not an apt source of inspiration. Its essence is too indigenous in nature.'[17] Schmitz's critique was echoed in a letter addressed to the Minister of Colonies in 1933 by Raymond Cloquet, one of the few Belgian architects residing in the Congo at that time. If even as gifted an architect as Lacoste had failed to design a convincing display for the Congo, this was, according to Cloquet, because the documentation assembled in museums and catalogues remained 'empty of life, if one had not experienced it on the spot'.[18] Cloquet, and Schmitz also in a sense, thus suggested that claims of authenticity

13 Vigato, op cit, p 30.

14 Lacoste's own comment on the design of the Congo pavilion is particularly revealing in this respect. See *L'Emulation*, no 12, December 1931 (theme issue devoted to the 1931 Congolese section).

15 See Gaetano Minnuci, 'Notiziario Tecnico: coperture a lamelle', *Architectura e Arti Decorative*, anno X, 1931, vol V-VI, p 408.

16 I am referring to what Pat Morton has described as 'hybrids', ambiguous architectural forms that ruptured a colonial power structure predicated on the strict segregation of things metropolitan and things colonial'. See Pat Morton, 'A Study in Hybridity: Madagascar and Morocco at the 1931 Colonial Exposition', *The Journal of Architectural Education*, vol 52 no 2, November 1998, pp 76-86.

17 Marcel Schmitz, 'Architecture coloniale', *le Bâtiment*, August 1931, pp 17-18 (Africa Archive, Brussels).

18 Letter from Raymond Cloquet to the Minister of Colonies, January 3, 1933 (Africa Archive, Brussels). Cloquet's critique, however, was not without bias hecause in his letter he was himself applying for the commission to design the Congolese section of the 1935 Brussels World's Fair.

19 Letter from Raymond Moenaert to the Minister of Colonies, November 3, 1931 (Africa Archive, Brussels).

20 The project, ambitiously entitled Reconstruction géohydrographique et climatérique d'un voyage d'exploration au Congo Belge', was also announced in the colonial press, see *L'Illustration Congolaise*, no 146, 1st November 1931, pp 4708-4715.

could only be made in reference to the contemporary situation in the Congo, not in reference to an invented past.

During the preparation of the 1935 Brussels World's Fair, two projects for the Congolese section were submitted to the Ministry of Colonies that reveal this shifting interpretation of authenticity. The first proposal had already been put forward at the end of 1931 by Raymond Moenaert, the architect who had won the competition for the construction of the new governor general's residence in Leopoldville, without doubt themajor public building commission in the Belgian colony. Moenaert regretted that the Belgian colony had until then always been represented by phantasmagoric images. 1n his view, a new concept was needed and he therefore proposed to build the governor general's residence at the 1935 Brussels exhibition. Even if the economic crisis had temporarily halted the construction of the actual residence in Leopoldville, this proposal, in his view, was the most authentic display imaginable: by reconstructing his residence project, the Congolese section would become 'a [contemporary] part of Kinshasa, imported and implanted in Belgian soil'.[19] If Schmitz had known of this proposal, he would surely have supported it, because at various occasions he had praised Moenaert's residence project and its' *'style hispano-colonial'* as a rare example of a truly contemporary colonial architecture for the Congo.

The contrast with the second proposal for the Congolese section in Brussels in 1935 could not have been more striking. Submitted by Henri Lacoste in 1933, the proposal consisted of a huge exhibition hall containing a *panorama atmosphérique* that would offer the visitor the experience of an expedition that crossed three climate zones in the Congo: the savannah, a tropical forest and the mountain range of the Ruwenzori.[20] Lacoste's proposal can be seen as a reinterpretation of the informal African villages at previous expositions, yet its claims of authenticity were even more emphatic: the latest engineering technologies, it was argued, would be used to replicate environmental conditions, and the panorama would generate visual, as well as tactile, olfactory and auditory sensations. Lacoste originally thought of masking the exhibition hall with an overblown version of his design for the 'Exposition Coloniale Internationale' of 1931. In the end, however, he changed the outer appearance completely and clad the gigantic hall with a striking modern façade. This change clearly reveals the ethno-centric character of the project.

Proposal for the Congolese section at the Brussel's World's Fair of 1935 (architect: Henri Lacoste) – the *panorama atmospheriques*, second project for the facade.
©Archives d'Architecture Modeme, Brussels, Belgium

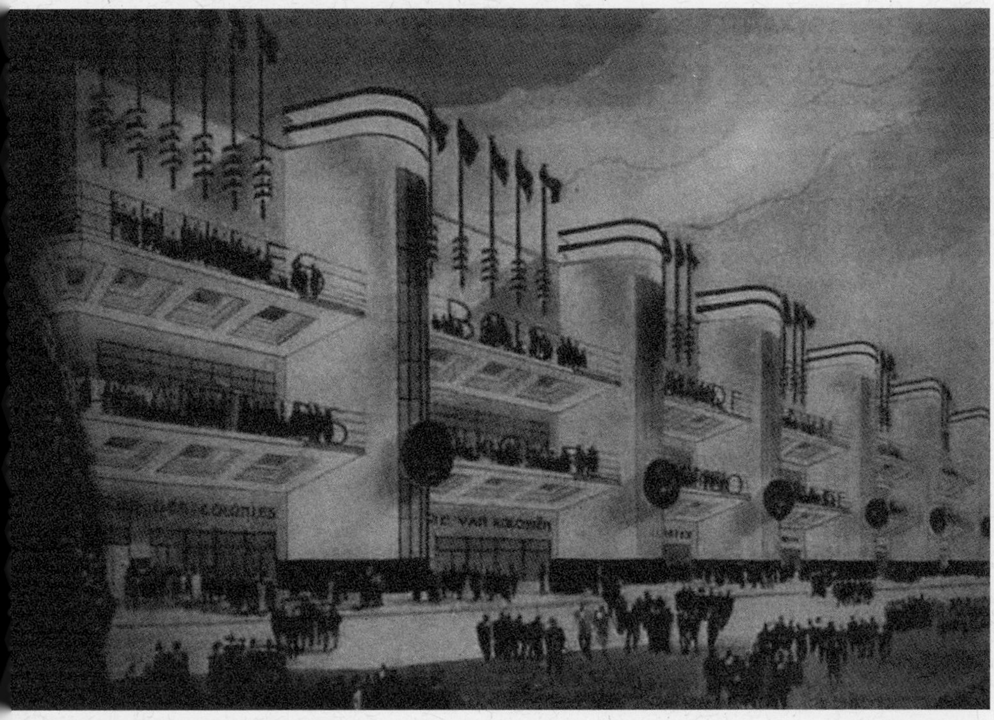

In fact, the *panorama atmosphérique* was based on the blunt confrontation of the so-called 'primitive' African regions, experienced inside, and the contemporary civilisation of the West, as presented at the exit, where an impressive view over the city of Brussels was offered. Thus, the panorama legitimised the civilising mission of Belgian colonialism in the same way as nineteenth century colonial sections had done. Within only two years, Lacoste seems to have lost all the subtlety and productive ambivalence that had marked his design approach for the Congo pavilion of the 1931 exhibition.

CELEBRATINGA CINQUANTENAIRE

The Brussels exhibition of 1935 marked the 50th birthday of Belgian colonialism.[21] It should have been a glorious event, but in reality, it was disillusioning. Because of the economic crisis, the colonial government made only a minor investment in the Congolese section. The proposals by Moenaert and Lacoste were rejected, and in the end the official Congo pavilion was built by an engineer-architect of the Ministry of Colonies, Rene Schoentjes. Schoentjes's design approach was an attempt to invent a native architecture, very similar to what Lacoste had done in 1931. Schoentjes used a wider range of references, however, combining sources from Central African, Islamic and Egyptian material culture. This approach was reviewed very differently by his contemporaries. While a prominent connoisseur and promoter of African art, Gaston-Denys Perier, was enthusiastic about the design, the *Commissaire Générale* of the exhibition harshly criticised the fact that Schoentjes applied decorative patterns from contemporary catalogues of commercial interior design, which, in his view, completely undermined the harmony of the design.[22] While Schoentjes's design shows several similarities with the 1931 Congo pavilion, a comparison of both projects quickly reveals the former's lack of subtlety and skill in the formal treatment as well as in the handling of space.

Furthermore, the Congo's representation at the 1935 Brussels exhibition lacked the unity that had been so characteristic of the Congolese section at the 'Exposition Coloniale Internat-ionale'. This was partly because the several parts of the Brussels section were designed by different architects. Two colonial pavilions flanking the official building were designed by Victor Bourgeois, the most prominent figure among Belgian modernist architects. On close analysis, Bourgeois's designs did not really address the issue of representing the Congo in an architectural manner. The 'Leopold II' restaurant stayed completely in tune with the

The front facade of the Congo pavilion at the Brussels World's Fair of 1935 (architect: Rene Schoentjes)

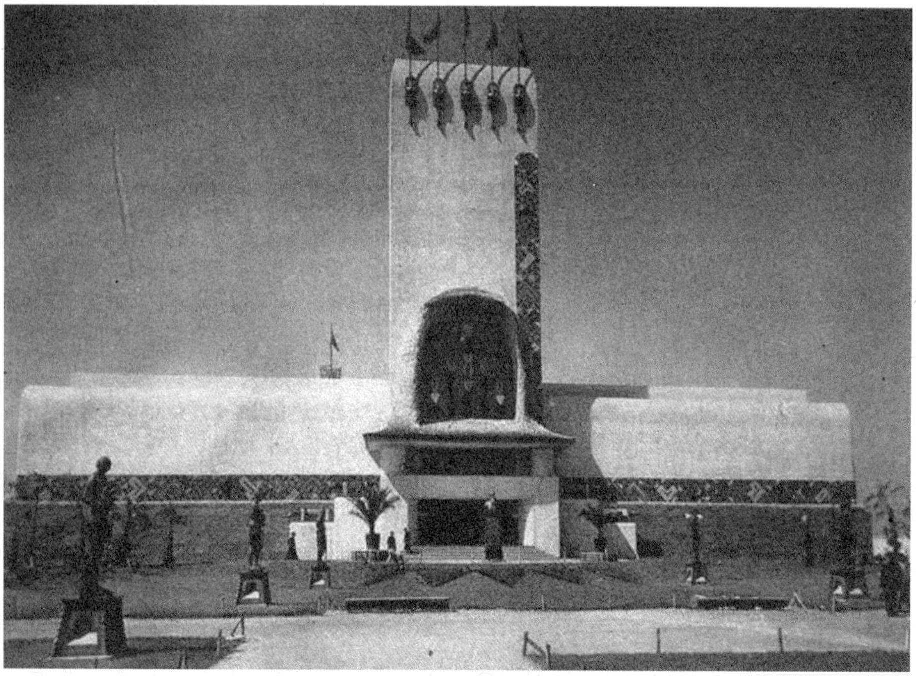

21 For a more extensive discussion of the Congolese section at the 1935 Brussels World's Fair, as well as a general survey of the architecture, see Johan Lagae & Jef Vervoort, *The Universal and International Exhibition* in Brussels, 1935, website, Department of Architecture and Urbanism, Ghent University, 2000. **arch.rug.ac.be/expo35**

22 See Gaston-Denys Périer, L'enchantement congolais à l'Exposition', *Revue du Touring Club de Belgique*, 15 April 1935, pp 116-120; and the correspondence between the *Commissaire Général* and the Minister of Colonies (Africa Archive, Brussels).

23 These frescoes were probably painted by the contemporary Congolese artist of Bapende origin, Massalai, who also decorated the colonial enterprises pavilion, a design by Schoentjes and Douret. Massalaï was one of the artists who at the time were promoted in the Belgian artistic milieu by Gaston-Denys Périer.

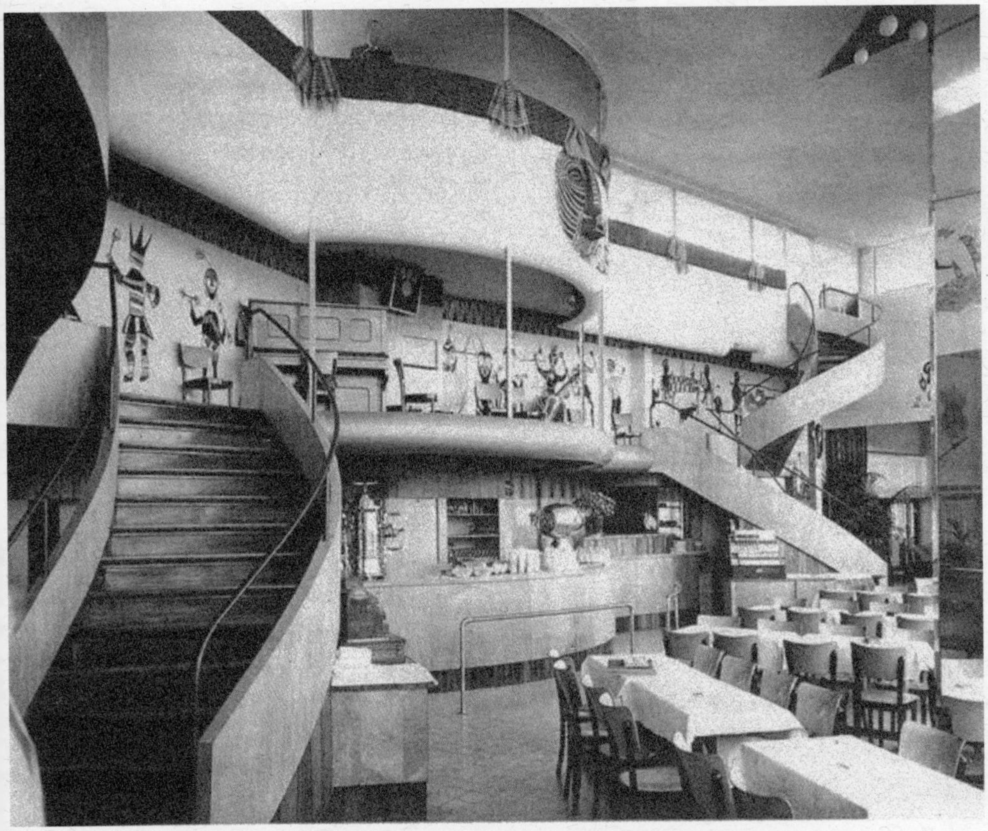

The Leopold II restaurant at the Brussel's World's Fair of 1935 (architect: Victor Bourgeois)

sober modernist style characteristic of Bourgeois's œuvre and, apart from the food served, only the frescoes in the interior, depicting curious Congolese figures, reminded the visitor of its connection with the colony.[23] But it is in the pavilion that housed the Congo's tourist industry displays that Bourgeois's failure to create an architectural language capable of referring to the colonial programme, while remaining in accordance with the tenets of modernism, is most apparent. At one stage of the design-process, Bourgeois even produced a design solution for the entrance reminiscent of the three cupolas of the 1931 Congolese section, which fails to be more than an immature paraphrase.[24]

REPRESENTING THE MODERN CONGO

For many visitors, the Congolese section at the Brussels exhibition of 1935 waspervaded with a sense of *déjà-vu*, because of the reuse of exhibits and displays from former exhibitions. Moreover, the section had not functioned as an architectural workshop in which a contemporary colonial architecture could be developed. Interest in the topic, however, was minimal among Belgian architects, even if, from the late 1920s on, initiatives had been made to stimulate a debate on colonial building. That colonial architecture was not a priority on the political agenda of the government — a fact most clearly illustrated by its decision to abandon, albeit temporarily, all initiatives for building the new governor general's residence in Leopoldville in 1932 — was no doubt a major reason for this lack of interest in the architectural milieu.[25] That the Ministry of Colonies had resorted to the approach of an invented native architecture for the 1935 Congolese section was probably also due to the public success of the 1931 section and the conviction that most visitors were still enchanted by the exotic exhibition architecture. Yet, Schoentjes's and Bourgeois's rather mediocre designs made it clear that such a display was gradually becoming untenable, as it was incapable of representing contemporary colonisation in the Congo.

This was the reason, at least in part, why the organisers of the Congolese section at the Paris 'Exposition des Arts et des Techniques dans la Vie Moderne' of 1937 explicitly chose an opposite strategy. They claimed to give the visitor an impression of the modern way of life in the colony, suggesting at

24 Bourgeois's contribution to the Brussels Congolese section blurs the image of Bourgeois as a 'master of modern architecture in Belgium', but one has to remember that Bourgeois's importance lies primarily in his activity as a critic and promoter of modernist ideology in Belgium, rather than in the quality of his architectural oeuvre.

25 In this respect, the situation in the Belgian Congo differs from that in French, British or Italian colonies. No comprehensive analysis of colonial architecture in the Congo has been made. For a brief introduction to the topic, see Anne Van Loo, 'Page Coloniale', *Paysages d'Architecture*. Archives d'Architecture Moderne, Brussels, 1986, pp 52-55.

the same time that 'ideas of tradition and exoticism by no means have to stand in opposition to a sense of transformation and new conceptions'. The colony was presented by means of an elegantly designed bungalow with an encompassing veranda, representing the ideal home of a Belgian colonial.[26] The pavilion was modelled on the colonial bungalows that had been imported in the tropics since the late nineteenth century and which had provided Europeans with comfortable living conditions in this tormenting climate. At he time of the Paris exposition, however, such bungalows were no longer the most common type of housing for white colonisers in Congo. Due to emerging urbanisation in the colony, they had been replaced since the early 1920s by designs that were based on the middle-class villas of Belgian garden cities.[27]

The 1937 Congolese section thus cultivated the romantic image of the domestic life of colonial pioneers, rather than offering an accurate view of contemporary daily life in the Belgian colony. It failed to define an architectural image for the 'new Congo' that was characterised by gradual modernisation. In fact, the section placed only a minor focus on technological progress; and the visitor was reminded only in a subtle way of the importance of the expanding industries in the Congo. Delicately arranged displays illustrated how many contemporary products were derived from raw materials of Congolese origin. In comparison, the display of technological progress in the Congolese section at the 'Exposition Coloniale Internationale' had been far more straightforward. In the interior of the pavilions of the 1931 section, the different infrastructural networks and mining exploitation in the colony had been presented through impressive stands that showed part of a bridge, for example, and an aeroplane. This interior display of the modernised Congo formed an ambivalent alliance with its exterior design that aimed at representing Congo's native culture. In this sense, the Congolese section at the 'Exposition Coloniale Internationale' of 1931 exemplifies an 'architectural ambivalence' in the sense that the 'invented hybrid exterior acts as mediator between a prestigious western presence in the interior and an absent, native environment, considered not worth showing'.[28]

THE END OF AUTHENTIC DISPLAYS?

If representing the Belgian Congo by means of an authentic display of the colony's native culture had been a primary concern at the 1931 'Exposition Coloniale Internationale', by the end of the 1930s such concern for authenticity was no longer considered important. Colonial propaganda now almost

Fragment of a bas relief on the outside of the Belgian pavilion that marked the Congolese section at the New York World's Fair of 1939 (sculptor: A. Dupagne)

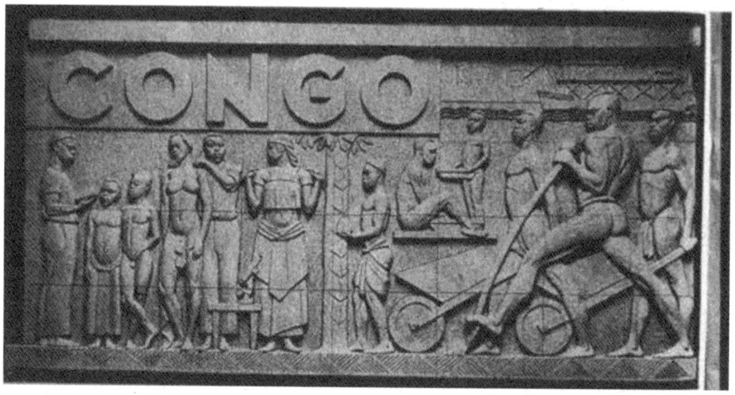

26 See 'Congo Belge', in *Exposition Internationale des Arts et des Techniques dans la Vie Moderne, Paris 1937. Rapport Général présenté par Ed. Labbé*, Paris, 1938-1940, Tome 9, pp 106-110. The design was by the architect Fernand Petit,

27 See Johan Lagae, In search of a "comme chez soi". The Ideal Colonial House in Congo: a survey', in Jean-Luc Vellut (ed), *Irruptions de la modernité dans l'ancien Congo Belge c. 1900-1950*, Tervuren / Louvain-la-Neuve (forthcoming 2000).

28 I am quoting a definition of the notion of 'architectural ambivalence', as suggested by Hilde Heynen and André Loeckx in their comment on Pat Morton's discussion of the Madagascar pavilion at the 1931 'Exposition Colonial Internationale': see 'Scenes of Ambivalence: Concluding remarks on Architectural Patterns of Displacement', *The Journal of Architectural Education*, vol 52 no 2, November 1998, p 103.

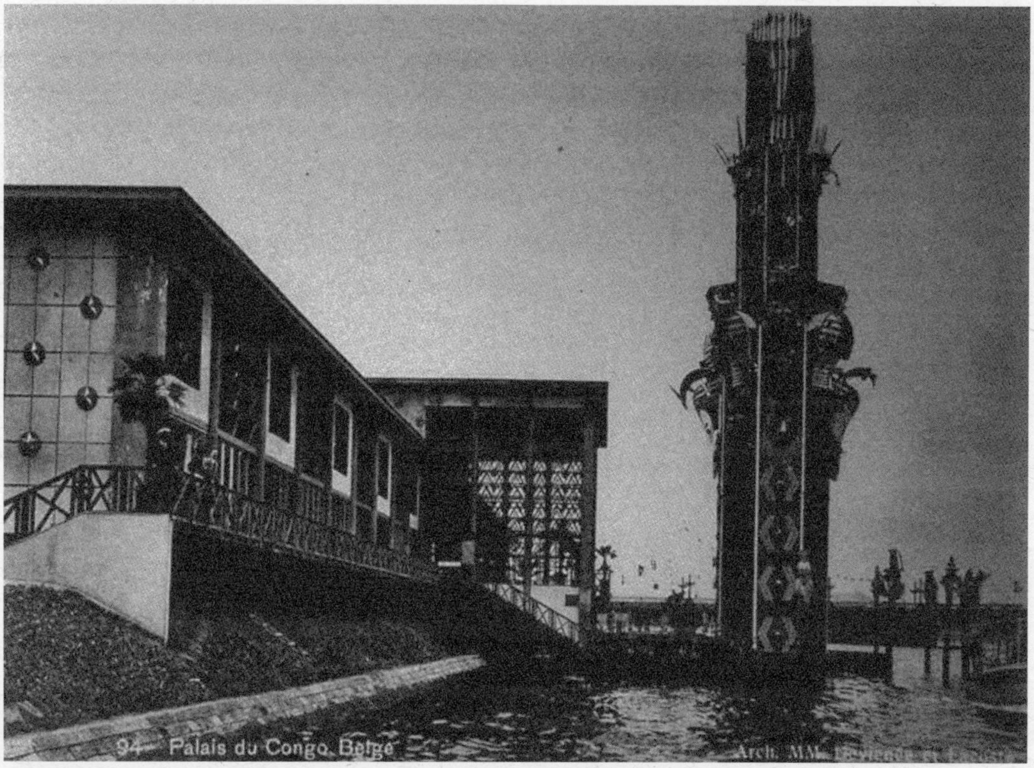

The Congolese section at the *Exposition Internationale de la Technique de l'Eau*, Liège, 1939 (architect: Henri Lacoste), contemporary postcard (collection: Denys Lacoste)

exclusively focused on the modernisation of the Congo - a shift in attention which can be illustrated by reviewing the two Congolese sections that were designed for international exhibitions in 1939. The first section was built at the New York World's Fair, organised on the theme 'The World of Tomorrow'. As the presence of the Belgian colony at this fair was primarily a marketing strategy to promote the Congolese diamond industry in the United States, the organisers did not make any efforts to create an authentic display. The Congolese section was not even housed in a separate building, but formed a part of the Belgian pavilion. The architects, who included Victor Bourgeois, had avoided all exotic formal vocabulary and used a modernist idiom. On the outside, only a bas-relief revealed the presence of a Congolese section. In the luxurious but sober interior, elements referring to Congo's native culture were restricted as much as possible.[29]

The representation of the Belgian colony in New York contrasted greatly with the Congolese section at the 'Exposition Internationale de la Technique de l'Eau', held in Liege the same year. At this event, the Congolese section was meant to promote Belgium's civilising mission in the colony by displaying the progress made in hydraulic engineering, water purification and water supply. The overall architectural co-ordination of the exposition was given to a team of young architects who imposed strict design rules, based on a functionalist doctrine.[30] This did not, however, prevent Henri Lacoste, commissioned to design the Congolese section, from repeating his design approach of 1931. He submitted a proposal for a phantasmagoric Congolese setting, placing four gigantic golden elephants in the canal running in front of the pavilion.[31] Due to financial restrictions, the design was strongly simplified, and, in the end, the elephants were replaced by a huge, totem pole-like construction, decorated with Congolese masks and armoury. If such an approach had been apt for

29 The Congolese section in New York, designed by Victor Bourgeois and Léon Stynen under the supervision of Henry Van de Velde, was commented on in detail in *L'Illustration Congolaise*, nos 213 & 215, 1939, Pp 7352-7353 & 7439-7442. For the official ambitions of both the New York and Liège exhibition, see *L'Illustration Congolaise*, no 214, 1939, pp 7404-7405, 7417.

30 See G Dedoyard, 'L'Architecture à l'Exposition', in *Exposition Internationale de la Technique de l'Eau, Liège 1939. Rapport Général*, pp 75-107; and Xavier Folville, 'Le Corbusier, le Groupe Equerre et 'Exposition de l'Eau' [1939], in P Burniat (ed), *Le Corbusier en Belgique*, CFC-Editions, Bruxelles/ Fondation LC, Paris, 1997, PP 187-198.

31 Design note by Henri Lacoste (Africa Archive, Brussels). Further information on the Congolese section in Liège was found in the *Rapport Général*, the Lacoste files in the Archives 'Architecture Moderne, Brussels, and the personal archives of the Lacoste family.

the 'Exposition Coloniale Internationale' in Vincennes — which, in the end, was the ultimate 'Theatre des Colonies' — it was rather out of place at the Liège exhibition. Lacoste's design was not capable of grasping the essence of the 'Exposition de l'Eau', which was purely a celebration of technological progress, nor did it create a meaningful image of the emerging 'new Congo'.

In only a few years, the strategy of inventing a Congolese architecture had been outstripped. But the Congolese section at the New York World Fair could hardly be regarded as a suitable alternative, as the mental connection with the colony's culture was established not through the architectural design but by purely decorative means. The architectural representation of the Belgian Congo thus remained problematic, all the more so because from 1945 onwards, indigenous populations' struggles for independence could no longer be neglected. The Congolese section of the Brussels World's Fair of 1958, however, made it rather shamefully clear that this new situation was not yet fully understood.[32]

OPPORTUNITIES FOR CREATIVITY

One can legitimately criticise the various Congolese sections I have discussed here for their underlying ethnocentrtc preconceptions. The 'voice of the colonised' was totally absent in these representations of the Congo. Moreover, the general assumption that the Congo did not have a native architectural tradition worthy of attention was never questioned by architects, most of whom had never even been to the colony. Given his projects for the 1935 and 1939 expositions, not even Henri Lacoste fully deserves to be noted as an exception, despite the fact that his design for the 1931 'Exposition Coloniale Internationale', in my view, offers a rare glimpse of hybridity, capable of breaking open fixed notions of colonialist imagery. Because of the general acceptance that a native architectural tradition was non-existent in the Congo, there were no appropriate models available for the Belgian architects who were commissioned to design a Congo pavilion. But this situation should not necessarily be regarded as restrictive: it actually offered architects a rare opportunity for creativity and imagination. While the native architectures of north or west African colonies offered French architects ample inspiration, just as the built heritage in India provided models for the British, designing these pavilions could easily become a dangerous routine. Sylvianne Leprun has rightly blamed the '*déssèchement créatif*' in French colonial sections.[33] As the many divergent design solutions discussed here illustrate, in Congolese sections this 'desiccation of creativity' was much less to be feared. This is not to say that Belgian architects always succeeded in designing pavilions that were innovative from an architectural point of view, or that they offered that rare quality of hybridity. Still, I believe that analysing these colonial displays offers particular opportunities to reveal specific aspects of contemporaneous arcpitectural practices. Tlu-ough such analysis we might gain a more nuanced understanding of architecture as visual representation and as a discipline, as well as of the role of architecture in the realm of colonialism.

This article is an extended and reworked version of a paper presented at the 52nd Annual Meeting of Architectural Historians in Houston, Texas, 14th-18th April, 1999. I would like to thank Lisa Schrenk, Mil De Kooning and Jean-Luc Vellut for their comments during the various stages of this research. Unless otherwise noted, translations are my own.

---

32 1956 marked a turning point regarding the indigenous population's claims for independence in the Belgian Congo, and many historians consider the 1958 Brussels fair as a catalyst for Congo's struggle for independence, leading to the end of Belgian colonial rule only two years later. Yet, within most of the colonialists's minds, the idea of Congo becoming independent in Tune 1960 was inconceivable as late as 1958.

33 Leprun, op cit, p 212.

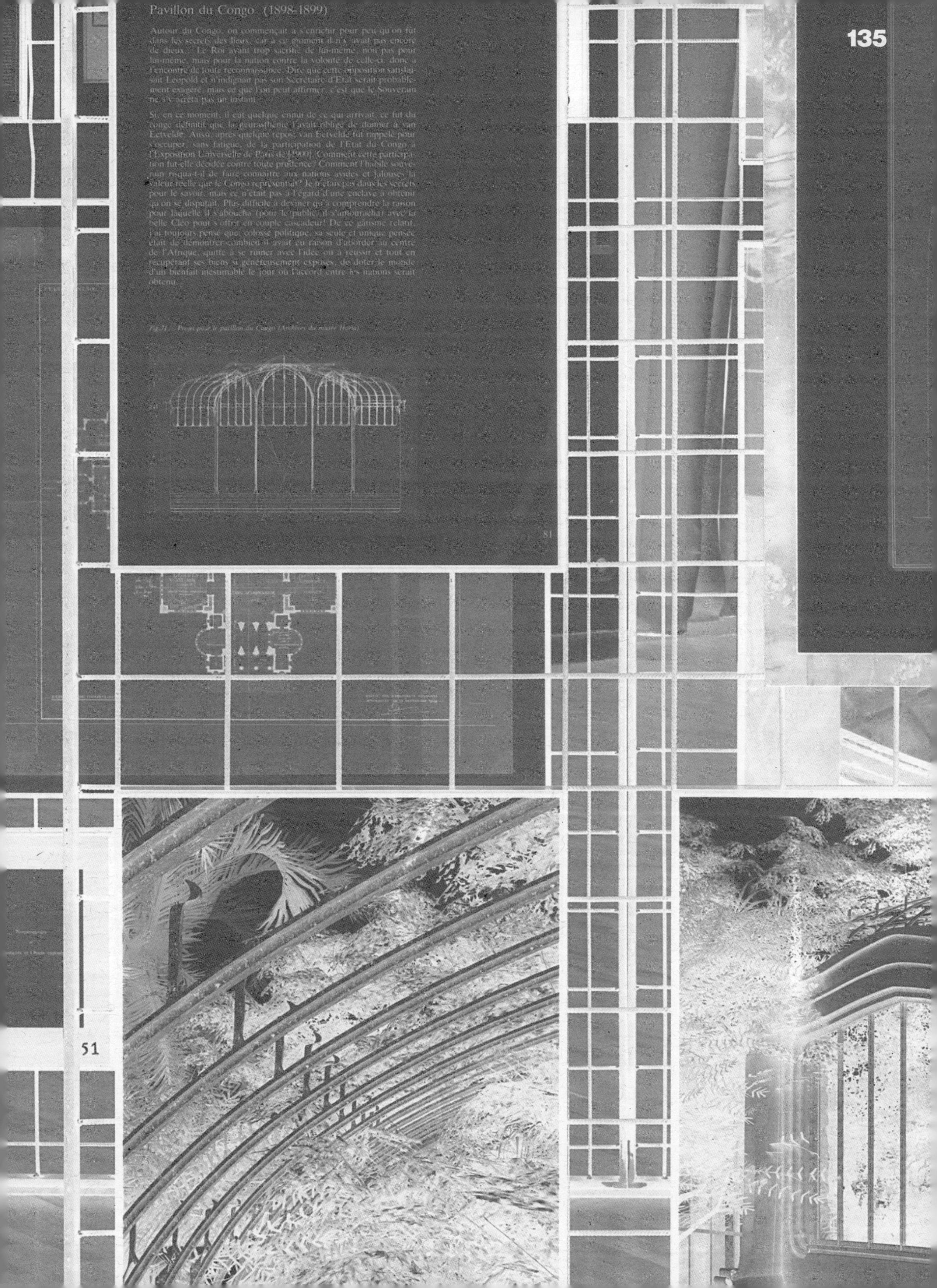

Pavillon du Congo (1898-1899)

Autour du Congo, on commençait à s'enrichir pour peu qu'on fût dans les secrets des lieux, car à ce moment il n'y avait pas encore de dieux... Le Roi ayant trop sacrifié de lui-même, non pas pour lui-même, mais pour la nation contre la volonté de celle-ci, donc à l'encontre de toute reconnaissance. Dire que cette opposition satisfaisait Léopold et n'indignait pas son Secrétaire d'Etat serait probablement exagéré, mais ce que l'on peut affirmer, c'est que le Souverain ne s'y arrêta pas un instant.

Si, en ce moment, il eut quelque ennui de ce qui arrivait, ce fut du congé définitif que la neurasthénie l'avait obligé de donner à van Eetvelde. Aussi, après quelque repos, van Eetvelde fut rappelé pour s'occuper, sans fatigue, de la participation de l'Etat du Congo à l'Exposition Universelle de Paris de [1900]. Comment cette participation fut-elle décidée contre toute prudence? Comment l'habile souverain risqua-t-il de faire connaître aux nations avides et jalouses la valeur réelle que le Congo représentait? Je n'étais pas dans les secrets pour le savoir, mais ce n'était pas à l'égard d'une enclave à obtenir qu'on se disputait. Plus difficile à deviner qu'à comprendre la raison pour laquelle il s'aboucha (pour le public, il s'amouracha) avec la belle Cléo pour s'offrir en couple cascadeur! De ce gâtisme relatif, j'ai toujours pensé que, colosse politique, sa seule et unique pensée était de démontrer combien il avait eu raison d'aborder au centre de l'Afrique, quitte à se ruiner avec l'idée ou à réussir et tout en récupérant ses biens si généreusement exposés, de doter le monde d'un bienfait inestimable le jour où l'accord entre les nations serait obtenu.

Fig.71 — Projet pour le pavillon du Congo (Archives du musée Horta)

81

51

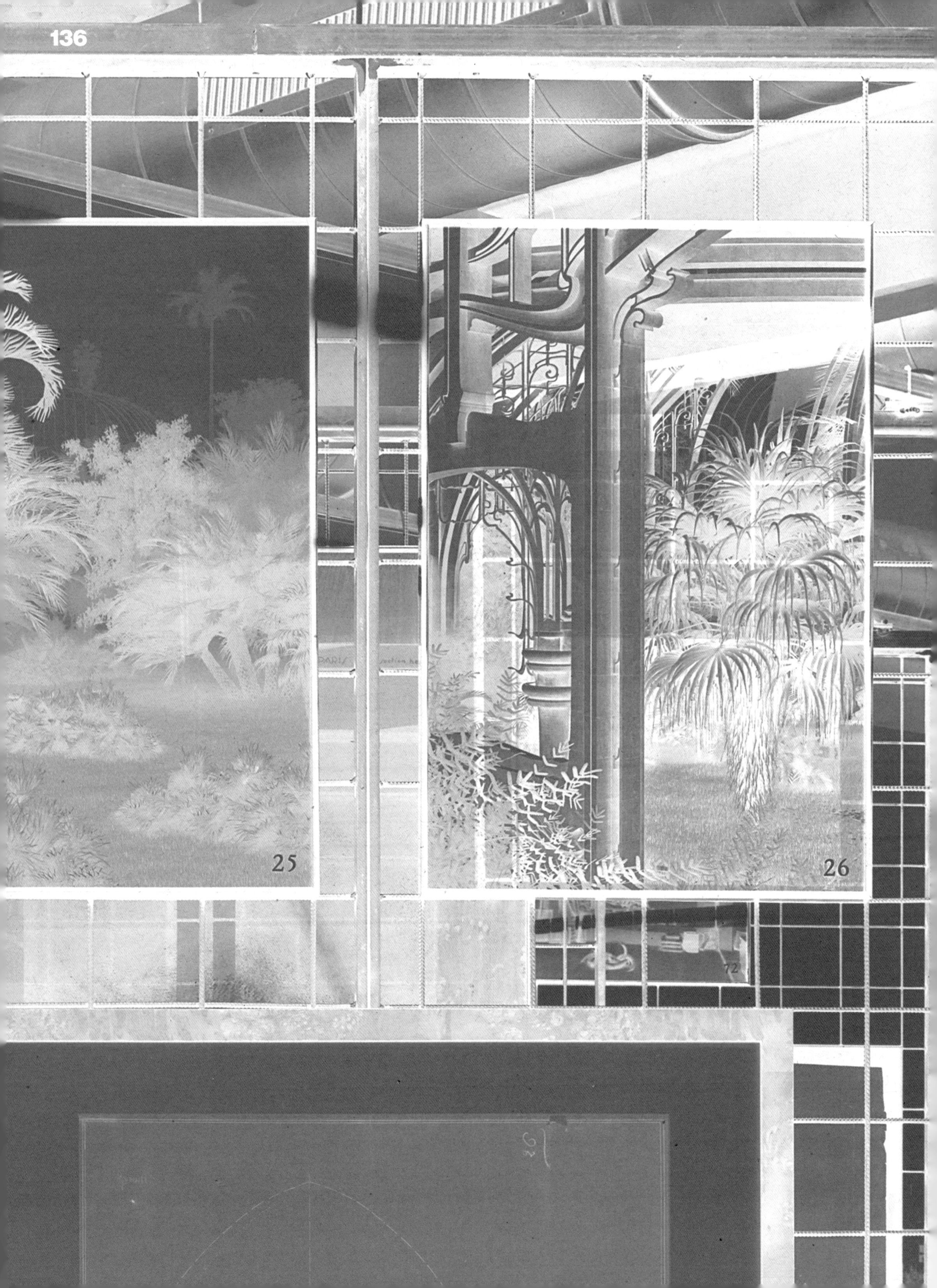
25
26
72

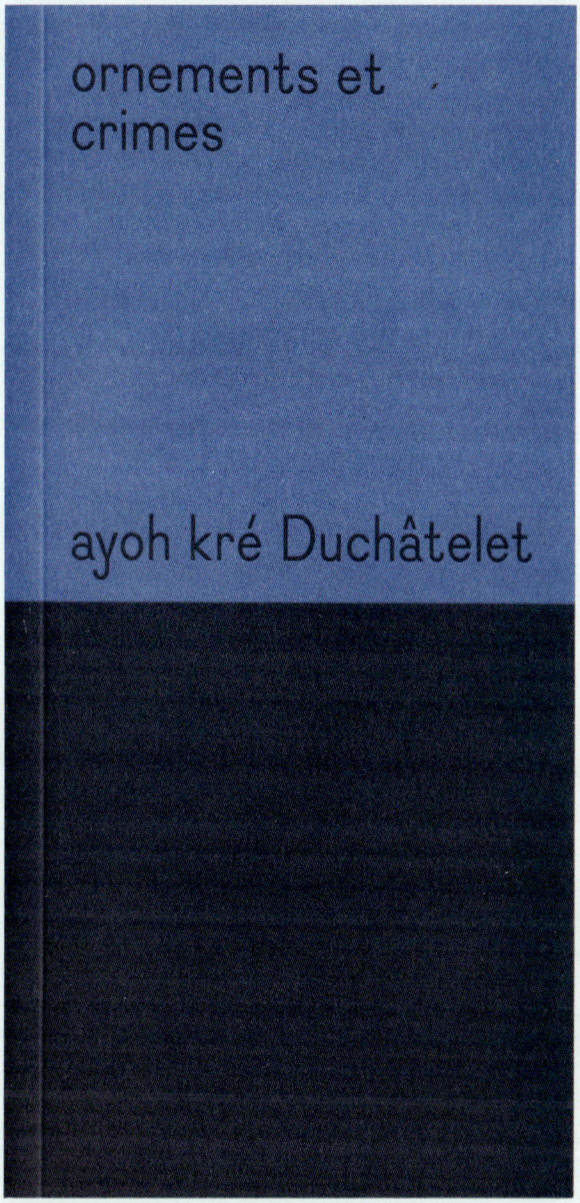

ayoh kré Duchâtelet, *Ornements et Crimes*, 2023. Novel.
Courtesy of the artist

In the textual work entitled *Ornaments and Crimes*, ayoh kré Duchâtelet tells the story of an investigation into a mysterious image disease that spread between Belgium and the Congo Free State at the end of the 19th century. The story unfolds around Art Nouveau ornaments found in Brussels and the crimes committed along the Matadi-Kinshasa railway line. The installation shown in the exhibition materializes a scene from this narrative, in the manner of a movie set. It is presented as a listening room for a sound composition produced from recordings taken in the former colonial ABC Hotel (Hôtel Alimentation du Bas-Congo), built at the beginning of the 20th century with prefabricated iron elements in the Art Nouveau style, which was then converted into a courtroom in the small Congolese town of Mbanza-Ngungu, near the railroad. This second story can be perceived as the soundtrack to a film whose scenes are to be imagined by the listener. The installation is part of the series entitled *hearing rooms*, which traces the troubled relationships between the wide range of images produced both inside and out of the body by the hallucinatory delirium of the colonial era. The two drawings hanging in the installation also deal with these issues, depicting fragments of chryselephantine statues presented in the Congolese pavilion of the 1897 International Exposition in Brussels: Charles Van der Stappen's *Mysterious Sphinx* and Philippe Wolfers' *The Caress of the Swan*.

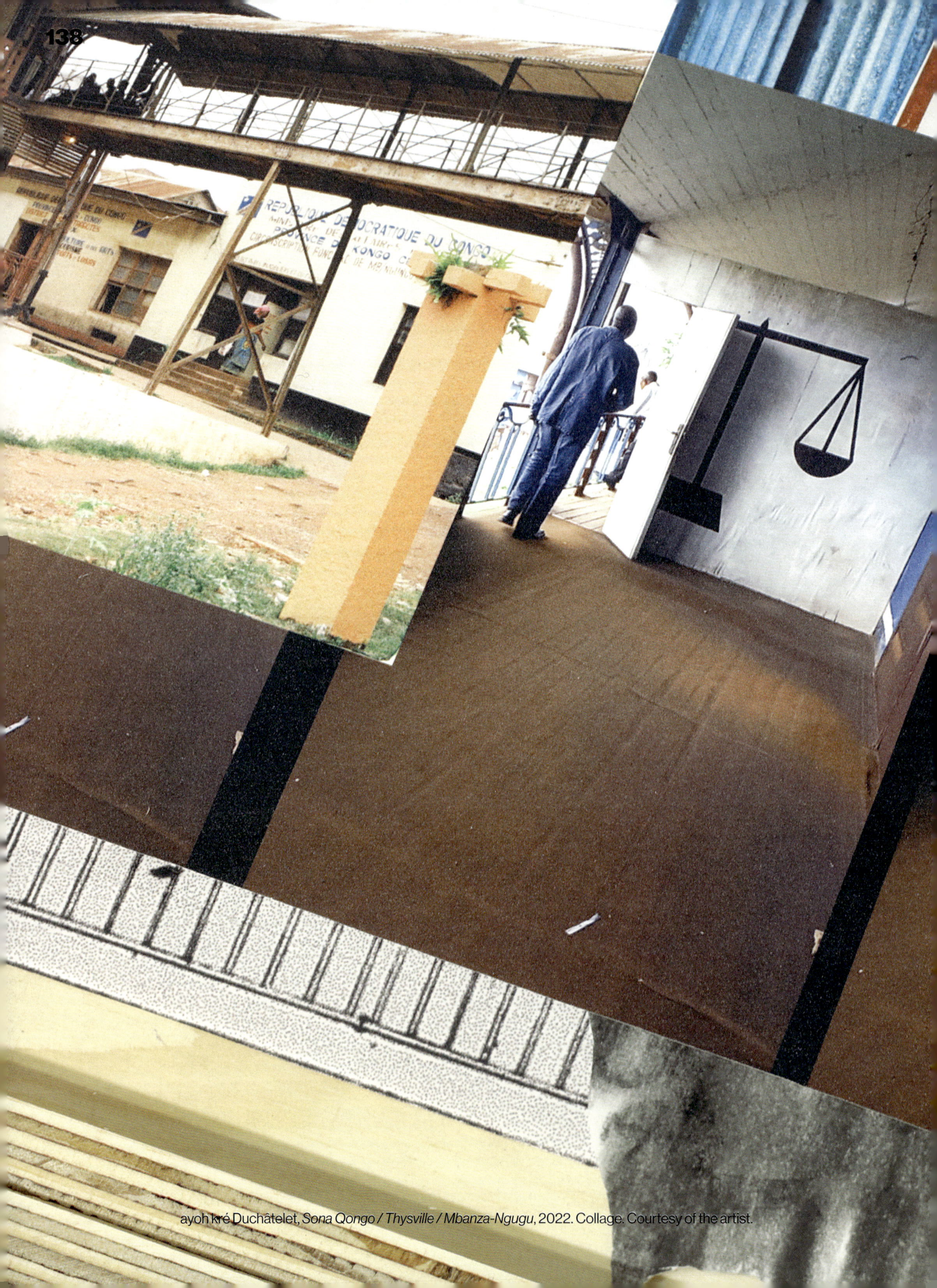

ayoh kré Duchâtelet, *Sona Qongo / Thysville / Mbanza-Ngugu*, 2022. Collage. Courtesy of the artist.

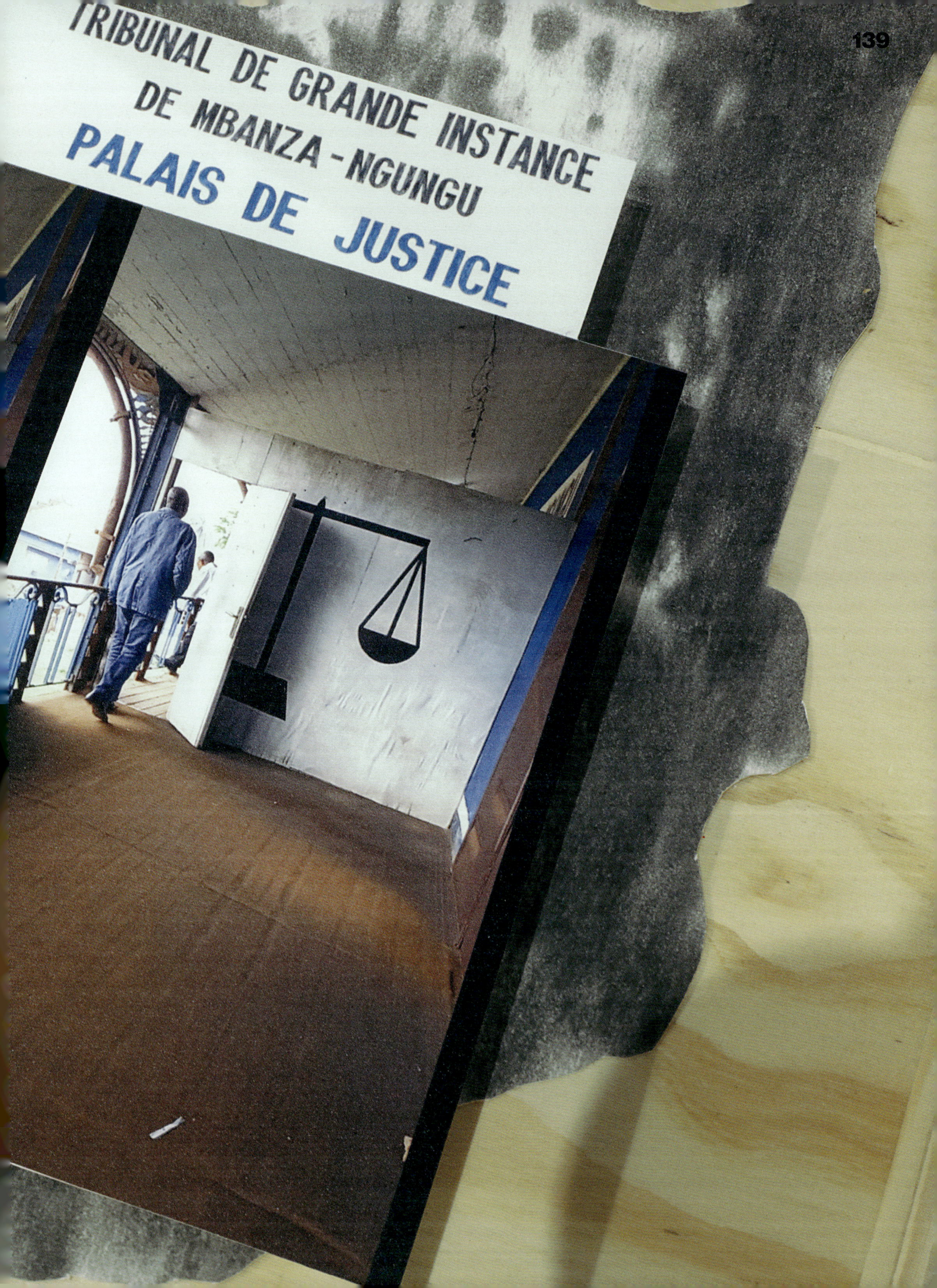
TRIBUNAL DE GRANDE INSTANCE
DE MBANZA-NGUNGU
PALAIS DE JUSTICE

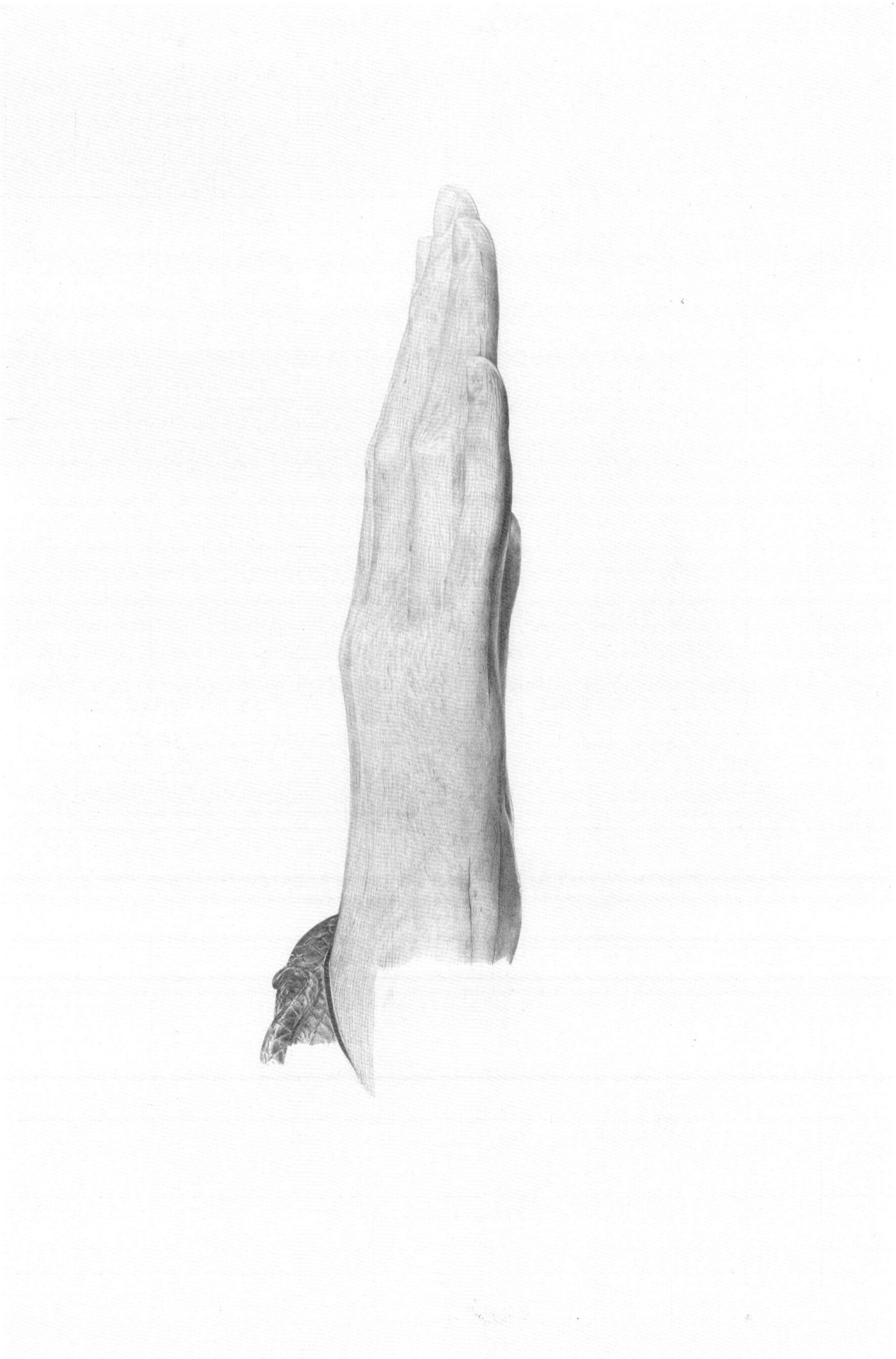

ayoh kré Duchâtelet, *Ornements et Crimes*, 2023. Graphite on paper. Courtesy of the artist

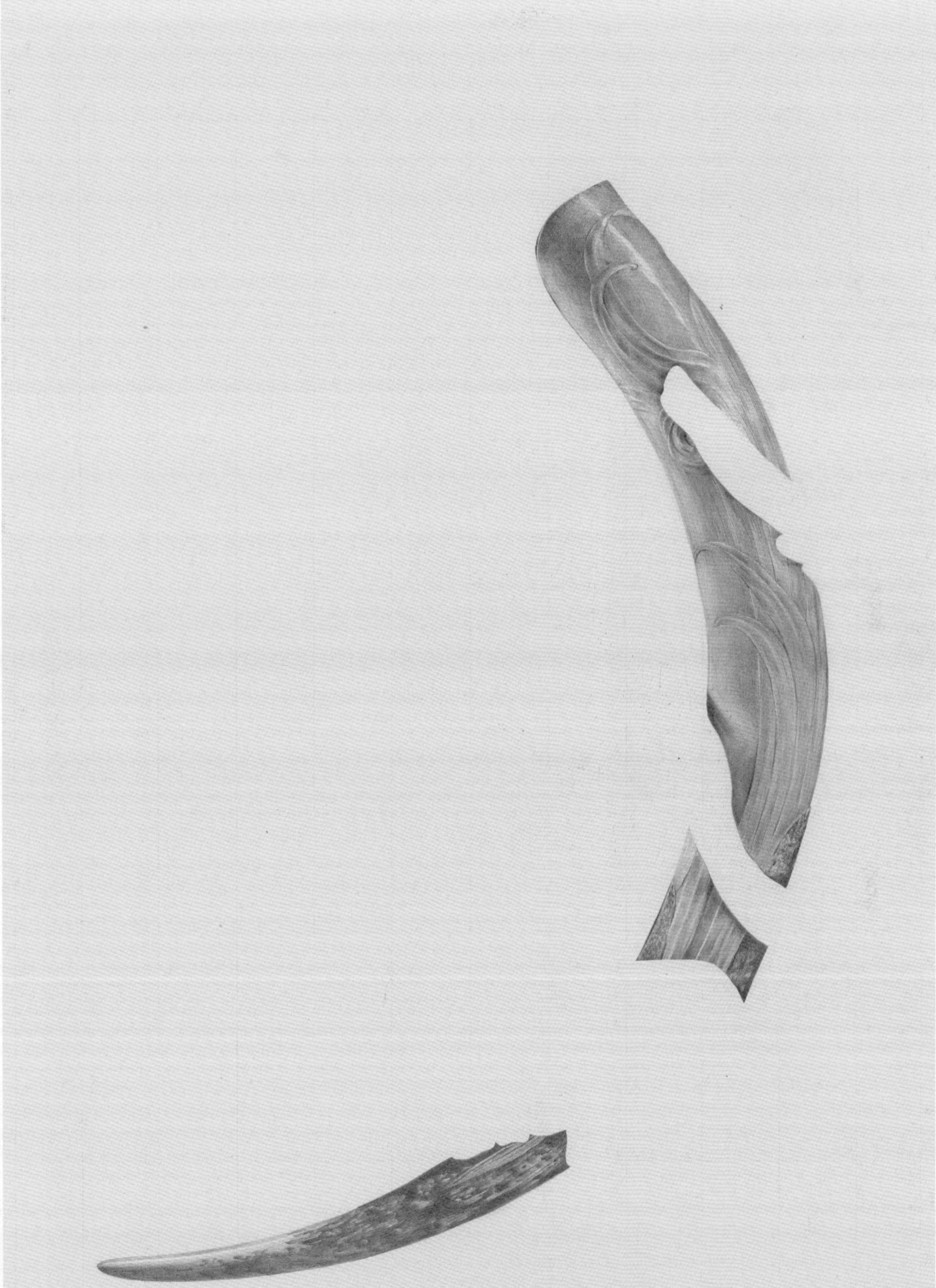

ayoh kré Duchâtelet, *Ornements et Crimes*, 2023. Graphite on paper. Courtesy of the artist

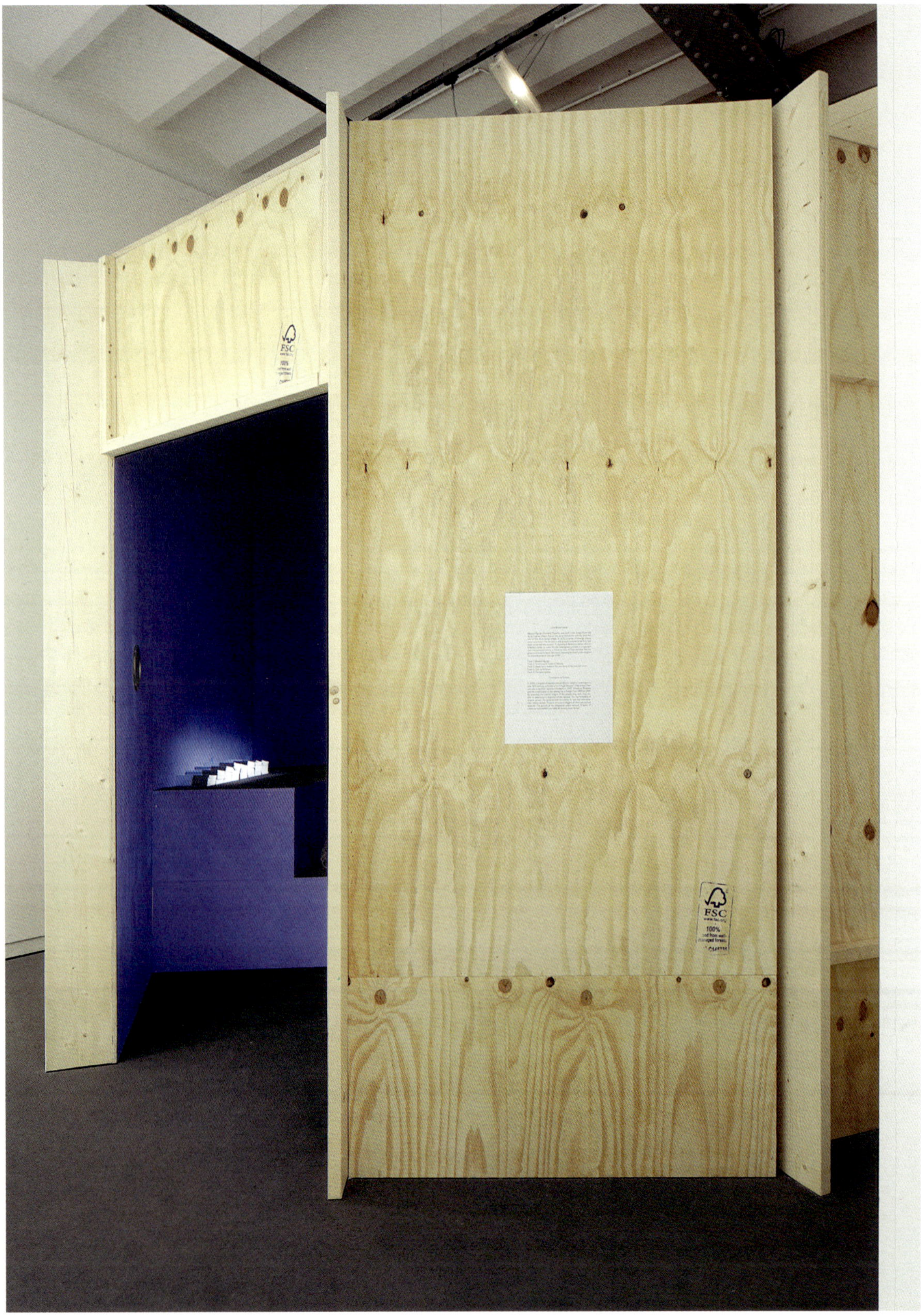

ayoh kré Duchâtelet, *Le tribunal hanté*, 2023. Sound installation. Courtesy of the artist

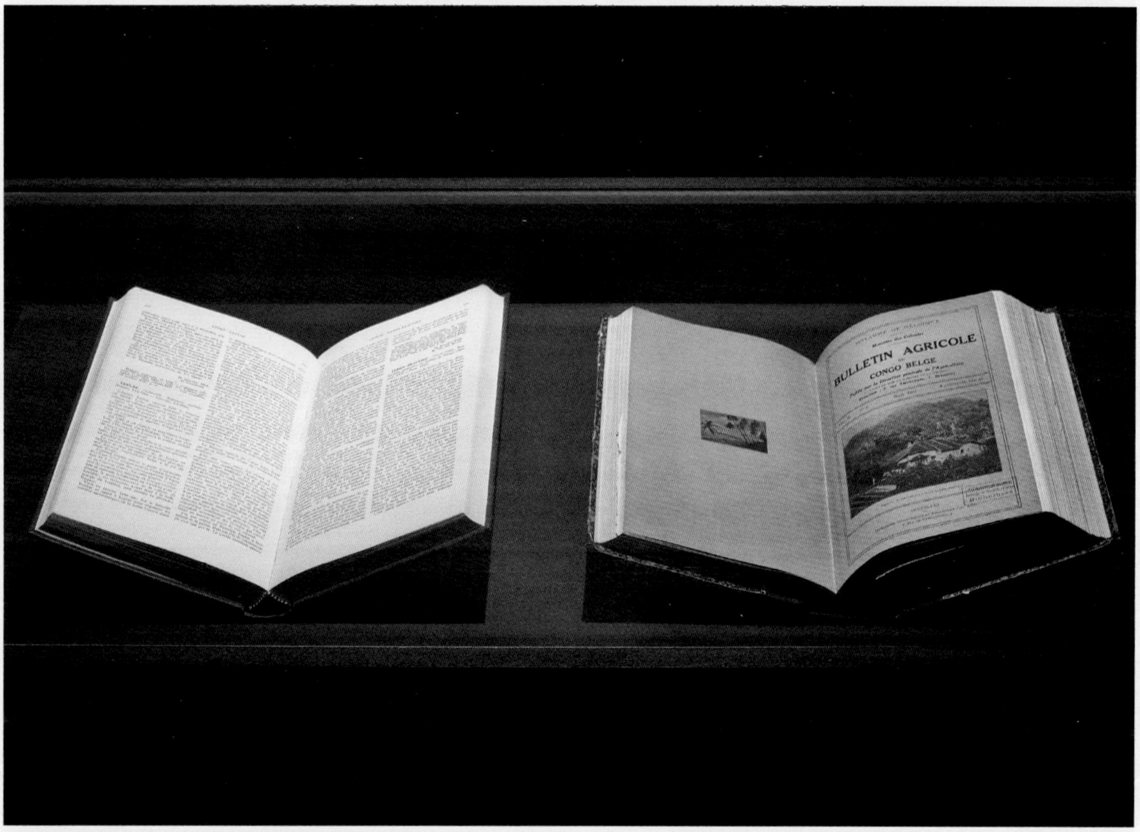

Edmond Leplae, Bulletin Agricole du Congo Belge, vol. 1., 1911 and M. Van den Abeele, Edmond Leplae. Biographie Coloniale Belge, vol. IV, Brussels, 1955 in Paoletta Holst and Johan Lagae, *"Objects that are dear to him"*, 2023. Courtesy of the artists

In 1911 a seventy-seven-page file entitled "Plans et photographies d'habitations pour plantations coloniales" was featured in the Bulletin Agricole du Congo Belge. Authored by Edmond Leplae (1868 - 1941), the first director general of the Agriculture Department of the Belgian Ministry of the Colonies, and consisting of documentation collected during a trip to the tropics, it made a case for the coloniser's house as the key instrument for a successful mise en valeur (exploitation) of the colony. This dwelling should not only ensure safety and a healthy hygienic environment, but also contribute to morality and counter feelings of discourage-ment and (mental) fatigue. Moreover, "it should allow [the coloniser] to bring his wife and children to the colonies and to live without danger in a familial environment, surrounded by the people and objects that are dear to him." For Leplae, it seemed important lessons were to be learned from British and Dutch colonial experiences. In a double screen video installation, a close and critical reading of Leplae's file on colonial houses from 1911 is placed in dialogue with a photo reportage from his mission to Katanga between 1910 and 1914. With comments by Donatien Dibwe dia Mwembu (Université de Lubumbashi, DRC) and Johan Lagae Gent University).

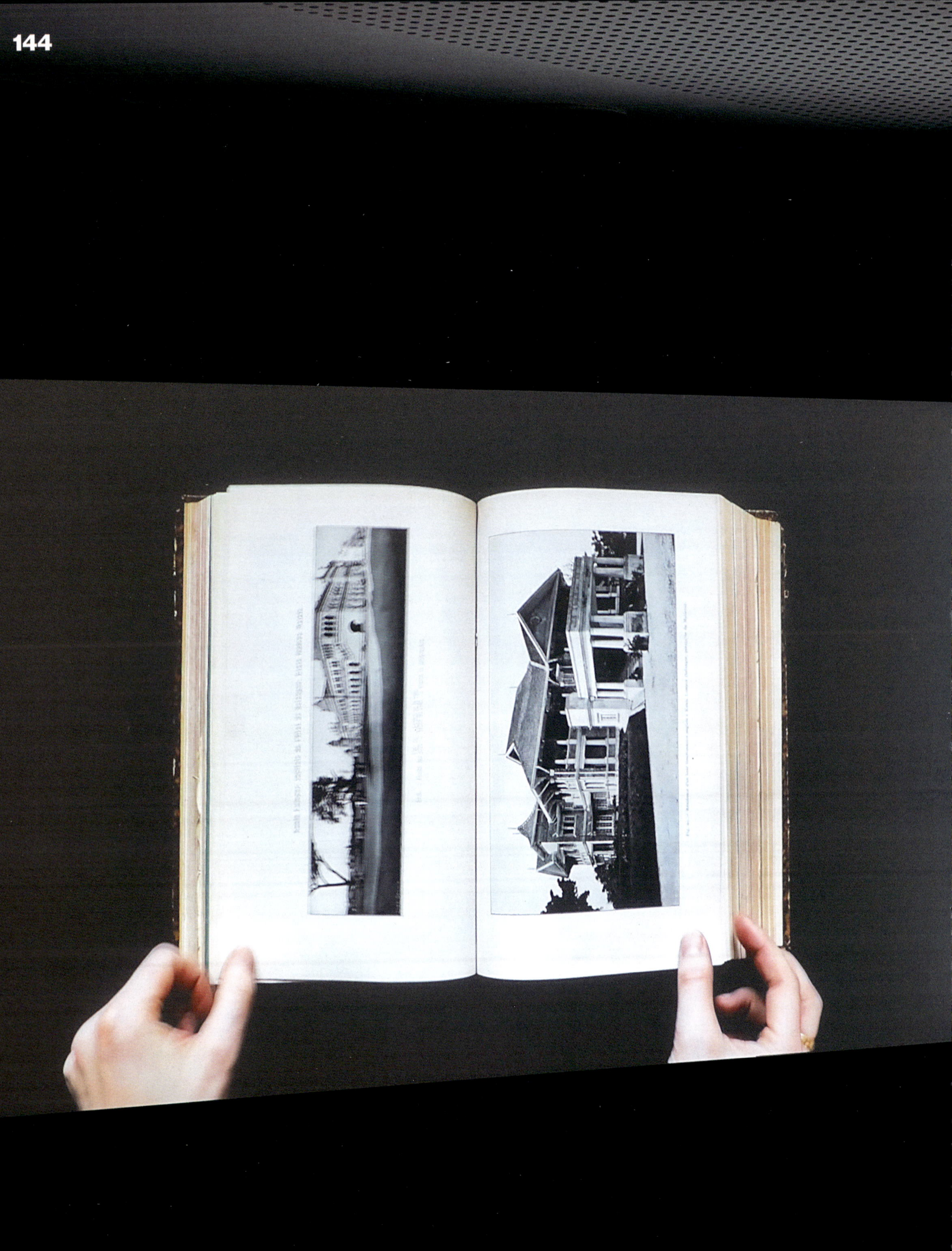

Paoletta Holst and Johan Lagae, *"Objects that are dear to him"*, 2023. Double screen video installation. Courtesy of the artists

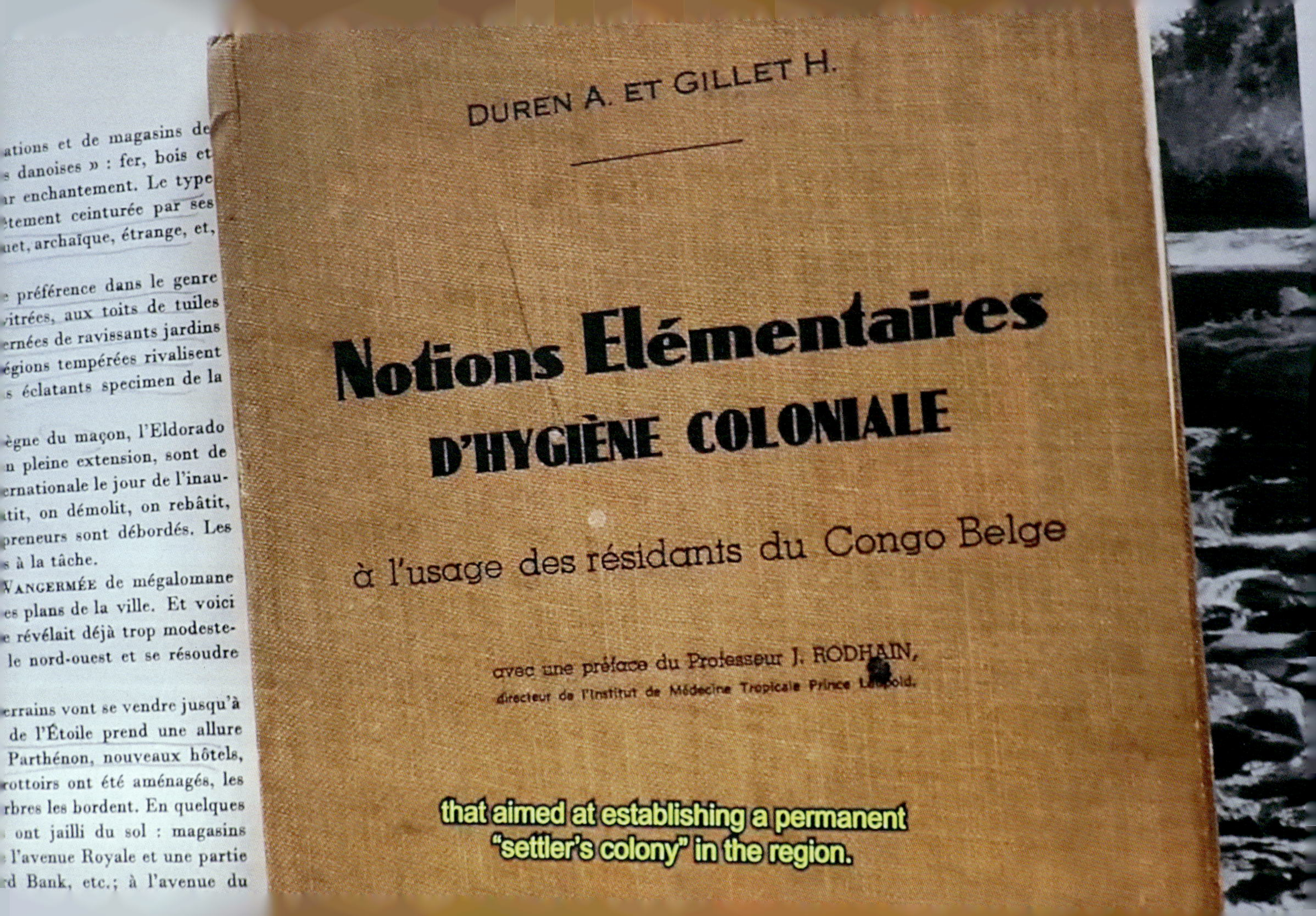
DUREN A. ET GILLET H.
Notions Elémentaires
D'HYGIÈNE COLONIALE
à l'usage des résidants du Congo Belge
avec une préface du Professeur J. RODHAIN,
that aimed at establishing a permanent
"settler's colony" in the region.

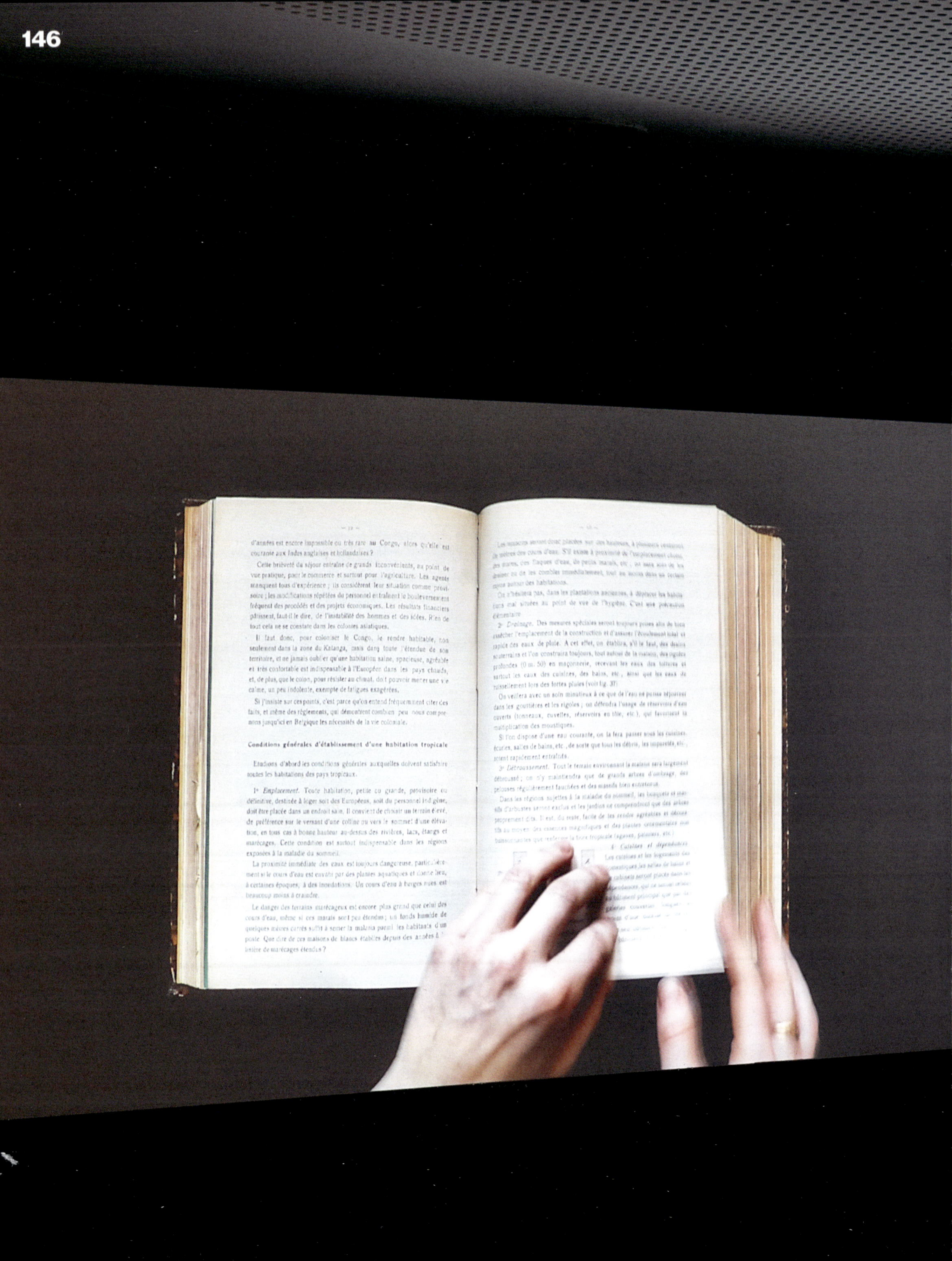

Paoletta Holst and Johan Lagae, *"Objects that are dear to him"*, 2023. Double screen video installation. Courtesy of the artists

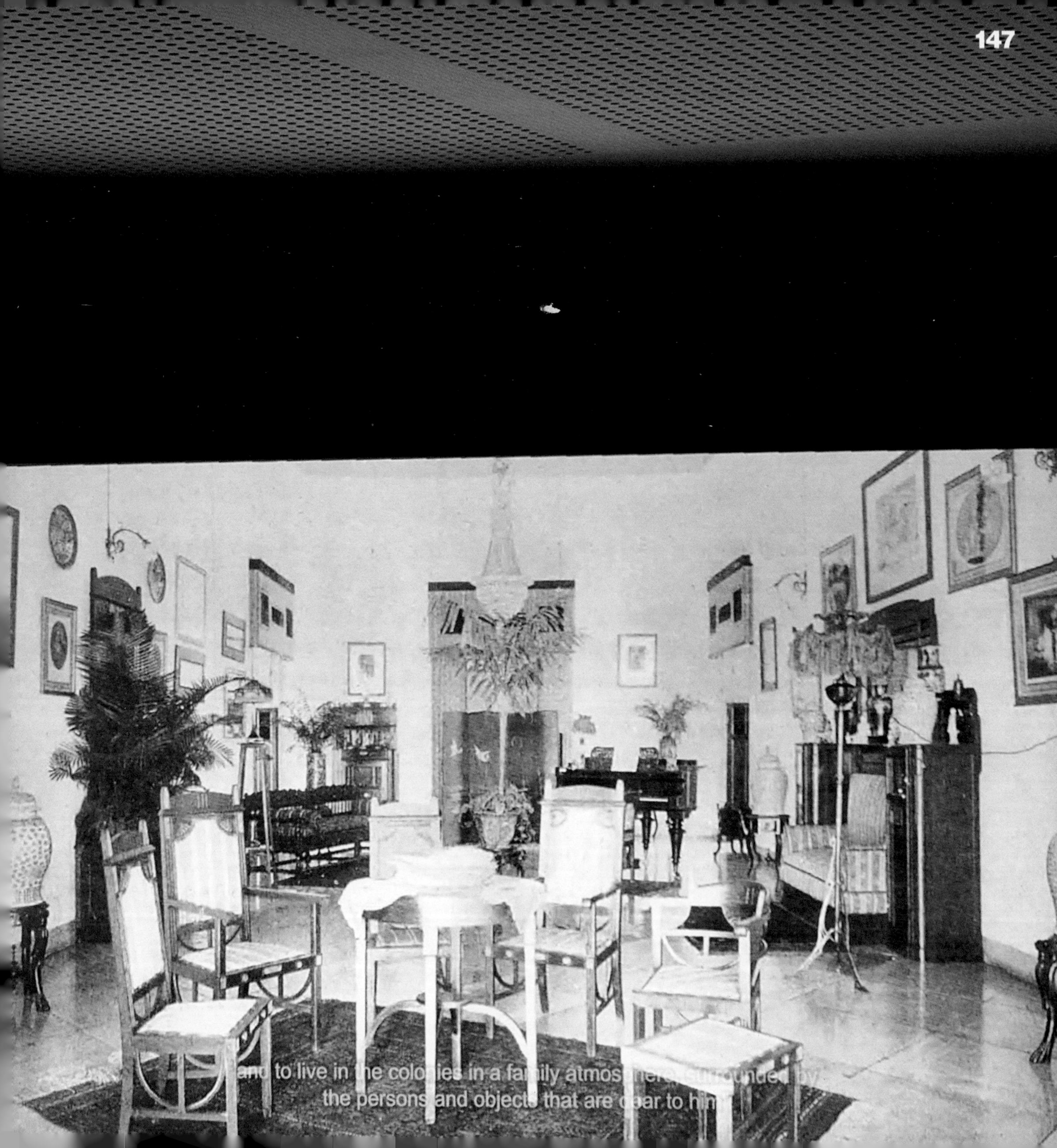
and to live in the colonies in a family atmosphere, surrounded by
the persons and objects that are dear to him.

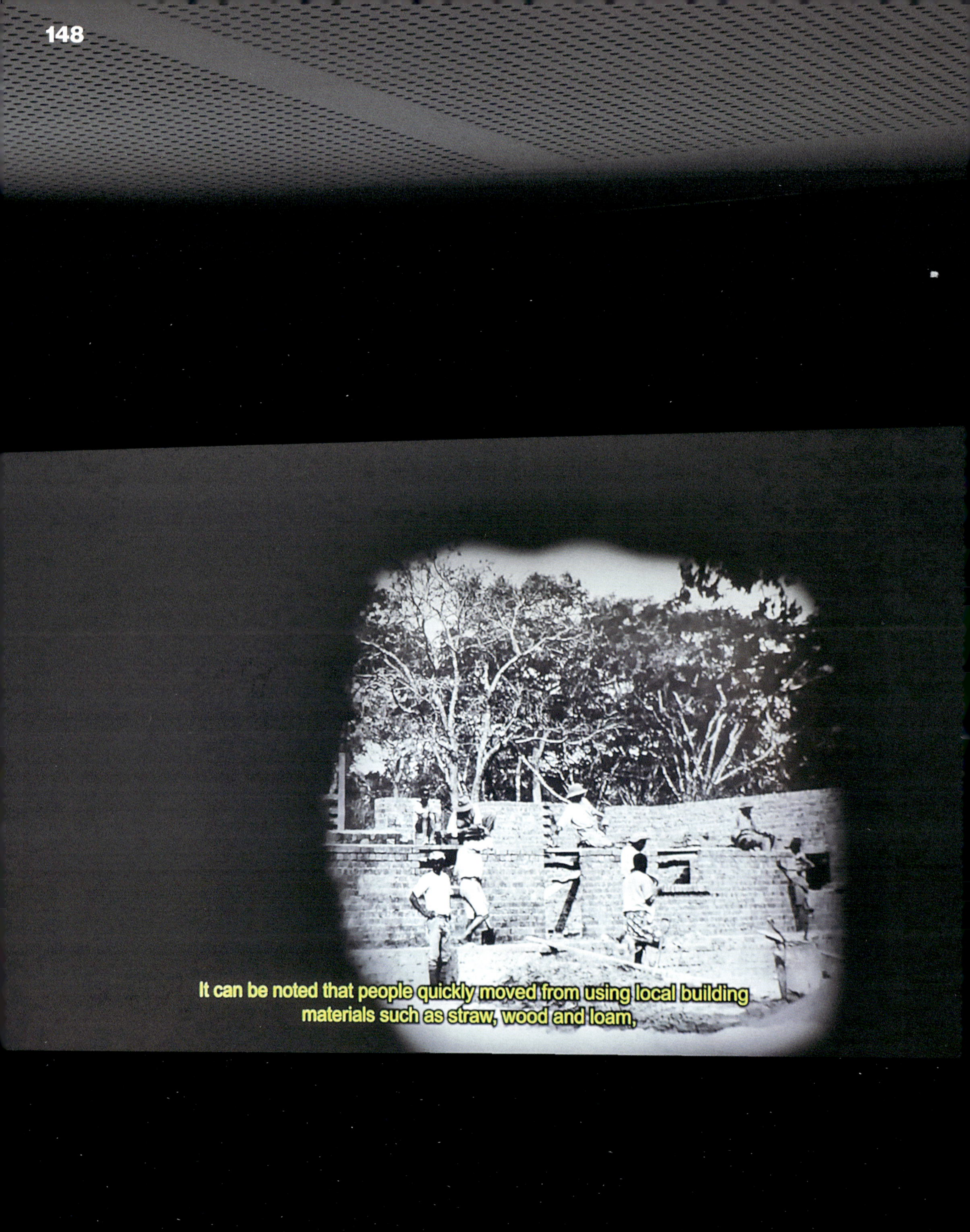

Paoletta Holst and Johan Lagae, *"Objects that are dear to him"*, 2023. Double screen video installation. Courtesy of the artists.

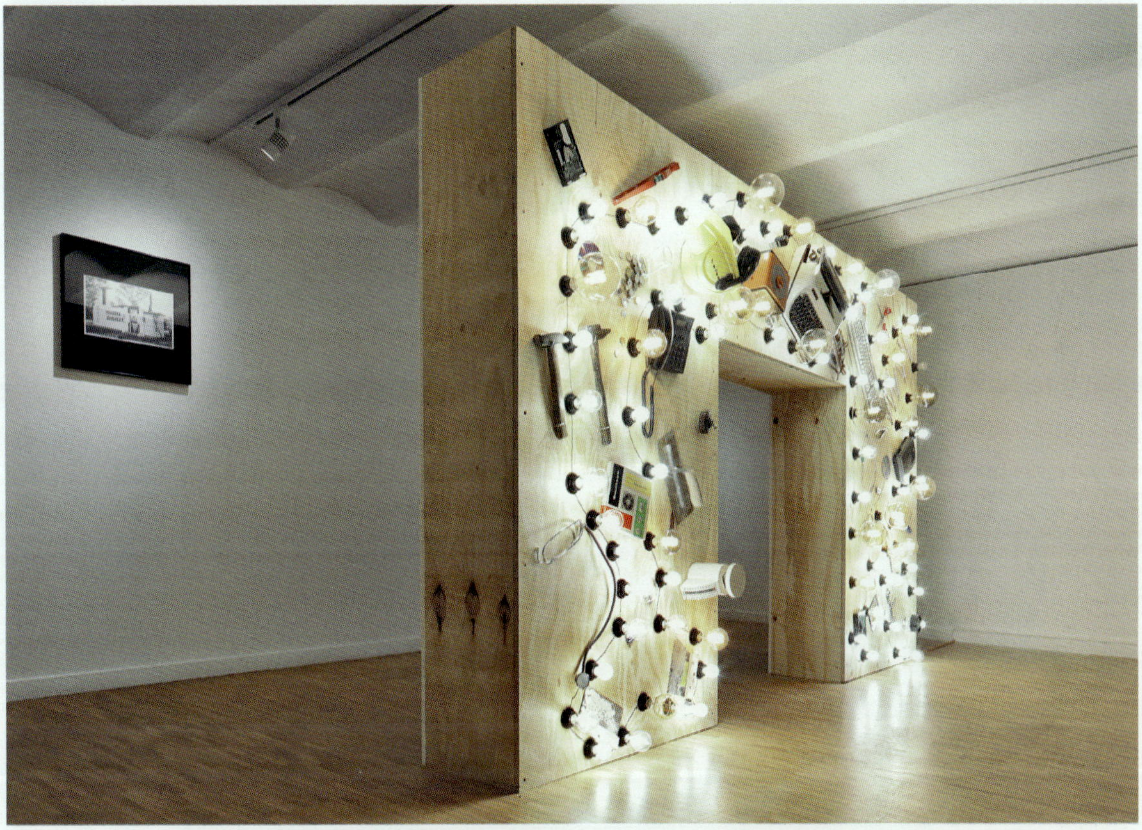

Jean Katambayi Mukendi, *Au-dedans des murs*, 2023. In situ mixed media installation, including archives from the MRAC Tervuren Collection and National Archives of Belgium. Courtesy of the artist

In his in situ installation for CIVA, Jean Katambayi asks why the 1931 International Exposition in Elizabethville (now Lubumbashi), held in the name of progress, did not ultimately result in every Congolese household having access to daily electricity by 2023. Indeed, the participation of powerful companies such as *Union Minière du Haut Katanga* (Mining Union of Upper-Katanga) in the exhibition was intended to posit the city as a model for economic growth. Elizabethville was heralded as an example for the region, creating connections not only between the city and other inland regions, but also with neighboring countries such as South Africa. Here, the artist addresses economic, political, and societal problems, describing the promises of urban and architectural development, industrial progress, and economic development that should have led to an improvement in the living conditions of the people of Lubumbashi as a "failed handover". It is through the lens of such deep disappoint-ment that Jean Katambayi stages a mural made up of various discarded objects illuminated by light bulbs that symbolize the miracle of electricity that never came to pass.

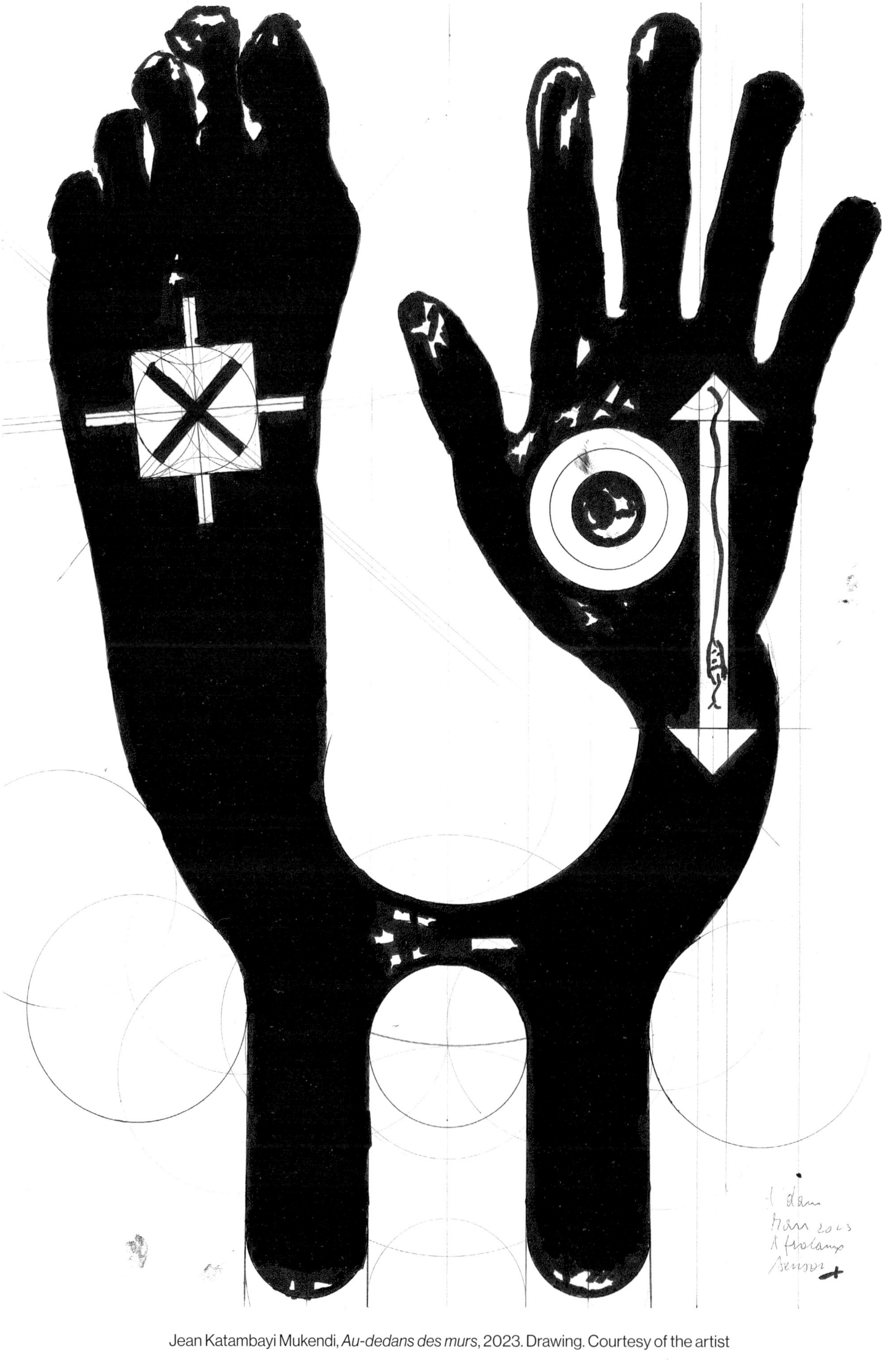

Jean Katambayi Mukendi, *Au-dedans des murs*, 2023. Drawing. Courtesy of the artist

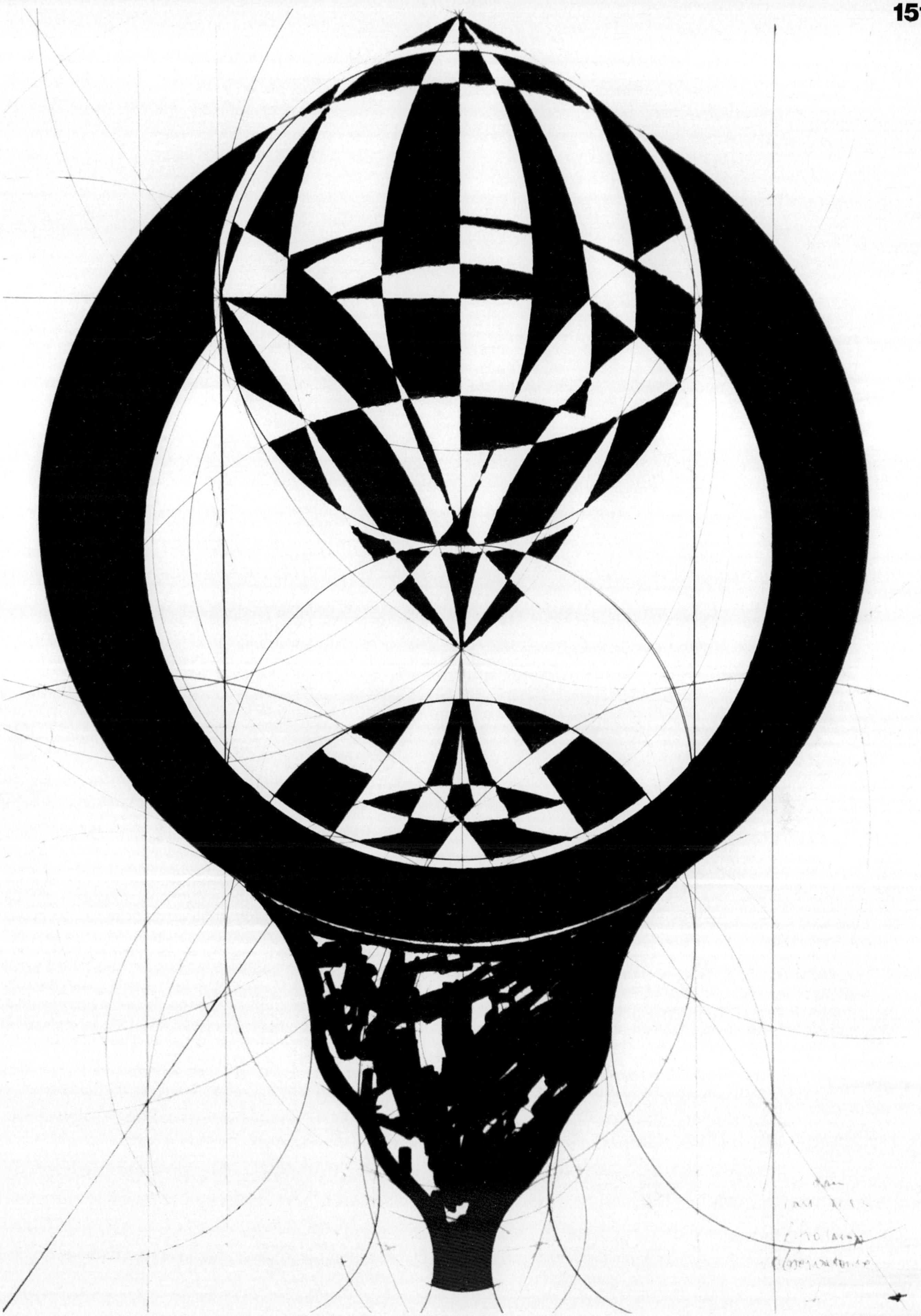

Jean Katambayi Mukendi, *Au-dedans des murs*, 2023. Drawing. Courtesy of the artist

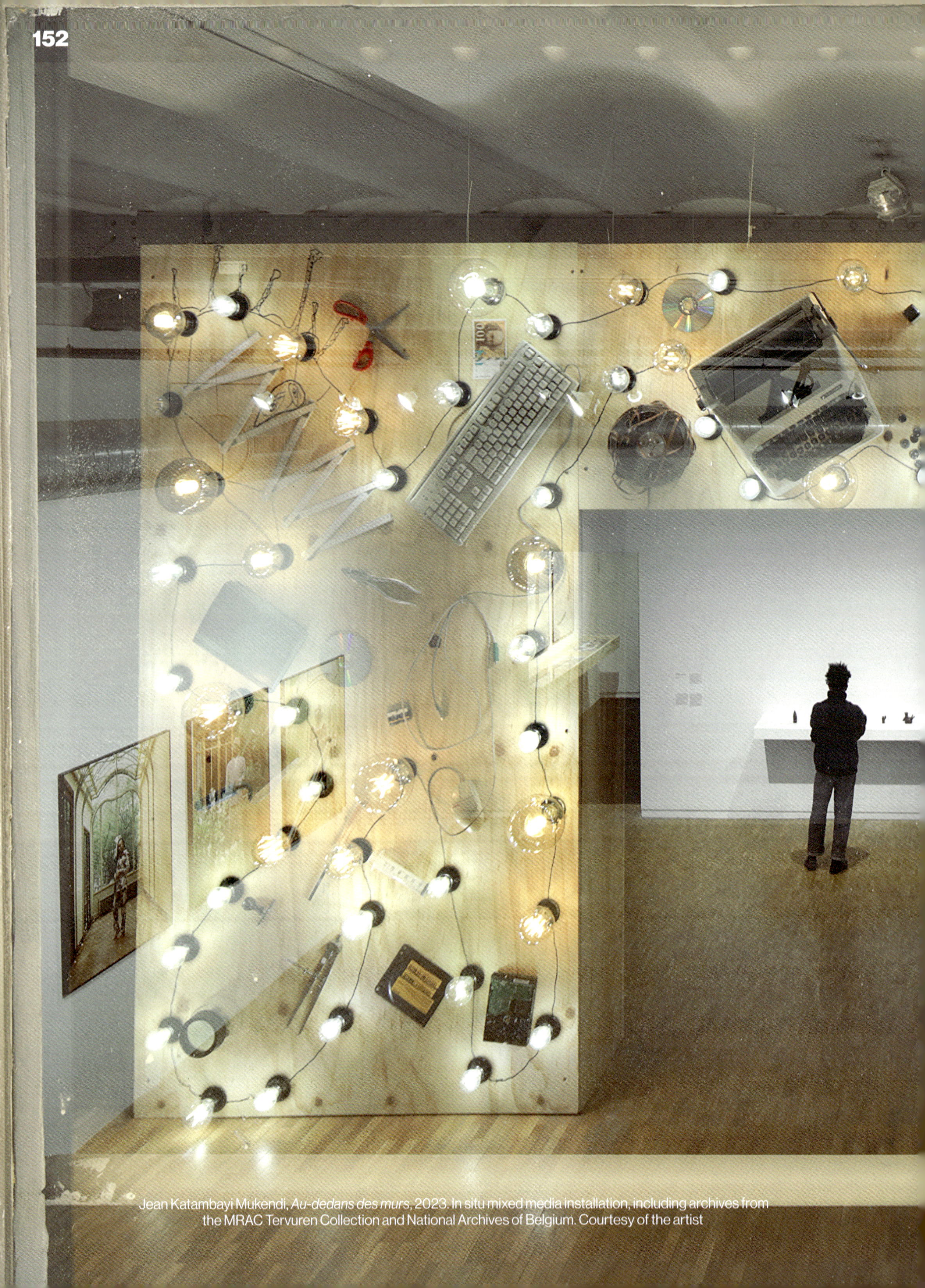

Jean Katambayi Mukendi, *Au-dedans des murs*, 2023. In situ mixed media installation, including archives from the MRAC Tervuren Collection and National Archives of Belgium. Courtesy of the artist

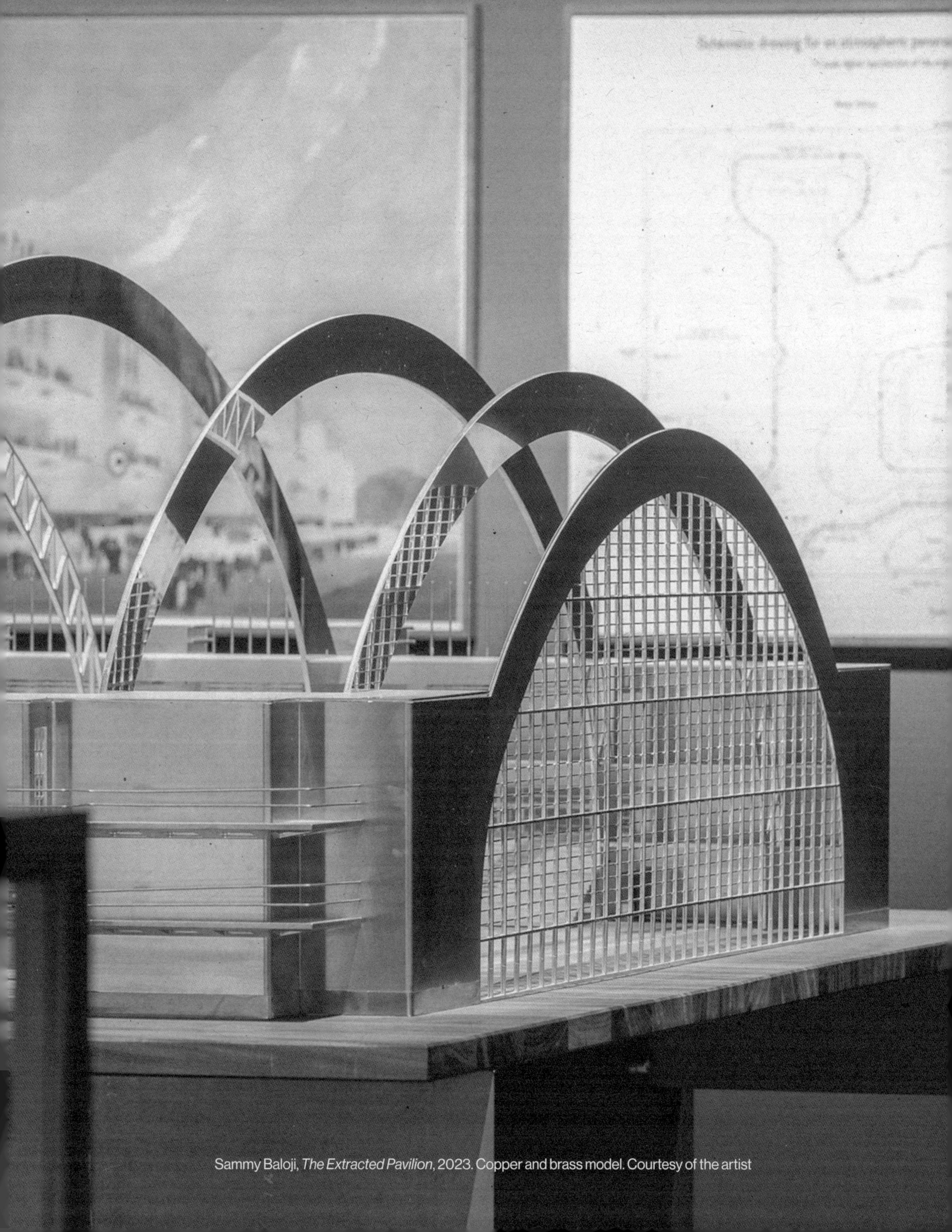

Sammy Baloji, *The Extracted Pavilion*, 2023. Copper and brass model. Courtesy of the artist

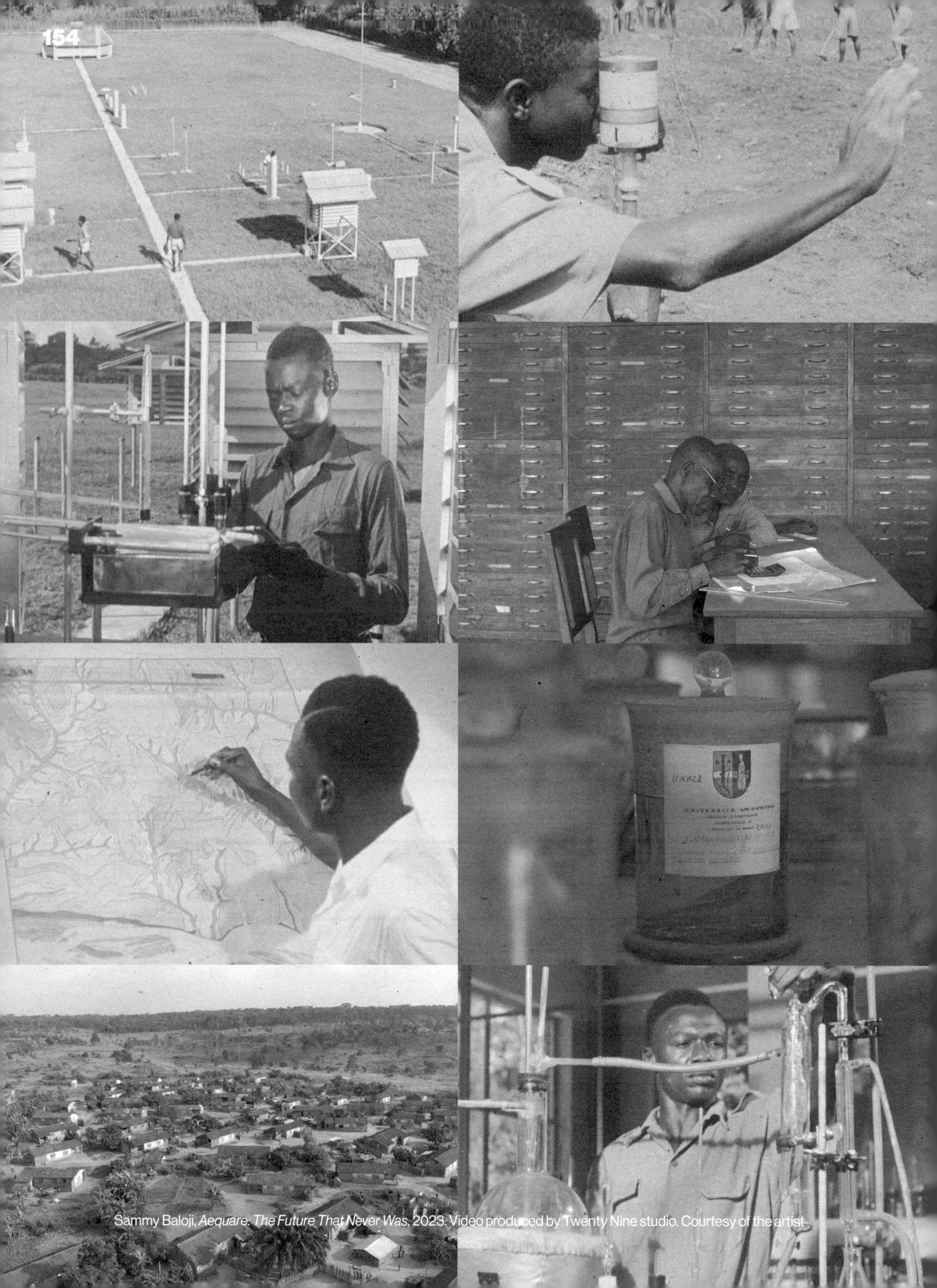

Sammy Baloji, *Aequare: The Future That Never Was*, 2023. Video produced by Twenty Nine studio. Courtesy of the artist

After a two-minute long flight over the town of Yangambi in Congo's Equatorial forest, a drone camera in one of the rushes of Sammy Baloji's feature film descends amidst a group of locals, who excitedly run toward the celestial object. Landing in a small cloud of dust, the camera continues to record the curious faces of the young and older inhabitants of the land from the ground up. Montaged with what appears like muffled and unfathomable sounds, that scene's effect is to silo spectators from the forest surroundings and the populations, as if watching from within an airtight and soundproof vessel returning to Earth, aliens to what they see. A disconnect from an environment as overpowering as the second-largest tropical forest in the world, and the colonial history of that estrangement and its heritage are at the heart of Baloji's work for the 2023 Venice Biennale of Architecture. At a time when, in Bruno Latour's words, climate change urges humans to regain a long lost "down to Earth"[1] approach towards our planet, the artist reflects upon the origins of that disorientation in colonial modernity. The paradox of this alienation—which grows from Western settlers' acclimation, scientific control, and territorial appropriation of Africa—is probed through the thick and uncanny atmosphere of past and present film footages of the Equatorial forest and the Yangambi scientific centre in its midst: A geography that entangles as much of the stigmas of ecological destruction as the poetic and atmospheric potential of futurity.

1
Bruno Latour. *Down to Earth: Politics in the New Climatic Regime*, Cambridge, 2018.

Sammy Baloji's *Aequare. The Future That Never Was* is a response to a dialogue that we initiated in 2019 when I was the curator of the 6th Lubumbashi Biennale, co-founded by the artist. I conceived of the event as a poetic repurposing of Congo's cartography, one that claimed the segment of the Equator that crosses it—the longest in an African country—as its redefining axis. Differently from its globe-bisecting role, the Equator was re-interpreted as a line that profoundly binds hemispheres rather than divides them (the Congo River's serpentine outline weaves them together by straddling the parallel twice). From here, the sun rises and sets quicker than anywhere else, with swift transitions from nighttime to daylight. These recomputed coordinates anchored the Congo at the pulsing heart of the globe rather than at its long-assigned "off-world" periphery, and it propelled the region into a realm of possibilities for renewed horizons, unmoored from the mineral determinism dictated by its rich underground and colonial aftermath. Moving the compass as close as possible to the median parallel, Baloji's installation *Aequare. The Future That Never Was* focuses on this decolonial map's neuralgic centre: the immense tropical rainforest region. A paramount actor in the reduction of humanity's carbon emissions and in the survival of biodiversity, the forest and its territory connect more than any other to this reconfigured cartography centralising the Congo. Owing to its cardinal role in the planet's common climatic destiny and its potential to regenerate our atmosphere, the Equatorial forest is literally one of the main actors of our planet's future. However, with *Aequare*, a title inspired by the Latin etymological root of the word equator which means "making equal", Baloji unwinds how the emergence of these new geographies keeps being impeded by the disequilibrium caused by old imperial networks and their vestiges.

The film swings between archival film clips dating from 1943 and 1957, sourced from INEAC's colonial propaganda, and 21st century captures of the same Yangambi premises, like a pendulum that never moves time forwards. An acronym for the former National Institute for the Agronomic Study of the Belgian Congo, its post-colonial successor, the Institut national pour l'Etude et la Recherche Agronomique (INERA), is on film so suffused with past, colonial "coordinate systems" that the present looks inert and at a standstill, as if held hostage by frames of knowledge that refuse to abdicate. Decades after decolonization, that persistent hold is made explicit by an imposing and intact map of the Belgian Congo hung high on the wall, and by all the remaining rusty machines, labelled test tubes and rotting reports and specimens, dusty instruments of measure, and laboratories. Against the crumbling of these infrastructures, a devoted population of Congolese clerks seem to assist the preservation of the collected data and methods, in a choreography of gestures that the montage reveals to be inherited from the colonial decades. Amidst images of farmers burning trees to make the charcoal sold at surrounding markets, or those of clerks' motivational posts proudly professing the exactitude of their pursuit, the atavism of colonial ecology seems apparent.

Baloji's sophisticated work on sound saliently makes palpable the uninterrupted ecological catastrophe initiated by the colonial presence during the 20th century. Mostly foreign and asynchronous to the images shown, Aequare's soundtrack functions like a buffer rather than a conduit to the forest milieu, and this sensory gap registers a profound disjunction and inability to relate to the environment. In the archival film clips, natural sounds are altogether absent and subsumed by exoticizing tam tams, orientalizing arpeggios of Rimsky-Korsakow's Sheherazade, and the permanence of a triumphant and self-indulgent voice-over. In the same breath rejoicing in the war's effect upon the demand for Hevea tree rubber and in agriculture's necessary "attack on an untamed nature", the scripted comments proudly declaim all the misguided arrogance and ominous folly of their authors. A spectacle of complacent images showing large-scale deforestation, monocultures, and pesticide spraying are supported by boastful assertions that the richness of the forest does not exist before man turns it into productivist agriculture. The echoes of these colonial voices and sounds overlap with the contemporary filmed images, as a basso continuo that continues to underlie and erode the present landscape. But throughout the film, other tracks of haunting sounds merge with it. In recordings by the artist Chris Watson, fading birdsong is layered with enigmatic and increasingly distressing noises as one comes to understand that these are the noise of Earth's melting ice caps. This is the soundtrack of imperialism's tragedy and its consequences which are precipitated around the globe. In unison, these sounds compose an anxious polyphony cutting across Earth's atmosphere from the equator to the poles.

The doomed fate of what Malcom Ferdinand has called "colonial inhabitance" (l'habiter colonial) is mostly understood through the extreme violence exerted upon the land and its people, and the long-term devastation that it has provoked.[2] Fundamentally, it is also a modality of inhabitance that condemned colonisers to the inadequacy and artificiality of their relation to the occupied environment. Colonial and tropical architecture show how a core element of their conceptual and spatial organisation was the sensory removal of Europeans' white bodies from African surroundings. Curated by Johan Lagae (architectural historian and professor at Ghent University where he conducts research on 20th century architecture and urbanisation in Central-Africa), a display of colonial books and manuals deploys how the highest degree of physical detachment from the Congolese soil was a foundation of Belgian building philosophy in the colony. The construction of verandas, the systematic elevation of the floor, the conditioning of air and thermal control, the brise-soleil, mosquito nets, and tight metallic lattices were all intended to accrue a comfort as great as the distance between the European settlers and the African climate and people. Added to the core deceit that attempted to justify colonial presence, such sensorial excision

2
Malcom Ferdinand. *Une écologie décoloniale. Penser l'écologie depuis le monde caribéen.* (Paris: Edition du Seuil, 2019).

made the colonial experience one cut off from reality and quite literally, one that has been physically out-of-touch. Despite the fact that the ramifications of imperial white supremacy within contemporary racism are nowadays largely recognized, a central question in Baloji's installation is how this idea of being impervious to the African atmosphere can be appreciated as part of a larger attempt to desensitise us to the root of our contemporary ecological crisis.

It is deeply ironic that colonisers who spent so much energy making themselves immune to African sensorial contacts in the Congo, so obsessively attempted to recreate them abroad, in their homeland. International and Universal Exhibitions and their colonial pavilions were unmistakable opportunities for Belgian authorities to plunge their nationals into a recreated Congolese landscape. In that respect, the project of Henri Lacoste for the 1935 World Fair in Brussels, the Panorama Atmosphérique, is one of the ultimate expressions of that desire. Unrealized despite the strong interest of the administration, the "Atmospheric Panorama" sought to reproduce the three main climatic zones of the Congo: the savannah, the tropical forest and the mountain ridge of Ruwenzori. While Lacoste's project once again confirms that the Congo was seen as "never better experienced than at a distance" (as advertised in the colonial press of the time), it also discloses two important subtexts to the colonialist environmental approach. First, it foregrounds the idea and its deleterious effects that "nature" could be turned into a spectacle to be manipulated and recreated at will. Second, that the benevolent and allegedly rational and scientific management of the land was always subaltern to financial returns. On the façade of Lacoste's preparatory sketches, the names of Congo's most lucrative natural resources and their extractive activities—"oil", "copper", "plantations", "wood", "coffee"—greeted visitors in massive golden letters, before they could enjoy the picturesque replica. The preeminence of that hierarchy—profit over environmental sustainability or appreciation—concealed by the hypocrisy of colonial discourse, is unveiled and solidified in Baloji's hands. The artist entirely casts the structure of Lacoste's pavilion in copper, one of the most profitable minerals in the history of the Belgian Congo. This unsettling alchemy shows how the "atmosphere" in the colony was never pure; how the air was always saturated with mineral dust and toxic emanations; and how imperialism turned the world's celestial vault and the canopy of trees into mineral ceilings.

In spite of the global scale of their ecocidal history, Western societies continue to brandish the monopoly of reason to the rest of the world. Such discourse is repeated like a confident chorus alongside the backdrop of deforestation, monocultures, and poisoned soils in the colonial films montaged into *Aequare*. In them, the European "rationalisation" of agriculture and forest management is opposed to "irrational" indigenous modes of cultivation, in spite of the very mixed results of colonial agricultural techniques in the Congo. Science, which will be needed more than ever if humanity is ever to survive climate change, is not what is on trial in the film. Rather, it is science's denaturation in its allegiance to unbridled capitalism in the fundamentally unethical system of colonialism, and the contempt it has held for any indigenous knowledge. In the words of Ariella Aïsha Azoulay, "what we have learned with imperialism is that knowledge is the permission to violate everything."[3] The Yangambi scientific centre, like others, have been engaged in this botany of death, and in Baloji's films, nothing shows that this past is being questioned. On the contrary, the present-day Congolese that roam the buildings look like guardians of the past, extras in a scenario that they have not chosen, in a history that seems as arrested as the leaves that fill the herbarium that they tend to.

3
Ariella Aïsha Azoulay, *The world like a jewel in the hand*, 2022 (3:30), 58 mn

There is no trace of local and indigenous knowledge's participation in the healing of our dying world, and the future belongs exclusively to one hemisphere, which will eventually become either the Earth's gravedigger or its saviour. If time passes like a river flows, the long tracking shots going up and down the Congo River fit the pendulum-like movement of a continually returning time, while the re-enchanting potential of the equatorial cartography keeps being ruined by the resurgence of old maps. In recent years "rediscovered" by the international scientific community, the archives and data gathered in Yangambi in the colonial era have proven to be extremely precious aids in understanding the evolution of our changing climate. However, rarely is it mentioned that a place like the INEAC contributed to the derailment of the climate it set out to study. Today, the urgency of climate change makes the bypassing of this responsibility all the more invisible, in another Western move to innocence.

Yet, equatorial geography continues to offer ways to transcend the impasses in which imperialism has trapped the world. Today, officially recognized as a UNESCO biosphere, the Yangambi forest counts a spectacular tree informally known as the "tree of authenticity" (Pachyelasma tessmannii)[4] and its characteristics present uncanny parallels with what a viable human and environmental future might look like. Scientists call that species "paradoxical" as it is capable of storing a large amount of carbon while growing rapidly, doubling the benefit of carbon capture and the efforts of stabilising the Earth's climate. No explanations were found as to why "authenticity" is the tree's given name, but it inscribes together in its bark the quality of being true and authentic with the possibility of purifying the very air that we breathe. That miraculous tree rises for us to realise that one more coördinate needs to be taken into consideration for the equatorial map's telluric revolution to advent: the authentic examination of our present's roots.

4 https://www.africamuseum.be/en/see_do/temporary_exhibition/extra_muros/ensuring_the_future. Accessed on April 3rd, 2023.

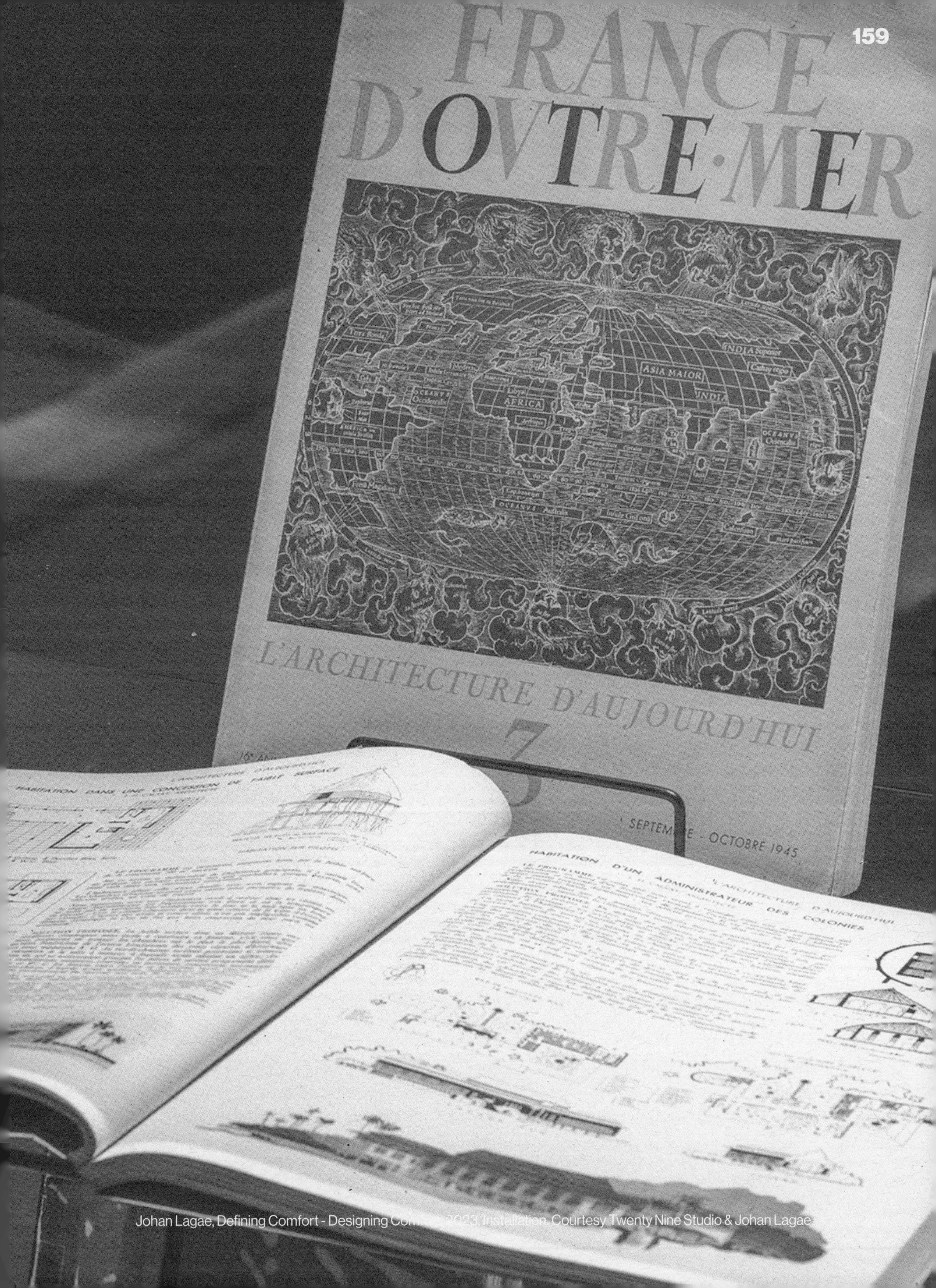

Johan Lagae, Defining Comfort - Designing Comfort, 2023, Installation. Courtesy Twenty Nine Studio & Johan Lagae

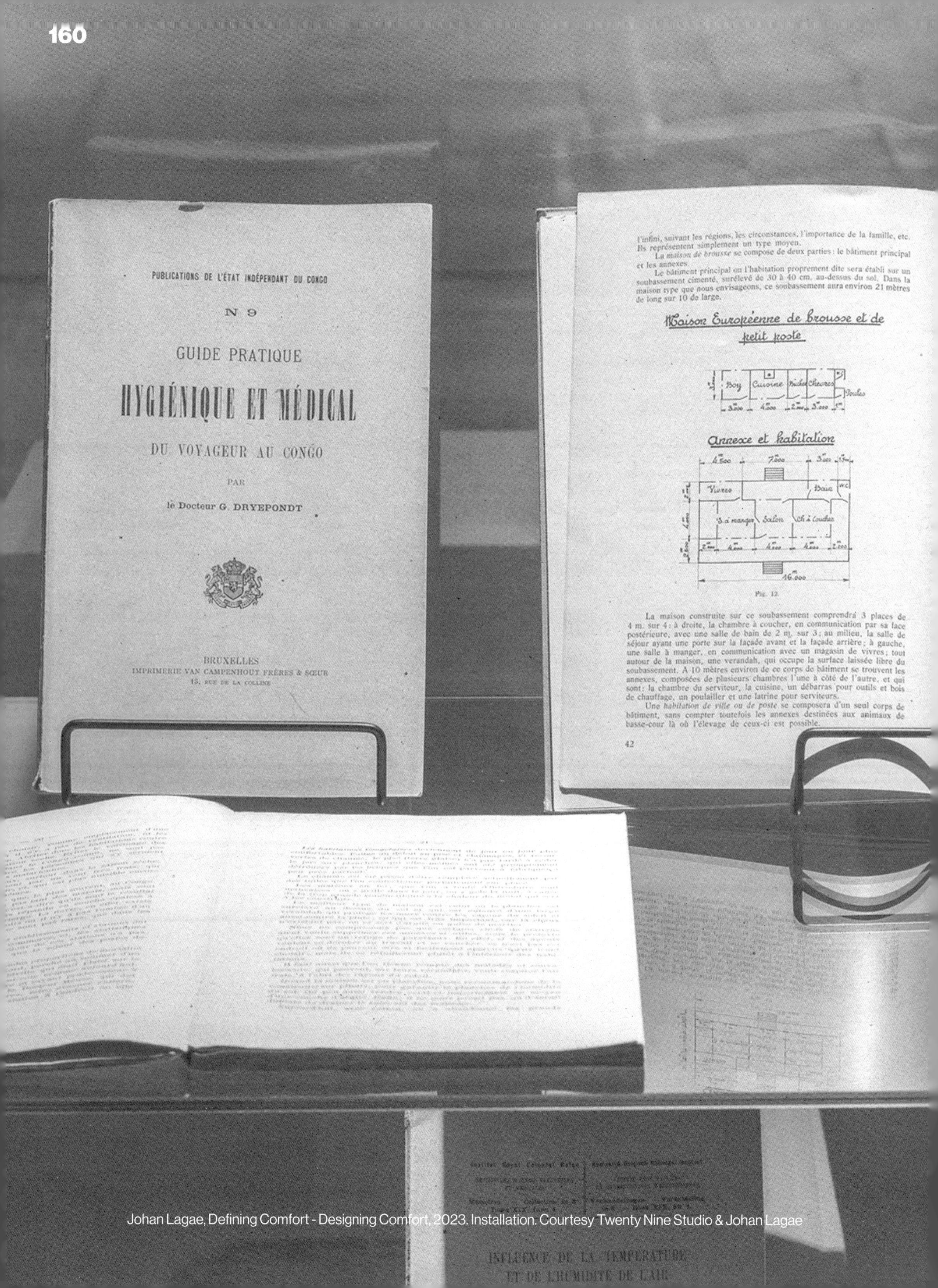

Johan Lagae, Defining Comfort - Designing Comfort, 2023. Installation. Courtesy Twenty Nine Studio & Johan Lagae

Rolando Vázquez Melken
What was the main intention behind your exhibition *Style Congo: Heritage & Heresy*?

Sammy Baloji
A lot of communities in Brussels don't have Belgian roots, but they are living in the city, and make the city what it is. KANAL asked my studio and I to create an exhibition that could bring visibility to the Congolese community, in relation to the colonial history that brings these two communities together: the Belgians and Congolese. One of the things I was interested in was the Black Lives Matter movement and the idea of destroying colonial monuments in public space. There were all these debates going on: should we leave these colonial monuments in the street, or should we remove them? I felt it was really important to dig into these questions, because it wasn't only one or two monuments that needed to be taken down, but the whole colonial system that needed dismantling. One of the things that system does is appropriate and transform object cultures, which colonial propaganda transforms into a modern landscape of progress. I wanted to look at how buildings, materials, artifacts, etc. from Congo have been instrumental to this framework of "progress," but have largely remained invisible within its narrative.

RVM How is this project grounded in your ancestral roots?

SB I was accompanied in this investigation by the architectural historian Johan Lagae, with whom I have been working with for more than ten years, primarily in Lubumbashi—the city where I was born and raised. In Lubumbashi, industry centers around the extraction of mineral resources like uranium and cobalt. The city was basically built around and for extraction by two major companies: a huge mining company called Union Minière du Haut-Katanga, and the Compagnie du chemin de fer du Katanga, a railway company that transported all the minerals to Cape Town, South Africa. From there they brought raw materials to Europe or China via the Indian ocean, which is still the case today. I remember in 2006, while I was working with Johan Lagae, he wrote an article around the idea of "shared heritage."[1] He reflected on how the city has been reappropriated by indigenous people in ways that were contrary to the intentions of the colonists and the architects who designed it, and questioned whether colonial buildings should be protected as heritage. If we want to save and protect these buildings, are we talking about a shared heritage? Do the indigenous have the same experience that the colonists had with the city? With the exhibition, I wanted to question all the buildings that were constructed through this relationship with the Congo, and ask whether they are somehow part of a shared heritage.

RVM How did you encounter the world exhibitions as a site to reveal these colonial questions?

SB I was interested in international exhibitions not only because they had human zoos, but also Congo pavilions that were created in order to display objects. I approached CIVA because they have archives related to these international exhibitions. I was interested in Congo pavilions as speculative spaces in terms of displaying objects, goods, or cultural productions, all of which were introduced as "progress activities." Those were the main ideas that we wanted to address with Traumnovelle and other artists that were ready to look at these pavilions as spaces designed to raise money to reinvest in the colony. For me, these were spaces of speculation, which linked Brussels to the exploitation and extraction of human and natural resources. Most of the architects who made exhibition pavilions were inspired by objects in the Africa Museum, which was built after the international exhibition of 1897. Through the lens of their proposals, we can see how elements coming from Congo were incorporated into the modern practices that gave birth to Art Nouveau and Art Deco.

RVM The pavilions that you show in the exhibition are part of what we can call "white speculation." There's a lot of talk and celebration today of speculations and imaginaries, but not all speculations and imaginaries are liberating. I'm worried about these words being used without qualifications. Whose speculation and whose imaginaries are these? We need to be grounded and positioned. Your exhibition speaks of how colonialism was a manifestation of a "white imaginary," of this incredible hubris of owning and representing the world. These pavilions show how the white speculation of modernity, modernisms, progress, and civilization, was implicated in the destruction of the lives of others and the extraction of the life of Earth. In world exhibitions, this speculation is made concrete as an architectural reality, and becomes a choreography where people could experience this white, imperial imaginary. The pavilions had a very concrete function, which is to control the representation of the world. They enacted a racist and anthropocentric mode of representation that legitimized and enabled the appropriation of the lives of others and the life of Earth. Here is where we need to question how Western aesthetics mobilized pleasure and enjoyment as a tool of oppression.

SB How so?

RVM The wisdom of the peoples of the Americas, of "Abya Yala," teaches us to read Western modernity and capitalism as a system built on the extraction of life, human life, and the life of Earth and Earth beings. One of the big paradoxes or even perverse paradoxes of the modern/colonial system is that it creates beauty and aesthetic enjoyment, it gives pleasure to the senses, on the basis of the suffering of others.[2] It is a pleasure that comes from the power to consume the lives of others, the life of Earth and Earth beings.[3] What we call "decolonial aesthesis" is concerned with how the destruction of life is legitimized and enabled by an aesthetic system that produces pleasure out of the destruction of the lives of human and non-human others.[4]

SB This is quite evident in the Congo pavilions that Belgian architects made for international exhibitions.

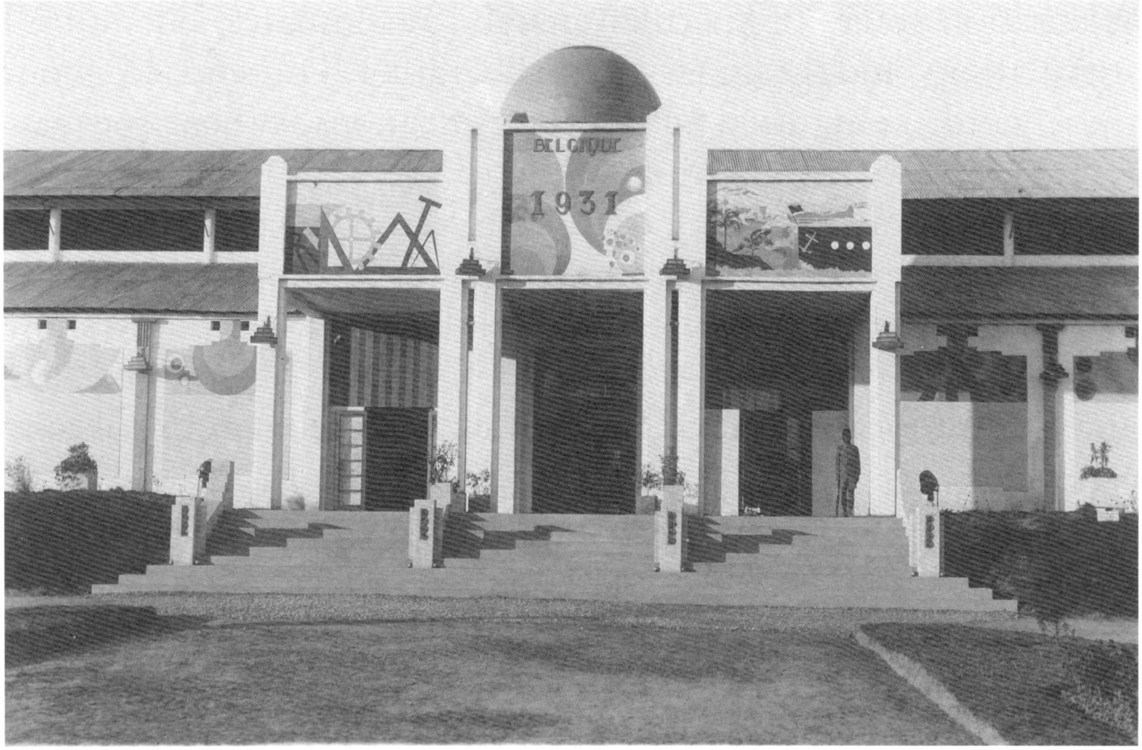

Belgian Pavilion, Exposition internationale d'Elisabethville 1931. Collection MRAC Tervuren - Photo L. Gabriel

RVM Yes. In *Vistas of Modernity*, I speak of the extraction of aesthetic resources that made possible all sorts of modernisms in painting but also in architecture and design.[5] In your exhibition, we see how Art Nouveau, that as you recall was referred to as "Style Congo," extracted the aesthetic worlds of others, the life-worlds of others—just like mining resources from Earth—to produce the aesthetics of modernity.[6] For example, in the Congo Pavillion, we see how Henry Lacoste appropriates the aesthetic resources and materials from Congo, sometimes just in his "white" imagination of the "other." But by doing this, he appropriates these resources and turns them into his own property. He becomes the author, the architect. Another striking example of this is when Picasso declared that all he "needed to know about Africa is in those objects." He was not interested in the cultures where African masks come from, only their aesthetic value. He just needed the aesthetic resources from other worlds to push the borders of Western modernity forward, to go beyond tradition, to be in the "now." This is why I am critical of the notion of the "contemporary," because to invoke the contemporary is to sanction a space of power that says we are in the now, while the other is in the past or outside of history. When Art Nouveau was not a novelty anymore, it gave place to other modernisms that in turn incorporated and differentiated themselves from the other worlds by affirming their own positions in the now of history.

SB How do you understand or feel about the idea I mentioned before, of "shared heritage"?

RVM I think we need to be very careful when we say we have shared histories, because one part might celebrate that shared history and say, "we are all entangled and it's all complex." But what decolonizing does is to say "no," this entanglement is not just any entanglement. There is a colonial difference. There is a history of violence and suffering. There is an underside that has been made invisible, like the extraction of aesthetic resources, like the production of pleasure through the suffering of others.

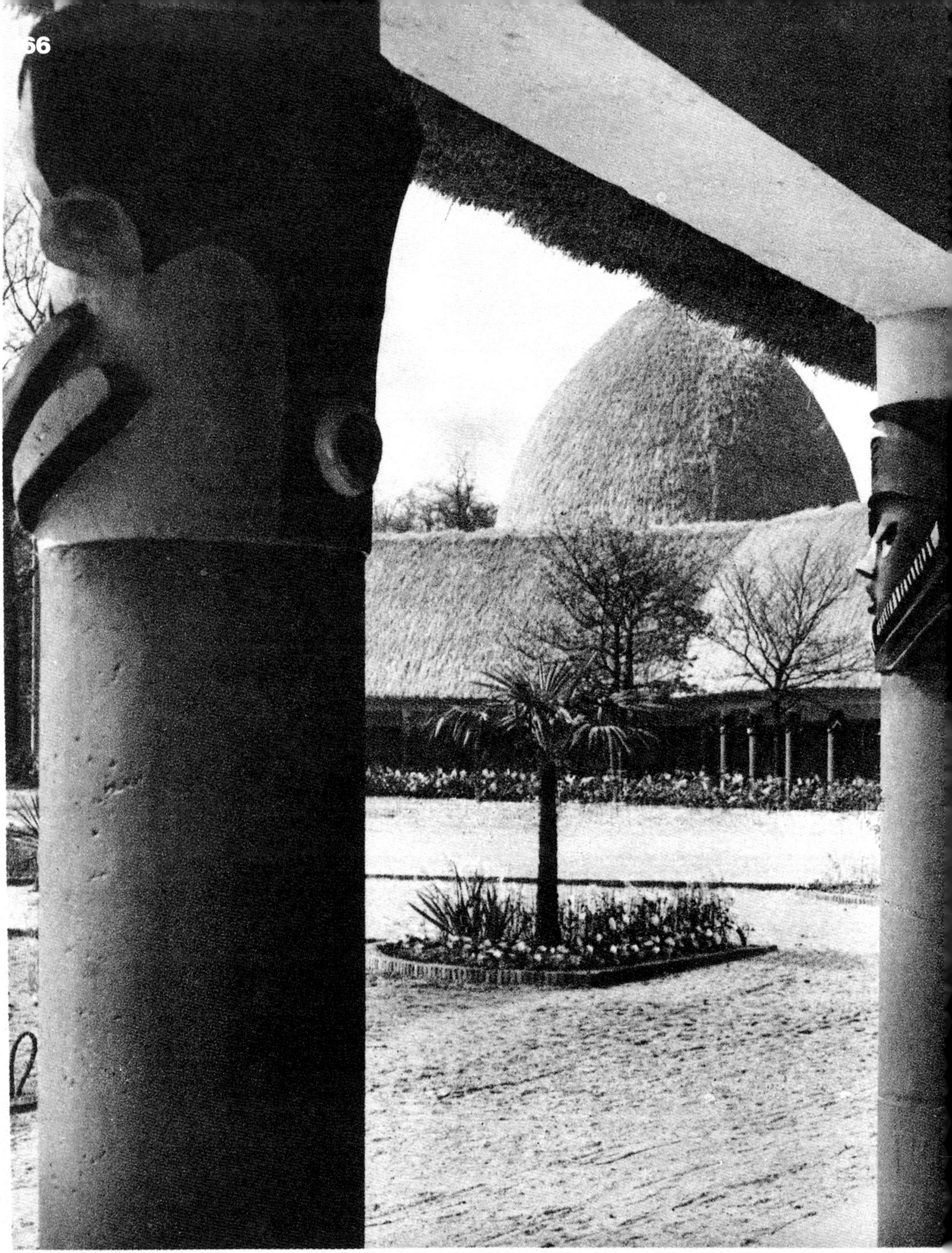

H. LACOSTE. ARCH. S. A. D. G.

Henry Lacoste, *Le Congo Belge – Vue de prise du portique des industries de luxe vers le pavillon d'honneur,* Paris International Colonial Exhibition, 1931. CIVA Collections, Brussels

7 P LE CONGO BELGE - VUE PRISE DU PORTIQUE D

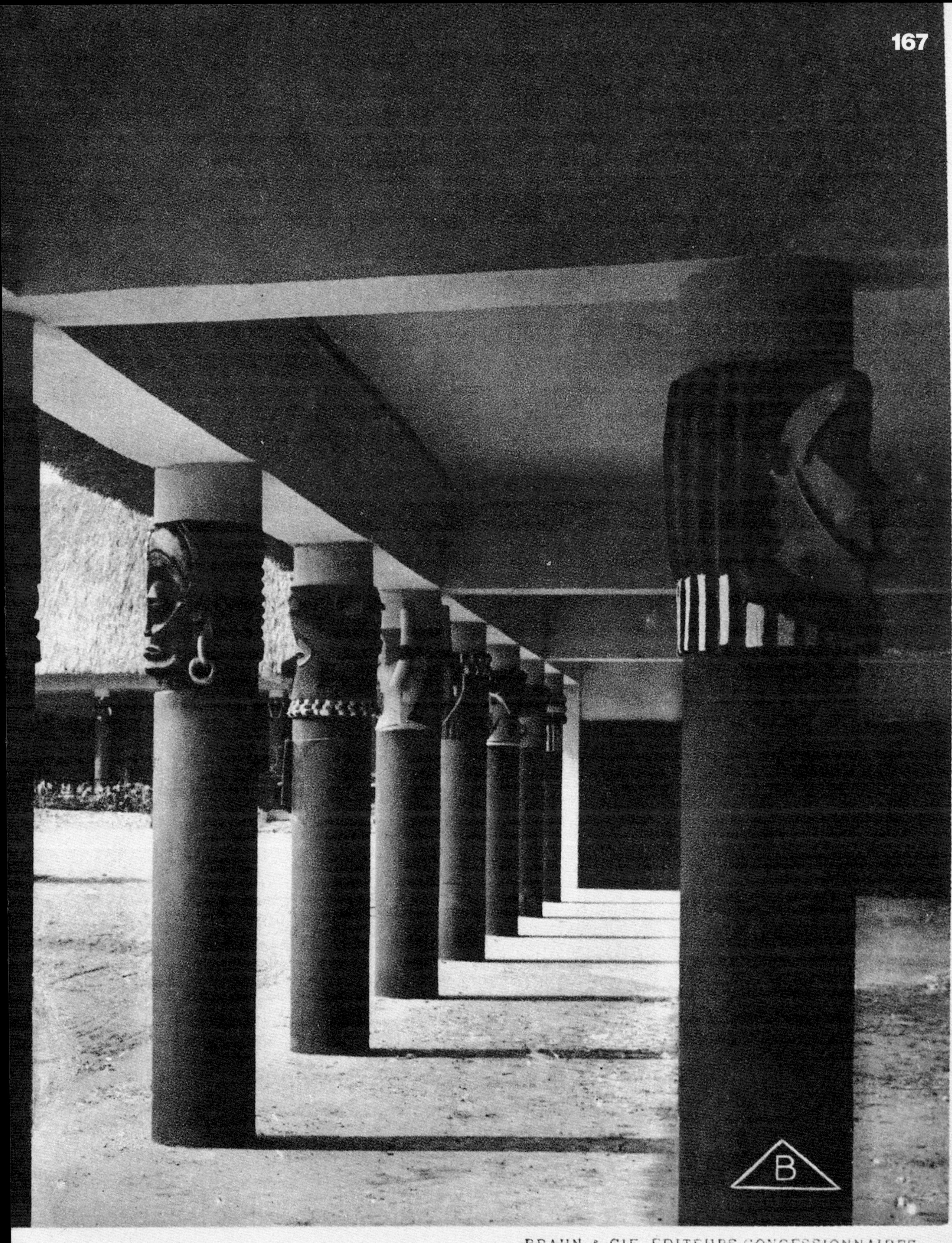

BRAUN & CIE, ÉDITEURS-CONCESSIONNAIRES

NDUSTRIES DE LUXE VERS LE PAVILLON D'HONNEUR

There is an entangled history, but to say that it is "shared" is a bit difficult for me, because sharing carries an ethics of giving and receiving, of the gift. But here, "sharing" means something else. It means that there is a modern/colonial history, and coloniality is the darker side. Your exhibition looks at the underside of Art Nouveau, and shows that it is implicated in the destruction of peoples' lives, of worlds, of cultural heritage, of languages, of other forms of living on Earth, with Earth. It is what we call "epistemicide" or "aesthesicide." Dominant history is enabled by massive destruction and erasure. When we say shared, the term may evoke the idea that there is a parallel, a semblance of equality, when in reality there is none.

SB How do you propose we approach such issues?

RVM We need to speak about being implicated, and how the history of modernity is deeply implicated in suffering across the world.[7] Instead of moving towards an idea of a speculation and relativism or entanglements, we should move towards positionality. "Yes" we are part of an entangled history, but we have very different positions. Whiteness, in this sense, is not a racist term, but a particular historical position that has not been sufficiently located. Whiteness is a historical position in the modern/colonial order.[8] It's also today the consumer in the supermarket, it's the people who enjoy Art Nouveau with indifference, without the awareness of being implicated. It's the people who do not sense the extraction of resources from the forests, or the oceans. It's the people who have not experienced or no longer recall the loss of their mother tongue through school systems, the church, or mass-media. Positionality requires us to know who is speaking, who is representing and who is represented, who is enjoying and who is suffering across the colonial divide. Your exhibition brings about a gaze that is different from the white gaze and its aesthetics. If the people that designed the international exhibition pavilions you speak about would have created this exhibition, even with all the same elements, it would be very different.

SB We hope that this exhibition can be a starting point from where reactions or positionality can originate. But how do you deal with this positionality which is not a shared identity? How do you express it and work with it?

RVM I will bring in an example that I want to connect to something you said about the reappropriation of colonial buildings and colonial monuments. In *Black and Blur*, a book on Black radical thought, Fred Moten shows how the object of capital—the commodity—can be subverted and performed as resistance. Similarly, it is possible to reappropriate dominant architectural objects, like the pavilions, and make them do what they were not designed to do. They can, for example, become an undeniable evidence and testimony of coloniality. For instance, international exhibition pavilions were designed to produce pleasure. It is a pleasure that comes from the power to consume the lives of others, and the life of Earth and Earth beings. I have explained this mechanism previously in my analysis of the coloniality of the commodity, namely how the commodity's magical appearance and pleasure is an expression of the power it bestows over the consumption of life.[9] When we take a pavilion, like the Congo Pavilion, or its documentation and we make it tell the story of coloniality, we are reversing its function, because its function was to produce the pleasure of empire, of coloniality. By reappropriating it, we are also re-functioning it.

SB Reappropriation is a delicate matter, though, isn't it? It doesn't always work as intended.

RVM Absolutely. It is very difficult for me when exhibitions reproduce racist images, images that typify peoples of the world, which were very common in the colonial period. In my analysis, they were about the production of whiteness. The ethnographic museum was about the production of whiteness, the "Human Zoo" was about the production of whiteness. It was not about encountering the other; it was about becoming the self. It was about being the center of the world, being in the now, being in

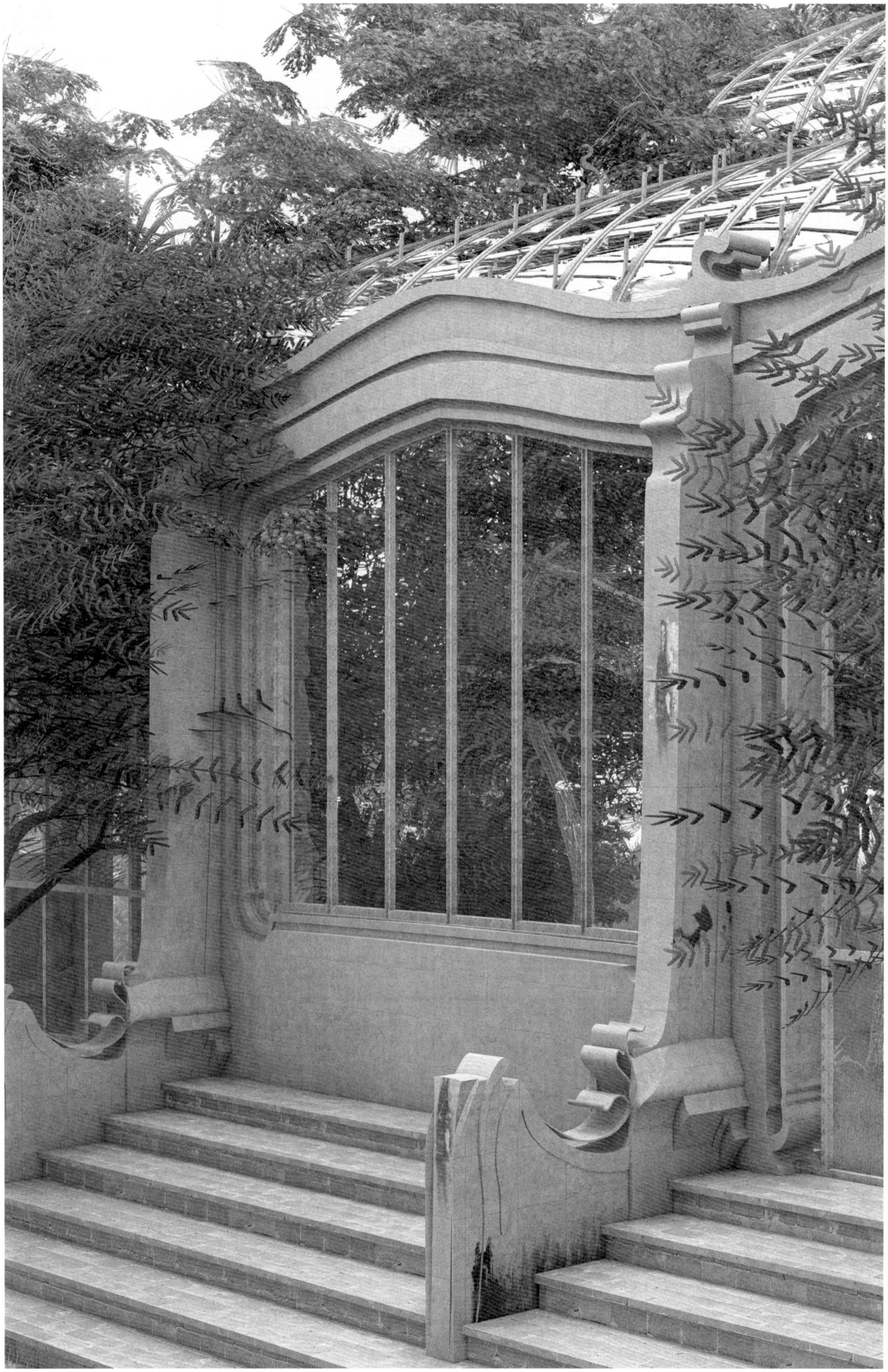

Victor Horta, Design for the Congo Pavilion, 1900, uncompleted. Simulation by Traumnovelle, 2023.
Courtesy of the architects.

the world exhibition, being in an ethnographic museum, being in the metropolis. It was never really about encountering others and being transformed by our relation with others. It was about consuming the other as a spectacle to produce and re-produce whiteness. That's why it's important to speak of whiteness as a positionality. The same artifact that was produced for pleasure and for whiteness to become the center of civilization, can certainly be used for a decolonial intervention to reveal and denounce these mechanisms. But it is complicated to replicate racist images in exhibitions, like those portraying peoples of the world as "types," because the public still carries that white gaze that derives pleasure from the consumption of "others." These images often have the effect of reproducing the pleasure of racism. It is very difficult to use those images and make sure that they become functional for denouncing the suffering, the injustice of coloniality. It's a big challenge for many decolonial artists today to reveal the underside of the splendor and beauty of modernity, because the public will often still come and consume it as a spectacle. We must be aware that the reproduction of those images often ends up reproducing their violence.

SB There is also this idea of showing coloniality in order to repair or make clear what was, or even still is happening. You've recently been working on Henry Lacoste's *Panorama Atmosphérique*, his proposal for the Congolese section at the 1935 Brussels World's Fair, which did not only display human resources, it also reproduced the climate and other atmospheric elements.

RVM Yes. Lacoste's *Panorama Atmosphérique* has to do with something I wrote about the Philips Pavilion by Le Corbusier and Yannis Xenakis at the 1958 World Exhibition in Brussels.[10] It is an attempt to control the senses, to create an artifice. It is the drive to control the senses, to design the experience of people. In the case of the *Panorama Atmosphérique*, it was designed to make people experience that power of empire, of being in all the climates of Earth that the Empire holds under its sway. Botanical gardens are part of this same history, like the Crystal Palace in London. In the metropolis, through these devices you could experience the power of accessing and controlling the worlds of others, of owning the worlds of others. It reproduced the idea of the sovereign-individual as the owner of the world. In big cities today, we experience this at the supermarket. We don't need to go far. We can consume the world just by strolling through a supermarket. As consumers, we can exercise and enjoy that enormous power over the life of others and the life of Earth. We are at the center of the world, and we are the owners. The imaginary of the world exhibitions, like the one of the *Panorama Atmosphérique*, belongs to that history of the hubris of modernity and empire.

SB Within this context, what does it mean to practice what you call a "decolonial aesthesis"?

RVM When we speak of "decolonial aesthesis," we mean that we need to move away from a logic of aesthetics as representation and ownership and instead move towards a logic of reception, listening, and offering; of owing instead of owning. For example, as Indigeneous philosophies teach us, we do not own Earth, we owe our life to Earth. It sustains us. All the water and minerals, every element in our bodies come from Earth. This is very present in the ontologies or philosophies of Abya Yala, for which modernity is an absurdity that has reduced Earth to property. How can we think that Earth is an object of consumption instead of a motherhood that requires our gratitude and our care? We're in a relationship of owing. In the history of Western arts and Western representation, including architecture, there is that exercise of the power of representation and of owning Earth and the worlds of others. In the *Panorama Atmosphérique*, people were supposed to experience owning the world instead of a relationship of owing, of gratitude, of offering, of reception… Reception is liberatory because it liberates us from the single self.[11] The self which owns is a very poor thing. To be an owner is to be enclosed in a single self, hungry to own more and more. In contrast, the plural self, is a self that owes, receives, and offers, and that is much broader than a single self.

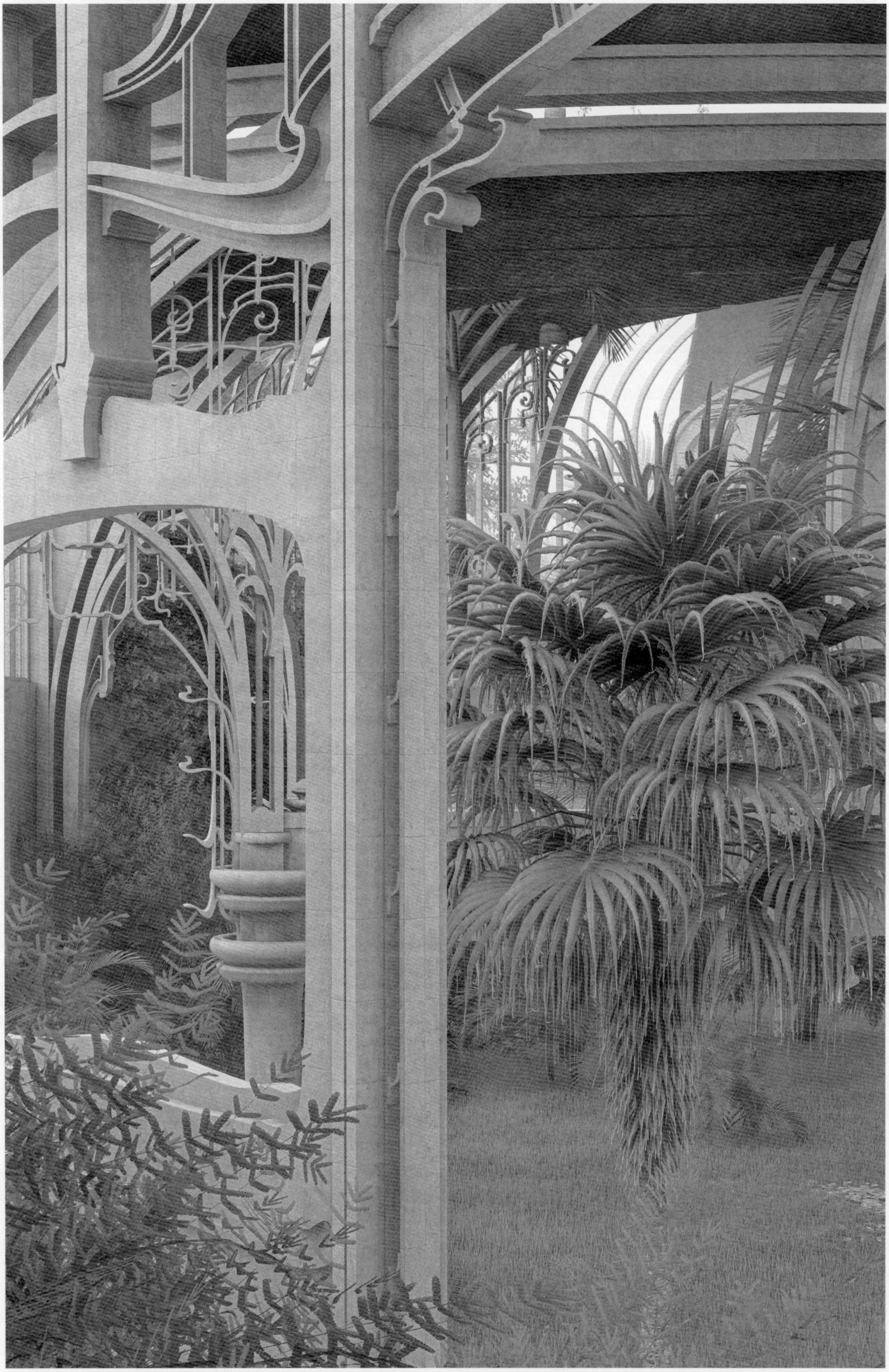

Victor Horta, Design for the Congo Pavilion, 1900, uncompleted. Simulation by Traumnovelle, 2023. Courtesy of the architects.

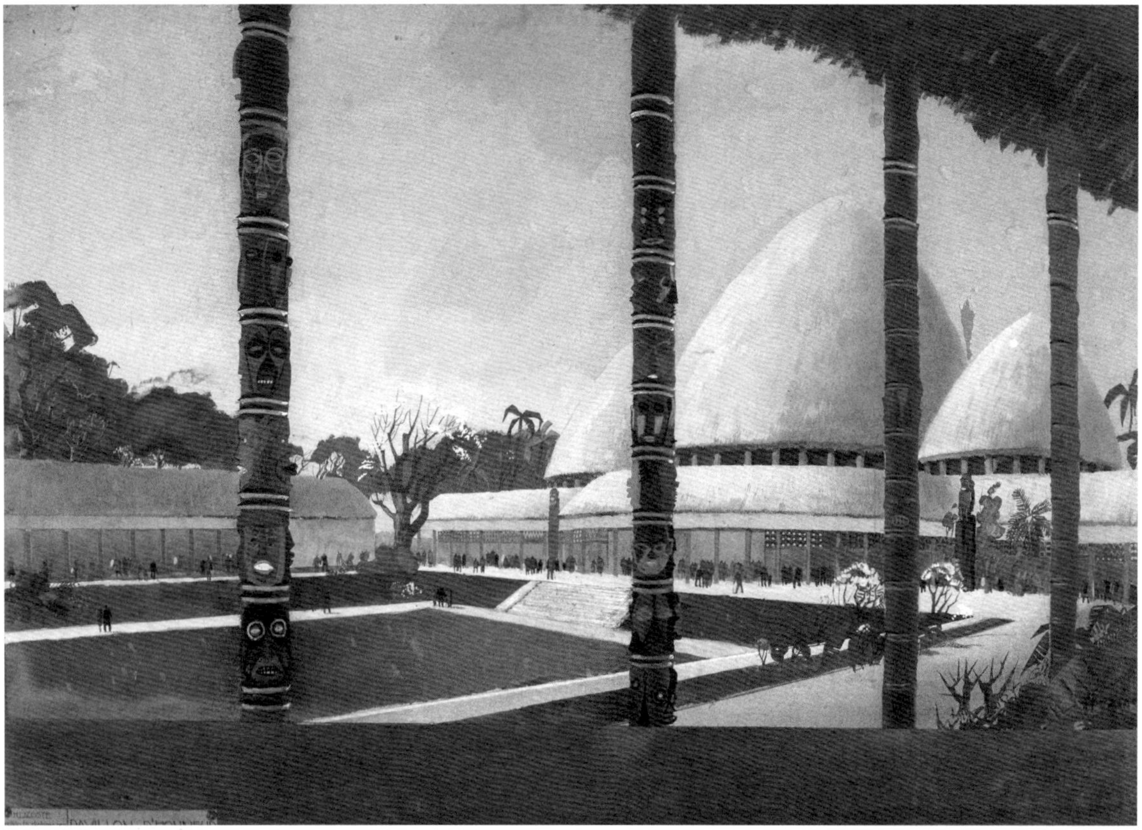

Henry Lacoste, *Le Congo Belge – Vue de prise du portique des industries de luxe vers le pavillon d'honneur,* 1931.
CIVA Collections, Brussels

It is a self that cherishes the plenitude of life. That is the proposal of decolonial aesthesis. Decolonial aesthesis aims to overcome modern aesthetics and the practices that are implicated in the extraction from Earth and the worlds of others.

SB In a recent article of yours, you talk about overcoming the contemporary and knowing otherwise.[12] Can you speak about how you suggest working with, or overcoming the contemporary?

RVM For us, the contemporary is just a reinstalment of that notion of modernity, of being in the present, of owning the present and sanctioning what belongs to the present. That's why the subtitle of my book is "the end of the contemporary." We need to end that logic of owning the present. That was the logic of imperial power. We need to move towards an aesthesis of pluriversality, of relationality.[13] Decolonial aesthesis doesn't seek to be contemporary, but rather seeks out processes of healing the colonial wound, processes of re-emergence. The decolonial response to the violence of modernity or the modern/colonial order is not to become modern or to become contemporary, because we know that they are both complicit with coloniality. The solution is not to enter the system, but to go beyond it, to delink from the system.[14] Like how the Zapatistas in Mexico clearly say that they don't want to be part of the project that is destroying the life of others and of Earth. That's why we question if it's possible to have an ethical life in a world where our wellbeing and sense of self depends on the suffering of others and the destruction of Earth.

SB And what does it mean to "know otherwise"?

RVM Knowing otherwise is knowing through relations and through remembering. It is a knowing in which we inhabit other temporalities. For example, for most of the peoples that are fighting coloniality, ancestrality is fundamental. Ancestrality is not a matter of superstition, but is the reality of those who have suffered before us, of those who have known a different relation to Earth.

That's why the cultivation of that relation and the fight against erasure is fundamental. What these pavilions and world exhibitions did was erase. They mined aesthetic resources, and they erased the memories of the peoples, the memories of the forests, of the oceans, of the mountains... It is this fight against erasure that marks the decolonial. It is a process of healing. It is not a process of becoming contemporary.

1
"Colonial encounters and conflicting memories: shared colonial heritage in the former Belgian Congo," https://www.tandfonline.com/doi/pdf/10.1080/1360236042000230161

2
In an article titled "The Delicious Pleasures of Racism," Egbert Alejandro Martina analyzes this perversity. https://processedlives.wordpress.com/2013/10/15/the-delicious-pleasures-of-racism/

3
I explain this mechanism in my analysis of the coloniality of the commodity in my text on "Decolonizing Design", namely how the commodity's magical appearance and pleasure is an expression of that power it bestows over the consumption of life. https://www.tandfonline.com/doi/abs/10.1080/14487136.2017.1303130

4
For the decolonial use of the 'we' voice see Vázquez Melken, Rolando. 2020. Vistas of Modernity: Decolonial Aesthesis and the End of the Contemporary. Essay / Mondriaan Fund 014. Amsterdam: Mondriaan Fund. Pp xx-xxi. Mignolo, Walter, and Rolando Vázquez Melken. 2013. 'Decolonial AestheSis: Colonial Wounds/Decolonial Healings'. Online Journal. Socialtextjournal. Org. 15 July 2013. https://socialtextjournal.org/periscope_article/decolonial-aesthesis-colonial-woundsdecolonial-healings/.

5
Vázquez Melken, Rolando. 2020. Vistas of Modernity: Decolonial Aesthesis and the End of the Contemporary. Essay / Mondriaan Fund 014. Amsterdam: Mondriaan Fund.

6
On the extraction of aesthetic resources and Primitivism see Susan Hiller, 'Editor's introduction', in: Susan Hiller (ed.), The Myth of Primitivism, Perspectives on art, London/New York: Routledge, 1991, p.12.

7
María Lugones, Pilgrimages/Peregrinajes: Theorizing Coalition Against Multiple Oppressions, , Lanham: Rowman & Littlefield, 2003.

8
Walter Mignolo, Local Histories/Global Designs, Coloniality, Subaltern Knowledges, and Border Thinking, Princeton, New Jersey: Princeton University Press, 2000

9
Vázquez Melken, Rolando (2017), Precedence, Earth and the Anthropocene: Decolonizing Design. *Design Philosophy Papers*, DOI: 10.1080/14487136.2017.1303130

10
Vázquez Melken, Rolando. 2020. Vistas of Modernity: Decolonial Aesthesis and the End of the Contemporary. Essay / Mondriaan Fund 014. Amsterdam: Mondriaan Fund.

11
María Lugones, Pilgrimages/Peregrinajes: Theorizing Coalition Against Multiple Oppressions, , Lanham: Rowman & Littlefield, 2003

12
"Recalling Earth, Overcoming the Contemporary, Knowing Otherwise."

13
Arturo Escobar, Designs for the Pluriverse, Durham/London: Duke University Press, 2017

14
Walter Mignolo, 'Geopolitics of sensing and knowing: on (de)coloniality, border thinking and epistemic disobedience', in: Postcolonial Studies 14:3 (2011), pp. 273-283.

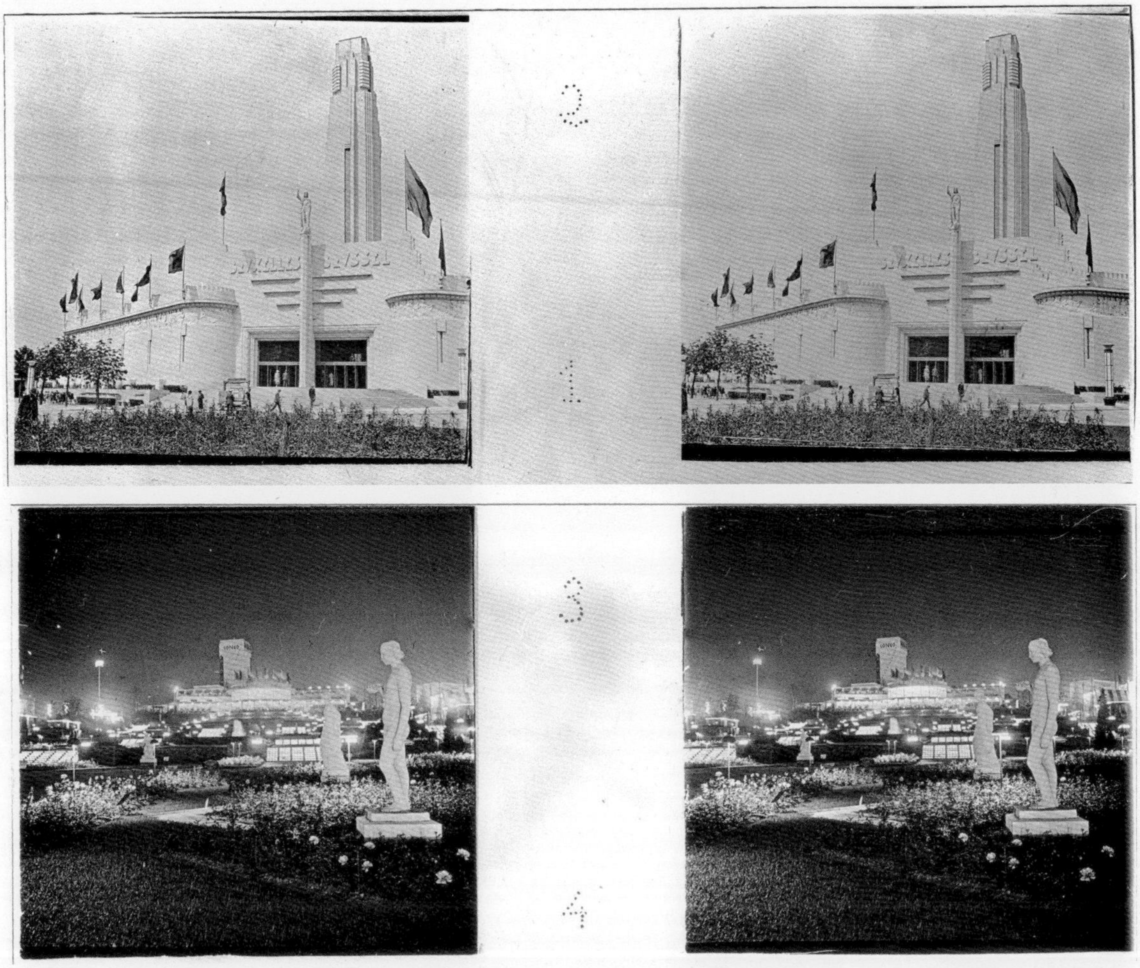

Rossella Biscotti, *Congo Congo Bruxelles Brussel*, 2007. Silver gelatin prints on baryta paper.
Courtesy of the artist, Private Collection, Aachen

Two enlarged prints show two mirroring pavilions built in front of each other on the occasion of the Brussels Universal Exhibition of 1935: the Brussels pavilion and the Congo pavilion. The Palace of the City of Brussels, designed using classical proportions by the architect François Malfait, contained works by members of the Académie Royale des Beaux-Arts of Brussels as well as a series of exhibitions showcasing the modernization of the Belgian capital.
The Congo Pavilion was designed by the architect of the Ministry of Colonies, René Schoentjes, as an attempt to illustrate vernacular architecture as a combination of sources from African and Islamic material culture. The exposition marked the fiftieth anniversary of Belgian colonialism. Brussels-based artist Rossella Biscotti found a set of stereoscopic images in a flea market, alongside a small stereoscopic machine, which were part of a box set created for the 1935 Brussels International Exposition. She selected these paired images and decided to enlarge and print them to emphasize the contrast between the representation of the "self" and the representation of "others" in an exhibi-tionary context crucial for the building of national identity.

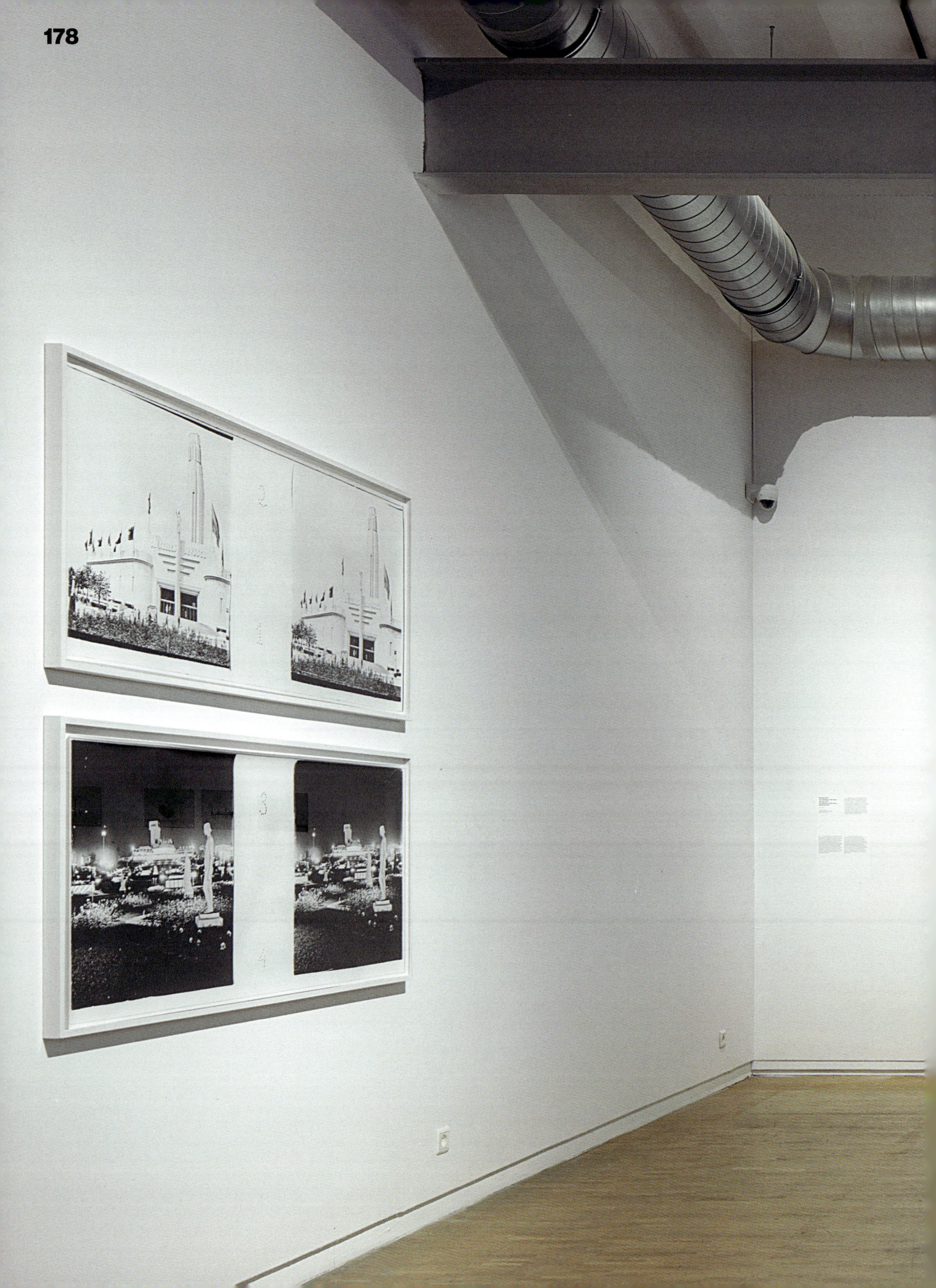

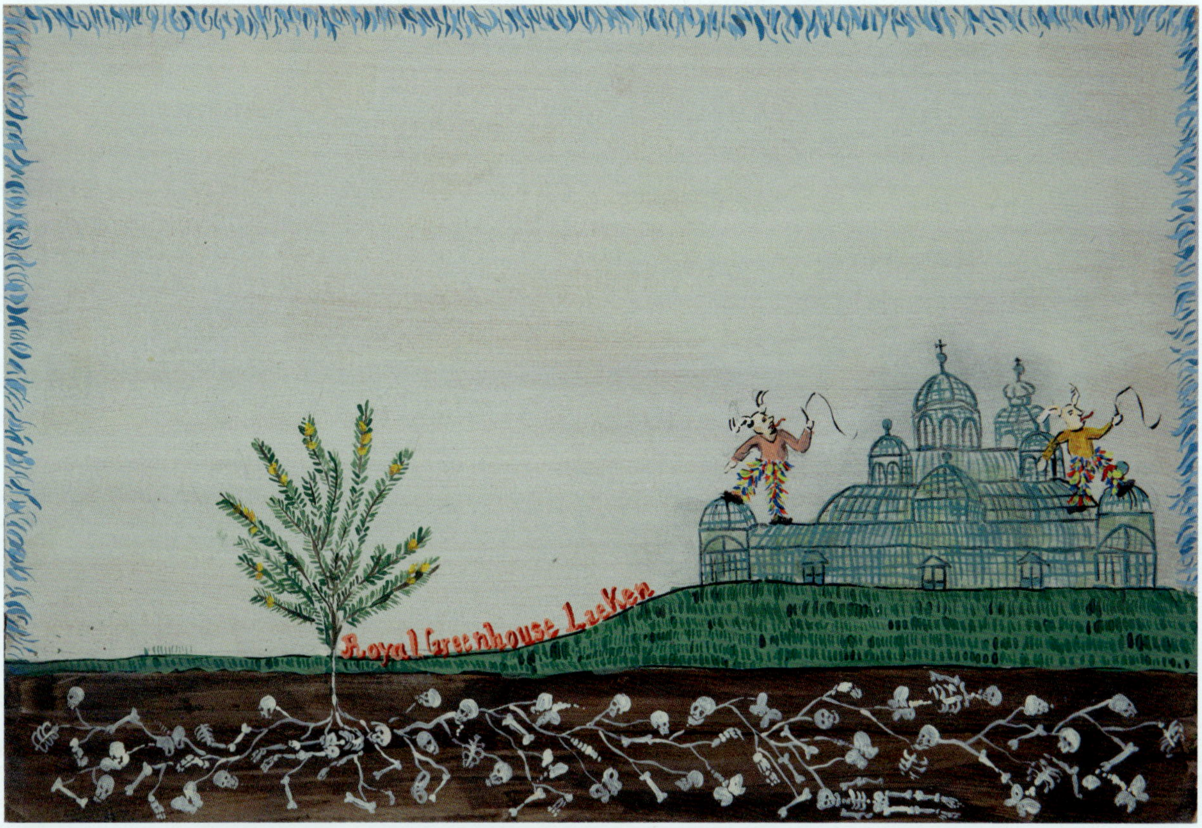

Daniela Ortiz, *The Rebellion of the Roots*, 2021. Acrylic on wood. Courtesy of the artist, AkzoNobel Collection, Amsterdam; Kadist Collection, Paris

Daniela Ortiz's series *The Rebellion of the Roots* explores the botanical gardens and greenhouses built for Great Universal Exhibitions and International Expositions in the nineteenth century. These events propagated the narrative of an industrial and civilized Europe, manifested in monumental industrial buildings such as the Crystal Palace and the Eiffel Tower. In symphony with those constructions were greenhouses and botanical gardens, whose main function was to complement such narratives through the import and containment of tropical plants and animals. Ortiz's series of 14 painted panels draw upon the aesthetic of ex-votos, depicts various tales in which tropical plants are kept in captivity across European cities. In the paintings, plants are imagined to be protected and nurtured by the spirits of those who experienced violence and death at the hands of colonial powers.

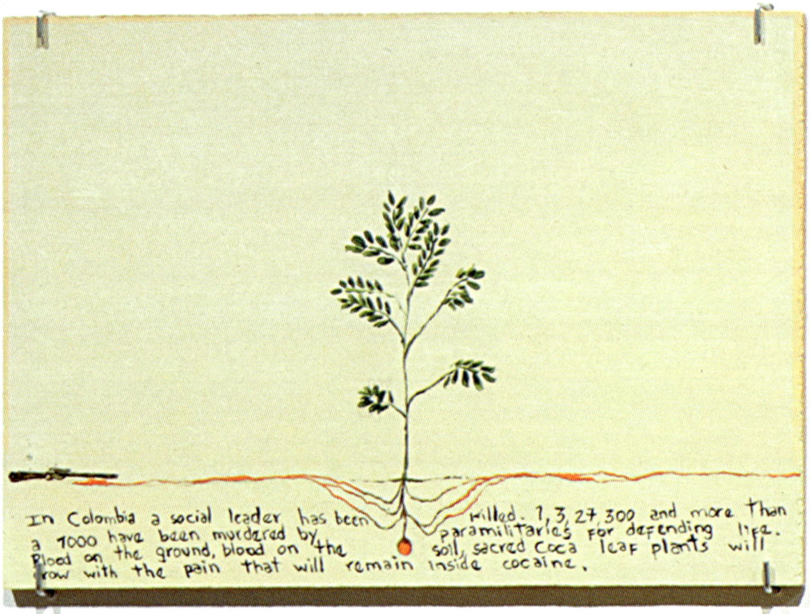
In Colombia a social leader has been killed. 1, 3, 27, 300 and more than
a 1000 have been murdered by paramilitaries for defending life.
Blood on the ground, blood on the soil, sacred Coca leaf plants will
row with the pain that will remain inside cocaine.

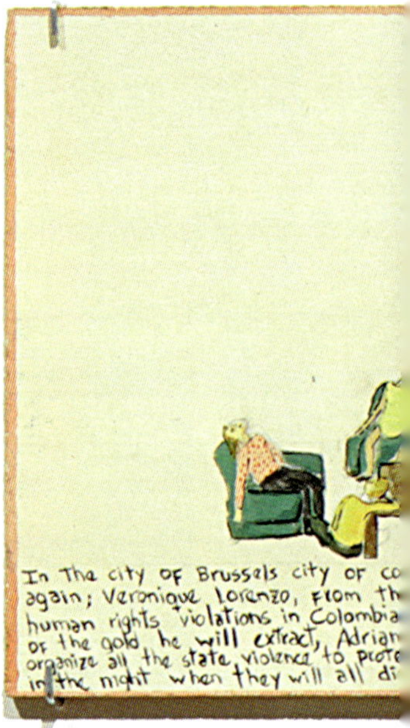
In The city of Brussels city of co
again; Veronique Lorenzo, from th
human rights violations in Colombia
of the gold he will extract, Adrian
organize all the state violence to prote
in the night when they will all di

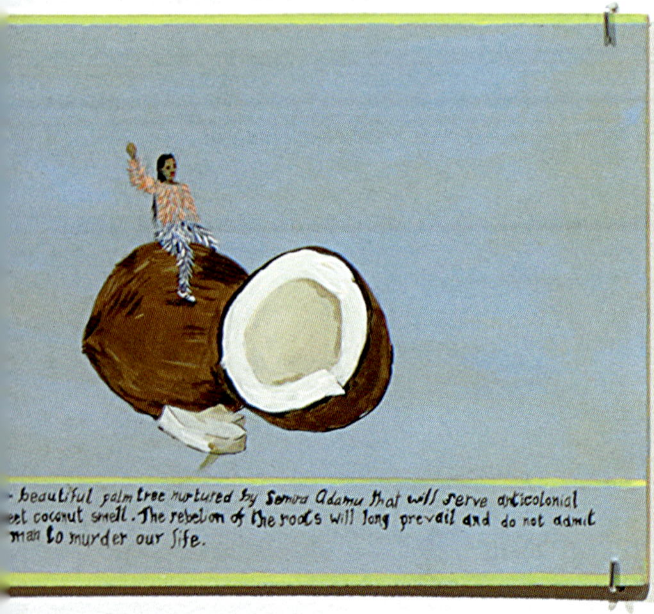
beautiful palm tree nurtured by Semira Adamu that will serve anticolonial
eet coconut smell. The rebelion of the roots will long prevail and do not admit
man to murder our life.

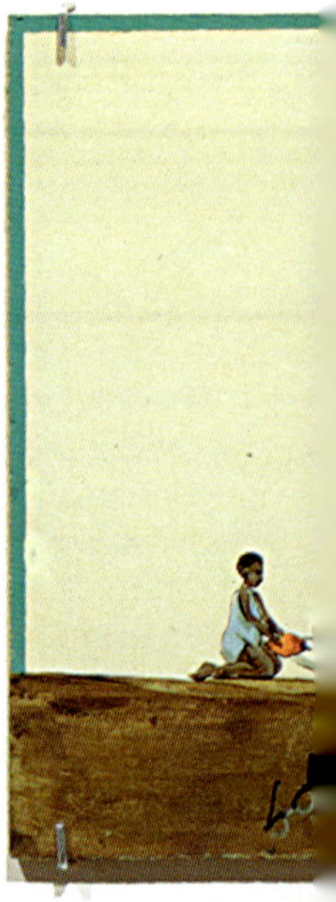

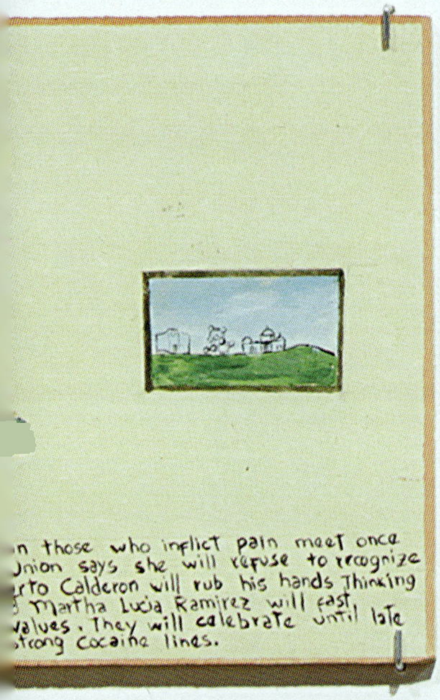
n those who inflict pain meet once
Jnion says she will refuse to recognize
rto Calderon will rub his hands Thinking
Martha Lucia Ramirez will fast
values. They will celebrate until late
strong cocaine lines.

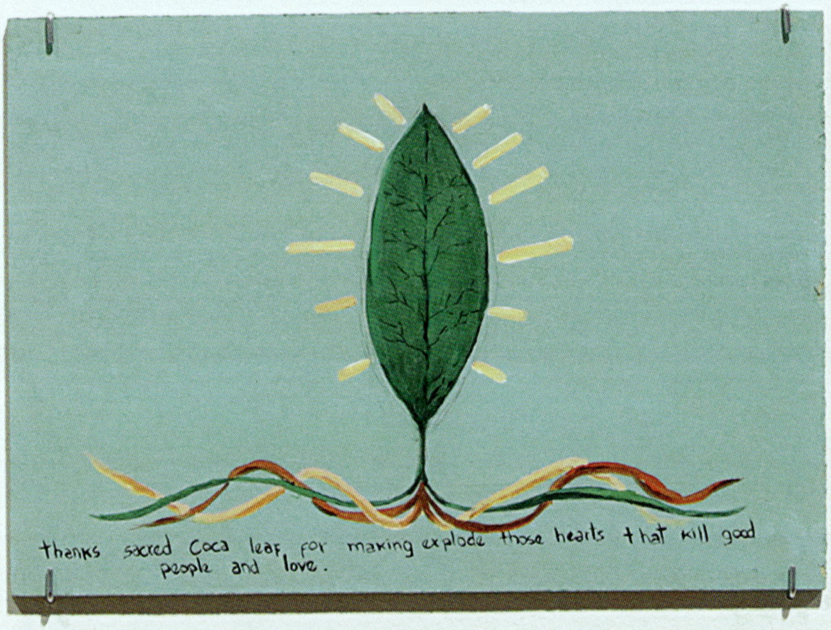
thanks sacred Coca leaf for making explode those hearts that kill good
people and love.

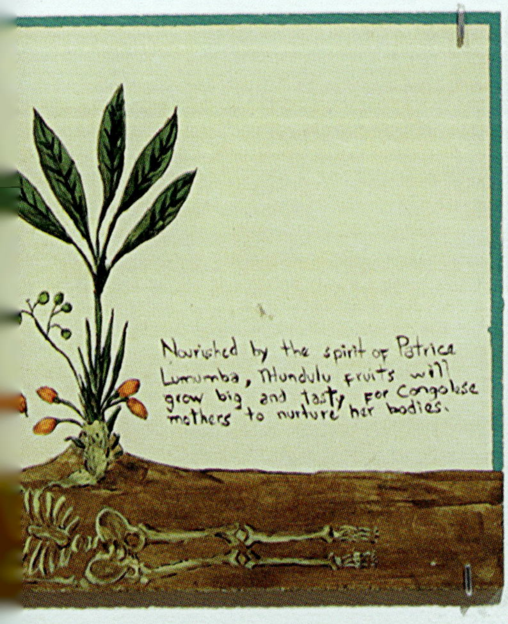
Nourished by the spirit of Patrice
Lumumba, Ntundulu fruits will
grow big and tasty for Congolese
mothers to nurture her bodies.

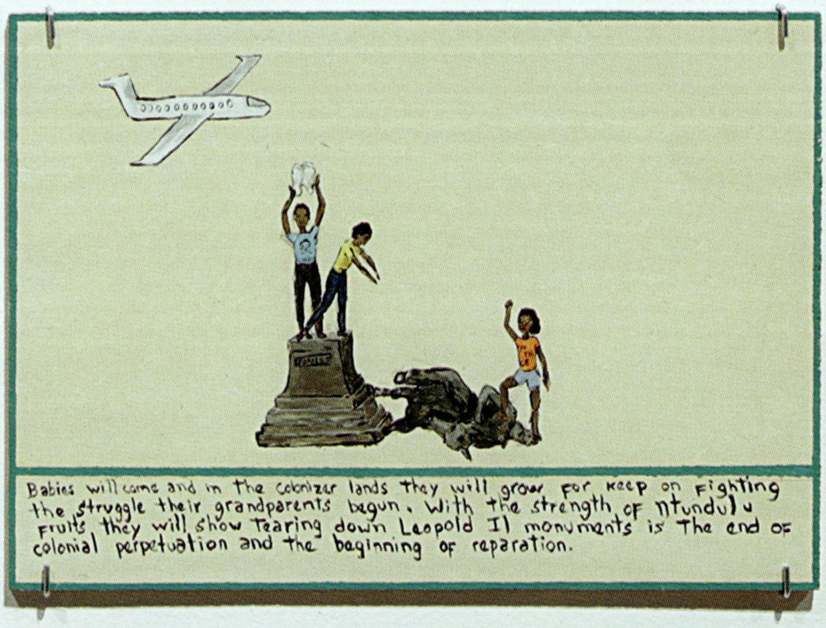
Babies will come and in the colonizer lands they will grow for keep on fighting
the struggle their grandparents begun. With the strength of Ntundulu
fruits they will show tearing down Leopold II monuments is the end of
colonial perpetuation and the beginning of reparation.

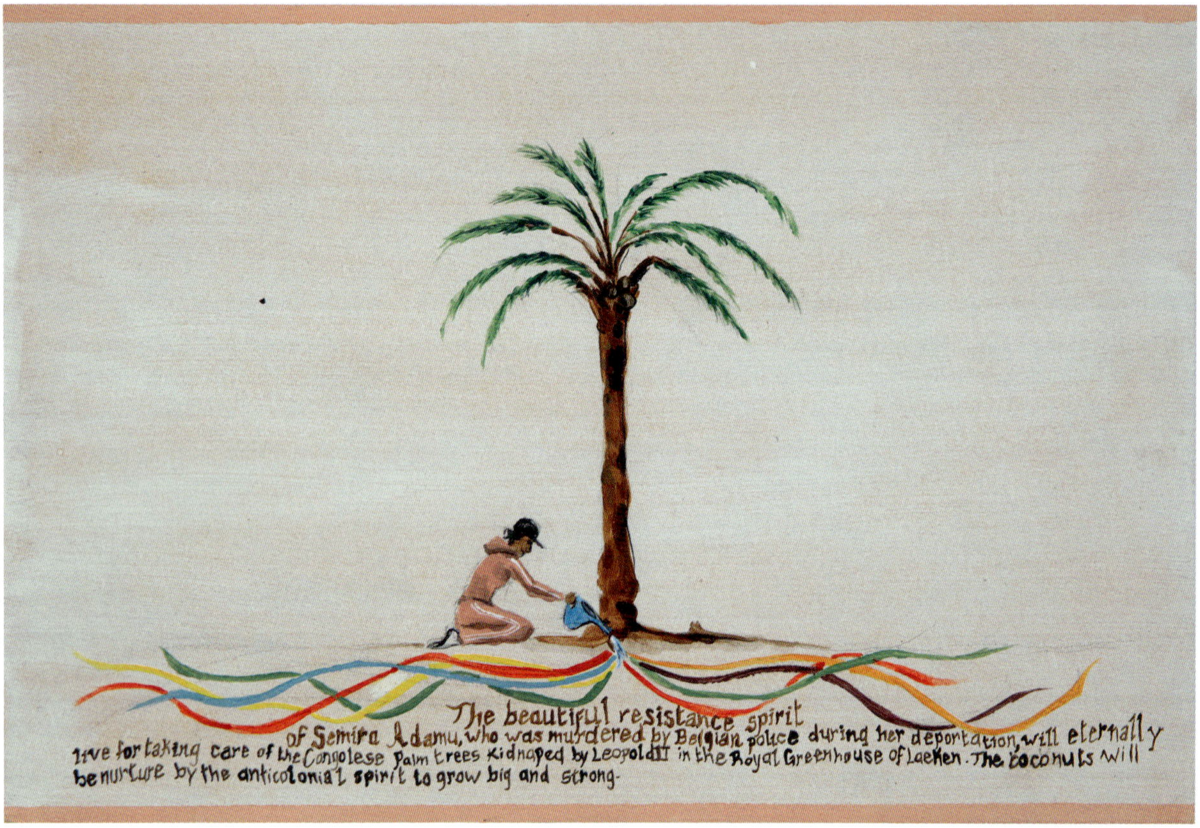

Daniela Ortiz,The Rebellion of the Roots, 2021. Acrylic on wood. Courtesy of the artist, AkzoNobel Collection, Amsterdam; Kadist Collection, Paris

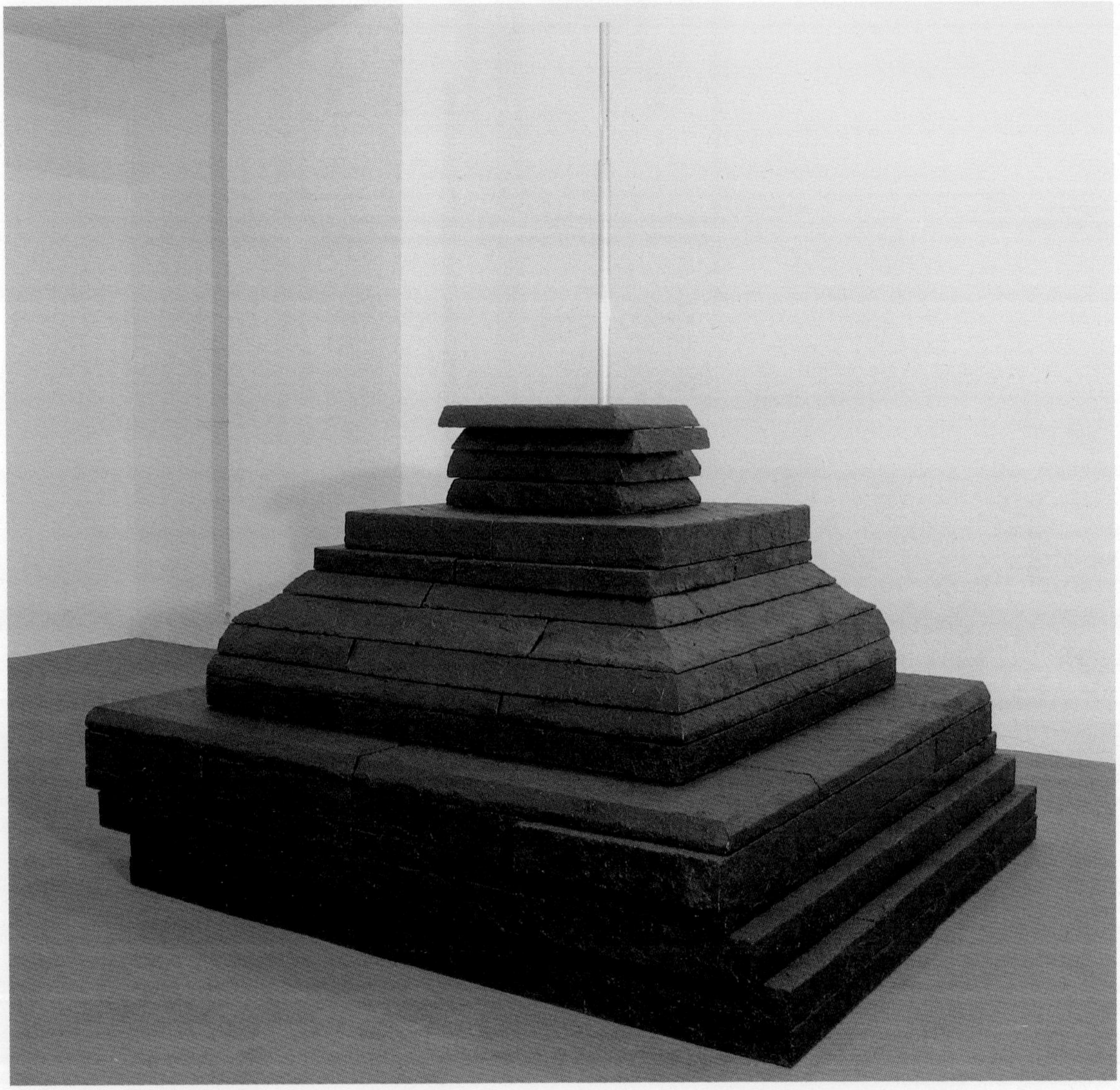

Peggy Buth, *Monument*, 2005. Styrofoam. Courtesy of the artist, FRAC Alsace Collection

Peggy Buth's *Monument* is a fragment of her multipart mixed media installation, *Desire in Representation (2005–12)*. The point of departure for this group of works is Buth's two-volume artist book, *Desire in Representation*, which is based on her extensive research on the Royal Museum for Central Africa in Tervuren. The book and her photo series *Tervuren* are also part of this exhibition. *Monument* consists of an empty plinth, whose function as structure for symbolic representations is purely self-referential — as all the figures of power who could be atop are seemingly "knocked off their pedestals." The massiveness of this substructure turns out to be an elaborate surface lamination — a farce — at the core of which are multiple layered polystyrene sheets. Deception, illusion, stage, and scenery are imbued in this sculptural object.

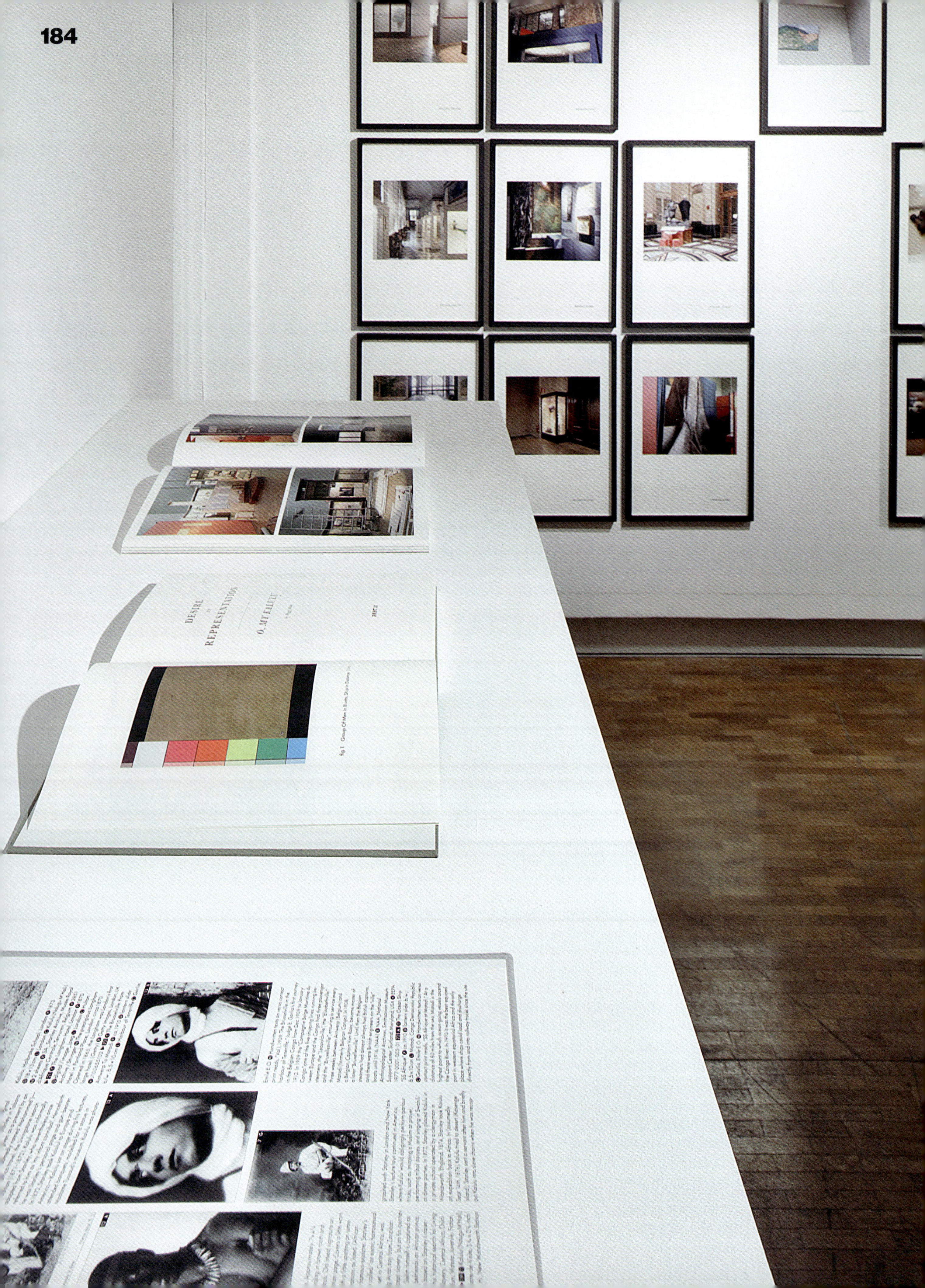

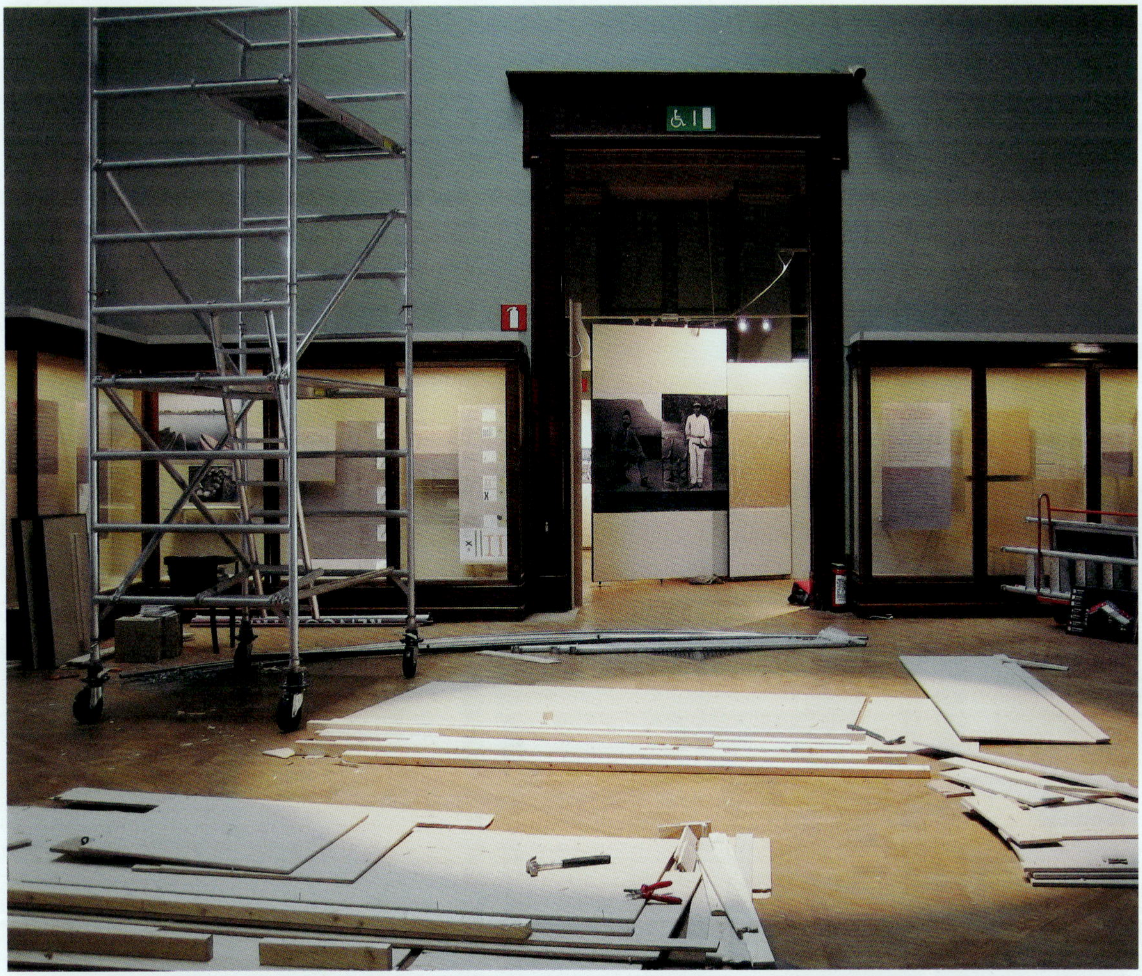

Peggy Buth, *Desire in Representation. Tervuren*, 2004–08. Photo series and artist books.
Courtesy of the artist, Klemm's Berlin

In her two-volume artist book, *Desire in Representation*, Peggy Buth examines the afterlife of colonial representation. The book is displayed in combination with her photo series *Tervuren*, for which the artist spent several years following the transformations of the Royal Museum for Central Africa in Tervuren. In her photographs, Buth shows exhibition displays and spatial arrangements as they undergo museological change while the museum grapples with how to represent the cultural legacy of Belgian Congo. Overlapping traces of past displays and vacant spaces disclose an ongoing process of historical reevaluation. The museum contains belongings and papers from the estate of Henry Morton Stanley, who worked for King Leopold II during his exploitation of Congo. In 1874, Stanley published a novel, *My Kalulu, Prince, King, and Slave: A Story of Central Africa* that Buth uses as the basis for the two parts of Desire in Representation, respectively titled *Travelling through the Musée Royale: Index/Register* and *O, My Kalulu*. She presents the story of the romantic friendship between the son of an Arabian slave trader and an African prince. Photographic stagings, which draw in equal measure on Western painting, popular book illustrations, and homoerotic photographs, reveal the allure of male initiation rites, ethnicity and slavery in Stanley's fiction.

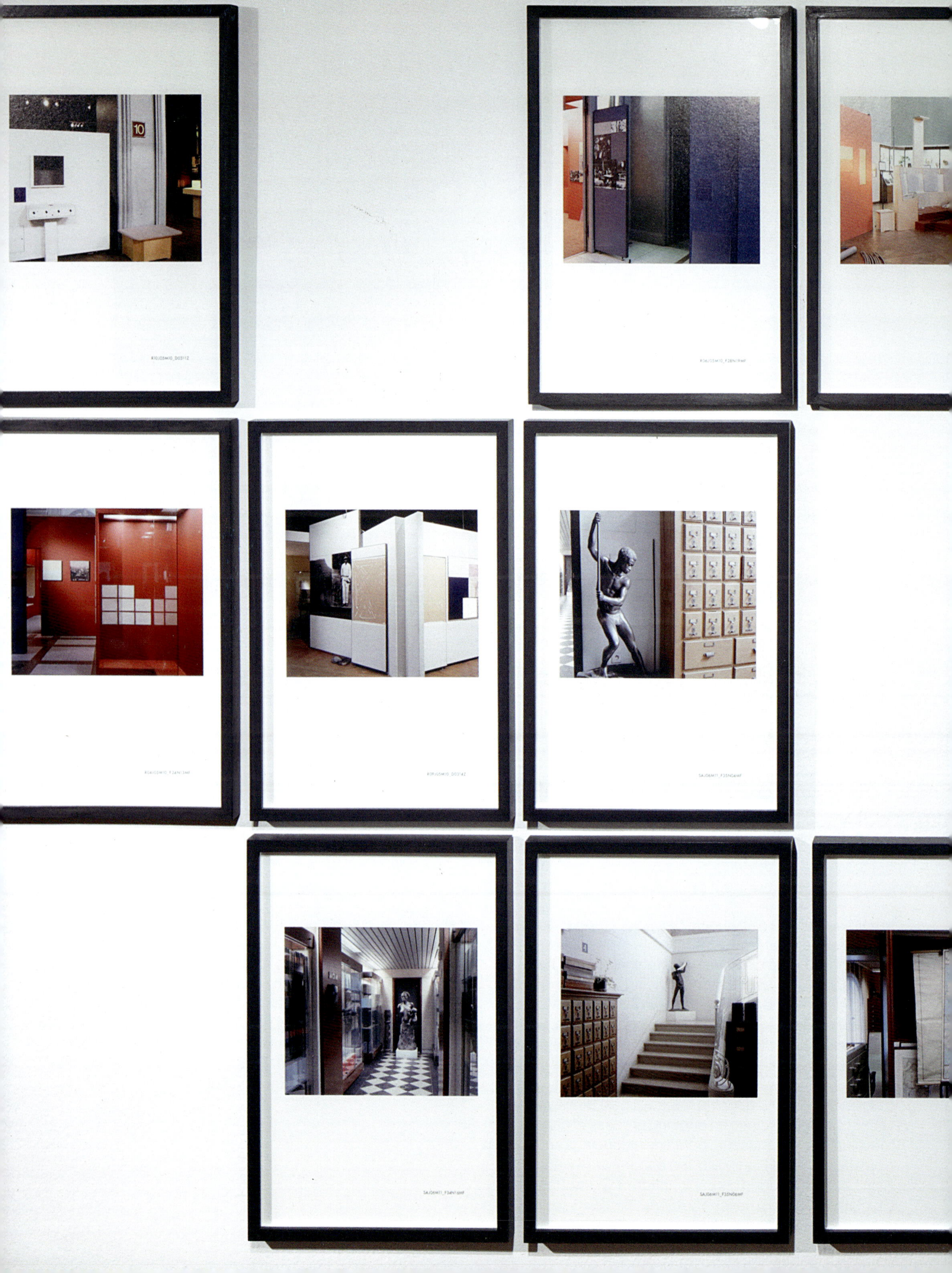

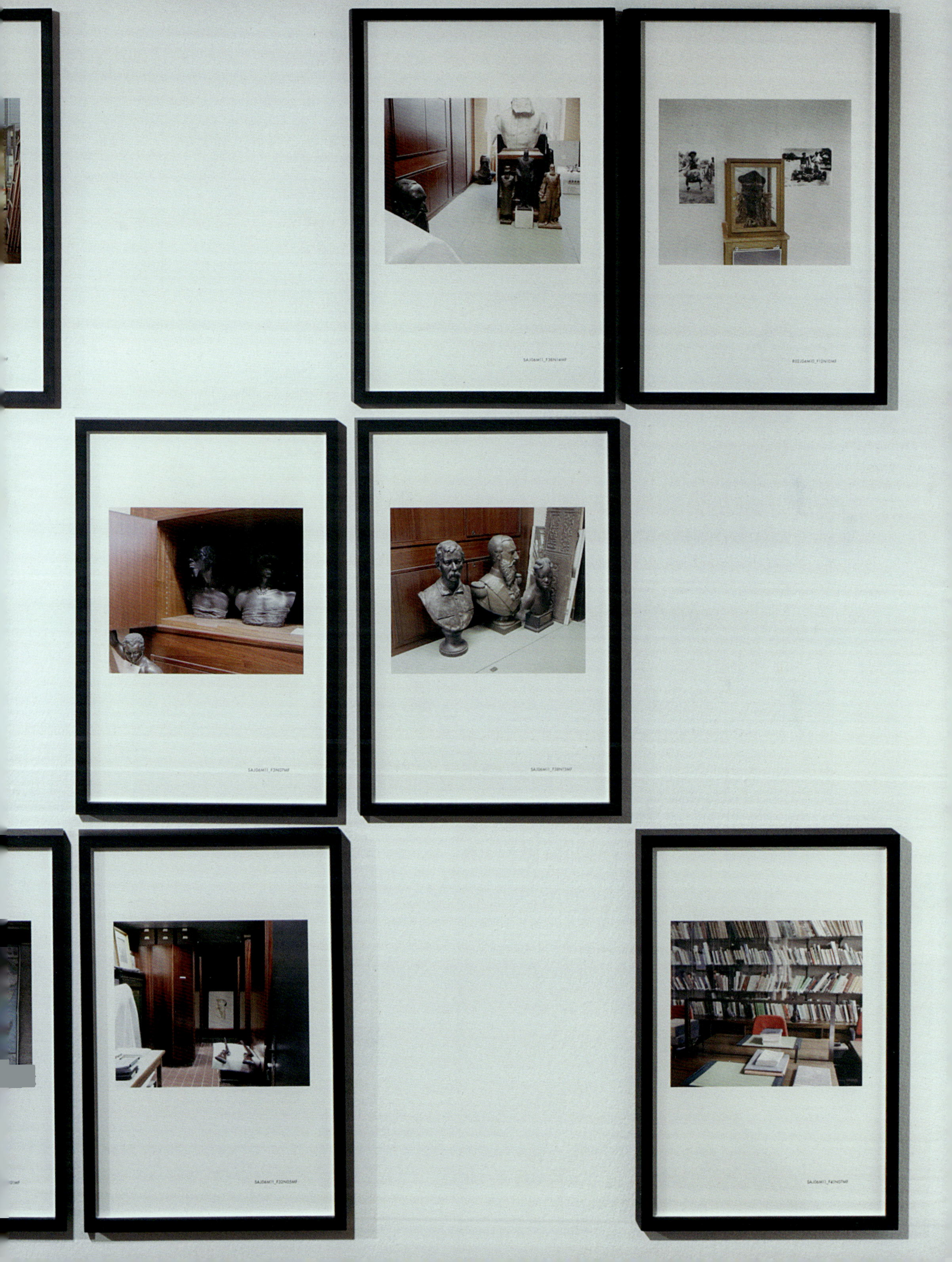

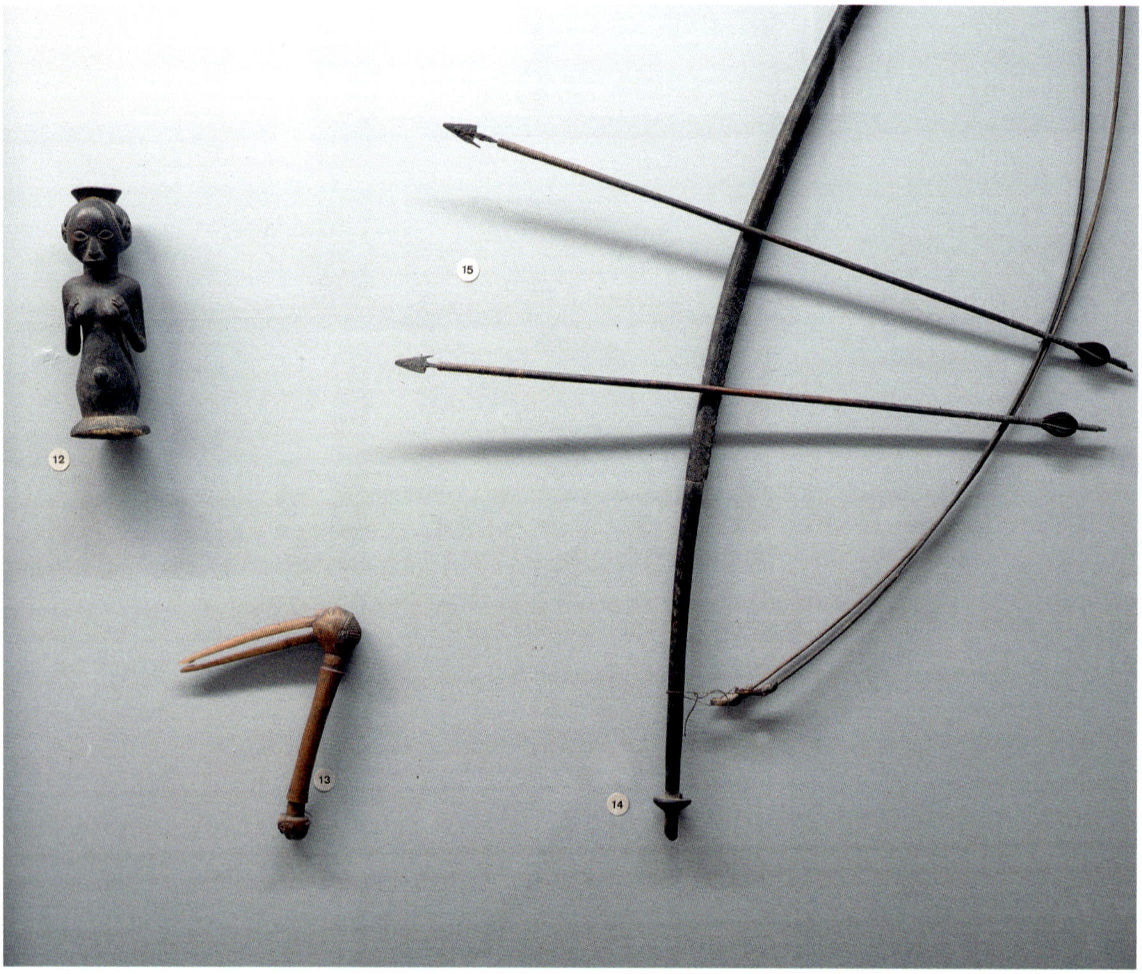

Peggy Buth, *Desire in Representation. Tervuren*, 2004–08. Photo series. Courtesy of the artist, Klemm's Berlin

Sammy Baloji

Sammy Baloji is a Brussels-based artist. His work involves ongoing research on the cultural, architectural, and industrial heritage of the Katanga region, as well as a questioning of the impact of Belgian colonisation in Congo. His use of archives allows him to manipulate time and space, comparing colonial narratives with contemporary economic imperialism.
A Chevalier des Arts et des Lettres, he was a laureate of the Rolex Mentor and Protégé Arts Initiative. In 2008 Baloji co-founded the Rencontres Picha/Biennale de Lubumbashi. He has had solo exhibitions at Palazzo Pitti, Florence (2022); the Beaux-Arts de Paris (2021); Lund Konsthall (2020); Framer Framed, Amsterdam (2018); The Power Plant, Toronto; and WIELS, Brussels (2016-2017). He participated in the Venice Biennale of Architecture (2023); the Sharjah Biennial (2023), Sydney Biennial (2020); documenta 14, Kassel/Athens (2017); and the Venice Biennial (2015).

Judith Barry

Judith Barry is a New York-based artist and writer who combines a number of disciplines including installation and project-based research, film and video, architecture and exhibition design, performance art and dance, sculpture, photography, and digital media. She has exhibited at documenta 13 (2012); at the Sharjah Biennial (2011); the São Paulo Biennale (1994); the Berlin Biennale (2004); Carnegie International (1991); the Venice Biennale (1990); the Whitney Biennale (1987); and the Sydney Biennale (1982), amongst others. She was awarded "Best Pavilion" – Cairo Biennale (2001), as well as the Frederick Kiesler Prize for Architecture/Arts (2000); and was the laureate of the Guggenheim Fellowship (2011).

Rossella Biscotti

Rossella Biscotti is a Brussels-based artist. Her work deals with the exploration of forgotten or untraced events. Places which have been tapped historically by forms of mining, exploitation, and confinement are often the backdrop of her artistic explorations. Biscotti has taken part in international exhibitions, including the 55th Venice Biennale (2013); the 13th Istanbul Biennale (2013); documenta 13, Kassel (2012); and Manifesta 9, Genk (2012). Her work has been presented in solo exhibitions at Mor Charpentier gallery (2022); Kunstinstituut Melly, Rotterdam (2019); Fondazione Ratti, Como (2019); daadgalerie, Berlin (2019); Kunsthaus Baselland, Basel (2018); Protocinema Istanbul (2018); GULAG History State Museum, Moscow (2016); Museion Bolzano (2015); WIELS, Brussels (2014); Sculpture Center, New York (2014); and Secession, Vienna (2013).

Peggy Buth

Peggy Buth is a Berlin-based artist and professor of intermedia and artistic photography at Kunsthochschule Kassel. She studied art and photography at the Hochschule für Grafik und Buchkunst in Leipzig and was a fellow of the Jan van Eyck Academy in Maastricht. Buth's transmedia approach is process-based and often involves extensive research. Her mixed media body of work "Desire in Representation" (2008-2012), explores the afterlife of colonial representation. In her work "Vom Nutzen der Angst" (2014-2019) she asks questions about the meaning of solidarity and empathy, about the history and memory of emancipatory movements and their decline in the course of (de-) industrialisation and globalisation.

Sandrine Colard

Sandrine Colard is Assistant Professor of Art History at Rutgers-Newark University in the United States, and Curator-at-large at KANAL–Centre Pompidou, Brussels. She holds a PhD from Columbia University (2016) and is a historian of African, modern, and contemporary arts, as well as a historian of photography. Her research has been published internationally and has been supported by grants from the Musée du Quai Branly, the Institut National d'Histoire de l'Art, the Ford Foundation and the Getty/ACLS foundation for her publication project on the history of photography in colonial Congo. In addition to other exhibitions, Sandrine Colard curated the 6th Lubumbashi Biennale entitled *Future Genealogies: Tales from the Equatorial Line* (2019).

ayoh kré Duchâtelet

ayoh kré Duchâtelet is a Belgian-Ivorian artist who lives and works in Brussels. His approach involves documentary research into instances of colonial and contemporary history. This research gives rise to heterogeneous fictional assemblages including texts, images, videos, sounds, and document-based installations. After a career as a graphic designer and set designer for cultural institutions, associations, and artists, ayoh kré gradually committed to an artistic practice from 2017. Since then, he has taken part in a number of exhibitions and residencies in the following institutions: Laboratoire Kontempo, Kinshasa; Laboratoires d'Aubervilliers, Paris; iMAL, Brussels; Galerie de l'Erg, Brussels; Constant, Brussels; La Bellone, Brussels; and KANAL-Centre Pompidou, Brussels.

Silvia Franceschini

Silvia Franceschini is a curator at CIVA in Brussels. Previously, she served as a curator at Z33-House for Contemporary Art, Design and Architecture, Hasselt. She has curated exhibitions for institutions such as SALT, Istanbul; V-A-C Foundation, Moscow; Futura—Center for Contemporary Art, Prague; Centre Pompidou, Paris. Additionally, she was part of the curatorial team of The School of Kyiv — Kyiv Biennial (2015). Franceschini is editor of *Curator Without a System, Viktor Misiano: Selected Writings* (Sternberg Press, 2022); *The Politics of Affinity, Experiments in Art, Education and the Social Sphere* (Cittadellarte-Fondazione Pistoletto, 2018); and *Global Tools 1973–1975, When Education Coincides With Life* (Nero Publishing, 2019).

Nikolaus Hirsch

Nikolaus Hirsch is the Artistic Director of CIVA, Brussels. He has previously held the positions of Dean at the Städelschule, Frankfurt and Director of Portikus Kunsthalle, Frankfurt. His architectural work includes the Dresden Synagogue, Hinzert Document Center, Cybermohalla Hub in New Delhi, and Do We Dream Under The Same Sky (with Rirkrit Tiravanija) at Art Basel and LUMA, Arles. Hirsch curated "Gwangju Folly", Gwangju Biennale (2012); Wohnungsfrage, HKW Berlin (2015) and the German Pavilion at the Venice Biennale (2021). He is the author of *On Boundaries* and *Cybermohalla Hub*, editor of the Critical Spatial Practice series at Sternberg Press, and founder and editor of e-flux Architecture.

Paoletta Holst

Paoletta Holst is a Brussels-based artist and architectural historian. She is a PhD candidate at Ghent University since March 2022, her PhD research focussing on late colonial housing politics and domestic cultures in the former Dutch East Indies through an artistic mobilisation of the "colonial archive." Since September 2022 she is an associated researcher at the a.pass Research Center in Brussels.

Johan Lagae

Johan Lagae is full professor at Ghent University where he teaches 20th Century Architectural History with a global focus and currently acts as Head of the Department of Architecture and Urbanism. His research interests are (post)colonial architecture and urbanism, built heritage, and photography in (Central-) Africa. He is currently involved in a large research project re-calibrating the discipline of Construction History. Alongside Nina Berre and Paul Wenzel Geissler he recently edited the volume *African Modernism and its Afterlives* (2022). He has also co-curated and contributed to several Congo- and Africa-related exhibitions and has collaborated with several artists from The Democratic Republic of the Congo.

Estelle Lecaille

Estelle Lecaille is an art historian, museologist, and curator at mòsso, Brussels—an independent collaborative platform for contemporary artistic practices that designs and supports international projects in Europe with countries in the global South. Between 2013 and 2020, she developed *dokountin*, an artistic exchange project whose title translates as "where the wealth is". Since 2019, she has managed the Brussels-based Twenty Nine studio, which designs and produces the work of artist Sammy Baloji. In 2021, in collaboration with ayoh kré Duchâtelet—member of la Villa Hermosa design studio—she created *sika*, an editorial project in the form of a free online magazine. She is the Associate Curator of the 8th Rencontres Photographiques de Guyane (2023) on the theme "Our landscape as its own monument".

Jean Katambayi Mukendi

Jean Katambayi Mukendi is a Lubumbashi-based artist. His practice is imbued with his fascination for mathematics, engineering, and geometry. Marked by his upbringing in the workers' camp of his mining hometown, Katambayi creates fragile and complex installations and drawings inspired by sophisticated electrical circuits and technological studies. Often made of recycled and impermanent material, such as cardboard and recycled electronic material, the artist's poetic pieces attempt to address its country's depletion of its enormous energetic resources. He has had solo exhibitions at Enough Room for Space, Brussels (2016) and at Stroom, The Hague (2017). He has taken part in numerous group exhibitions, notably the 11th Dak'Art biennial in Dakar (2014); the 12th Havana Biennial; the 4th Lubumbashi Biennale (2015); and the Taipei Biennale (2020).

Chrystel Mukeba

Chrystel Mukeba is a Brussels-based photographer and a graduate of ARBA ESA, Brussels. Her photographic work, which is mainly film-based and takes the form of portraits, focuses on intimacy and those close to her, capturing them in images where time stands still. His first series, *Confrontation*, was exhibited at Recyclart, Brussels (2011) and at BIP, Liège (2012). More recently, she exhibited Les Instants at Eté 78, Brussels (2022) and published a book of the same name (Arp2 Editions, 2022). She has also exhibited at the Centre Culturel Jacques Franck/ Musée de la Photographie, Charleroi (2023).

Daniela Ortiz

Daniela Ortiz lives and works in Cusco, Peru. Through her artistic work she generates visual narratives in which the concepts of nationality, social class, and genre are explored. Her projects have often dealt with migratory politics and its links to colonialism. Active in the world outside of her artistic practice, Daniela Ortiz is also an activist and the author of various publications and has held workshops and lectures internationally. She had solo exhibitions at Fondazione Sandretto Re Rebaudengo (2022); La Virreina – Centre de la Imatge, Barcelona (2020); the Middlesbrough Institute of Modern Art, UK (2017); Fabra I Coats, Barcelona (2017); and the Van Abbemuseum, Eindhoven (2016).

Ruth Sacks

Ruth Sacks is a visual artist and academic based in Johannesburg, with a PhD from Wits Institute for Social and Economic Research (2017). She has exhibited extensively, with a focus on writing, artist books, and installation, including M KHA, Antwerp (2019); ZKM, Karlsruhe (2011); Performa 09, New York (2009);and Venice Biennale (2007). She has participated in the organisation of artist-run projects in public spaces such as Response-ability, Joubert Park Greenhouse, Johannesburg (2020-2021) and Regions A-G, Johannesburg Public Library, (2012). Recent academic publications include the monograph *Congo Style: From Belgian Art Nouveau to African Independence* (Michigan University Press, 2023). Sacks is a member of faculty at the University of Johannesburg.

Debora Silverman

Debora Silverman is Distinguished Professor of History and Art History at UCLA, where she holds the University of California Presidential Chair in Modern European History, Art and Culture. Her books include *Selling Culture: Bloomingdale's, Diana Vreeland, and the Aristocracy of Taste in Reagan's America*; *Art Nouveau in Fin-de-Siècle France: Politics, Psychology, and Style;* and *Van Gogh and Gauguin: The Search for Sacred Art.* Her recent publications explore Gustav Klimt's marble mosaic frieze in the Palais Stoclet; the impact of The Congo Free State on *fin-de-siècle* Belgian modernism; and the history and politics of memory of the Tervuren Royal Museum for Central Africa.

Traumnovelle

Traumnovelle is a Brussels-based architecture studio founded in 2015 by Léone Drapeaud, Manuel León Fanjul, and Johnny Leya. Their work questions the relationships between architecture and politics and investigates architecture's civic role through all forms of space-making. Traumnovelle believes that collective narratives are constructed – and as such they should be questioned, deconstructed, and redefined. Traumnovelle is committed to critical design thinking and is determined to foster inclusive world-making. The studio represented Belgium at the Venice Architecture Biennale (2018). Among their projects are a community/office space in Charleroi (2019) and the scenography of the exhibition "Kinshasa N'tonga" at KANAL–Centre Pompidou in Brussels (2022). Traumnovelle's members teach at La Cambre in Brussels.

Rolando Vázquez Melken

Rolando Vázquez Melken is a founder and contributor to the movement of Decolonial AestheSis and Thought. He is associate professor of sociology at University College Roosevelt, affiliated to the research institute for Cultural Inquiry (ICON) and the Gender Studies Department of the University of Utrecht. Alongside Walter Mignolo he has coordinated Middelburg Decolonial Summer School for the past decade. In 2016, in collaboration with Gloria Wekker *et al.* he wrote the report of the Diversity Commission of the University of Amsterdam. His work seeks to transgress the dominion of contemporaneity, heteronormativity, and modernity/coloniality. Developing the questions of "precedence" and "the end of contemporaneity" he seeks to contribute to the decolonisation of institutions and subjectivities, epistemologies, and aesthetics.

Congolisation Traumnovelle

1885 Antwerp

Congo(lese) as Guest?

fig. 1 Congolese arrived in Antwerp to participate in the World's Fair, in particular, King Massala, from the vicinity of Vivi, accompanied by his son Mango, May 12, 1885, Extract from *Mouvement géographique*, Belgium, May 1885. Collection MRAC Tervuren

fig. 2 Zala, one of King Massala's lovers, Extract from Z. A. Etambala, «Carnet de route d'un voyageur congolais : Massala à l'exposition universelle d'Anvers en 1885», *Afrika Focus*, 1-2, 1994. Ghent University Library

fig. 3 King Massala at the photographer, Extract from Z. A. Etambala, «Carnet de route d'un voyageur congolais : Massala à l'exposition universelle d'Anvers en 1885», *Afrika Focus*, 1-2, 1994. Ghent University Library

1894 Antwerp

The Congo Section as a "Human Zoo"

fig. 4 Collection of plates of the Congolese Section of Antwerp Universal Exhibition, "Section de la Belgique", Extract from *Afdeling Congo, tentoonstelling Antwerpen,* 1894. Rijksmuseum Fonds, Amsterdam and the Egbert Kunstfonds – Photo Th. Lantin

fig. 5 Collection of plates of the Congolese Section of Antwerp Universal Exhibition, "Femmes Congolaises", Extract from *Afdeling Congo, tentoonstelling Antwerpen,* 1894. Rijksmuseum Fonds, Amsterdam and the Egbert Kunstfonds – Photo Th. Lantin

fig. 6 Collection of plates of the Congolese Section of Antwerp Universal Exhibition, "Section du Congo", Extract from *Afdeling Congo, tentoonstelling Antwerpen,* 1894. Rijksmuseum Fonds, Amsterdam and the Egbert Kunstfonds – Photo Th. Lantin

fig. 7 Collection of plates of the Congolese Section of Antwerp Universal Exhibition, "Musée et Village Congolais", Extract from *Afdeling Congo, tentoonstelling Antwerpen,* 1894. Rijksmuseum Fonds, Amsterdam and the Egbert Kunstfonds – Photo Th. Lantin

1897 Brussels

Style Congo and (the Display of) Imperial Ambitions

fig. 8 Fernand Khnopff, "Vis Superbae Formae", Design for the title page of the exhibition catalogue: *L'Etat indépendant du Congo. La sculpture chryséléphantine*, 1897. KBR

fig. 9 Paul Hankar, Ethnography room in the Colonial Palace, Extract from *Exposition congolaise de 1897,* Collection of plates. CIVA Collections, Brussels – Phototypie Alexandre Bruxelles

fig. 10 Idem.

fig. 11 Collection of plates offered to Paul Hankar, author of the interior design of the Congolese Section with Gustave Serrurier-Bovy, Georges Hobé and Henry van de Velde. CIVA Collections, Brussels

fig. 12 Paul Hankar, Ethnography room in the Colonial Palace, Extract from *Exposition congolaise de 1897,* Tervuren. CIVA Collections, Brussels – Phototypie Alexandre Bruxelles

fig. 13 Attributed to Ernest Acker, Glasshouse in the Colonial Palace, Extract from *Exposition congolaise de 1897*, Tervuren. CIVA Collections, Brussels – Phototypie Alexandre Bruxelles

fig. 14 Georges Hobé, Field crops room in the Colonial Palace, Extract from *Exposition congolaise de 1897*. CIVA Collections, Brussels – Phototypie Alexandre Bruxelles

fig. 15 Paul Hankar, Georges Hobé, Gustave Serrurier-Bovy, Henry van de Velde, Ramp and Wildlife in the Colonial Palace, Extract from *Exposition congolaise de 1897*. CIVA Collections, Brussels – Phototypie Alexandre Bruxelles

fig. 16 Paul Hankar, Ethnography room in the Colonial Palace, Extract from *Exposition congolaise de 1897*. CIVA Collections, Brussels – Phototypie Alexandre Bruxelles

1900 Paris

Horta's Paper Project for a Congo Palace

fig. 17 Victor Horta, Design for the Congo Pavilion, elevation plan of the façade, uncompleted, ca. 1900. Archives du Musée Horta

fig. 18 Victor Horta, Design for the Congo Pavilion, uncompleted, Extract from C. Dulière, *Victor Horta: mémoires*, 1985. CIVA Collections, Brussels

fig. 19 Victor Horta, Design for the Congo Pavilion, uncompleted. Simulation by Traumnovelle, 2023. Courtesy of the Architects

fig. 20 Victor Horta, Design for the Congo Pavilion, uncompleted, Extract from C. Dulière, *Victor Horta: mémoires*, 1985. CIVA Collections, Brussels

1905 Liège

A Modest Presence

fig. 21 Congo Pavilion in the Jardin d'Acclimatation *Le Quartier des Palais*, Extract from catalogue of the Etablissements Jean Malvaux S.A., 1905

fig. 22 Léon Sneyers, Design for the Congo Pavilion, uncompleted, 1905. CIVA Collections, Brussels

1910 Brussels

An Incomplete Educational Project

fig. 23 J. Gilbert and P. Van Brempt, *Exposition universelle de Bruxelles, Section coloniale parc de Tervueren*, 1910. Collection MRAC Tervuren

1913 Gent

Celebrating the Belgian Nation as a Strong Colonial Power

fig. 24 Alfred Bastien, Paul Mathieu, Drawings of the circular "Panorama du Congo" in the Colonial Palace, Extract from *Panorama du Congo par les peintres Paul Mathieu et Alfred Bastien,* Édition d'Art E. Mertens, ca. 1913. Ghent University Library, Creative Commons

fig. 25 Joseph Caluwaers, "Palais Colonial", Extract from *Tekhné*, 51, 1912. CIVA Collections, Brussels

1930 Antwerp

Displaying Colonial Modernization in an Era of Economic Crisis

fig. 26 Joseph Caluwaers, "Palais du Congo Belge", Extract from *De Bouwgids, 10,* 1930. CIVA Collections, Brussels
fig. 27 Joseph Caluwaers, Palace for Belgian Congo, 1930. CIVA Collections, Brussels
fig. 28 Palace for Belgian Congo. Official Guide, Extract from *Palais du Congo belge. Guide Officiel, 1930.* Collectie M UKHA I Collectie Vlaamse Gemeenschap
fig. 29 Idem.
fig. 30 Idem.

1931 Paris

A Phantasmagoric, yet Erudite and Functional Architectural Response

fig. 31 Henry Lacoste, Pavilion of Honor of the Belgian Congo in the Belgian Section, design for the central rotunda. CIVA Collections, Brussels
fig. 32 Henry Lacoste, Monument to the dynasty in the hall of honor of the Belgian Congo in the Belgian Section. CIVA Collections, Brussels
fig. 33 Henry Lacoste, Entry to the Belgian Section. CIVA Collections, Brussels
fig. 34 Henry Lacoste, Pavilion of Honor of the Belgian Congo in the Belgian Section. CIVA Collections, Brussels
fig. 35 Henry Lacoste, The Pavilion of luxury industries in the Belgian Section. CIVA Collections, Brussels
fig. 36 Maréchal Hubert Lyautey, «Le sens d'un grand effort», *L'Illustration*, May 1931; Maxime Alexandre, Louis Aragon, André Breton, René Char, René Crevel, Paul Éluard, Benjamin Péret, Georges Malkine, Georges Sadoul, Yves Tanguy, André Thirion, Pierre Unik, *Ne visitez pas l'Exposition Coloniale*; Tract against colonialism, particularly against the prefect Chiappe, guilty of having expelled a student from Indochina. CIVA Collections, Brussels
fig. 37 *Exposition Coloniale 1931 Paris. 60 Aspects de l'exposition coloniale*, Collection of plates with exhibition pictures, Cover, 1931. CIVA Collections, Brussels
fig. 38 Henry Lacoste, Gallery of the Pavilion of luxury industries in the Belgian Section, Extract from *Exposition Coloniale 1931 Paris. 60 Aspects de l'exposition coloniale, Arts et métiers graphiques*, 1931. CIVA Collections, Brussels – Photo M. Cloche
fig. 39 Jacques Cury, Fernand Leroy, Colonial Woods Pavilion. *Exposition Coloniale 1931 Paris. 60 Aspects de l'exposition coloniale, Arts et métiers graphiques*, 1931. CIVA Collections, Brussels – Photo M. Cloche
fig. 40 Henry Lacoste, Pavilion of Honor of the Belgian Congo (left) and Pavilion of luxury industries (right) under construction, in the Belgian Section. CIVA Collections, Brussels – Photo M. Cloche

1935 Brussels

Celebrating a *Cinquantenaire* in Uncertain Times

fig. 41 Henry Lacoste, Pillar to the Belgian dynasty in the central hall of the Honor Pavilion of the General Commissariat in the Belgian Section. CIVA Collections, Brussels – Photo E. Sergysels
fig. 42 Victor Bourgeois, Restaurant Léopold II. CIVA Collections, Brussels Photo C. Vandenberghe
fig. 43 Henry Lacoste, Belgian arts and crafts exhibited in the dining room of the Pavilion of Honor of the General Commissariat in the Belgian Section, Extract from "Le Livre d'or de l'Exposition universelle et international Bruxelles 1935", éd. *Bruxelles: le Comité exécutif de l'Exposition* 1935, 1935. CIVA Collections, Brussels – Photo E. Sergysels
fig. 44 *Bruxelles 1935*, Album published as a supplement to the book *La Belgique Centenaire 1830-1930. Encyclopédie Nationale*, 1935. CIVA Collections, Brussels
fig. 45 René Schoentjes, Pavilion of the Belgian Congo, Extract from *Bruxelles 1935*, suppl. *La Belgique Centenaire 1930-1930, Encyclopédie Nationale, 1935.* CIVA Collections, Brussels
fig. 46 Douret, René Schoentjes, The Pavilion of the colonial propaganda auxiliary Society «Soprocol» in the Belgian Colonial Section, Extract from *Le Livre d'or de l'Exposition universelle et international Bruxelles 1935*, éd. Bruxelles: le Comité exécutif de l'Exposition 1935, 1935. CIVA Collections, Brussels
fig. 47 *Exposition de Bruxelles 1935, Pavilion du Congo*, éditeur Michiels-Leblicq (Thill-Nels), 1935. Collection MRAC Tervuren
fig. 48 Henri Lacoste, Design for an atmospheric panorama for the Colonial Grand Palais in the Belgian Colonial Section, Simulation by Ruben Van de Walle, Bachelor's thesis, Universiteit Gent, Vakgroep Architectuur & Stedebouw, 2002-03 (promotor: prof. Mil De Kooning; ass. Johan Lagae)

1937 Paris

Romanticizing Colonial Life in Modern Congo

fig. 49 Jean-Jules Eggericx, Diorama room in the Belgian Pavilion. CIVA Collections, Brussels – Photo E. Sergysels
fig. 50 Arthur Dupagne, Door leaf of the chapel in the Pavilion of the Belgian Congo (Fernand Petit). CIVA Collections, Brussels
fig. 51 Jean-Jules Eggericx, The Belgian Pavilion. CIVA Collections, Brussels
fig. 52 Jean-Jules Eggericx, Diorama in the Belgian Pavilion. CIVA Collections, Brussels – Photo E. Sergysels
fig. 53 Idem.
fig. 54 Fernand Petit, Pavilion of the Belgian Congo. CIVA Collections, Brussels
fig. 55 Jean-Jules Eggericx, Hall of Honor of the Belgian Pavilion. CIVA Collections, Brussels – Photo Lumière

1939 Liège

An Exoticizing Decorated Shed on the River's Edge

fig. 56 Henry Lacoste, Design for the Palace of the Belgian Congo. CIVA Collections, Brussels
fig. 57 Henry Lacoste, Design for a Trophy and masks in front of the Palace of the Belgian Congo. CIVA Collections, Brussels
fig. 58 Idem.
fig. 59 Idem.

1958 Brussels

An Unanticipated Swan Song of Belgian Colonialism

fig. 60 René Pechère, Travel diary *Congo Belge, René Pechère, Architecte-Paysagiste chargé de Mission*, 1956-58. CIVA Collections, Brussels

fig. 61 René Pechère, *Choix d'arbres d'alignement, Région Stanleyville*, Binder, 1953. CIVA Collections, Brussels

fig. 62 René Pechère, Tropical Garden in the Belgian Congo and Ruanda-Urundi Section. CIVA Collections, Brussels – Photo Roland D'Ursel, Les Frères Haine, Willy Kessels, SADO, Sergysels & Dietens

fig. 63 René Pechère, Basketry design for the Tropical Garden in the Belgian Congo and Ruanda-Urundi Section, 1958. CIVA Collections, Brussels

fig. 64 René Pechère, Tropical Garden in the Belgian Congo and Ruanda-Urundi Section, decoration details, 1958. CIVA Collections, Brussels – Photo Willy Kessels

fig. 65 René Pechère, Tropical Garden in the Belgian Congo and Ruanda-Urundi Section. CIVA Collections, Brussels – Photo Roland D'Ursel, Les Frères Haine, Willy Kessels, SADO, Sergysels & Dietens

fig. 66 Idem.

fig. 67 Picture of a termite mound taken by René Pechère during his research trip in Congo in 1956 and reconstitution of a termite mound in the Tropical Garden in the Belgian Congo and Ruanda-Urundi Section. CIVA Collections, Brussels – Photo SADO

fig. 68 Constantin Brodzki, Wildlife Pavilion. CIVA Collections, Brussels

fig. 69 Constantin Brodzki, Wildlife Pavilion, Model. CIVA Collections, Brussels – Photo Jacques Donatil

fig. 70 Pierre Coulon and André Noterman, Mining Industry Pavilion, 1958. CIVA Collections, Brussels

fig. 71 Lucien de Vestel, Project for the Belgian Congo and Ruanda-Urundi Section, uncompleted, CIVA Collections, Brussels

fig. 72 Georges Ricquier, Palace of the Belgian Congo and Burundi, 1958. CIVA Collections, Brussels – Photo Sergysels and Dietens

fig. 73 A Congolese soldier responsible for guarding the Congolese pavilion visiting Expo 58 with his family, September 10, 1958. Archives Photo Belga

fig. 74 Georges Ricquier, Palace of the Belgian Congo and Burundi, 1958. CIVA Collections, Brussels – Photo Sergysels and Dietens

fig. 75 Julien De Ridder and Yvan De Ridder, Catholic Missions Pavilion, 1958. CIVA Collections, Brussels – Photo Sergysels and Dietens

Note fig. 8, 11, 19, 22, 23, 25, 27, 30-34, 56-59, 60-61, 70 have been converted to black and white and do not represent the original colors of the documents.

Artwork Credits

pp. 19-22 **Judith Barry, *The Work of the Forest*, 1992**
Three-channel video projection panorama. Installation Design: Ken Saylor, Projection Design: David Sirola, Executive Producer/Curator: Bartomeu Mari, Picture and Sound Finishing Provided by: GOLDCREST POST NY, Archive Specialist: Maurice Schecter, Color and Restoration: Jane Tolmachyov, DI Assist: Dan Dragicevich, Data I/O Manager: Aaron Kelly-Penso, DI Producer: Linda McDonnell Re-recording Mixer: Allan Gus, Audio Department Manager: Nicole Tessier, Head of Production: Wade Rudolph, Managing Director: Dom Rom

p. 142 **ayoh kré Duchâtelet, *Le tribunal hanté*, 2023**
Sound installation. Sources for the audio piece: Excerpts from Departure and Virginia by DRC Music, Congo Avenir by Tabu ley Rochereau, Godee by Docteur Nico, L'African Fiesta, Tabu Ley Rochereau and Kwami.

pp. 144-148 **Paoletta Holst and Johan Lagae, *"Objects that are dear to him"*, 2023**
Double screen video installation. Sources for the film: Edmond Leplae, "Plans et photographies d'habitations pour plantations coloniales" *Bulletin Agricole du Congo Belge*, vol.1. no.2, 1911; M. Van den Abeele, "Edmond Leplae", *Biographie Coloniale Belge*, vol. IV, Brussels, 1955, pp. 515-518.; and a series of 31 photographs taken by Leplae on his mission to the Katanga region in Congo between 1910 and 1914, Colonial Office Collection, MRAC Tervuren.

p. 153, 159, 160 **Archivio Storico della Biennale di Venezia**
Photos by Andrea Avezzù, Jacopo Salvi, Marco Zorzanello, Matteo de Mayda

p. 154 **Sammy Baloji, *Aequare: The Future That Never Was*, 2023**
Video. Editing: Luca Mattei, Sound mix: Frédéric Furnelle, Yangambi footages: Frank Moka, Sound: Chris Watson, Production: Twenty Nine studio, Brussels

Exhibition Views

pages 2, 19, 20, 22, 23, 24, 27, 31, 35, 45, 51, 55, 57, 61, 69, 77, 85, 95, 101, 121, 122, 135, 136, 139, 143, 144-148, 149, 152, 178, 180-181, 184, 186-187, 195
Photos by Filip Dujardin

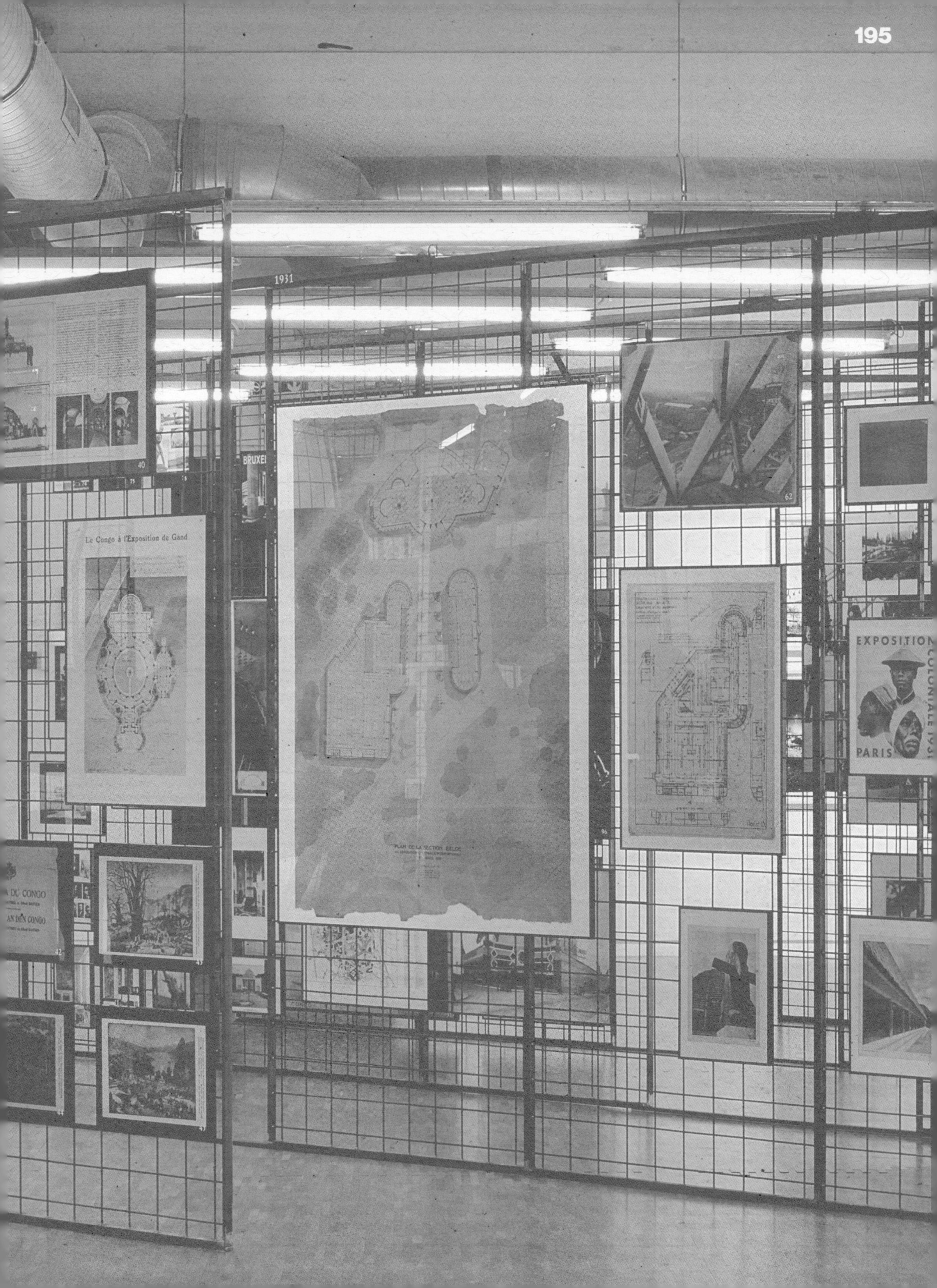
1931
Le Congo à l'Exposition de Gand
EXPOSITION
PARIS

CIVA
President: Rabab Khairy
Artistic Director: Nikolaus Hirsch
Secretary General: Jeremy Uhr

Editors
Sammy Baloji
Silvia Franceschini
Nikolaus Hirsch
Estelle Lecaille

Authors
Sandrine Colard
Johan Lagae
Debora Silverman
Traumnovelle
Rolando Vázquez Melken

With Works by
Judith Barry
Rossella Biscotti
Peggy Buth
ayoh kré Duchâtelet
Paoletta Holst & Johan Lagae
Jean Katambayi Mukendi
Chrystel Mukeba
Daniela Ortiz
Ruth Sacks
Traumnovelle

Exhibition Photos
Filip Dujardin

Graphic Design
Boy Vereecken
with Antoine Begon

Managing Editor
Tania Garduño Israde

Archives and Collections
Archivio Storico della Biennale di Venezia, Bibliothèque royale de Belgique, CIVA Collections, Brussels; Collection AkzoNobel Art Foundation, Collection FRAC, Alsace; Collection M HKA, Antwerp; Collection MRAC, Tervuren; Fondation Jean Delhaye et Archives du Musée Horta, Fonds pour l'architecture, Ghent University Library, KADIST Collection, Klemm's Berlin, Rijksmuseum, Amsterdam.

Translations and Copy Editing
Nick Axel
Blurbs
Pierre Bouvier
CTRL TAAL DELETE &
Transpardinus
Nathalie Tabury
Catherine Warnant
Leah Whitman-Salkin

Printing and Binding
Graphius, Belgium

Published
August 2023

CIVA
Rue de l'Ermitage 55
1050 Brussels
www.civa.brussels

Spector Books
Harkortstraße 10
04107 Leipzig
www.spectorbooks.com

This book is published on the occasion of the exhibition *Style Congo. Heritage & Heresy* (17.03 - 03.09.2023), curated by Sammy Baloji, Silvia Franceschini, Nikolaus Hirsch, Estelle Lecaille; organized by CIVA and Twenty Nine Studio. In collaboration with KANAL-Centre Pompidou, in the framework of Living Traces.

C I.II.III.IV. A
Culture — Architecture

KANAL Centre Pompidou

TWENTY NINE

The publication and exhibition were kindly supported by the Brussels – Capital Region, urban.brussels, Fédération Wallonie – Bruxelles, Wallonie – Bruxelles International and Flanders State of the Art

BRUSSELS CAPITAL-REGION

urban.brussels

Thanks to
Werner Adriaenssens
Nick Axel
Mihaela Bacu
Thierry Belenger
Christine Bluard
Marion Cambier
Francis Carpentier
Bambi Ceuppens
Jan Claerhout
Stéphanie De Blieck
Minne De Meyer Engelbeen
Jacques Deneuville
Gratienne Dubois
Drucila Clément
Bambi Ceuppens
Fondation Frison
Flavien Gillié
Yves Goldstein
Jan Goossens
Guy Gypens
Mohamed Ikoubaân
Séverine Janssen
Caroline Kadziola
Jeremy Kayoka
Agnès Kena
Pierre Labergue
Debora Levyh
Lesley Lokko
Anna Loporcaro
Lionel Maes
François Makanga
Jean Pierre Müller
Badibanga Ndeka
Leonie Ngoie
Lewis Ossoko Hang
Clément Paillion
Kasia Redzisz
Valérie Roucou
Benjamin Sauviac
Anna Serio
Simon Thielen
Aude Tournaye
Mouhamad Tshimbalanga
Jeremy Tshiyembi
Jeremy Uhr
Dieter Vanthournout
Guilliana Venlet
Robin Vinois
Benjamin Zurstrassen

The public program of *Style Congo. Heritage & Heresy* included
Sepake Angiama
Lotte Arndt
Ariella Aïsha Azoulay
Alexandre Chevalier
Sandrine Colard
Jessica De Abreu
Clémentine Deliss
Georgina Dibua
Samia Henni
Hannah Ishmael
Mbala Lusunzi Vita
Yannos Majestikos
Bruce Mateso
Ayoko Mensah
Jonelle Twum
Som•m•e Of Us
Phillip Van Den Bossche
Eric Van Hove
Francoise Vergès
Salomé Ysebart
Yasmina Zian

In the context of *Style Congo: Heritage & Heresy*, CIVA collaborated with e-flux architecture on the series *Appropriations*, www.e-flux.com/architecture/appropriations/

Distribution
Germany, Austria:
GVA, Gemeinsame Verlagsauslieferung Göttingen GmbH & Co. KG,
www.gva-verlage.de
Switzerland:
AVA Verlagsauslieferung AG,
www.ava.ch
France, Belgium:
Interart Paris, www.interart.fr
UK:
Central Books Ltd,
www.centralbooks.com
USA, Canada, Central and South America, Africa:
ARTBOOK | D.A.P.,
www.artbook.com
Japan:
twelvebooks,
www.twelve-books.com
South Korea:
The Book Society,
www.thebooksociety.org
Australia, New Zealand:
Perimeter Distribution,
www.perimeterdistribution.com

First edition, 2023
Printed in the EU

ISBN ENG: 978-3-95905-775-2
ISBN FR: 978-3-95905-774-5
ISBN NL: 978-3-95905-776-9